DOMINGO F. SARMIENTO:

PUBLIC WRITER

(BETWEEN 1839 AND 1852)

DOMINGO F. SARMIENTO:
PUBLIC WRITER
(BETWEEN 1839 AND 1852)

by

William H. Katra

Center for Latin American Studies

Arizona State University

1985

It is rather for us the living . . .

Domingo F. Sarmiento: Public Writer (Between 1839 and 1852)

Library of Congress Cataloging in Publication Data

Katra, William H
    Domingo F. Sarmiento: Public Writer (Between 1839 and 1852).
    Bibliography: p. 213
    Includes index.
    1. Sarmiento, Domingo Faustino–1811-1888–Literary Art.
    2. Argentina–History–1817-1860–Historiography.
    3. Liberalism–Argentina–History–19th Century.
    4. Literature and History
I. Title
F2846.S26K38

1985

982'.05'0924

85-11120
ISBN 0-87918-061-7

CONTENTS

Acknowledgements ix
Foreword xi
Chapters
  1. The Formative Years 1
     Ideas and Social Change 11
     Sarmiento: Military Leader 18

  2. The Making of a Public Writer 27

  3. Ideological Bricoleur 41
     The Linguistic Organization of Subjective Experience 52
     Discourse Production and Authority 57

  4. 'Facundo': Historical Context and Derivative Aesthetics 71
     The Definition of a Militant Aesthetics 75
     An Aesthetics in Practice 81
     The Romantic Struggle Between Civilization and
       Barbarism 85
     The Prose of Progress. 90
     Romantic Poetry. 92

  5. 'Facundo': An Exercise in Bricoleur Historiography. 105
     Historicism's Enlightenment Roots. 110
     Historicism and the Prescription for Progress. 121
     Romantic Historicism: Society's Telluric Foundations 126

  6. Determinism, Idealism and the Web of History 143
     Philosophical Materialism 145
     Philosophical Idealism and the Future of Society 149
     Liberalism and the Mythical Power of the Idea 152
     Idealism, Materialism and the Education of Man 158

  7. European Civilization and American Barbarism:
     Historiography on the Periphery. 167
     Sarmiento: Critic of Neo-colonialism. 169
     The Europeanization of South America. 174
     The Philosophy of History 182
     The Genesis of a Mystifying Historical Antithesis 186

  8. Epilogue: Sarmiento's Contradictory Voice in the
     Argentine Liberal Tradition. 197

Select Bibliography 213
Index 229

ACKNOWLEDGEMENTS

I appreciate the invaluable assistance of Washington State University's College of Sciences and Arts, Holland Travel Grant Fund, Humanities Research Center, Research and Arts Committee and Systems and Computing Center, which have have underwritten the necessary expenses for researching, writing and producing the manuscript. The Berkeley-Stanford Joint Center for Latin American Studies generously provided funds for a summer of library consultation. Thanks is due to Thomas Faulkner, Director of WSU's Humanities Research Center, for his ever-available time and impeccable guidance in the computer production of the camera-ready copy. I am also indebted to those individuals who, in some moment along the way, have given of their time to criticize my draft copies: Rodolfo Borello, Angelo Cantera, Eloy González, John Kicza, Virginia Tejera de Lavayen, Wolfgang Luchting, John Schmitt, Dennis West, Frances Wyers, my two anonymous reviewers for the Arizona State University Press, but especially Iván Jaksić and Armando Zárate. My thanks to Liz Finelli, Jim Grunewald, Ralph McQuillan, Lori Nyegaard, Carol Reeves, Charlotte Sanborn, Debbie Sheldon and Evelyn Smith de Gálvez for assistance in typing and proofreading the manuscript. I owe my profound gratitude to David William Foster and Juan Loveluck, who have continually provided moral support for my sometimes tenuous critical undertakings. Lastly, I am most indebted to my *compañera*, Sara, and two children, Dani and Esti, on whose account a project such as this becomes meaningful.

Chapter Four, in shortened form and in Spanish translation, appeared as "El *Facundo*: contexto histórico y estética derivada," in *Cuadernos Americanos*, 236 (1981), 151-76.

FOREWORD

In the *Summa Theologiae,* it is denied that God can unmake the past, but nothing is said of the complicated concatenation of causes and effects which is so vast and so intimate that perhaps it might prove impossible to annul a *single* remote fact, insignificant as it may seem, without invalidating the present. To modify the past is not to modify a single fact; it is to annul the consequences of that fact, which tend to be infinite. . . . As for myself, . . . I have guessed at and set down a process beyond man's understanding, a kind of exposure of reason; but there are certain circumstances that lessen the dangers of this privilege of mine. For the present, I am not sure of having always written the truth. I suspect that in my story there are a few false memories.

Jorge Luis Borges

"La otra muerte," *El aleph*

Domingo F. Sarmiento, at the age of forty-one in 1852, stood at the threshold of historical action. He was already an accomplished writer. *Facundo, De la educación popular, Viajes, Recuerdos de provincia,* and *Argirópolis* are by any standard the most important writings that he would produce in a long career, and all of them were conceived, written, and published during the previous decade of intense journalistic and political activity in Chile. But the acts and events which still lay ahead of him would assume an even more important position in his nation's history: his break with Urquiza and his subsequent opposition to the goals of the Confederation; his solidarity with Buenos Aires and his contribution to that province's final victory over the Confederation; his fervent advocation and then leadership in the "pacification" of the interior; his complicity in the persecution and then brutal killing of Angel "El Chacho" Peñalosa; his troubled governorship of San Juan; his enlightened but frustrating term as the nation's president; his promotion and then termination of the War of the Triple Alliance against Paraguay; his government's bloody military interventions in Entre Ríos and the Andean provinces; his fiscal dependence upon British capital for the construction of Argentina's railroads; his lifelong commitment to popular education, free trade, and European immigration to the Río de la Plata region; his break with Mitre; and his final disillusionment with the cattle-exporting oligarchy, whose interests he had long defended. This list could be extended, but the point has been made: the year 1852 marks the transition in his life from relative obscurity to national and international prominence, from writer and theorist to political actor and statesman.

Domingo F. Sarmiento: Public Writer

The demarcation between theory and praxis, or between writing and action, in Sarmiento's career creates special difficulties for the historian who studies the earlier period of his life, the years between 1839 and 1852. First, there is the traditional philosophical issue of the relationship one assumes to exist between consciousness and acts. Then, there is the problem of determining the degree of unity or consistency in the values, ideas, motivations, and indeed, identity, of a man whose activity spanned different historical or biographical periods. Does the continuity between two such moments exist only through the illusion granted by memory or writing? Is it merely the historian's perverse curiosity which invents his subject's precursors—as Borges would have us believe? At the very least, Borges makes us question the methodological basis of any historical investigation. History, because it is always written with retrospective knowledge, actualizes the present. History, he suggests, is the stuff of *ficciones.*

Indeed, a superficial survey of the vast body of critical writings which treat Sarmiento might lead one to conclude that his ideas and acts are the stuff of invention. Biographers and critics present dramatically differing perspectives. The vast majority have recreated the circumstances of his life according to the logic and necessities of their own times and struggles. In Argentina's charged ideological environment, almost every word written about a figure such as Sarmiento has been converted into ammunition for one group or another in the social and political forray.

Authors of the voluminous writings on Sarmiento concur with regard to only two issues: the superb quality of his writing style, and his inspired analyses of Argentine culture and society in the works he wrote and published before the fall of Rosas. Unitarians and Federalists, liberals and conservatives, porteños and provincials alike, have been in relative agreement that his early works occupy a foremost position in Argentina's, and even Latin America's, cultural history. About this there is universal agreement; all other events and contributions of the man are subject to continued and heated polemic.

David Viñas (in *Rebeliones populares)* has identified two traditional perspectives—the "heads" and "tails" of bourgeois thought, as he calls them—which have led to particularly distorted treatments of Sarmiento's life and thought: first, nationalist revisionism, with its variants of aristocratized nationalism of the national left and populism, whose followers denounce Sarmiento for his crimes; and second, orthodox liberalism, with its interpreters of the liberal left or liberal Marxism, all of whom exalt Sarmiento for his promotion of Europeanized and elitist "civilization" against local "barbarism." It is not difficult to identify representative studies which exemplify these ideological tendencies. Manuel Gálvez, Leopoldo Lugones, and Ricardo Rojas have written studies which could be classified under the label of aristocratic nationalism. Juan José Arregui, Fermín Chávez, Eduardo Luis Duhalde, Pedro Paoli, Rodolfo Ortega Peña, and J. M. Rosa could be said to typify a populist approach to nationalist revisionism. Orthodox liberal writers, who constitute the largest group, include Héctor Félix Bravo, Carlos Octavio Bunge, American critic Allison Williams Bunkley, Juan Pablo Echague, Martín García Merou, José H. Guerrero, José Ingenieros, Alberto Palcos, Félix Weinberg, and José María Zuviría. Two examples of liberal Marxists favorably treating Sarmiento are Aníbal Ponce and French critic Noël Salomon.

Another group not mentioned by Viñas because it includes himself, are Marxists who criticize Sarmiento on account of his association with Argentina's liberal elite, which has dominated the national political scene more or less since the fall of Rosas. Writers in this group, in addition to Viñas, are Atilio García Mellid, Leonardo Paso, Milcíades Peña, and Roberto Tamagno.

Needless to say, many of the critics named above have made significant contributions to Sarmientine studies, regardless of their respective political orientations. To their credit, Rojas, Lugones, and Gálvez generally go beyond ideology in their presentations of Sarmiento within the complex and multifaceted parameters of living. Similarly, Mellid, Paso, Salomon and Viñas present convincing and well documented accounts. Other writers who evade easy classification into one of the three general categories, as mentioned above, and whose works have proven useful for the present work are Enrique Anderson Imbert, José S. Campobassi, Ezequiel Martínez Estrada, and Paul Verdevoye. Lastly, the historians whose works have been useful for understanding the socio-historical and intellectual contexts of Sarmiento's time are Alejandro Korn, Raúl Orgaz, James R. Scobie, and especially Tulio Halperín Donghi.

The present work builds largely upon the works mentioned in this last paragraph. I share with the revisionists a discomfort in contemplating Sarmiento's role in the forceful imposition of Buenos Aires over the interior provinces subsequent to 1852. I share with the liberals an admiration for Sarmiento's disinterested struggles against tyranny and his lifelong, although not entirely consistent, defense of political and economic democracy. I also share, to a great degree, the platform of the Marxists in my reservations about the value of Argentina's dependent-liberal regime over the last 130 years.

The present work goes beyond the objectives of the works just cited in its attempt at constructing what Fredric Jameson calls a "history of consciousness," or in Jean Franco's words, "discourse analysis." I have largely eschewed the diachronic development of Sarmiento's ideas, with all the shortcomings this entails, in order to focus on a limited number of prominent topics or orientations in his writings.

Jean-Paul Sartre has provided indispensable models for my treatment of false consciousness, *mauvaise foi*, and, in general, the role of the imagination with regard to social and material forces. The ideas of Louis Althusser and his followers, in addition to the works of Fredric Jameson, have provided an invaluable orientation for analyzing an individual's psychological mediations in front of class ideology. In the works of Jacques

Derrida and Michel Foucault, I have found relevant discussions treating the relationship between discourse production and sociopolitical power. And lastly, readings from Roland Barthes and Jorge Luis Borges have provided the theoretical basis for my literary readings of political discourse and my political readings of literature.

Sarmiento expressed on one occasion that his *Facundo* united aspects of "poema, panfleta, historia," a statement that characterizes not only his public writing in general, but also his concerns as a leader in society: in different moments he was engaged in the promotion of culture, the exercise of journalism, and the investigation of the present conflicts of his land. What is of particular interest about his activities as public writer is that these different domains of inquiry (the aesthetic, the political, the social-scientific) frequently join together on the same page. His writing is most appropriate for an interdisciplinary study. Inevitably, political goals affected his discussion of aesthetic or historical issues; his social-scientific data is presented with rhetorical or literary devices.

The fusion and confusion of constituent ideologies in Sarmiento's writing has elicited different responses in the reading public. Whereas, literary readers recognize the heightened value of a work such as *Facundo* on account of the interpenetration of discourses, other observers have concluded that the same mixture of disciplines lends a demagogic character to his writings on social and historical matters. On the one hand, Sarmiento has been praised as a master of political and literary writing. On the other hand, critics have rightfully pointed out that his strong prejudices and idiosyncratic impulses many times outweighed a conscious resolve to describe and judge with objectivity.

In this study, Sarmiento's texts constitute the principal material for my analysis. However, they acquire their fullest meaning only when viewed in relation to the sociopolitical and intellectual contexts in which they were produced. No writing is ever completely self-referential, for a writer's values, ideas, and intentions are formed, and then subsequently become functional, in relation to his time. Sarmiento's ability to communicate depended largely upon the success of his writing in addressing the values, procedures, and ideologies which he shared with the reading public. Taking this into account, I attempt to study the dialectical unity of Sarmiento's early texts and multiple contexts; my goal is to study biography and the subjective dimension of his experience in relation to the social and historical backgrounds of his community. Sometimes these relationships are revealed upon analyzing an unrepresentative utterance; on occasion the unexpected contact between apparently distinct categories finds dramatic formulation. In more than one instance, a particular character trait or utterance will lend itself to two, or more, interpretations which are equally convincing. Contrary to the advocation of Ortega y Gasset, I explore the "human content" of Sarmiento's writing and treat as secondary its aesthetic aspects and epistemological content. I attempt a holistic view of the writer engaged in the labor of constituting his texts.

Since Sarmiento's lifelong crusade was the promotion of liberal ideas and institutions, it is not surprising that the subsequent critical response to the man has more or less paralleled the critical response to dependent liberalism in Argentina. The early 1970s witnessed that regime's near collapse, on account of its inability to deal successfully with grave political and economic crises and an armed guerrilla threat. There then followed what is popularly referred to as the "dirty war," lasting from approximately 1974 to 1980, which witnessed the armed forces' brutal persecution of the political left and the drastic reshaping of the nation's economic priorities according to laissez faire doctrines. Argentina's dependent-liberal order has survived one more crisis, but at what price? Once again, the imperatives of the present lead us to analyze the historical past. One organizing principle of the present work is my belief in the continuity existing between the post-Rosas liberal order of Sarmiento's time and that which continues dominant today. The historians mentioned above have already demonstrated that continuity, whether explicitly or implicitly, through the analysis of the social, economic, and political data. This work attempts to demonstrate that same continuity in the areas of culture and history of ideas.

Sarmiento, as writer and more generally as intellectual, was not a member of the bourgeoisie in the strict sense, although his writings offer what is now regarded as one of the clearest and most passionate defenses of the liberal program for national organization in his century. The association of Sarmiento with liberalism is significant: his life bridges the transition from its utopian to its dependent period.

Briefly considered here (but treated more extensively in the last chapter), utopian liberalism in Argentina, which prevailed more or less up to the fall of Rosas in 1852, received its most representative expression in the *Dogma socialista* of Echeverría. This work and others reiterated many of the goals of Latin America's independence movement and the European Enlightenment: the desire for a harmonious and progressive social order based on representative democracy, equality in politics and economics, liberty of assembly and expression, laissez faire organization of production and commerce, and universal public education. Utopian liberalism remained an abstract and idealistic dream since its young advocates among the Generation of 1837 (Echeverría, Alberdi, Sarmiento, etc.) wrote from exile in protest of Rosas' heavy-handed authoritarian practices, and hardly took into account the possibilities for incorporating these goals into actual institutions and practices.

After the fall of Rosas in 1852, most of these worthy objectives were either compromised or abandoned, when their advocates directly confronted the impossibility, and at times the undesirability, of implementing such radical changes in a largely unreceptive context. The previous defenders of enlightened liberal ideals became agents of accommodation in front of the cattle-producing oligarchy of Buenos Aires. Liberalism's contradictory legacy in this "dependent" period was that its defense of economic liberty took the form of a defense of economic privilege; its laissez faire policies resulted in Argentina's structural dependency vis-à-vis European imperialism (financial penetration and technological dependence, an economy emphasizing cattle exports for manufactured imports, and opposition to local industrialization and financial control), its promotion of modernized—or in the language of the time, "civilized"—institutions justified the violent imposition of port-city priorities over the native population and the political structures of the interior.

Sarmiento's destiny was to be protagonist in this dramatic transition from utopian to dependent liberalism. His early writings express the revolutionary promise of the former, and his acts as national leader subsequent to 1852 largely followed the advocation of the latter. Central to this study is the thesis that the young Sarmiento, in idea and act, anticipated what was to come; that his early writings expressed the essense of utopian liberal thought, but also the seed of liberalism's dependent future. Many of his contradictions as an individual were related to the contradictions of the philosophical and political movement which he advocated and to which he devoted his lifelong energies.

Nature made Sarmiento great. She gave him the unity of a mountain . . .; she made his structure an agglomeration pintoresquely composed of rock, abyss, forest and water. This chaos, as seen from close up, seems to express a type of ancient suffering reduced to the disorder of granite.

Leopoldo Lugones

His writings seem always to be a product of the occasion, and without a carefully matured plan. The subjective necessity of his aesthetic temperament and the objective necessities of that uncultured environment carried him by the hand, without giving him truce, but also without imposing upon him a sacrifice; writing was as indispensable for his spirit as breathing for his body.

C. O. Bunge

His written work is journalistic, militant, apostolical, and has the external variety and disorder of the deeds that it itself comments or illuminates . . . .

Ricardo Rojas

There was no clearcut division between his attitude, upon putting himself to write, and that which he adapted while living. For this reason his written work at the same time is chronicle of his country and autobiography . . . .

Ezequiel Martínez Estrada

His habits were those of a journalist, not those of a writer.

Enrique Anderson Imbert

Soldier with the pen or the sword, I combat in order to write, for writing is thinking; I write as means and as an arm of combat, because through combat one realizes his ideas.

Domingo F. Sarmiento

CHAPTER 1

The Formative Years

Domingo Faustino Sarmiento was born in the Province of San Juan in 1811, only months after the outbreak of the country's independence movement. The initial impetus for independence from Spain was provided by a small minority of intellectuals in Buenos Aires who proposed a continuation of the colony's centralized political structure, but this time according to liberal principles of the Enlightenment. The uncultured masses of the coast and the interior initially followed their lead, but later rebelled against the efforts at political centralization and cultural modernization. Their protest arose from a centuries-old distrust of urban authority and a traditional orientation based on the values and customs of the past. This conflict between two distinct civilizations led to a political dispute between Unitarians and Federalists, as the two sides came to be called. By 1820 these conflicting interests had worn away the governing structures previously uniting the country, and the separate provinces established their own governments, which were controlled, frequently, by local strongmen or *caudillos*. 1827 marks the last attempt by the Europeanized elites, led by Bernardino Rivadavia, to impose their leadership over the country. His fall in that year plunged the country into anarchy. Out of this morass of civil disorder, Juan Manuel de Rosas emerged as the strongman of the Province of Buenos Aires.

These events in the political realm were accompanied by an equally important transformation in Argentina's role vis-à-vis the world economy, which also profoundly affected the affairs of Buenos Aires and the interior provinces. Of foremost importance in this transformation was the progressive decline of the commercial network which for centuries had linked Argentina's northern regions with Bolivia and Peru. Traditionally, the southern regions had provided the Andean mining areas with food stuffs, textiles, and beasts of burden, in exchange for currency and a limited quantity of manufactured goods, which came by pack train via Peru. By 1776, this trade pattern was already in crisis on account of the growing commercial importance of Buenos Aires, a fact which was formally recognized that year by the creation of the Viceroyalty of the Río de la Plata. Subsequently, the growth of Buenos Aires paralleled the decline of Peruvian mining activities. The independence movement from Spain in the first decades of the nineteenth century brought to an end the Spanish trade monopoly and the trans-Andean commercial relationship of

Argentina's northern provinces. Argentina, in short order, became firmly entrenched in England's trade system. These changes would have lasting effects in the internal organization of the newly independent country.

In the post-independence period, Argentina's coastal regions, and in particular the area in and around Buenos Aires, experienced a growing prosperity. Demand in Europe progressively increased for Argentina's traditional exports of hides and dried beef. In addition, markets rapidly expanded, beginning in the 1820s for salted beef. The *saladero,* or salted meat plant, quickly became a highly profitable venture, and came to exercise a prominent role in the country's formation. In the 1790s the yearly slaughter of cattle for salted meat had been at 7000 head. This grew to 60,000 in 1822, and then to 350,000 by 1827.[1] Profits accumulated rapidly for the large landowners of the coast who since colonial days had strong ties to the urban centers. The growing power of these local groups, both in the economic and political domains, was shared by exporters and importers of commercial goods who were predominately of foreign origin.

The rise to power of Rosas was made possible by this power coalition of regional landowners and foreign (principally British) commercial interests. His program of government largely corresponded to the interests of these groups in its promotion of British trade, defense of cattle ranching and large landholdings, opposition to agriculture and sheep herding, transformation of the vagabond gaucho population into a rural proletariat, and the domination of the country's ports and commerce.[2] Born into a landowning family, Rosas understood more clearly than most the commercial possibilties offered by the technological innovations in the preservation and transportation of meat, and the increased European demand for the Río de la Plata's exports. Combining entrepreneurial ability to political astuteness, his innovations in the *saladero* won him a wide influence and control over the meat exportation activity in the region.

During his first decade in power, the despot enjoyed the nearly unanimous support of the people in the Province of Buenos Aires. He earned the title of "El restaurador" for having successfully unified the region under a central authority, pacified the Indian frontier, and provided a desperately needed peace and stability to the political order. He financed his endless military campaigns with the revenues derived from his monopolized control of the customhouse of Buenos Aires, through whose doors the great majority of the country's imports and exports passed. In periods of declining revenues, he terminated many of the publicly sponsored institutions which had been founded by his liberal predecessors: the national bank, agencies for land distribution, programs for attracting and assisting immigrants. Censorship of the press and impingements upon public assembly increased. His resistance to the French and British blockades of the port city won the applause of his supporters and the wrath of his detractors. For almost twenty years he resisted any effort at institutionalizing his system through a national constitution. During his latter years, he depended more and more on the calculated application of coersion and terror in order to maintain his unlimited power in and around Buenos Aires, and his authority in the provinces of the interior.[3]

During the first half of the century, many of the same factors which caused the ascension of Buenos Aires meant ruin for the economies of the interior. Upon independence the latter were faced with a crisis resulting from the loss of their traditional markets in Peru and the influx of European goods into their own region. Newly accessible cloth and manufactured goods from the industrialized European countries competed advantageously with the higher-priced textiles from Argentina's interior cities, and many local producers were forced out of business. Similarly, the commercial interests of the coast were able to take advantage of the relatively low trans-Atlantic shipping costs for Europe's wine, cereals, and dried fruits, in comparison to the higher costs for similar products produced in the Andean regions of the country—San Juan, San Luis, Mendoza—and transported by a sixty to ninety day wagon caravan trip across the pampas. As a consequence, the importers of the coast quickly gained for themselves the country's most lucrative markets, and displaced the producers from the provinces. Up through the period of Sarmiento's youth the economy of the interior provinces languished, and in some regions declined precipitously. Lacking markets for its agricultural production, the local population could ill afford to import articles, tools, and books from Europe or even from the coast. In spite of a slow and substantial population increase, the great majority of the population continued to dedicate its energies to subsistence agriculture.[4]

San Juan, which in colonial times had been the most important city of the Cuyan region in the northwest corner of the country, began a rapid decline in 1778 as a consequence of Spain's decision to lessen its control on international commercial activity in the region.[5] Whatever means the provincial leaders attempted in order to adjust to the new market conditions of a vast world were doomed to failure. In the period of Sarmiento's youth the regional society continued its slow disintegration, although it still maintained the vestiges of colonial life which had been developed to an advanced degree. In his *Recuerdos de provincia* one can read the unforgettable description of some old and illustrious families of the region, fallen into poverty, consoling their misery in defensive appeals to the nobility of their blood line. Up through Sarmiento's youthful years, the old aristocracy was able to preserve its relative prominence in the wine production and commercial activities and ensure a government of eminent and cultured men. In spite of the province's overall decline over the previous century, it still enjoyed relative progress in relation to the other provinces of the interior. In his youth, Sarmiento was witness to a society which promoted education and the arts, and had made significant strides in the modernization of its institutions. All of this announced to the outer world the existence of a cultural enclave which held its own in the midst of a general decline throughout the country's interior.[6]

The country's subsequent fall into civil war, however, accelerated the general crisis of the interior. In *Facundo* Sarmiento provides a vivid description of the new set of circumstances which marked the definitive disintegration of his native region, but he is less enlightening concerning its causes. He describes how the deteriorating social, economic, and political situation caused the emigration of some two hundred citizens to Chile in 1831, among whom were several of the region's most noted doctors, lawyers, small businessmen and youth. He personally witnessed similar problems in San Luis, Santiago de Estero, and Santa Fe. His pessimistic assessment of life in the interior cities is summarized in the observation that all that was left there were "esqueletos de ciudades, villorios decrépitos y devastados" (VII, 62).[7]

In analyzing the causes for this rapid disintegration, Sarmiento gave only slight attention to how the long-term historical changes in the patterns of production and commerce had for the most part relegated his native region to marginality in the economy of the continent. Somewhat surprisingly, he did not place the blame for Cuyo's economic decline directly on the elimination of trade barriers by first the Rivadavia government, and later the Rosas adminstrations, those measures which had caused considerable damage to small industries in other regions of the country.[8] Undoubtedly the relative geographical isolation of San Juan from the rest of the country accounted for, at least in part, the lessened effect of those domestic and international factors which had contributed to the accelerated decline of the other interior provinces. His silence or ignorance on this issue was undoubtely a result of his intellectual formation in a largely isolated setting. He was an astute observer of those events and trends affecting his region, however, his limited firsthand knowledge of other areas of the country accounts for his overall vision of the nation's social crisis –at least up through 1845 and his writing of *Facundo* –which was generally Cuyan in focus.[9]

In the first three decades of the nineteenth century the interior provinces were subjected to severe strains, which accounted in great part for the disintegration of the colonial elite's hegemony and the advent of civil war. The changing economic conditions destroyed the fortunes of many prominent families, who previously had constituted the mainstay of provincial rural and urban life. In addition, the protracted struggle for independence gave rise to a new class of military leaders, who, with support from Buenos Aires, commanded armies of underclass soldiers and extracted money and cattle from the producers of the region. The provinces' declining economic situation, in addition to the war, impoverished the cities of the interior, and set the scene for a shift in political power to the wealthy landowners from the rural zones.[10]

Sarmiento would describe in idealist terms the declining fortune of the old colonial elite and the rise of the *caudillo*. That is to say, in his writings he remained almost silent about the economic causes for the rise of Rosas and the *saladero* economy on the coast. According to him, the recent social clashes in the country resulted from a struggle pitting the countryside against the cities: "En la República Argentina se ven a un tiempo dos civilizaciones distintas en un mismo suelo; una naciente, que sin conocimiento de lo que tiene sobre su cabeza, está remedando los esfuerzos ingenuos y populares de la edad media; otra que sin cuidarse de lo que tiene a sus pies, intenta realizar los últimos resultados de la civilización europea. El siglo XIX y el siglo XII viven juntos; el uno dentro de las ciudades, el otro en las campañas" (VII, 46). The city versus the countryside: each had its corresponding population, customs, and institutions, and each had committed itself to the other's annihilation in order to insure its own survival.[11] For him, the ruin of provincial life was due to the invasion of the cities by the barbaric countryside. He believed that the reforms offered by the Unitarian governments in the decade following Argentina's independence had slowly succeeded in overcoming the dead weight of colonial stagnation. However, those gains were largely undone in the subsequent period of civil conflict.

By 1830 civil authority had been reestablished to a great extent, but government control was now exercised by local *caudillos,* who, in their majority, opposed the liberal reforms of the previous period. Disdaining their disrespect for democratic institutions, Sarmiento mistakenly called them gaucho tyrants, a name which demonstrated his confusion between two distinct social groups. First, there were the *terratenientes,* who owned the land and directed the productive activites of the different regions. Second, there were the landless and at times lawless gauchos, who progressively were becoming transformed into a rural proletariat. In social fact, only individuals from the former group had claim to social power and became *caudillos.* In his analysis, Sarmiento grouped these two social classes together. His thesis was that rural society had risen up against the urban centers, which historically had been the focus for progress. Rural institutions and values which dated back to colonial times had been able to withstand the brief period of reform in the cities. But with civil authority in crisis and the cities devastated, the countryside had successfully surged forth and extended its domination over the cultured urban sector. For the most part, Sarmiento ignored the fact that the opening of his country toward the exterior world, as a result of the changes in the world economy and the corresponding liberal program of the independence movement, was the principal cause for the decline of the interior provinces, and not what he depicted as their growing isolation.[12]

The equation of the countryside versus the cities figured prominently in the world view of the young Sarmiento, who began his public writing activities in 1839, which was shortly before his leaving the region of Cuyo and establishing himself in Chile. Although raised among Federalists, at an early age he became a convert to Unitarian principles and that party's program for national transformation.[13] He believed admirable the goals of the governments headed by Bernardino Rivadavia of promoting European immigration, dividing state lands, and encouraging colonization for the purpose of crop farming. He shared with the early Unitarian leaders the belief that an increased population density was necessary for the country's economic, social, and cultural well-being. A major objective was the replacement of the cattle-producing economy by crop farming, which in turn would cause the demise of the criollo class of large landowners and would stimulate the growth of urban centers thoughout the country. Indeed, from Sarmiento's perspective, similar patterns of settlement, immigration, and crop farming, as supported by the Unitarian governments a generation before, were precisely what accounted for his own region's relative prosperity and progressive civil institutions in relation to the rest of the country. So beginning in the 1840s, Sarmiento's renewed support for the old Unitarian project of national transformation was based primarily on the theoretical conviction of the correctness of that old banner, as demonstrated by the relative success of many of those principles in his native Province of San Juan.

His fundamental values in civics and politics derived in large part from his early childhood experiences. From birth he had been inculcated with a sense of class superiority with regard to the other population groups in the region. Both of his parents hailed from distinguished families of Cuyo, whose economic fortune had of late been on the decline. "La posición social de mi madre estaba tristemente marcada por la menguada herencia que había alcanzado hasta ella" (III, 133), he wrote. His maternal grandfather had been owner of half the valley of Zonda, and of troops of wagons and mules. Upon his death, Sarmiento's mother, one of a dozen children, had received little more than some unsettled lands and a firm respect for the family's superior social position. The situation of Sarmiento's father was very much the same: he was the survivor of a wealthy family which had fallen into hard times. Sarmiento wrote that the only inheritance he would receive from his father's side of the family was a passion for liberty, an accentuated self-respect, and a hardheadedness for demanding his own way. Both parents instilled in him an awareness of their superior social status, pride, and sense of community obligation. While these attitudes had survived from the family's aristocratic roots in the colonial past, the family itself had retained little or none of the material resources which made those attitudes a living reality. Only the resourcefulness of his dedicated and hardworking mother mitigated the frequent economic deprivation, almost to the point of misery, of Sarmiento's childhood home. He would later write: "En el seno de la pobreza, criéme hidalgo . . ." (III, 135).

Adolfo Prieto, in _La literatura autobiográfica argentina,_ provides perhaps the most penetrating study of the play between conservative aristocratic orientation and progressive liberal ideas that characterized the young Sarmiento. The contradictory psychological disposition of one like Sarmiento is usually a result of a pervasive contradiction that characterizes the society as a whole: "El liberalismo, triunfante en la faz política, inflama los sentimientos, tiñe con nuevos colores algunas formas del vivir, pero se vuelve inoroso en la disolución de varios de los principios en que se asienta la sociedad colonial."[14] Prieto emphasizes the important role of Sarmiento's semiconscious aristocratic values, in spite of the man's intellectual conversion to liberal ideals. Those values, probably fostered by his mother in his childhood home, are discernable in the ornamentation and high tone of his descriptions of his early childhood environment in San Juan which one finds in *Recuerdos de provincia*. Sarmiento revealed his traditional world vision when he referred to his family geneology, and also in apparently unguarded bursts of sentiment, which were not uncommon in his writing. For example, in *Recuerdos* he exclaims: "¡Costumbres patriarcales de aquellos tiempos, en que la esclavitud no envilecía las buenas cualidades del fiel negro!" Rationally embracing many of the ideas of the Enlightenment, Sarmiento certainly believed that any form of slavery demeaned man, but Prieto observes that "El Sarmiento evocador se ha arrojado a la infancia como a un estanque, y trae a la superficie profundas aguas de extraño, alquitarado sabor . . . ."[15]

As a youth and as mature thinker, Sarmiento's aristocratic orientation often flavored his interpretation of liberal goals, with which he became familiar primarily through his readings. Both the aristocratic and liberal traditions placed an emphasis on the desirability of cultural pursuits and the respect for private property; in his time, however, culture and property ownership were the near-exculsive domains of society's elite. Both traditions placed an emphasis on education, but Sarmiento's paternal, and at times authoritarian, practices in that area are reminiscent of the aristocratic sentiment of *noblesse obligée*. One finds in both traditions an expressed need for public order, but Sarmiento's interpretation of liberal consitutional democracy implicitly called for the predominance of society's cultured elite who resided in the cities, and were educated in European ways. And lastly, Sarmiento's at times rhetorical affirmation of liberty went hand in hand with his personal disdain for the ideas and social institutions associated with the popular classes and even his call for their vigorous repression by governmental authorities (VII, 52).

If Sarmiento's advocation of liberty was contradictory and at times strictly limited to the pursuits of society's social and cultural elite, then he had little or nothing to say about the realization in the society of his time for the other ideological pillar of liberal thought: *equality*. As Noël Salomon observes, Sarmiento alludes to the concept in passing, but only in a relatively theoretical way.[16] This is not surprising, if one takes into account the violent hatred which he felt for not only the gauchos and Indians, but in general for the popular classes in the society of his time. Adolfo Prieto suggests that perhaps this attidude grew out of an irrational fear of failure which he experienced as a child and as a young man. His family, still enjoying the prestige of its upper-class background, was constantly tormented by a perilous economic situation that bordered on poverty. The smallest misfortune and his family would have fallen to the level of the most miserable of the common families of the town. Prieto suggests: "En las ambiguas zonas de deslinde el temor a la confusión es obsesivo. Y el miedo transfiere fácilmente su signo al odio."[17] Sarmiento's hatred for "la chusma," gauchos, Indians, and the subclasses of his society,

can therefore be compared to the reaction of the petite bourgeoisie during
Peronism who spilled venom against the "cabecitas negras" or popular
classes. It was the result of an internalized fear of his own loss of prestige
and wealth.

Another convincing explanation for Sarmiento's irrational hatred of
the lower classes has to do with his very unpleasant memories of San
Juan's first experience with the civil wars which came to disrupt the entire
country. The occupations of his native Province of San Juan, Sarmiento
reminds us in the pages of *Facundo,* were almost exclusively agricultural
or commercial in nature; not having "campaña" or the large open plains
which served admirably for cattle production, the province withstood
for a long time the domination of *caudillos* (VII, 62). That is to say,
Sarmiento's social contacts in his native province throughout the period
of his youth were limited by and large to small peasant or pre-bourgeois
agricultural producers and the urban residents of the city proper. It is
possible that he had never witnessed to any large degree the effects of
extreme poverty upon a landless and powerless rural proletariat. For the
first eighteen years of his life, the typical horse and cattle-centered culture
of the gaucho, the latter's garb, language and customs, were but elements
of a distant, folkloric culture for the ambitious young man.

Then, in 1827, the peace and security of his childhood years were sud-
denly overturned. At the door of the store he tended, Sarmiento witnessed entering into the town some 600 "salvaje" *montonera* troops under
Facundo Quiroga:

> ¡Que espectáculo! . . . Los caballos briosos y acaso más domestica-
> dos que sus caballeros se espantaban de aquellos ruidos y encuentros
> extraños, y en calles sin empedrar veíamos los espectadores avanzar
> una nube de denso polvo, preñada de remores, de gritos, de blas-
> femias y carcajadas, apareciendo de vez en cuando caras más em-
> polvadas aún entre greñas y harapos, y casi sin cuerpo, pues que los
> guardamontes les servían de ancha base, como si hubiera también
> querubines de demonios medio centauros. He aquí mi visión del
> Camino de Damasco, de la libertad y de la civilización. Todo el mal
> de mi país se reveló de improviso entonces: ¡la Barbarie! (XXII,
> 244-45)

Overnight the peaceful and progressive environment of the provincial capital plummeted into disorder; inner security became a treasured memory
of the past. In short, the advent of Facundo's gaucho cavalry traumati-
cally ended the period of his idyllic youth. Sarmiento would later explain
in somewhat romantic fashion that the result of this experience was his
immediate passage from Federalist to Unitarian ranks (this is his explanation in the continuation of the passage quoted above). Regardless of when
his political conversion did occur, there is no doubt that Sarmiento was
deeply shocked by this event. But there are reasons to believe that his
unpleasant surprise was due to more than just the ferocity of Quiroga's
mounted warriors. The mere sight of an alien and lower class culture,
with radically differing values, codes of behavior, and style of dress, must

have caused as much panic in the young Sarmiento as did the anticipation of violence. On the unconscious and semiconscious levels, all those diverse reactions became mutually supporting. Irrational hatred or historical mystification would thereafter prevail whenever he wrote about Aldao, Facundo Quiroga, the *caudillo*, the *montonera*, and the gaucho, and in general the lumpen or rural proletariat of his country. In his literary writings he would compare Facundo to the marauding Gengis Khan, and the gauchos to the primitive Bedouins of North Africa. In truth, the gaucho was nearly as exotic to the young Sarmiento as was the nomadic Arab. For him, all were one and the same; more precisely, all inspired in him the same fear of radical cultural differences, the same dread of social and political anarchy. All symbolized for him his definitve and abrupt separation from childhood security.

In *Mi defensa* Sarmiento offers a vivid description of the abrupt transition that occurred in provincial life in 1830, from a state of "profunda tranquilidad" to one of brutal and unprovoked terror (III, 14-15). His favored Unitarian Party had recently occupied the provincial government following an uprising of the local militia. Shortly thereafter reaction set in. Several of what he calls "bandits" both inside and outside of the prison, surprised and then killed a number of guards. They were quickly joined by "la chusma y el pueblo gaucho," all of whom demonstrated fierce hostility to the province's liberal leaders and the wealthier families of the region. Landowners were killed and their properties ransacked. The uprising was finally suffocated, but only through a bloody confrontation and the execution of several rebels. Sarmiento justifies the stern actions taken and criticizes any who would call those military officials assassins on account of the severe justice rendered in such threatening circumstances. He states, and then repeats in emphatic and somewhat defensive language, that the struggle was social in origin and not political: it was a clash whose character was "puramente de vandalaje" (III, 17). It was important to him at the time of writing that he justify his participation on the basis of his solidarity with the decent and educated families of the region and his stalwart opposition to the threat of social chaos and the violent acts of the lower classes.

Sarmiento's reservoir of unconscious aristocratic values influenced to a great extent how he interpreted the new social order that arose from the chaos of the civil wars.[18] A far cry from the paternalistic system of the propertied and cultured elite was the new provincial order that came to predominate in the next few years. The government was headed by Benavides, the local strongman who was obedient to Rosas. Sarmiento recognized that Benavides was far more respectable than the governing *caudillos* in other provinces. Nevertheless, he was

un hombre frío . . . . Tiene un excelente corazón, es tolerante, la envidia hace poca mella en su espíritu, es paciente y tenaz. Después he reflexionado que el raciocinio es impotente en cierto estado de cultura de los espíritus . . . . Como la generalidad de los hombres de nuestros países, no tiene conciencia clara del derecho ni de la justicia.

Le he oído decir candorosamente, que no estaría bien la provincia sino cuando no hubiese abogados . . . . La provincia de San Juan, salvo La Rioja, San Luis y otras, es la que más hondamente ha caído; porque Benavides le ha impreso su materialismo, su inercia, su abandono de todo lo que constituye la vida pública, que es lo que el despotismo exige. Coman, duermen, callen, rían si pueden, y aguarden tranquilos, que en veinte años más . . . sus hijos andarán en cuatro pies (III, 186).

The social disorder of the province, according to Sarmiento, was due to the decline of his own class and the usurpation of position and privilege by military strongmen at the head of uncultured and undisciplined gauchos. He notes that the officers under Benavides, Quiroga, and Aldao, who, were Cuyo's principal strongmen, rarely, if ever, hailed from the prominent families of the region. Many of the new officer class, on the contrary, had questionable antecedents and some even had criminal records. Admittedly, many youthful military leaders from poorer families admirably aspired an improvement in their social position. But given the lower class origins of the majority of officers in the provincial armies, it was no wonder that the "escoria de la sociedad" was putting asunder the province's legacy of political order and cultural refinement.

Sarmiento's elitist social values governed to a great degree his opinion that the social conflict of his time was primarily the result of the rude rural population rebelling against the cultured elites of the cities. There is only a faint echo in his writings of the thesis usually applied in order to explain the origins of the nation's internal conflict, namely the dispute between Unitarians and Federalists. Sarmiento, writing in the 1840s, suggests that the dispute between those two parties and their respective programs for organizing the country corresponded to a period of national history that had been largely superceded.[19] That is to say, Rosas initially represented the anti-urban, anti-centralization forces of the Federalists. However, during his long tenure in power, he utilized the superior commercial, productive, and military resources of the Province of Buenos Aires to slowly bring the local *caudillos* of the other provinces under his authority. The paradox of Rosas is that while utilizing the slogans of the Federalists, he in fact accomplished the Unitarians' political goal of unifying the country under Buenos Aires leadership. In order to avoid the trap of focusing on the differences between the political programs of those two parties, Sarmiento emphasized the social effect of Federalist rule: the *caudillo* leadership in San Juan, supported by Rosas, was overseeing the province's regression; crude and violent leaders, responding to the desires of the unschooled and uncultured masses, were gaining control over the civil authority:

Así han trastornado la sociedad en la República Argentina, elevando lo que está deprimido, humillando y apartando lo que es de suyo elevado; así triunfó la federación y así se sostiene, llena de miedo siempre, teniendo necesidad para vivir de humillar, de aterrar, de cometer nuevas violencias y nuevos crímenes. Benavides no tenía ministro entonces, todos los federales le huían el bulto y él sólo con sus tropas llevaba adelante el insano designio. ¡Así toman el nombre de los pueblos para llamarse gobiernos, después que los han envilecido y ajado! (III, 187)

According to Sarmiento, two outstanding characteristics of the province's general decline in recent years were the rising militarism and the passing of provincial leadership from the educated elites to the uncultured *caudillos*. For Sarmiento, the *caudillo* tyrants attacked any institution defending the fertile interchange of ideas and democratic association; their cattle-based economy and feudal social institutions stymied the efforts of the nascent bourgeoisie to found a new order based on democratic principles and the continual development of the country's commercial and agricultural potentials.

Ideas and Social Change

In *Recuerdos de provincia,* Sarmiento makes an inciteful observation regarding the dual existences and ambiguous ideologies of men such as Dean Funes, who, a generation before, had guided Argentina toward independence (III, 132). The men of Funes' period, he states, were doubly colonial and republican in outlook, a situation which correlated with the transitional moment in which they lived. In a similar fashion, Sarmiento's early years bridged two epochs: first, there was the period lasting up to the early 1830s when the Province of San Juan still enjoyed the leadership of the propertied elite. And then, there was the subsequent period of civil turmoil during which the educated minorities fought their losing battle for social prominence with *caudillos* and their gaucho followers. In the earlier period he assimilated many of the values typical of his parents' patrician class, a class which continued to dominate regional life during his youth. Then, it was in the latter period of civil struggle that Sarmiento acquired his arsenal of liberal, and later *socialista,* ideas.

Sarmiento's acquaintance with the ideas of the Enlightenment came principally through reading, although a number of people also had a direct and early influence. His father had been perhaps his earliest inspiration, in his love of liberty and dedication to free speech and democratic institutions. A later association with Domingo de Oro and other members of San Juan's cultural elite continued to fuel Sarmiento's love for republican principles. An avid reader since childhood, he read any book that came into his hands. By an early age he had gained a firsthand familiarity with the limited public and private library holdings of the region. In addition to early Biblical and theological readings, one text which had an especially important impact on his developing consciousness was the *Life of Franklin.*

Yo me sentía Franklin; ¿y por que no? Era yo pobrísimo como él, estudioso como él, y dándome maña y siguiendo sus huellas podía

un día llegar a formarme como él, ser doctor *ad honorem* como el,
y hacerme un lugar en las letras y en la política americana. . . .
Alienta tanto su ejemplo, está tan al alcance de todos la carrera que
él recorría, que no habría muchacho, un poco bien inclinado, que
no se tentase a ser un Franklincito, por aquella bella tendencia del
espíritu humano a imitar los modelos de la perfección que concibe
(III, 168).

In the 1830s Sarmiento had further opportunities to develop his ideas
on free trade and liberal social reform. He became familiar with more
contemporary writers, principally from Europe and North America, and
he acquired a reading knowledge of French, Italian, and later English.
The world of ideas rapidly expanded before him. By 1839, he and a few
other energetic youths of San Juan were meeting almost nightly in order
to debate the new doctrines of progress which they assimilated through a
systematic plan of readings. They were already in contact with the *Joven
Argentina,* that group of progressive youths in Buenos Aires headed by
Esteban Echeverría, Juan Bautista Alberdi, Juan María Gutiérrrez, and
others. Manuel Quiroga Rosas, of Cuyan origin, provided a personal
link betweeen the two groups. Sarmiento tells in *Recuerdos de provincia*
of Quiroga Rosas' return to San Juan from Buenos Aires, armed with
a select library of modern writers: Jouffroy, Lerminier, Guizot, Cousin,
Tocqueville, Leroux, and others. Out of this conglomeration of influences
they formulated their *socialista* program of national reconstruction, which
at the same time united them in a common struggle against the tyrannical regime of Juan Manuel de Rosas. Within a year, when Sarmiento
began his public writing career in earnest, he had achieved intellectual
maturity. Throughout the next decade of Chilean exile he would become
the staunch defender and advocate of Chile's and Argentina's transformation according to *socialista,* and more generally, liberal principles. Nevertheless, many of the patriarchal values which he had learned in early
childhood continued to influence his perceptions and acts.

Perhaps the most important value learned early in life and then reinforced by his liberal creed, was Sarmiento's culturism, that is to say, the
high esteem he always held for writing's transformational power in society. Sarmiento was convinced that the written dissemination of ideas was
fundamental to the nation's development, whether accomplished by San
Juan's progressive propertied class in the post-independence period, or by
the exiled intellectual vanguard of a few decades hence who would struggle against the system of *caudillos.* This belief in the insurrectional power
of ideas, and more precisely, the written word, explains in great part his
voracious reading habits and his respect for the most advanced ideas of
the time. It also accounts for his lifelong promotion of public education
and career choice of public writing in the daily and weekly press.

During Sarmiento's childhood, the principal institution in the Cuyo
region for disseminating ideas and influencing opinion had been public
oratory. He recounts in *Recuerdos de provincia* the "fascinación mágica"
which the words of one like Domingo de Oro had over the listener (III,

77). Among a predominantly illiterate or non-reading population, Oro had provided the standard for leading the society of his time: he provided "el modelo y el tipo del futuro argentino, europeo hasta los últimos refinamientos de las bellas artes, americano hasta cabalgar el potro indómito, parisiense por el espíritu, pampa por la energía y los poderes físicos" (III, 80). By combining a European outlook to his largely creole spirit, he was the ideal spokesman for progress in his age. His means of communication was adequate to his situation. Sarmiento notes that he himself had analyzed in detail the rhetorical qualities that accounted for Oro's persuasive power and had transcribed a few of the latter's most memorable sermons. Only through writing, Sarmiento believed, could the glories of oratory be communicated to future generations.[20]

Sarmiento was among the first on his continent to perceive journalism's emerging function as the preferred medium of communication for society's new class of leaders. It was no coincidence, he would later point out, that his generation's rise to power paralleled the displacement of oratory by the press as the principal medium of communication in society:

> El diario es para los pueblos modernos, lo que era el foro para los romanos. La prensa ha substituido a la tribuna y al púlpito; la escritura a la palabra, y la oración que el orador ateniense acompañaba con la magia de la gesticulación, para mover las pasiones de algunos millares de auditores, se pronuncia hoy ante millares de pueblos que la miran escrita, ya que por las distancias no pueden escucharla. Por el diarismo el genio tiene por patria el mundo, y por testigos la humanidad civilizada (I, 58).

Somewhat simplistic was his association of oratory with the "magia de la gesticulación" and a supposed arousing of the passions in the listener, all of which he opposed to the rational reaction of the reader of newspapers. Nevertheless, he was convinced from an early age of the importance of the press for spreading liberal ideas and preparing its readers for democracy.

Sarmiento's own development paralleled the decline of oratory and the rise of writing as the predominant means of social discourse in the provincial capital of his time. His later writings indicate the close association he believed existed between the spread of literacy and his own rise to prominence in the community. At the age of five, his family had paraded him from house to house in the neighborhood to demonstrate his exceptional abilities at reading, and in turn receive the applause of the community. A few years later, in San Juan's newly founded school, he was ascended to the position of "primer ciudadano" among his classmates for his exceptional academic endeavors. The next chapter would occur in Chile between 1840 and 1842: in *Mi defensa* he wrote with pride of the local citizenry's enthusiastic response to his articles treating public issues which he published in the local press. In these early junctures of his social development, his accomplishments in the written culture elevated him above his peers and bolstered his self-confidence. It was a period when writing, in the form of newspapers and pamphlets, was becoming the primary means of social discourse in the cosmopolitan world into which Chile and

Argentina were being inserted. Sarmiento became progressively aware that his skills related to assimilating and disseminating a written culture qualified him for leadership in the society that was then emerging.

It is also significant that from an early age he committed his energies to the establishment of educational institutions. At the age of fifteen he helped to establish a school in the city of San Luis, for which he, younger than all the students, was the teacher. Some eleven years later, in 1839, he founded an institution for young women in Santa Rosa, for which he was the director and principal instructor. This audacious experiment in women's education ended a year later when the school was closed due to the province's decaying political situation and Sarmiento's subsequent exile to Chile. Then, an Argentine émigré in Santiago, Chile, he was entrusted by the government with the important task of directing the national preparatory school for teachers. All of these experiences in promoting education were motivated by his larger goal of social and political progress. He wrote in *Recuerdos de provincia* that his efforts on behalf of education had "un tema único, cambiar la faz de la América, y sobre todo de la República Argentina, por la sustitución del espíritu europeo a la tradición española, y a la fuerza bruta como móvil, la inteligencia cultivada, el estudio y el remedio de las necesidades" (III, 224).

Sarmiento's conviction of the effectiveness of the daily and weekly press as an instrument of social progress followed logically from his ideas on literacy and education. In the 1830s, the Province of San Juan, similar to many other areas of the continent, had experienced a rapid growth in the reading public, and for the first time had united the financial and technological means for supporting a regional press. Sarmiento, writing decades later, realized that the writer, who reached literally thousands of readers, could singlehandedly marshal support and perhaps sway the public on a particular issue or concern. The press could take those "ideas que están en germen e incubarlas, animarlas, y allanarles el camino para que marchen . . . hasta convertirse en preocupación pública" (III, 209-10). Although somewhat exaggerated, this conception of writing's power nevertheless reveals the enthusiasm with which Sarmiento came to view journalism as the instrument par excellence for promoting progress among a ready and willing public.

His early writings on education and journalism suggest that Sarmiento believed in the almost mythical power of the written word to precipitate events and influence people's actions. Although many readers would doubt this strict causal relationship linking writing to historical events, Sarmiento had concrete reasons for believing it. The ideas he had learned from books had indeed transformed his own life, so why couldn't reading, that "instrumento poderoso" (III, 151), do the same for society? An example of writing's power in his own life was the letter he wrote denouncing Facundo Quiroga's brutality, which subsequently was read to the assembled representatives of his province. In response to this written denouncement, he became the target of insults and life threats at the hands of Quiroga's henchmen (III, 25). That letter did indeed incite the *caudillo* and provoke a reaction. A mere letter had almost cost the young Sarmiento his life! In his autobiographical writings he provides many other examples which enable the reader to understand why the skills associated with literacy came to occupy in his mind such a lofty position in the hierarchy of human activities. In his own experience, writing had indeed demonstrated its insurrectional power to anger or enthuse individuals, and thereby lead them to political action. Sarmiento, like many others of his generation, believed that the education of the public was a principal means of inspiring the successful political action which would bring about society's development. Little separates Sarmiento from the many revolutionary leaders of the twentieth century in this regard. Indeed, Latin America's revolutionary experiences in recent decades testify to the importance which leaders still accredit to literacy campaigns and increased public involvement in written communication as an integral part of society's overall transformation.

Sarmiento's commitment to the civilizing ideal was most intense. As a youth he already manifested two character traits that he would retain throughout his life: an unshakable faith in his own convictions, and the will to overcome adversity. Unlike many writers and social activists, he rarely was immobilized by the contradictions of promoting progress in the midst of underdevelopment, of defending culture while surrounded by illiteracy and backward customs. At times, his zeal for reform and his love of an abstract European ideal clashed head on with an obstinate American reality that resisted change. His idealized and abstract set of principles, some times in complete conflict with his existing situation, were often treated with ridicule by his contemporaries. But, by and large, when he succeeded in adapting the goals of his cultural mission to the possibilities and limitations of his situation, he found fertile terrain for action.

In many ways, Sarmiento typifies the "ambiguous" intellectual of an underdeveloped country who exists in constant tension on account of the contradiction between his progressive goals and the backwardness of his physical setting.[21] This tension was aggravated by a sensed inferiority, at least in his younger years, on account of his provincial origins and his unsystematic intellectual formation. These two sources of anxiety explain in large part his often strident and uncritical defense of "civilized" values and his desperate need to gain social recognition in a more cosmopolitan setting. Adolfo Prieto relates these traits to the nascent bourgeois society of his time: in fame and in economic advancement, capitalism's competitive environment produces winners as well as losers. Sarmiento's anxiousness to succeed was dialectically related to his fear of marginality.[22] Success in society signified the reward bestowed upon he who possessed the right combination of personal characteristics; and failure signified the lack of those qualities or the frustration of one's efforts. The "organized insecurity" which he experienced in his childhood home stimulated the development of a series of positive values that fortified him well for his later struggles against adversity. These tensions of his childhood and youth would leave their imprint on the man's mature thought.

Undoubtedly related to these tensions was the duality with which he came to perceive not only his own situation, but also many aspects of Argentinian history and society. He and his community were inevitably suspended between an undesirable past and an idealized future. His intellectual and social environments consisted of both positive and negative, civilized and barbaric elements. His discourse has in common with that of other writers of his generation the inclusion of both demoniac and utopian elements.[23]

The region's underdevelopment can be considered one of several "demoniac" elements which affected his formation as an intellectual, and later, as a public writer. Prevalent in his writing is the sense of humiliation over the backwardness of Argentina and other South American nations after three centuries of Spanish colonial rule.[24] Before independence, the Spanish American colonies, like the Spanish metropolis, had hardly participated in the pan-European cultural dialogue, and had scarcely been affected by Europe's incipient social transformation and industrialization. Spain had relegated its colonies to self-perpetuating stagnation. The long-standing intellectual censorship in the colonies and the subsequent restrictions on the commerce of European books and journals in the newly independent republics were superficial indications of a profoundly isolated cultural life. Sarmiento identifies in *Facundo* what was perhaps an even more pervasive manifestation: the Ecclesiastic mentality that predominated in the country's institutions and what were euphemistically called "centers of learning." He quotes from Dean Funes, who had described the intellectual life of the university in which the majority of the newly independent country's theologians and doctors had been trained: "Razonamientos puramente humanos, sutilezas, sofismos engañosos, cuestiones frívolas e impertinentes, esto fue lo que vino a formar el gusto dominante de estas escuelas" (VII, 95). This frozen scholasticism, a throwback to the country's colonial past, had adversely affected social institutions and legislation. Alejandro Korn writes: "El rasgo saliente de esta legislación es su afán por entremeterse en el sagrado de la conciencia y establecer no sólo una regla de derecho, sino un precepto moral, fundado en valores éticos inmutables, para que la ley humana sea un reflejo de la divina . . . ."[25] Surviving aspects of a paralyzed scholasticism were still evident in the thought and social institutions of his day which accounted in part for the resistance of many people to the ideas of progress.

Recent events had demonstrated to Sarmiento that the benefits of civilization accumulated primarily in Buenos Aires and that the pampas were a bad conductor for disseminating progress throughout the provinces (VII, 23). According to the demoniac dimension of his thought, the immense underpopulated plains were largely to blame for the countryside's resistance to the ideas of liberty and democracy. Unfortunately, he admits, the savage natural environment and its crude gaucho inhabitants would determine the course of development in the interior regions of the country for some time to come. Upon extending his vision over the cultural landscape of his homeland, he perceived only deserts. Inspired by the liberal mythos of revolution, he interpreted the mission of his generation as that of tearing society away from its historical roots; what was necessary was an apocalyptical separation of the present from the past in order to start anew.[26] The question posed in 1855 by his liberal Chilean cohort, Benjamín Vicuña Mackenna, expresses well the abhorrence which the young Sarmiento also felt for those institutions related to an unredeemable past: "¿Cómo puede salvarnos y absolvernos el pasado, si el pasado es nuestra anatema, nuestra condenación?"[27]

Not finding in his country's intellectual heritage an orientation for national reconstruction,[28] Sarmiento consequently turned his attention to the thought of European writers. Like other Latin American intellectuals of his time, he must have become quite frustrated upon searching through the written testimony of three centuries of intellectual production from local learning centers for information relevant to regional history, people, and social institutions. In European literature he attempted to glean what would be useful for the struggles which he proposed to wage in his own land. He was convinced of the necessity of assimilating into his own thought the most prestigious historical and social theories of that tradition. Intentions, however, do not always transfer into acts. Andrés Bello, who was one of the most progressive thinkers of his age—but who, ironically, also enjoys the reputation as traditionalist—criticized those young Argentine and Chilean intellectuals who refused to turn their gaze inward and instead sought in Europe the intellectual foundations for Latin American culture. Perhaps Bello had in mind the likes of Sarmiento, whose outstanding tendency was to promote European or North American practices with the goal of "civilizing" South American society.

The utopian direction for Sarmiento's ideas on progress complements his demoniac interpretation of Argentina's underdevelopment. He is akin to the provincial or the *nouveau riche,* who, out of a subliminal need for status disdains his own origins and seeks the intellectual refuge amid the symbols of progress. David Viñas has identified the resulting psychological tensions of one such as Sarmiento who was torn between an idealized and an existing reality: his "recogimento"—or his defensive turn inward—and his fear of being violated by others went hand in hand with his bookish pedagogy and his authoritarian violence.[29] Thus his conviction that if Argentina's institutions evolved according to the most recent intellectual acquistions of universal culture, then his nation would be able to leave behind its ignominious origins and forge a new and redeemed identity. The ascent of his society along the path indicated by its "chosen" leaders would require a dramatic uprooting from tradition and a forced change of orientation. This transformation promised to be violent, but how else could a society achieve such a lofty objective?

Paradoxically, there was another, and opposing, direction for Sarmiento's revolutionary action. The liberal in him spoke to the necessity of freeing the future from a decrepit past, but the aristocrat in him spoke of the need to recover the honorable traditions of a bygone period which in recent years had been systematically torn apart by gaucho barbarism.

Four pages of *Facundo* are dedicated to the description of the high level of culture attained by the residents of San Juan in the two decades following independence: the area had enjoyed a "wealth" of civilized men, a progressive government, and the nation's most advanced system of primary education (VII, 62-65). Then came the scourge of gaucho leaders with their instinctive hatred of decency and civilized customs. Only the history of the Arab's conquest of Greece presented examples of as rapid a *barbarización,* he explains. Now, the struggle was one of "regaining" what had been lost. Argentina's cities of the interior had to "reivindicar glorias, civilización y notabilidades pasadas" (VII, 66). The struggle would be easier for Buenos Aires, which enjoyed constant contact with European civilization. But for the cities of the interior, the struggle would be far more fierce: "Dos siglos no bastarán para volverlas al camino que han abandonado, desde que la generación presente educa a sus hijos en la barbarie que a ella le ha alcanzado. Preguntásenos ahora, ¿por qué combatimos? Combatimos por volver a las ciudades su vida propia" (VII, 66). Here, the vision Sarmiento expressed for the future of his country was decidedly reactionary: it sought a *return* to past norms and the reestablishment of an anterior stage in its development.

Sarmiento's revolutionary vision, which combined both progressive and reactionary ideological currents, offered a uniquely apocalyptical vision of the sociopolitical reality of his time. The liberal vision promised a utopian future, and his aristocratic values sought a return to an idyllic past. Although so strikingly different, these two visions coincided in their condemnation of the present. Both visions prescribed the eradication of Argentine society as it was presently constituted. Both visions justified violent means for their respective goals, but that justification, in the case of Sarmiento, would become more and more irrational after 1852, when, free to act at last, he would have to reconcile the conflicting goals of the revolution that consumed the country and inflamed his contradictory spirit.[30]

Sarmiento: Military Leader

Sarmiento's passionate involvement in his country's civil struggles began at an early age. In 1827, the sixteen year old youth repeatedly had to close the store he tended in order to participate as an ensign in the local militia forces, which had the mission of protecting the town from the growing disorder in the region. In that year, the young man, already impetuous in his criticism of the army's heavy-handed oppression of the local population, came into direct conflict with the Federalist governor of the province. His brief imprisonment had the opposite effect of what his jailers intended: he came out converted to the Unitarian political faction and intensely committed to the struggle against the brutal forces that were extending their domination over the region.

After the defeat of Rosas in 1852, his writings and acts would demonstrate his deep anger and profound bitterness toward the rudimentary gaucho society of his country's interior provinces and what he depicted as its savage *caudillo* leaders. These attitudes had an unmistakable origin in his personal experiences with the civil war beginning in about 1829. With the war's eruption in that year, he quickly enlisted in the forces that had risen up against Facundo Quiroga. In the next two years he was to witness first hand the carnage of personal friends and fellow combatants. He himself narrowly escaped from death on at least two occasions. He undoubtedly came to realize that the savage wars of the pampas had little to do with the noble battles described in his classical readings, nor with the wars of independence of the two Americas, which had occurred a generation or more in the past. The leadership of the opposing forces were no longer guided by a respect for human life and a code of honor or decency in battle. "Jamás la naturaleza humana se me había prestado más indigna" (III, 179) he writes about the deceitful tactic of El fraile Aldao, who, after having entered into negotiations for peace, attacked Unitarian forces and caught them completely offguard. Sarmiento, with extraordinary luck, escaped unharmed from that "laberinto de muertes." But several of his fellow combatants suffered a more terrible end: the illustrious Laprida, former president of the congress of Tucumán, was slain on the field of battle; José María Villanueva, taken prisoner, had his neck slit open by his captors three days later; several of Sarmiento's personal friends and fellow representatives of San Juan's most respected families were executed by firing squads within a week.

One of Sarmiento's most profound lessons from these struggles, for which he had been both witness and participant, was that in the war of the pampas mercy had no role. The *caudillo* leader of the gaucho forces, he realized, held as his goal the total extermination of the enemy. In Mendoza he had personally observed the atrocities of Aldao, who ordered the execution of 200 unhappy victims, among whom were twenty of Sarmiento's personal friends. Similar massacres committed by Facundo Quiroga were already the stuff of improvised songs by gaucho singers throughout the interior provinces. Sarmiento himself could not help but be repelled by this thirst for blood. He never demonstrated a desire to personally commit violent acts in retribution, but would fully approve of the acts of others when he felt the situation justified.

In the 1837 to 1839 outbreak, he approved of the execution of several leaders of local insurrections–"bandidos de profesion" (III, 180) he called them–an act ordered by Coronel Benavides of the Federalist forces and later loyal Rosas henchman and governor of San Juan. He came to believe that in time of war violent acts against society justly deserved a violent punishment. During these trying moments of his adolescence the perpetrators of social and political violence were easily identified, and his own growing hatred found obvious, and perhaps justified targets. In later years, however, his bitterness hardly abated, and he would continue to seek out the culprits for a social reality which fell far short of his dreams.

His determination to find someone to blame for the backwardness of Argentina's customs and institutions was compelling. After he exchanged the rifle for the pen, he would continue through the press, which was his newfound weapon of ideological warfare, his advocation of the principle of harsh punishment for those who he believed perpetuated the degrading social and political environment in the interior.[31]

The young Sarmiento, with Hemingway-like spirit, thrilled to the sounds of military battle, in spite of the death and destruction that would inevitably result. War, for him, was an exciting adventure, one of life's truly unique and exciting experiences. The description he gives of one of his first battles captures the enthusiasm which he experienced:

> Pero la guerra con todas las ilusiones que engendra, y el humo de la gloria que ya embriaga a un capitán de compañía, no me han dejado impresiones más dulces, recuerdos más imperecederos, que aquella campaña de Mendoza, que concluyó en la tragedia horrible de Pilar. Fue para mi aquella época la poesía, la idealización, la realización de mis lecturas. Joven de dieciocho años, imberbe, desconocido de todos, yo he vivido en el éxtasis permanente del entusiasmo, y no obstante que nada hice de provecho, porque mi comisión era la de simple ayudante, sin soldados a su mando, era o hubiera sido un héroe, pronto siempre a sacrificarme, a morir donde hubiese sido útil, para obtener el más mínimo resultado (III, 176).

War was an intriguing novel, with exciting incidents and singular scenes.[32] The adventure of the moment caused in him a mental intoxication which was addicting in its power. Upon remembering that past action, he would forget the horror and magnify the glory and excitement of direct involvement. Such was the stuff of great literature, which, like the monument in the public plaza, perpetuated the memory of heroic encounters.[33]

War, in addition, was for Sarmiento a school for society's future citizens and its leaders. One must merely read the passages already indicated from *Recuerdos de provincia* in order to form a desirable list of the moral qualities which he believed a combat situation cultivated. The common soldier became "constant" under stress and "valiant" in spite of fear. His "pure patriotism" reciprocally engendered a willingness to engage in battle. If he followed his capable leaders with "blind obedience," then he would win "glory" whatever the outcome of the battle.[34] The experience of battle also educated society's more "elevated" or "influencial" citizens in the responsibilities of leadership. Sarmiento expected that those ordering the common soldiers also experienced the thrill and passion of battle, but not at the price of circumspection. The leader was the one who had to plan strategy, foresee difficulties, and later reflect upon results. While others could give themselves over to the vertigo of the moment, it was the leader who had to keep his head clear in order to calculate the next move, in order to "know" what was happening in front and behind the lines of combat. One could say that the leader of soldiers was for Sarmiento like Hemingway's *matador* against the bull. Both depended on their professional skill, courage, and grace in the face of pressure. Both governed the passions and instincts of their respective situations through the iron control of the intellect. For both, their honor and their art depended upon the degree of brilliance with which they conducted themselves when confronted by death.

Not uncharacteristic of Sarmiento was his conviction, from an early age, that he himself united all of the qualities of a successful battlefield leader. In *Recuerdos de provincia* he makes an implicit comparison between himself and Napoleon (III, 161) in his ability to plot battle moves and foresee consequences. Pages later he recounts his fearlessness and his cool style of leadership under extreme danger. His supreme satisfaction at the conclusion of the childhood skirmish he had led against a rock-armed neighborhood gang, was due to the esteem he had won as leader: "Cesó con esto el combate y se acercaron los más inmediatos hacia mí, silenciosos y más contentos de mí que de su triunfo" (III, 162). This self-infatuation as military leader would grow to gigantic proportions in subsequent years. In 1852 it caused no small problem when he, expecting to be named to the general staff by Urquiza, received instead the relatively insignificant commission of army *boletinero*. Later, his pretensions as military chief often provoked the satirical comments of his contemporaries.[35] But, in 1861, he accepted the first of several military assignments which largely fulfilled his own ambitions. In that year he was named "Auditor de Guerra" for Paunero's military expedition to the interior, which had the objective of quelling a rebellion in San Juan. In 1863 he briefly exercised the responsibilities of "Director de Guerra" against "El Chacho." Then, in 1868, upon assuming the presidency of the country, he, as Commander in Chief of the country's armed forces, directed several important "pacification" campaigns in the interior.[35] Throughout his life, Sarmiento thought like a soldier and fought like one, too: the only thing that mattered was total victory. This goal fueled his early writing onslaughts against Rosas, against Urquiza, and then against Alberdi, as much as it later inspired his fierce campaigns against "El Chacho" and López Jordán.

Notes for Chapter 1

1. See Tulio Halperín Donghi's *Revolución y guerra: formación de una élite dirigente en la Argentina criolla* (Buenos Aires: Siglo Veintiuno, 1972), and James R. Scobie, *Argentina: A City and a Nation,* 2nd ed. (New York and London: Oxford University Press, 1971), pp. 76-87, for interesting discussions concerning the relationship between the local and national influence of Juan Manuel de Rosas and the rise of the regional economy that was based on the *saladero* (the salted meat industry).

2. John Lynch, *Argentine Dictator: Juan Manuel de Rosas, 1829-1852* (Oxford: Clarendon Press, 1981), pp. 143-53.

3. James R. Scobie, *La lucha por la consolidación de la nacionalidad argentina, 1852-1862,* trans. Gabriela de Civiny (Buenos Aires: Hachette, 1964), p. 8. Lynch, *Argentine Dictator,* pp. 201-46, discusses in detail the terror and intimidation tactics used by Rosas in order to fortify his control.

4. Aldo Ferrer, *The Argentine Economy,* trans. Marjory M. Urquidi, (Berkeley and Los Angeles: University of California Press, 1967), pp. 65-73.

5. Halperín Donghi, *Revolución y guerra,* p. 26.

6. This is also the argument of Noël Salomon, "El *Facundo* de Domingo Faustino Sarmiento: manifiesto de la preburguesía argentina de las ciudades del interior," *Cuadernos Americanos,* 39, No. 5 (1980), pp. 170-76.

7. All references to Sarmiento's writing, unless otherwise noted, are from his *Obras Completas* (Buenos Aires: Luz del Día, 1948-1956), and will be indicated by volume and page numbers in the text of the monograph.

8. Miron Burgin, *The Economic Aspects of Argentine Federalism 1820-1852* (Cambridge: Harvard University Press, 1946), p. 245, states that after the failure of the tariff of 1835

> There was [for the population of the interior] hardly any difference between Rosas and Rivadavia, between porteño federalism and unitarism. Rosas no less than Rivadavia became the representative of Buenos Aires, the defender of its special interests, willing and ready to sarifice the most vital needs of the provinces. And to the porteño middle class Rosas revealed himself as the champion of the wealthy landowners, cattle breeders, and meat producers, who were the real beneficiaries of the federalist regime.

The complex issue of the effects of the Rosas administrations' protectionist policies upon the interior provinces (and the revisions it has suffered at the hands of historians) is treated by Salomon, "El *Facundo,*" pp. 170-76.

9. Salomon, "El *Facundo,*" p. 175. Sarmiento was torn between the theoretical conviction of the benefits brought about by trade (even before his 1846 meeting with Cowden in Barcelona) and the destruction of the interior economy on account of those measures. States Salomon, p. 149: "Aunque el liberalismo económico de D. F. Sarmiento en el *Facundo* no es absoluto—lo matiza un leve

proteccionismo con vistas a defender la 'industria naciente' del interior–puede decirse que constituye algo medular en el panfleto anti-rosista." Roberto Tamagno, *Sarmiento, los liberales y el imperialismo inglés* (Buenos Aires: A. Peña Lillo, 1963), quotes a number of Sarmiento's texts written between 1842-1844 which demonstrate his protectionist stance for internal commerce and nascent industries in Chile and Argentina.

10. Halperín Donghi, *Revolución y guerra*, pp. 285-87.

11. "Había antes de 1810 en la República Argentina dos sociedades distintas, rivales e incompatibles; dos civilizaciones diversas; la una española, europea, civilizada; y la otra bárbara, americana, casi indígena; y la revolución de las ciudades sólo iba a servir de causa, de móvil, para que estas dos maneras distintas de ser de un pueblo, se pusiesen en presencia una de otra, se acometiesen, y después de largos años de lucha, la una absorbiese a la otra" (VII, 54).

12. *Ibid.*, p. 126.

13. José S. Campobassi, *Sarmiento y su época 1811-1863* (Buenos Aires: Losada, 1975), I, pp. 78-83, quotes from Sarmiento's writing in order to document the latter's conversion to Unitarianism. Although he supported almost one to one the reforms advocated by the old Unitarian party, some of which were put into practice during Rivadavia's administrations, he nevertheless was highly critical of the rigidity of thought of the "old" Unitarians and their inability to come to grips with certain aspects of the national reality that impeded the realization of their otherwise worthy program. On one occasion he even accredited Rivadavia's ineptitude and lack of practical sense for having made possible twenty years of Rosism. In 1853, he would say to Mitre: "Yo soy federal de convicción" (p. 400, Campobassi), out of his belief that Argentina ought to imitate as closely as possible the federal system of the United States, which he admired.

14. Adolfo Prieto, *La literatura autobiográfica argentina* (Rosario: Editorial Biblioteca, 1968), p. 31.

15. *Ibid.*, pp. 65-66.

16. Salomon, "El *Facundo*," pp. 156-57.

17. Prieto, *Literatura autobiográfica*, p. 68.

18. *Ibid.*, pp. 65-66.

19. Juan Draghi Lucero, ed., *Cancionero popular cuyano* (Mendoza: Best Hermanos, 1938), comes to the same conclusion on the basis of his study of the surviving popular songs and poems of the period.

20. Sarmiento stresses in many passages (see, for example, III, 57, 72, 131) the superiority of writing over other modes of communication on account of its permanence and the record it provides for posterity. He also valued oratory as a means of persuasion. See Alberto Palcos, *El 'Facundo.' Rasgos de Sarmiento. Génesis y peripecias del 'Facundo.' Sarmiento y Rosas. Sarmiento íntimo. Sarmiento y el voto secreto* (Buenos Aires: El Ateneo, 1934), pp. 124-138; and Tulio Halperín Donghi, "Prólogo" to *Campaña en el Ejército Grande Aliado de Sud América* by Domingo F. Sarmiento (México: Fondo de Cultura Económica, 1958), pp. xxxvi-xliii.

21. Fernando Morán, *Novela y subdesarrollo: una interpretación de la novela hispanoamericana y española* (Madrid: Taurus, 1971), provides a discussion of the "ambiguous" intellectual.

22. Prieto, *Literatura autobiográfica*, pp. 40, 61.

23. Hernán Vidal, *Literatura hispanoamericana e ideología liberal: surgimiento y crisis (una problemática sobre la dependencia en torno a la narrativa del boom)* (Buenos Aires: Hispamérica, 1976), p. 21. In addition to the demoniac and utopian myths, Vidal posits yet a third: the Adamic myth, which in relation to Sarmiento's thought would correlate to the social program by which his society would travel from the demoniac to the utopian.

24. Adolfo Prieto, *Literatura y subdesarrollo: notas para un análisis de la literatura argentina* (Buenos Aires: Biblioteca, 1968), pp. 180-83.

25. Alejandro Korn, *Obras*, Vol. III: *Influencias filosóficas en la evolución nacional: ensayos y notas bibliográficas* (La Plata: Universidad Nacional de la Plata, 1940), p. 24.

26. Juan Guillermo Durán, "Literatura y utopía en Hispanoamérica," diss. Cornell, 1972, pp. 161-65, in treating the theme of utopia in Sarmiento's *Conflicto y harmonía*, calls attention to his vision of progress which had as its prerequisite the existing society's prior demolition.

27. Benjamín Vicuña Mackenna, *La Argentina en el año 1855*, introd. V. Lillo Catalán (Buenos Aires: Edición de la Revista Americana de Buenos Aires, 1936), p. 69.

28. Sarmiento, in *Recuerdos de provincia*, III, p. 118, states about the Argentine intellectual activities of the colony: "Aquello, pues, que llamamos hoy plagio, era entonces erudición y riqueza; y yo prefiriera oír por segunda vez a un autor digno de ser leído cien veces, a los ensayos incompletos de la razón y del estilo que aún están en embrión, porque nuestra inteligencia nacional no se ha desenvuelto lo bastante para rivalizar con los autores que el concepto del mundo reputa dignos de ser escuchados." .endend

29. David Viñas, *Literatura argentina y realidad política*. Vol. 1: *De Sarmiento a Cortázar* (Buenos Aires: Siglo Veinte, 1971), p. 17.

30. Ricardos Rojas, *El profeta de la pampa: vida de Sarmiento* (Buenos Aires: Losada, 1945), p. 446, details the intensification of his "disconcertante psicología" which culminated between 1861 and 1863 in his struggle against "El Chacho" Peñalosa: "su fantasía exaltose hasta el delirio" in his drive to exterminate the forces of gaucho insurrection.

31. "Las naciones pueden ser criminales y lo son a veces, y no hay juez que las castigue sino sus tiranos o sus escritores" (III, 207).

32. He describes several battles with the lexicon of the dramatist or novelist: "Salí por entre los enemigos, por una serie de peripecias y de escenas singulares . . . . Ordeno un tiroteo que sirva de introducción al capítulo; avánzome en seguida a provocar de palabras . . ." (III, 179). See especially his narrative recreation of when he and other children seriously imitated a battle of war (III, 159-62).

33. He concludes the episode of his childhood martial encounter between two gangs armed with stones: "¡Oh, vosotros, compañeros de gloria en aquel día memorable! ¡Oh, vos, *Piojoteo,* si vivieras! *¡Barrileto, Velita, Chuña, Gaucho y Capotito,* os saludo aún desde el destierro en el momento de hacer justicia al ínclito valor que hicisteis prueba! Es lástima que no se os levante un monumento en el puente aquel para perpetuar vuestra memoria" (III, 162).

34. See III, 160-62.

35. Vicuña Mackenna, *La argentina,* p. 89: "Vestía este jefe un 'frac' azul abrochado y estaba ahí echado para atrás con su bigote cano de teniente coronel, una gran parada de pretensiones militares, encogiéndose a cada instante de hombros como si sintiera sobre ellos el peso de las charreteras."

36. Among the works treating Sarmiento's military career, I have consulted Isaac Castro, *Sarmiento ante la montonera* (Corrientes: Edición del Museo Histórico y de Bellas Artes de Corrientes, 1937); and Augusto Rodríguez, *Sarmiento militar* (Buenos Aires: Edición G. Kraft, 1950). Works linking Sarmiento's military actions to the imposition of Buenos Aires' liberal government over the rest of the country are: Atilio García Mellid, *Proceso al liberalismo argentino* (Buenos Aires: A. Peña Lillo, 1957), and David Viñas, *Rebeliones populares argentinas.* Vol. I: *De los montoneros a los anarquistas* (Buenos Aires: Carlos Pérez, 1971).

CHAPTER 2

The Making of a Public Writer

In the period when Sarmiento began his writing labors, newspapers and journals were making slow but steady gains across the South American continent in the number of readers and the availability of publishing resources. The opposite was true for Argentina, however. The independence movement of 1810 had established the principle of freedom of the press and had initiated a period of rapid increase in publishing activity. The central government's increasing censorship after 1817 hardly interrupted this growth. But the long years of civil strife, in addition to the unenlightened and at times repressive policies of the country's government, drastically affected the flow of information and more particularly the level of publishing activity. Under Balcarce, the number of newspapers in the country rose to a high of forty-three in 1833, but then declined precipitously to fifteen in 1834.[1] The limitations on free expression continued following Rosas' return to power in 1835. Offsetting the decline in the number of publications in Buenos Aires was a corresponding gain in Montevideo, where exiled Unitarian leaders and others carried out their ideological attacks against the Buenos Aires dictatorship. In 1838 there were four publications in Buenos Aires and ten in Montevideo; in 1839, three and sixteen respectively; in 1840, six and thirteen; in 1842, three and fourteen; in 1846, four and eleven; in 1848, five and nine.[2]

Journals published during this period which did not have the explicit purpose of adulating Rosas generally came under official attack and folded promptly. One such journal was *El Semanario de Buenos Aires,* subtitled "periódico puramente literario y socialista; nada político,"[3] which appeared at the end of 1837. Members of the Salón Literario who followed the call of Esteban Echeverría and Juan B. Alberdi for Argentina's cultural renovation in publishing this journal, closed it after only four months. This effort was followed immediately by *La Moda,* a "gacetín semanal de música, de poesía, de literatura, de costumbres." This innocent denomination permitted its authors to disseminate new ideas through cautious means. It was through this latter journal that Sarmiento became familiar with the voice of Alberdi, whose pseudonym of Figarillo honored the legacy of Spain's great promoter of liberalism and critic of customs, José María de Larra.

The first of Sarmiento's experiences with journalism was typical with regard not only to his militant social objectives in writing, but also to the public furor which that writing caused. In 1839, he and his close friends, Manuel José Quiroga Rosas and Antonio Aberastain, founded in the city of San Juan the weekly journal, *El Zonda*. The provincial government under Benavides was not against the enterprise initially, since it made available to the young writers the province's printing facilities. In the editorial to the first issue, Sarmiento presented his definition of what a newspaper ought to consist. After enumerating the diverse types of notices and commentaries ordinarily printed, he wrote that "un periódico es, pues, todo, el gobierno, la administración, el pueblo, el comercio, la junta, el bloqueo, la Patria, la ciencia, la Europa, el Asia, el mundo entero, todo" (LII, 14). And then he added: "Un periódico es el hombre, el ciudadano, la civilización, el cielo, la tierra, lo pasado, el presente, los crímenes, las grandes acciones, la buena o la mala administración, las necesidades del individuo, la misión del gobierno, la historia contemporánea, la historia de todos los tiempos, el siglo presente, la humanidad en general, la medida de la civilización de un pueblo" (LII, 14-15). In short, the newspaper aimed at preparing the reading public for an intelligent role in deciding society's most urgent issues. The editors followed the lead of Alberdi and others of the young generation of Buenos Aires in clearly stating that the journal's primary objective was the promotion of the region's progress through their treatment of such nonpolitical topics as customs, public education, the arts, mining, and agriculture. In subsequent issues, however, it became evident that their enthusiasm for social criticism could not be totally contained. Benavides shut the press down and briefly incarcerated Sarmiento. Undoubtedly these acts were a reaction, at least in part, to the indignation which the social criticism of the young writers was provoking in the conservative provincial environment. It is also probable that Benavides followed the lead of Rosas in Buenos Aires. Rosas, threatened by the French blockade of that city a year earlier, had closed down several potentially critical presses and had suppressed at least one major conspiracy against the regime.

A few months later, Sarmiento's choice of Chile for political asylum was quite understandable. Historically, his native region of Cuyo had been intimately linked to Chile through political, as well as commercial, ties. Several times as a child or a young man he had crossed the Andes into Chile. First, it was for reasons of family business. Then, between 1831 and 1836, he had been forced to seek political exile with other members of his family and the survivors of a defeated Unitarian army of which his father was a member. A third time was with his uncle, the Bishop of Cuyo, who traveled to Chile's mountainous regions for reasons related to his religious mission.

Establishing himself in Santiago at the end of 1840, Sarmiento surveyed the possibilities for earning his living and at the same time continuing on with his promotion of progressive ideas. A rapid thinker, opinionated and confident, he stood out among the exiled Argentine community. He had only been in Santiago a matter of weeks before he began to manifest before his fellow exiles and the Chilean public his formidable abilities as a writer.

At the beginning of 1841 Sarmiento wrote and had published the article which was to launch him into a new career. The occasion was the anniversary of San Martín's victory over royalist Spanish forces at Chacabuco. In *Recuerdos de provincia* he recounts his fear and expectation over the public's possible reaction to his unsigned essay. He expresses his elation over the universal acclaim which the article later afforded him and concludes the passage with the exuberant realization that writing for the newspaper public was indeed a most suitable vocation, not only because of the facility with which he performed it, but also on account of it's promise of fulfilling his most deeply held goals: "¡Cuántas vocaciones erradas había ensayado antes de encontrar aquella que tenía afinidad química, diré así, con mi esencia!" (III, 194)

In spite of his inexperience, he had demonstrated a superior intellectual and writing talent. Within days his collaboration was solicited by at least two of the local political parties, each of which aspired to use the talents of the young writer for their own cause. To the surprise of many, Sarmiento rejected the bid of the liberal opposition and decided instead to support the Conservative Party of General Bulnes, whose authoritarian yet progressive orientation, and its past record for stable and honest government, he found attractive. Having been provided a press, he threw himself into his editing and writing activities.

His energetic example instantly caused envy among several young Chilean intellectuals. In the following years he courageously confronted the charges of *extranjero* which lesser spirits launched against him. However, his persistence and eloquence in defending his high ideals found their compensation in the support he received from some of Santiago's most important residents: Manuel Montt, governmental minister and later Chile's president; José Victorino Lastarria, a leader in Chile's youthful intellectual circles who would become that country's foremost literary historian; and several eminent Argentinians who also had left their native land for reasons of political opinion or personal safety.

Sarmiento quickly found his place in the rapidly expanding newspaper industry of Santiago and Valparaiso, and journalism became a way of life. In his writing few topics escaped his attention: historical issues, *costumbrista* sketches with reformist intention, reviews of theater productions, promotional pieces for public education, and the maintenance of the local highway systems. In 1842, he impetuously challenged the neoclassical ideas of Andrés Bello, Latin America's most important thinker who then resided in Santiago, in the renown polemics over language and romanticism. Over the next decade, Sarmiento would contribute to or share in the management of a long list of daily and weekly newspapers: *El Mercurio, El Nacional, El Progreso, La Crónica, La Tribuna, Sud América,* and *La Gaceta del Comercio.*

Writing in 1850 in *Recuerdos de provincia,* Sarmiento presents a somewhat romanticized image of his earliest writing activities in Santiago. He argues that from the very start his one overriding goal was to combat through journalistic means the system of *caudillos* which had usurped social, political, and economic power throughout his native land. He describes his first meeting with Manuel Montt, then Chile's Minister of Justice and Public Instruction, and who would soon become his employer: "Un punto discutimos larga y porfiadamente con el ministro, y era la guerra a Rosas que yo me proponía hacer, concluyendo en una transacción que satisfacía por el momento los intereses de ambas partes, y me dejaba expedito el camino para educar la opinión del gobierno mismo, y hacerle aceptar la libertad de imprenta lisa y llanamente como después ha sucedido" (III, 196). Sarmiento's assertion that he won Montt's permission to utilize the Chilean governing party's official press in order to carry on his struggle against Rosas is not born out by the available evidence. Indeed, the small number of articles he published in the first eight months of his Chilean exile, in addition to their moderate tone, attest either to his obedience to the Chilean government's official position of neutrality, or to his own discretion with regard to this matter.[4] However, his resolve to combat Rosas through the Chilean press would steadily grow until it assumed by 1844 the proportions of a crusade.

His agreement with Chile's governing party involved a related matter of primary importance: the government's commitment to defend free speech and the freedom of the press. In subsequent years, Sarmiento would make full use of this *carte blanche* in his writing activities. His vigorous articles on all subjects provoked opposition and at times the disfavor of individuals in the government who sponsored his journalistic activities. In an article of 1841, he theorized about the posssible social effects of his style of journalism. The newspaper, he states, "necesita irritar las pasiones, sublevar temores y desconfianzas, y aun ofender a las personas que perjudican a sus intereses. . . . La declamación más exagerada y virulenta, hace el fondo de estos escritos, y las palabras tiranía, despotismo, embarazan cada renglón y forman el fondo de cada página; porque se necesitan grandes estímulos para mover los ánimos indiferentes" (I, 63). He practiced what he preached. Through the press he launched his tempestuous attacks against injustices and stridently defended his progressive causes. He often ignored the bruised sensitivies of others and disdained the negative consequences to his own advancement that his frankness might cause. He believed that writing eloquence, which had limited utility in a society of rough-hearted and hard-minded citizens, became a formidable weapon for promoting progress in a more cultured environment like Chile (III, 200). In the government-sponsored press he even dared to criticize certain programs of the administration in power. With pride he rebutted in 1850 the accusation that his provocative writings had undermined the very concept of liberty in Chile: "Reivindico para mi aquella gloria del *Mercurio* de haber impugnado, al lado del gobierno, las ideas peligrosas a la libertad" (III, 197). He believed that his firey exercise of free speech in the promotion of progress and as a challenge to retrograde practices, provided a defense from within of Chile's budding democratic institutions.

In the next few years Sarmiento would undertake new writing projects with the same impetuosity that characterized his initial journalistic labors. What changed, however, was the scope of his vision. At first his energies were taken up with polemics over questions related to art and language with his Chilean peers, but toward the end of the decade his writings treated the most serious issues confronting Argentina as a nation: the need for free commerce, the unification of the country, and the content of its future constitution. In this spirit he believed that a decade of experience as public writer more than adequately prepared him for the much larger responsibilities of national statesman. "No soy periodista," he wrote in 1853 (XV, 207), responding to the charge by Juan Bautista Alberdi, that "la prensa periódica desempeñada por largos años, lejos de ser la escuela del Hombre de Estado, es ocupación en que se pierden las cualidades para serlo" (XV, 211). He therefore drew a careful line between mere journalism and his very personal idea of public writing. During his first crucial years he had accepted in full conscience the partisan defense of one Chilean political party over the others. However he was not a party man, and throughout his long public life he would never become one. He would later explain that professional responsibilities during his years in Chile had never caused him to detract from his primordial commitment of combating Rosas' tyranny (XV, 207). He made a distinction between journalistic professionalism and writing on behalf of progressive causes. The advancement of society would never take second place to personal interest or professional obligations. He would only expend his energies on behalf of partisan concerns if, in doing so, there existed the possibility of gaining one more ally for the struggles of his continent.

The doubt occasionally entered into his mind about the value for posterity of a journalism such as his which addressed the political issues of the day, but left aside concerns of a more lasting importance. What would survive of his public writing once the bitter memories of the Rosas tyranny belonged to the past? In an untypical instance of self-doubt, he communicates his fear that a writing so passionately composed, and then so hurriedly read, would hardly leave a trace in the collective memory of his continent: "¿Cómo podrán estas producciones [del diario] creadas de prisa, y sin más objeto que favorecer un intento del momento, desempeñar tan alta misión [de impulsar el progreso]? Puede el lector sensato esperar buena fe, examen filosófico y verdad en los hechos que sólo se le presentan para hacerlo interesarse en fines particulares?" (I, 65)

Sarmiento realized that a writing production oriented primarily toward social and political issues only with difficulty could address cultural issues of a more permanent or unchanging nature. The press excelled in the function of informing people of day-to-day issues, but it was less than ideal as a medium for expounding philosophical and scientific ideas. People, he knew, tended to read newspapers rapidly and superficially, and it was understandable that the journalist directed his energies toward causing a maximum and immediate impact on the reader. Given these conditions, he believed that the best way for the press to fulfill a progressive role in society was through the repetition and accumulation of those momentary impressions. The journalist wrote *sous rature* –or "under erasure"–knowing that his words, just like events in a progressive society, acquired importance only when they succeeded in generating an ever-evolving discourse. Paradoxically, he directed his words toward the future; but in that uncertain future those words would already belong to a forgotten past. The ally of the journalist (but from another perspective his worst enemy) was time itself, as Sarmiento observes: "El que escribe un libro puede cerrar con confianza los oídos a la crítica, no pasará mucho tiempo sin que el criterio público le haga justicia; el que escribe un periódico ni esa esperanza tiene, sus más brillantes escritos como los menos interesantes, mueren con el día en que ven la luz" (I, 332).

Undoubtedly Sarmiento exaggerated somewhat his point, because in his epoch there were many writers whose fame was based precisely on the quality of their articles published in the newspapers of the day. Sarmiento himself called attention to Larra, whose genius had found its appropriate expression in the columns of the daily and weekly press. Those articles were "dardos de su sátira punzante, enérgica y correccional, irritando de corazón contra los males de la sociedad . . ." (I, 115). Paradoxically, Larra's writing acquired universal value precisely for having addressed the most timely questions of his society: "dondequiera que haya gobierno por establecerse, costumbres añejas que combatir, quisquillas de nacionalidad que moderar, e ideas nuevas que introducir, Larra será el libro ameno, útil e instructivo" (I, 116). Sarmiento, then, believed in the transitory quality of words, but he still credited some journalistic writing with a value for posterity.[5]

The value of his own journalism, however, had to be determined according to the effectiveness in bringing about concrete results. If his writing were to disappear from public memory the next day, then so be it, provided that it first were to leave in its place tangible social and political gains. The promotion of progress outweighed any other objective. One is reminded of his early advocation of *socialismo,* or progress-oriented action: "El *socialismo,* perdónennos la palabra; el socialismo, es decir la necesidad de hacer concurrir la ciencia, el arte y la política al único fin de mejorar la suerte de los pueblos, de favorecer las tendencias liberales, de combatir las preocupaciones retrógradas, de rehabilitar al pueblo, al mulato y a todos los que sufren" (I, 310). *Socialismo* was the organizing principle for his actions as well as his writing. Sarmiento, in brief, refused to confine his writing energies to neat and independent disciplines. Unlike writers specializing in scientific, artistic, or literary issues, his program for composition meant channeling all disciplines of inquiry in pursuit of his social and political objectives.

His idea of *socialismo* indicates the "performative" mission of his writing.[6] He wrote with the goal of altering reality rather than merely describing it. Rarely, if ever, did he take the pen in hand with the idea that his words would constitute a value-free or impartial consideration of the relevant issues. On the contrary, writing for this ideological *bricoleur* was a type of action because it had the objective of transforming the social and political landscape according to a preconceived plan. In his works, regardless of whether individually classified as literature, biography and autobiography, travel correspondence, political pamphlets, remembrances, or quasi-sociological tracts, what stands out is the pragmatic goal he intended for them. *How* they effected the reader was often as important as *what* they said.

Being that the greater part of Sarmiento's extensive and varied writings were first published in the daily or weekly press, it is not surprising that the style, tone, and focus of these writings were influenced by that medium. He correctly observed in one work that there existed between himself and journalism "una afinidad química" (III, 194). Concerning the journalistic nature of his writing and thought, Leopoldo Lugones appropriately writes that Sarmiento was, before anything else, a journalist, a circumstance that chronologically determined, as is natural, the form which his writing, whether critical or literary, would take. Both the strengths and defects of Sarmiento's writing, Lugones affirms, can be traced to his newspaper activity, for Sarmiento subordinated his talents as a writer to the demands of the journalistic medium.[7] Sarmiento would have been in agreement. There was no higher calling than that of public writer, there was no more effective way of promoting society's progress than through the labors of the press. With his skills and his particular disposition, he was eminently suited for the tasks of the journalist. He wrote: "El espíritu de los escritos de un escritor, cuando tienen un carácter peculiar, es su alma, su esencia" (III, 211). These words communicate more, perhaps, than what he intended. The "spirit" of his writings, and perhaps the manner in which he perceived his personal and social situations, did indeed reflect his journalistic consciousness.

The journalistic influence is immediately evident when one observes how Sarmiento militantly promoted social progress when discussing even the most esoteric of topics. Writing for the press was his way of fostering an intellectual environment in which ideas were in constant movement. Although he recognized that the clash of ideas was integrally related to conflicts between material interests or rivalries for power, his idealist conception of history nevertheless led him to believe that those struggles were to be won or lost primarily on the ideological level. Out of this belief came his dedication to winning the hearts and minds of the public through journalism. With the same objective, he incessantly sought out polemics and entered into impassioned arguments. In addition to his desire of convincing others of his own conception of truth, he had the goal of provoking their reaction and thus encouraging their critical thought regarding important social and political issues. During his long years of exile in Chile, Sarmiento rarely avoided a dispute or lost an opportunity for stimulating readers' interest in public affairs. For him, the press caused the moral improvement of the individual not only because it propagated progressive values, but also because it encouraged a continual and ongoing consideration of ideas. Sarmiento accredited the newspaper with a formidable ability for moving the reader, a power that any social planner could use to his advantage in his own campaign for progress. The newspaper, he wrote, best fulfilled its destiny when it could "sacudir a las cabezas inteligentes del sueño de una inacción perjudicial" (I, 289).

A clear example of Sarmiento's pragmatic writing orientation is found in the articles he wrote during the literary polemics of 1841-1842, only months after his arrival in Chile. His goals were social, although the subject treated was literature. He lashed out against "las formas heladas y estériles" of past literary movements (I, 225), and especially those led by "los gramáticos [del lenguaje y de la sociedad quienes luchaban] para resistir a los embates populares, para conservar la rutina y las tradiciones" (I, 213). He also attacked "esa literatura reducida a las galas del decir, que concede todo a la expresión y nada a la idea" –in the borrowed words of Larra–(I, 249). He criticized writers of classicist tendencies (I, 293-94) for their continued use of antiquated modes of expression. In addition, Sarmiento promoted a simplified version of Castillian spelling, superior in his opinion to the writing system which Hispanic America had inherited from its colonial past. All of these issues spoke to his belief that writing was the appropriate expression of civilized society, and that the transformation of one necessarily required a modernization of the other.

Another aspect of the journalistic influence in Sarmiento's writing is the emphasis he gave to social and political themes. It is no coincidence that he referred to his vocation as "publicista" and "propagandista," given the manner in which his own ideological position with regard to social and political issues generally became the central concern for his writing. In most instances he willingly ceded the role of neutral investigator for that of partisan defender. He was largely undisturbed by the contradiction between his strong political convictions and his ambitions as historian, ethnologist, or literary writer. It was therefore inevitable that his total commitment to a *socialista* brand of progress came to influence nearly everything he wrote. Surprisingly few studies on Sarmiento have called attention to the complex relationship between political journalism, which was his preferred medium of idea dissemination, and the historical and even literary themes he treated.[8]

The political thesis in even the pages most acclaimed for their sociological and literary merits is especially obvious. *Facundo,* born of the Chilean "free press," was his contribution to the ideological struggle against *caudillo* tyranny in Argentina. Sarmiento paradoxically believed that the freedom of the press licensed intentional misrepresentation and one-sided presentations. He was later to admit that he intentionally distorted many details of the protagonist's career in an effort to heighten the work's propagandistic value.[9] The noble objective of combating gaucho tyranny, he believed, justified whatever procedure used, including the sacrifice of truth.

Later, his work on Angel "El Chacho" Peñalosa would exhibit a similar accumulation of negative evidence and the exclusion of any information not supportive of his own ideological position with regard to the circumstances surrounding the life and brutal assassination of his protagonist.[10] Public writing in this case served in the enterprise of justifying the controversial events in which he himself was a participant. He had a clear idea of writing's power for altering the appearance of reality. He utilized his own discourse for appropriating the facts. To write history was for him the recreation of history. It was one means of imposing his own truth over not only the society of his day, but also posterity.

Recuerdos de provincia (1850) is not as vivid an example as *Facundo* and *El Chacho* of Sarmiento's self-serving or partisan writing practice, but it does exemplify another aspect of his practice of writing "libros de combate." The work had the explicit objective of confronting the accusations of his political opponents and counterbalancing the pressure which the Rosas government was applying to Chilean officials for his extradition. But that same work had, as Ricardo Rojas observed, the implicit intention of "suplantar a Rosas" with himself in the position of national leadership for the approaching constitutional period.[11] These two works take their place along side of *Argirópolis, Campaña en el Ejército Grande,* and *Las ciento y una,* as powerful literary statements which were written with political effectiveness as their initial and principal objective. Perhaps García Merou exaggerates in his opinion that Sarmiento never reached a higher level of culture than when he wrote inspired by hatred.[12] But there is no doubt that Sarmiento's most inspired writing was a faithful product of his impetuous character. The journalistic pen was his sword of combat, as Sarmiento's words of 1852 confirm: "Soldado, con la pluma o la espada, combato para poder escribir, que escribir es pensar; escribo como medio y arma de combate, que combatir es realizar el pensamiento . . . ."[13]

Sarmiento attempted to demonstrate to his compatriots that his brand of writing was either an effective form of action or a prelude to personal involvement. In his way of thinking, the journalist was simultaneously the social activist, and the public writer was the future statesman. Typically, he stated on many occasions: "Actuar, hay que actuar, hazlo, aunque sea malo, pero hazlo . . . ."[14] His supporters could not help but observe his untiring energies on behalf of progressive causes. When he was not writing, he was organizing relief efforts for the victims of Rosas' tyranny or political action groups which would support a military confrontation against the dictator. Similarly, when not engaged in the combat against *caudillo* despotism in Argentina, he was busily promoting new ideas and institutions for the benefit of his Chilean neighbors. His detractors, however, pointed out the personal and social costs of such a plan of action based on continual and at times impulsive movement: Did an admirable objective justify questionable means or hasty acts, either of which might bring about harmful consequences? Didn't impetuous commitment to a program of action blind one to the need for self-criticism and evaluation of both means and ends?[15] Sarmiento was hardly alone in his advocating of a militant journalistic writing. His was a century of idealistic public writers–Fernández de Lizardi, Montalvo, Martí–who also believed in the progressive function of the press in promoting social and political change. Sarmiento correctly observed that Latin American culture had entered into a new phase of its development with the popularization, and then institutionalization, of the newspaper and its stepchild, the weekly or bi-weekly magazine.[16] Almost overnight the middle class, now with increased numbers and greater political influence, had become avid participants in this new medium of communication. Although he didn't call the newly ascendant class by the name of the bourgeoisie, as it is known today, he nevertheless recognized the indispensable function that the press would play for that class in the society of the future. He stated in 1851: "Las publicaciones periódicas son en nuestra época como la respiración diaria" (III, 212). These are premature words if one reads them as a characterization of the newspaper's role in the larger society of his time. Surely the statement was written with only his small group of urban intellectuals in mind. The continuation of those words reveals his pride for having associated himself with that medium of communication which–as he uncannily predicted–was destined to play an integral role in the integration of his country into a world system based on liberal economic principles. He wrote: "Ni libertad, ni progreso, ni cultura se conciben sin este vehículo que liga a las sociedades unas con otras y nos hace sentirnos a cada hora miembros de la especie humana por la influencia y repercusión de los acontecimientos de unos pueblos sobre los otros." Under the spell of utopian liberalism, the young Sarmiento dreamed of utilizing the mass communications technology for overcoming ethnic and regional differences and for uniting the population centers of the world under the common banner of progress.

Through his writing, Sarmiento attempted to translate dreams into living reality. His rapid rise to national and international prominence in little more than a decade was due primarily to his persistent and persuasive advocation of progress and to his untiring journalistic warfare against the ideological foundations of Rosism. By the fall of the dictator in 1852 he had become widely known among Argentinians and was regarded by many of his peers to be one of the most capable of men for leading the nation into the promising era of constitutional government. His qualifications: an impressive list of books, newspaper articles, pamphlets, and his several years of experience as public writer.

Much of Sarmiento's public writing was conceived under the sign of political expediency. But he brought to this task the rare gifts of an uncanny intuition, a penetrating intelligence, and a dynamic style. Only with difficulty can one attempt to understand that writing practice without taking into account the objectives he held for it in the sociopolitical context of the time. Ricardo Rojas correctly associates Sarmiento's writing with the underdeveloped social and cultural environment in which he lived.[17] Sarmiento, he says, was neither artist nor philosopher, but rather a tutelary publicist in a tumultuous and semibarbarian country. It is therefore to be expected that his writing was journalistic, militant, and doctrinaire, and that it reflected in its essence the disorder of the social reality which it treated. Rojas cautions against seeking what Sarmiento's writing does not offer: the rational or systematic exposition of ideas. Writing for Sarmiento was, before all, a powerful instrument for transforming the relatively backward social environment and turbulent political life of his continent.

Notes for Chapter 2

1. Victor García Costa, *El periódico político* (Buenos Aires: Centro Editor de América Latina, 1971), pp. 39-46.

2. Félix Weinberg, "El periodismo en la época de Rosas," *Revista de Historia*, No. 2 (1957), p. 92, who cites Antonio Zinny, the foremost historian of Argentine journalism. Weinberg's bibliography at the end of the article lists the indispensable sources for a study of this issue.

3. Weinberg, "El periodismo," p. 88.

4. Sarmiento's commitment to combat Rosas through the Chilean press grew with the passing of the months, and was not what he later characterized as his urgent mission at the very beginning. Julia Ottolenghi, *Vida y obra de Sarmiento en síntesis cronológica* (Buenos Aires: Kepelusz, 1950), provides a chronological list by title of his articles and writings. On that list I have identified only five articles written during the first eight or so months which treated issues relevant to Argentine politics: "Campaña contra Rosas," *El Mercurio*, 17 March 1841 (signed "un emigrado"); "Política americana," *El Nacional*, 14 April 1841; "Condición de la República Argentina," *El Nacional*, 8 May 1841; "Vindicación de la República Argentina," *El Mercurio*, 7 June 1841; and a series of four articles from 9-15 October, 1841 in *El Mercurio*, which treated the issue of Argentine emigrants.

5. Writing in 1852 about the assassination of Florencio Varela (presumably at the hands of Rosas' henchmen), Sarmiento expresses an uncharacteristic faith in the value of the press for posterity, even though it fails in its short-run political mission: "De ahí nace que los gobiernos tiránicos y criminales necesitan, para existir, apoderarse ellos solos de los diarios .... U na conspiración puede ser ahogada en sangre, pero un libro, una revelación de la prensa, aunque haya un puñal como el que dio fin con Florencio Varela, queda ahí siempre; porque lo que está impreso queda estampado para siempre, y si en el momento presente es inútil y sin efecto, no lo es para la posteridad que, juzgando por el examen de los hechos y libre de toda preocupación y de toda intimidación, pronuncia su fallo inapelable" (III, 212). Whatever the merit of Varela's writing, it is unlikely that Sarmiento would have welcomed a similar eulogy for himself and his own writing production. Although not treating this precise issue, Alicia R. Bóo's article, "La realidad argentina a través de Varela y Sarmiento," in *Florencio Varela y el 'Comercio de la Plata,'* by Félix Weinberg and collaboraters (Bahía Blanca: Instituto de Humanidades, Universidad Nacional del Sur, 1970), pp. 83-110, compares the sociopolitical and artistic thought of these two important figures.

6. J. L. Austin, *How To Do Things with Words*, ed. J. O. Urmson (Cambridge, Mass.: 1962), pp. 2-8, contrasts "constative" to "performative" linguistic utterances. The first makes statements about facts and must be measured against the criteria of truth and falsehood. The second produces an action which must be measured against the standards of success or failure.

7. Leopoldo Lugones, *Historia de Sarmiento* (Buenos Aires: Otero & Co., 1911), p. 131, writes:

Sarmiento fue periodista antes de ser autor de libros, circunstancia cronológica que determina, como es natural, la formación del escritor, y con esto el examen crítico.

Las cualidades y defectos más prominentes de aquél, son rasgos de periodista. . . . El escrito de Sarmiento, es siempre urgente. La gala literaria, resultante de un temperamento nativo de escritor, le viene al correr de la pluma. Por esto es siempre fragmentaria y comúnmente de tosco engarce. El positivismo es también su calidad dominante, y de aquí la escasez de metáforas. El periodista debe decir las cosas directamente, interesando á su lector con el valor intrínseco de las mismas. Esto excluye también el sistema filosófico y literario. Las ideas, tanto como la literatura del periodista, dependen de la impresión de su día. Son fugaces por naturaleza, como la hoja en que las edita. Su lógica es la de los acontecimientos, no la de las ideas.

Sarmiento subordinó sus dotes de escritor á estos rasgos de periodista.

8. Regarding the journalistic bent of Sarmiento's writing, see César H. Guerrero, *Sarmiento: el pensador* (Buenos Aires: Depalma, 1979), and especially the chapter "Sarmiento y el periodismo." Two books which have been unavailable for my study are Alberto Fernández Leys, *Sarmiento y el periodismo,* and Efraín U. Bischoff, *Sarmiento, periodista.*

9. See Sarmiento's letter of 22 December 1845 to General Paz, as reproduced by Matías E. Suárez, *Sarmiento: ese desconocido* (Buenos Aires: Theoría, 1964), p. 264.

10. José Hernández, poet, Federalist politician, and Sarmiento foe, in 1863 wrote for *El Argentino* of Paraná, Entre Ríos, a series of articles entitled "Rasgos biográficos del General Angel Vicente Peñalosa," that later was published in book form as *Vida del Chacho.* Similarly, Olegario V. Andrade, poet and Federalist politician, reacting to Sarmiento's negative portrayal of Peñalosa, wrote in 1863 some biographical notes for the newspaper *El Porvenir,* of Gualeguaychú, of Entre Ríos. In subsequent years, Eduardo Gutiérrez dedicated some ballads, and wrote *El Chacho* (ca 1886). See José S. Campobassi, *Sarmiento y su época,* pp. 517-553, for a balanced account of Sarmiento's part in the events leading to the death of Peñalosa.

11. Ricardo Rojas, *El profeta de la pampa: vida de Sarmiento* (Buenos Aires: Losada, 1951), p. 365.

12. Martín García Merou, *Sarmiento,* introd. Rodolfo Trostine (Buenos Aires: Ayacucho, 1944), p. 37.

13. Domingo F. Sarmiento, *Campaña en el Ejército Grande Aliado de Sud América,* prol. Tulio Halperín Donghi (México: Fondo de Cultura Económica, 1958), p. 61, in the "Complemento" or introduction to his diary which followed.

14. A. Belín Sarmiento, *Sarmiento anecdótico* (Saint Cloud: 1929), p. 375. Sarmiento at times demonstrated his belief in the curious idea that a new statement could erase from public consciousness any memory of his previous words or acts. "I wasn't talking in earnest," he attempted to communicate to Echeverría in a letter of 1849 about some devastating words that he had written a few years earlier (V, 54). His actual words, in the modernized orthography he

advocated at the time: "Dije una vez que estaba V. enfermo de espíritu i de cuerpo i me aseguran que rebienta de gordo. Agregue V. eso a la fe de erratas garrafales que he cometido en mis viajes." Quoted by Alberto Palcos, *Echeverría y la democracia argentina* (Buenos Aires: El Ateneo, 1941), p. 204, from the letter of 12 December 1849.

15. Sarmiento documents the advances of journalism in "El diarismo," I, 57-66; "Sobre la lectura de periódicos," I, 77-85; y "Diálogo entre el editor y el redactor," I, 329-35.

16. Ricardo Rojas, *La literatura argentina: ensayo filosófico sobre la evolución de la cultura en el Plata,* Vol. I: *Los proscriptos* (Buenos Aires: Guillermo Kraft, 1957), p. 332: "De ser este hombre un filósofo, hubiera sido fácil sintetizarle, por el sistema de sus ideas, como a Spencer en su obra cíclica. De ser un artista, hubiera sido fácil sintetizarle también, como a Hugo en la suya poemática. Pero es Sarmiento, no artista ni filósofo, sino publicista tutelar de un país pletórico, semibárbaro y nuevo. Su obra es periodística, militante, apostólica; y tiene la variedad externa y el desorden de los hechos que ella misma comenta o ilumina, en largo medio siglo de aguerrida actuación, aun extendido más, hacía el pasado por su memoria de historiador, y hacia el futuro por su visión de profeta."

CHAPTER 3

Ideological Bricoleur

Ideas make the ordinary man, but the extraordinary individual, through conscious design and idiosyncratic gesture, goes beyond the pre-existing ideological context in pursuit of his own truth. Sarmiento exemplifies the latter. He had a clearer understanding than most of the causes of his country's conflicts and their possible resolution. This, in large part, is the reason for his initial rise to fame and his subsequent triumphs as a national statesman. But Sarmiento, perhaps more than other great leaders, had his personal demons. Certain personal tendencies and prejudices, some of which have been discussed in Chapter One, dramatically affected his actions in ways frequently unconscious to himself. Many of these were undoubtedly related to his own class experience, others typified his generation and the spirit of the age, and yet others belonged to him alone. The following pages interprete some of these personal demons in relation to his mode of perception, ideation, and writing production. A fundamental issue which must be considered before undertaking the study of textual content and its effect upon society is the manner in which the idiosyncratic gesture determines to some degree the organization of the writer's ideas.

Sarmiento was a self-taught man. As a youth he began a practice that he would continue for the rest of his life: the search through reading and personal observation for ideas that might prove useful for his society's march toward progress. The European intelligence of the previous hundred or so years had been presented to him–shall we say–in smorgasbord fashion. A rapid and selective reader, he assimilated those ideas which he perceived to be most applicable to the South American reality or potentially useful in the formulation of his own program for national reconstruction. He read with his attention geared to the immediate and long range needs of his society, and had neither time nor desire to involve himself in the gratuitous exercise of erudition.

He believed that progressive action need not be preceeded by an excessively thorough consideration of problems and potential effects. The region's needs in all spheres of life were so overwhelming and urgent that it did not matter where one who desired change should begin. This accounts at least in part, for the dispersion of his interests and physical energies into any number of fields. As a consequence, only on occasion did he provide in his writing a thorough and penetrating consideration of any one of these particular needs. There are notable exceptions however, for example his extensive treatment of issues related to education. He was a man in a hurry, and he threw himself into action many times without a prior consideration of consequences. One of his mottos is quite revealing in this regard: "Hacer las cosas: hacerlas mal, pero hacerlas."[1] One will make mistakes, he realized, but they would be insignificant in comparison to those accomplishments resulting from one's incessant energy and indomitable will to act.

His most important biographers agree about the "journalistic" rather than "philosophical" tendencies in Sarmiento's writing. His penchant for action, says Ricardo Rojas, went hand in hand with his lack of intellectual discipline.[2] The impetus to action overflowed, impeding him from becoming an ideologue, or for that matter, an artistic writer or systematized thinker. In a similar fashion, Lugones calls attention to how the rapid practice of writing for the daily or weekly press caused a refinement in his style, but not in the content of his ideas. His writing causes a favorable immediate impression, but upon analysis one realizes the fragmentary treatment of issues and the loosely connected ideas.[3] Gálvez was of the opinion that guiding Sarmiento's acts as well as his writing, there was more instinct than reflection, more improvisation than calculation, and more will than intelligence.[4]

His anti-philosophical orientation followed logically from the underdeveloped conditions of his environment and his total commitment to change. Not that he was opposed to the principles of ideological consistency and rigorous erudition; on the contrary, it was merely a matter of priorities. A respect for the differences between schools of thought and logical argumentation would have detracted from more urgent endeavors. His knowledge production favored breadth and volume over quality and thoroughness.

In this regard, Sarmiento, when considered as a writer, resembles what Claude Lévi-Strauss calls the *bricoleur*. Certain characteristics of his discourse, for example its lack of a unified system of thought or inconsistent methodological focus, suggest a comparison with what the French structuralist observes in primitive thought. In contrast to the "engineer," who utilizes empirical science in order to understand objective or social reality, the *bricoleur* possesses a closed universe of intellectual instruments:

> the rules of his game are always to make do with 'whatever is at hand,' that is to say, with a set of tools and materials which is always finite and is also heterogeneous because what it contains bears no relation to the current project, or indeed to any particular project, but is the contingent result of all the occasions there have been to renew or enrich the stock or to maintain it with the remains of previous constructions or destructions. The set of the '*bricoleur's*' means . . . is to be defined only by its potential use, or, putting this another way and in the language of the '*bricoleur*' himself, because the elements are collected or retained on the principle that 'they

may always come in handy.' Such elements are specialized up to a point, sufficiently for the *'bricoleur'* not to need the equipment and knowledge of all trades and professions, but not enough for each of them to have only one definite and determinate use. They each represent a set of actual possible relations; they are 'operators' but they can be used for any operations of the same type.[5]

The principal shortcoming of this otherwise useful description is that all men, and not merely the *bricoleur,* make due with "whatever is at hand" in the enterprise of conceptualizing experience. According to Hegel, man in general perceives situations according to a relatively reduced number of mental categories which he forms in the process of interaction with his situation: "it is from conforming to finite categories in thought and action that all deception originates."[6] More explicitly, Louis Althusser equates the concept of *bricolage* with ideology in general. Combining aspects of Freudian thought to his overall Marxian vision, he explains the process of conscious thought formation, or ideology, which is: "an imaginary assemblage *(bricolage),* a pure dream, empty and vain, constituted by the 'day's residues' from the only full and positive reality, that materially producing their existence."[7] This imaginary assemblage of ideas is necessarily influenced by the individual's lived experience vis-à-vis his social class—however remote that influence might sometimes seem. In this light, what Lévi-Strauss identifies as *bricoleur-* like ideation is a mental process common to men of any historical period. Taking the view of Hegel and Althusser into account, my application of the term *bricoleur* is in reference to those men whose thought tends toward the utilitarian norm identified by Lévi-Strauss, and in opposition to those who attempt to rigorously order their conscious world under the umbrella of empirical science or philosophical logic.

There are many aspects of Sarmiento's discourse which the Lévi-Straussian conception of *bricoleur* helps to identify and explain. Sarmiento manifested a *bricolage* orientation in his belief that the perception of fine distinctions or the comprehension of moral ambiguities stood in the way of decisiveness and movement. *Mi defensa* begins with a self-description which in content and in style breathes of his intrepid commitment to precipitate events without undue attention to possible consequences:

Lanzado repentinamente en la vida pública, en medio de una sociedad que me ha visto surgir en un día, sin saber de dónde vengo, quién soy, y cuáles son mi carácter y mis antecedentes; en dónde he templado las armas con que me he echado de improviso en la prensa, combatiendo con arrojo a dos partidos, defendiendo a otro; sentando principios nuevos para algunos; sublevando antipatías por una parte, atrayéndome por otra afecciones; complaciendo a veces, chocando otras, y no pocas reuniéndolos a todos en un solo coro de aprobación o vituperios; predicando el bien constantemente y obrando el mal alguna vez; atacando las ideas generales sobre literatura; ensayando todos los géneros; infringiendo por ignorancia o

por sistema las reglas; impulsando a la juventud, empujando brusca-
mente a la sociedad, irritando susceptibilidades nacionales; cayendo
como un tigre en una polémica, y a cada momento conmoviendo
la sociedad entera, y siempre usando un lenguaje franco hasta ser
descortes y sin miramiento . . . (III, 2).

There is an obvious contradiction between Sarmiento's impetuous style
of action, as this passage suggests, and the career of "public writer" for
which he believed himself to be so admirably suited. That is to say,
imperious movement makes difficult the careful introspection of one's own
motivations or the analysis of the potential consequences of one's acts.
One would hope that any public figure, and especially one involved in the
dissemination of information and the formation of opinion, be sensitive
to the need for comparing beginnings with conclusions and intentions
with results. Sarmiento, it would appear, was the promoter of ideas who
bypassed meticulous study; he was the "true believer" in reason and praxis
who many times acted out of intellectual passion.

Action, Sarmiento seemed to have believed, was only possible when
he restricted his field of vision, limited his alternatives, and committed
himself resolutely to the chosen path. His example contrasts with that of
the philosopher, who after carefully considering all possible ramifications
of an issue, rarely arrives at the threshold of decision. For the philosopher, thought has primacy over action; for the man of decision, however,
action takes precedence over thought. The latter describes the style of
Sarmiento, both in his personal and public lives: he acted first and sought
justification afterward.

A "man of action" with pragmatic goals, he followed a "patchwork"
program of action.[8] Because he placed priority on action, the succeeding
rationalizations or explanations for his acts were bound to be eclectic in
nature. The unarticulated motivations for his actions naturally became
transformed in practice. In many instances he seems to have recognized
the impracticality of ideological systems or meticulously defined programs
because of the very imperfect and constantly evolving social conditions in
which action had to prove its relevancy. This accounts for the frequent
attention given to concrete and tangible factors, and the corresponding
inattention paid to the theoretical interpretation of experience. The emphasis on what is immediate seems to typify not only individuals from
relatively underdeveloped circumstances, but in addition many persons
who are caught up in a particularly fluid social situation. It seems typical of many individuals whose group experience is not necessarily tied to
tradition and whose survival or social livelihood depends upon the ability
and willingness to take decisive action.[9]

An example from *Facundo*, Sarmiento's most famous work, will illus-
trate this mental trait of how an initially assumed position becomes flawed
with contradictions as it is subjected to the acid test of describing reality. Because work originally carried the title of *Civilización y barbarie en
las pampas argentinas* (in subsequent editions it, or its shortened form,

was relegated to the status of subtitle), one can assume that the opposition of civilization/barbarism originally served as one of the organizing principles around which the work was constructed. In the first chapters it appears that the writer is tracing a conflict whose contours are quite clear. Although he does not define either term, it is obvious that civilization has its residence in the cities, and barbarism in the countryside. The author then continues to accumulate associations for the two terms, which rapidly become conceptually unwieldy.

On the positive side, the opposition proved effective in polemic and as a guide to hasty, but nevertheless decisive action. The limitations of such an opposition are apparent to anyone who has had to reckon with the multifaced nature of society and human events. Sarmiento's discourse suffers from this very problem, as Chapter Five explains. Briefly here, the writer proceeds to accumulate attributes of either term, but in doing so, undermines the original opposition, which finally becomes excessively ambiguous and contradictory. The opposition finally breaks down and the writer is led into one futile justification after another in order to patch up, but not discard, his original opposition.

The idea of a "patchwork" philosophy comes together with Lévi-Strauss' idea that the *bricoleur* uses heterogeneous tools and materials, or whatever intellectual "operator" is at hand. Ideas, for the *bricoleur,* have value only to the extent that they serve in his mission of modifying the social or physical reality. In granting precedence to the transformation of reality, he believes that the intellectualization of that transformation is of secondary importance. Thought production is, so to speak, the rationalization after the fact; articulation, a stage which he rarely feels to be necessary, is accomplished in the most expedient manner. Articulation for him means leaving behind the familiar language of movement and entering into the fairly unknown terrain of ideas.

Paradoxically, Sarmiento and other select men of action did not find the world of ideas in all regards alien. At first appearance, indeed, it would seem that he, as one of the most prolific writers of his time, was precisely in his element when it came to philosophical discussion and, in general, the intellectual encounter with reality. However, there is a difference between the man who systematically organizes and articulates ideas for the sake of conceptual unity, and he who utilizes ideas merely as signs. Lévi-Strauss makes this useful distinction: the engineer (here, the engineer of ideas) "works by means of concepts and the *bricoleur* by means of signs. . . . [C]oncepts aim to be wholly transparent with respect to reality, signs allow and even require the interposing and incorporation of a certain amount of human culture into reality. Signs, in Pierce's vigorous phrase, 'address somebody.'"[10]

This relationship between signs, or discourse, and reality aids in understanding a further distinction separating the engineer from the *bricoleur.* The first accepts the external world as existing separate and independent

of the subject. He believes that his discourse, which consists of signs referring to that external reality, nevertheless belongs to an entirely different
plane. The engineer, according to Lévi-Strauss, uses language in order to
"make his way out of and go beyond the constraints imposed by a particular state of civilization . . . ."[11] For him, signification is an integral part
of external reality, which he may attempt to define or describe through
the signs he articulates, but will rarely, if ever, modify. The *bricoleur*, in
contrast, recognizes no conceptual barriers between discourse and meaning. As a pre-conscious phenomenologist, he ascribes to external reality
a secondary status in relation to his perception. For the *bricoleur*, order
or structure can only be said to exist because man, through his language,
bestows names on those sets which he carves out of the infinite chaos of
sensations. "Mythical thought builds structured sets by means of a structured set, namely, language," says Lévi-Strauss.[12] Discourse, then, is an
integral part of action; with both words and acts, the *bricoleur* assimilates
experience and transforms reality, thereby creating meaning.

The *bricoleur*, essentially idealistic in his conception of the universe,
rejects implicitly the engineer's belief in the existence of absolute laws
which govern the relationships between objects and men. Natural and
social realities, instead, are perceived as essentially haphazard or random
collections of ingredients which await the organizing vision of man. Truth,
then, is not some metaphysical Platonic form, but rather the intention
which man, through his praxis, utilizes in the construction of his universe.

The previously discussed example from *Facundo* illustrates further the
relationship which existed for Sarmiento between discourse and reality.
The work, a "libro de combate," was a tool for transforming his political,
social, and physical environments. He perceived his writing to be an
extension of his acts; it derived its meaning in relation to those acts.

A rigidly defined interpretation or set of ethics, such as the "civilization
versus barbarism" slogan, initially serves the *bricoleur* for restricting his
vision. It provides a pretext, and perhaps also a direction, for movement.
The shortcomings of that interpretation or ethical set become evident after movement has commenced, and when the actor calls upon that same
ethical set in order to rationalize or justify to others the completed action.
Having left behind the limited frame of reference which initially inspired
action, he confronts the dilemma of applying the original interpretation
to a newly emergent, and necessarily different, context. The *bricoleur* is
rarely one to stand on principle; because he is immersed in reality, his
ethical position is sacrificed to action. His program is revised continually.
Sarmiento's constant revisions resulted from the essential incompatibility
of his original suppositions with the reality in which he lived. With the
passage of time, the premises of his ideological edifice were continually
superceded. He quickly became a master of compromise, accommodation, and tolerance to internal contradictions. Américo Castro correctly
observes that Sarmiento's continual changes in essential positions were
hardly related to political or polemical issues, however he is unconvincing when he states that this trait was evidence of Sarmiento's intellectual

honesty.[13] More insightful is the assessment of Ezequiel Martínez Estrada that Sarmiento's attitude of struggle derived from an essentially static and ahistorical ethical position, which nevertheless was not inflexible. According to Martínez Estrada, one cannot forgive Sarmiento's natural duplicity, which was a result of his impetus for action adapting itself to the rigidity of his principles according to the necessities of the moment.[14]

Sarmiento, a *bricoleur* and not an engineer, was aware of the impermanent and relative quality of signification. He was convinced of his power to alter reality through his acts; he also demonstrated his awareness of the power to alter other's perception of a given reality even when he was powerless to affect a modification of that reality. Sarmiento seems to have been motivated by the realization that moral and even social progress would result from these two operations. His idea of "making war joyously"[15] is reminiscent of Nietzsche, who also expounded a program for preserving psychic order in the midst of objective chaos, for erasing the dilemmas of the past in order to keep abreast of a constantly evolving present. We see in the acts and writing of both the tautological circle of *bricoleur* logic, where the pre-conceived set of ethical principles also became the goal and final objective of praxis. Truth, for both, was the final destination of the journey for which nearly all paths were legitimate. Thus, we detect from his writing that Sarmiento was aware, at least in part, that an obedience to philosophic systems or specific methods of inquiry was an impediment to, rather than the necessary procedure for, arriving at truth. Chapters Five and Six demonstrate the eclectic combination of distinct, and sometimes contradictory, ideological currents in his historical thought. Furthermore, the reader detects in those pages most studied for their artistic value a sometimes unruly fusion of literary, sociological, and political objectives. Typical of his writing is a vacillating focus and an interweaving of contradictory ideas. What Noé Jitrik explains about the language of *Facundo* is equally true for Sarmiento's discourse in general: the goal of rational description or historical reconstruction is replaced by the intention of persuading the reader through seduction or enchantment.[16]

Jitrik's observation supports the contention that Sarmiento's writing always "addressed somebody"–to return to the idea expressed by Lévi-Strauss. Infrequently, if ever, did the man put words to paper with the intention of explaining an event, phenomenon, or personality from –shall we say–an academically neutral or uninvolved perspective. His writing did not have the goal of establishing an epistemological knowledge, a pursuit which he would have considered quite gratuitous and perhaps superfluous. On the contrary, he always considered his writing to be a means for achieving a predetermined objective. His writing necessarily pointed the way outside of its own textual space and into the sociopolitical context. Writing, and by extension, knowledge, was for him a tool for convincing, persuading, or teaching the reader about something. Truth was the product of discourse; only through discourse could it be produced. He was a "genio pragmático"–in the opinion of Ricardo Rojas–because he never took a step nor wrote a line without a practical objective in mind, be it pedagogical, political, instructional, or morally edifying.[17]

These pragmatic objectives explain in part a principal characteristic of his writing, namely, the indifference to many distortions in the use of ideas or in their opportunistic combination. On occasion, the reader observes the awkward inclusion of a variety of perspectives in passages treating historical or literary topics; his discourse many times combines dissimilar ideas into a totality which could be considered to be neither coherent nor systematic. In the world of ideas his discourse is—one could say—Machiavellian in its endeavor to rationalize and defend a predetermined program or objective. Anderson Imbert says quite succinctly that Sarmiento "no fue un estudioso, ni siquiera leyó sistematicamente. Al contrario, fue un improvisador fecundo y desaprensivo."[18] It would be easy, continues Anderson, to map the field of Sarmiento's readings on the basis of the many references he makes in his texts. Of greater interest is Sarmiento's romantic conception of history and other disciplines, that is to say, the original manner in which bookish sources are inextricably combined with ideas from the intellectual climate of his generation and tempered by his spontaneous and very original temperament.

Undoubtedly his activist temperament and his early commitment to social involvement affected the manner in which Sarmiento assimilated new ideas and placed them in the service of his social and political objectives. Anderson Imbert addresses himself to this dialectic between personality and environment: "Era un sentidor, no un teórico; y como leía u oía mientras peleaba a grandes saltos de un sitio a otro, su 'filosofía de la historia' no tenía coherencia sistemática."[19] Here, in essence, was Sarmiento's contradiction as a *bricolage* thinker: while it might seem that his immersion into the world of ideas had the objective of pursuing an epistemological truth, it becomes apparent that that knowledge and those ideas rarely constituted for him a theoretical stage which preceded action. Rather, he responded more to his senses or his intuitions; he thrust himself forward on the basis of semi-articulated beliefs and inchoate or partially formulated programs.

Impulsive, spontaneous, these words describe the man quite well. But the reliance on senses and intuitions suggests, in addition, a certain intellectual rigidity. Anderson Imbert succinctly observes: "En suma: que al iniciarse en el periodismo chileno, Sarmiento ya tenía respuestas para todas las cuestiones. Madurez temprana. O, si se quiere, inteligencia que, una vez que llega a cierto nivel teórico, pasa en seguida a la acción sin especular más."[20] Early in his life he had assimilated many ideas of eighteenth century liberalism, which later came to be combined with the ideological currents of his own day. *Facundo,* as his first important book, contains this mixture of historical and political ideas which he would treat time and again, and sometimes with little alteration, throughout his long and fertile writing career. That corpus of ideas, neither original nor complex, helps us to understand his high degree of self-confidence: with Messianic devotion, he strove to transform the social and material contours of his country according to what for him was an infallible doctrine.

In spite of this immovable center to his thought, Sarmiento is depicted by many historians as one who continually sought out opportunities to learn of new ideas in order to best guide the modernization of his country's institutions and culture. This apparent contradiction can be explained by comparing his *bricoleur* mode of ideation to what Howard Wiarda calls the "corporate" framework of Latin American political culture and institutions.[21] The corporate system responds to modernization by adopting some of its practice, but in doing so preserving unchanged the larger part of its traditional attitudes. The older system has the capacity of absorbing and assimilating the newer currents without being destroyed or significantly transformed in the process. Sarmiento, growing up and functioning in such an environment, shared many its characteristics in the organization of his own mental world.[22]

The metaphorical description which he gave for the formation of his own ideas has more truth to it than he perhaps intended: "¿Cómo se forman las ideas? Yo creo que en el espíritu de los que estudian sucede como en las inundaciones de los ríos, que las aguas al pasar depositan poco a poco las partículas sólidas que traen en disolución y fertilizan el terreno" (III, 172). Early in his life, Sarmiento developed a "bedrock" of ideas–to continue with his metaphor of the river bed. New readings and experiences did not alter significantly that foundation, but merely accumulated in eclectic fashion onto the base-structure of ideas and values. Like the earth strata underlying the river valley, the totality of his thought was in no way integral and systematic. Martínez Estrada is correct in spirit, but wrong in detail when he states: "A los treinta años había completado cuanto le fue permitido adquirir para su cultura; el resto de su vida se informará sucintamente, y es posible que muy pocos libros enteros haya leído en adelante. No es atrevido aseverar que con los años disminuía su acervo, borrándosele o esfuminándosele lo que adquiriera con febril avidez sin renovar el capital ni mejorarlo."[23] Untrue is the appraisal that Sarmiento read few new books; but substantially correct is the suggestion that new readings had little effect in transforming his most important orientations. Alberdi found in this same character trait the basis for his comparison of Sarmiento to Rosas: there predominated in the thought of both a hierarchy of values organized around an immovable center. Sarmiento, for Alberdi, paraded himself as liberal and republican, but was, in reality, little more than "un gaucho de la prensa."[24]

Singlemindedness, and in many instances dogmatism, characterized the young Sarmiento as an extremist: despite his rich intermingling with the stuff of experience, he nevertheless conceptualized man's social existence with a single transcendent meaning. He rejected the vision of a world in constant flux in favor of an orderly cosmos where human action was both possible and meaningful.[25] His somewhat restrictive conception of the moral and ethical values that ought to govern the lives of individuals reveals a quixotic side to his heroism. His firmly defined, and therefore somewhat inflexible, views regarding the means and ends of social progress reveal the romantic aspect of a deceptionally rational life.

In his articulated ideas Sarmiento revealed himself primarily as a social scientist and only occasionaly as a poet. His rejection of a multifaceted vision of human events went hand in hand with the contempt he felt for the type of literature which attempted to portray man in the moral and existential complexities of living. The following chapter considers his pragmatic view of fictional writing and poetry, those modes of discourse which in general seek an escape from the ordered contours of a narrowly defined ethical world. He often expressed the belief—which in typical *bricolage* fashion he contradicted in other passages—that expressive literature had little if any utility for the progress-minded citizen, except perhaps in the relatively insignificant function of exercising reading skills.

In many of his articles and works one can see evidence of this extreme commitment to truth. In the second part of *Facundo,* for example, Sarmiento, the rational writer, situates his protagonist in a closed universe. He eliminates all data which would contradict the one-dimensionality of this *tigre de los Llanos,* whose barbaric character had been determined by the telluric countryside. A second example is the description of the battle of the Tablada of Córdoba (as discussed more extensively in the following chapter). Sarmiento eliminates the greater part of what might be considered dramatic tension, and presents the battle, from beginning to end, as the enactment of Quiroga's predetermined fate. He thus demonstrates the preordained and providential victory of civilization, as incarnated in the armies of General Paz. Further examples are Sarmiento's biographies on "El Chacho" and Aldao, which also present an orderly, novelistic universe through the suppression of contradictory evidence. These examples demonstrate Sarmiento's tendency to avoid the portrayal of real-to-life tensions in the interest of preserving the ethical quality of his narrative.

That is what he intended. But Sarmiento, romantic writer *par excellence,* transcended in spite of himself the consciously imposed restrictions of form, the abandonment of contextual tensions, and the one-dimensionality of character. Out of the "painful necessity of esthetic wholeness,"[26] he created in *Facundo* a work which goes beyond any original intention he might have had, as many readers, including Sarmiento himself years later, have observed.[27] In the world of ethics and moral responsibility, the unbending commitment to principles brought upon Sarmiento continual tensions in his personal and public encounters; that commitment also won from others a deep respect and admiration.[28] He continually made exceeding, if not impossible, demands upon his colleagues and his situation, a practice that isolated him from many other public figures and at times made dialogue impossible. He was a man of few friends, and the friendships he did treasure prospered best when geographical distance made all but epistolary communication impossible.[29]

Quite understandingly, the corrupt oligarchial liberal order that survived him, and which he criticized severely in his latter years, has depoliticized his reputation and dehumanized his image. It has converted him into something simple and safe: a moral icon for youth. If in death as well as in life he cannot be ignored, at least his image can be contained. Generations of schoolchildren have revered his example of moral integrity and disinterested service in the context of a grade school history lesson or an officially sanctioned public holiday, but only occasionally is he remembered in relation to the uncontainable parameters of daily living.

If the unbending commitment to principles is the stuff of heroism, then it is also the source of parody. Fictional literature records various examples of the ethical visionary, who, because of the narrow definition of his ontological position, is transformed from character into parable.[30] In truth, there is little that separates the heroism inspired by firmly held beliefs from the anti-social *raideur* of the comic, as defined by Henri Bergson.[31] The social actor uncritically believing in the adequacy of his ethical beliefs and personal guiltlessness runs the danger of confronting circumstances that will reveal the flaw of his system and his inherent vice and folly. This is one explanation for why many of Sarmiento's contemporaries irreverently bestowed upon him the nickname of "loco" and reacted to his seriousness with uncomfortable laughter.[32]

An essential aspect of Sarmiento was the commitment to presupposed values or intuitions, those psychological givens that subsequently played an important role in the structuring of his discourse, and by extension, the determination of his acts. Lévi-Strauss is partially correct when he refers to the thought process of the *bricoleur* as "imprisoned in the events and experiences which it never tires of ordering and re-ordering."[33] However, what seems to escape the French anthropologist here is the idea that meaning for the *bricoleur* is already predetermined, and that only after having established meaning does there occur this relatively inconsequential ordering and reordering of signs. The *bricoleur* does not so much rearrange his materials in the "search to find them a meaning," as Lévi-Strauss goes on to say, but rather to adorn the predetermined meaning with documentation in order to impress or convince the observer. So, instead of considering the *bricoleur* as a semi-passive intellectual agent, it seems more correct to view him as an ideological tyrant, as one who seizes upon his limited range of images and symbols and disposes of them in successive and cumulative attempts in order to rationalize past acts or to fulfill his desire.

This desire which guides the impulsive assimilation of images from the external world into an all-encompassing subjective vision has been described by a number of theorists. Hoffer, whose ideas we have already considered above, claims that the "patchwork" thinker, contrary to his articulated motivations, acts—and here discourse is an aspect of action—in order to "possess" the world.[34] In a similar fashion Murray Krieger states that the literary protagonist with the single ethical set

is necessarily insisting on its exclusive rightness, its right to dominate all other sets, to impose itself upon them and demand their
capitulation. His ethical set, through its exclusive and absolute
rightness, dares through his agency be just as tyrannical over all
individuals. They now exist, not as persons, but as things, unindi-
viduated particulars to be subsumed under this or that universal.
Their full and dynamic existential reality is reduced to an opera-
tional function to be encouraged, tolerated, or obliterated as the
rules of the ethical set dictate.[35]

This quote suggests a number of well-known character traits or writing
practices of Sarmiento: his egomania, his contempt for ideas contrary to
his own, the continued effort to assert himself as a protagonist of history, his *idée-fixée* about moral and social progress, and the reductive
process he practiced when writing on historical and biographical topics.
What Krieger's words suggest about the ideation process is fundamental
for understanding Sarmiento and others of his type. In his case, idea formation, and its resulting articulation in discourse, had not so much the
engineer's objective of defining reality, but rather the functional role of
creating meaning by means of an imposition of order and structure over
reality.

The Linguistic Organization of Subjective Experience

Did Sarmiento defend too insistently his vision of a universe governed
by the regularity of the machine and the rationality of the spirit? That
is to say, can there be at the base of his protest a sense of insecurity and
a belief in the inherent disorder of things that would cause him, in his
defensiveness and perhaps frustration, to plea for the public consumption
of these myths? Sarmiento, it would seem, is to man's reason and the
proposed technological conquest of nature, what Unamuno's San Manuel
Bueno is to God. Both Sarmiento and San Manuel sensed—and in lucid
moments articulated—a desperate need for imposing an order, any order
perhaps, over the unending flow of perceptions through which the social
and physical realities made their presence known to man. Both became
ritual priests for the collective myth that granted to the masses an assurance of cosmic order.

Sarmiento's identity as a man of action seems to confirm the truth of
these speculations. The *bricolage* organization of his mental world also
reinforces the idea of his instinctive rejection of an absolute or a priori
structure to events. Only marginally did he share the realizations of Marx
and Freud, who in their own ways laid the foundations for the philosophical decentralization of reason in twentieth century thought. Marx, who
was Sarmiento's contemporary, clearly understood the illusory quality of
ideology, that body of conscious thought which was governed—sometimes

directly, but generally quite indirectly—by man's lived experiences in society. Freud, in quite another fashion—but with the same result of casting into doubt the organized nature of man's supposedly rational faculties—traced the dislocations and displacements of conscious thought to the mediatory functions of the mind's unconscious domains. These thinkers would articulate the alarm and perturbation of their contemporaries, but Sarmiento lived in a situation in which he could readily pass over intuited doubts and plow forward in a life characterized by motion, and only at times movement. He was, in this regard, a good example of Derrida's practitioner of "active forgetfulness," who was "like a doorkeeper, a preserver of psychic order, repose and etiquette: . . . there could be no happiness, no cheerfulness, no hope, no pride, no present, without forgetfulness."[36] In Sarmiento we detect an existential need—which also had its social utility—of projecting both the beginnings and endings of his own thought. He had the need to perceive his own ideas and his own life in terms of intentions and projected results. Reality, however, is never so perfect. He who can perceive it as such must necessarily restrict his own perception. In short, forgetting helped to provide Sarmiento with the comforting self-illusion of psychic wholeness; it helped him in the enterprise of interpreting his existence in the context of a vast metaphysical design.

Derrida's idea of an existential need for psychic unity suggests another dimension of *bricolage* ideation which also seems applicable to Sarmiento: his psychological need for producing discourse. Sarmiento fully ascribed to the myth, which constituted a cornerstone of bourgeois ontology, that written discourse possessed a formidable power over men's ideas and motivations.[37] Consequently, he believed that writing wielded an immense influence in the social and political struggle. At the same time, his personal affinities for the writing profession were due, at least in part, to its mediating role between consciousness and lived experience.

Typical of Sarmiento's pre-positivistic age was the manner in which he viewed the relationship of language to being, that is to say, the role of man's rational intelligence, through its vehicle, language, in the determination of social and political circumstances. At issue are the contradictory views regarding the nature of bourgeois ontology which prevailed in nineteenth century intellectual circles, and which Sarmiento accepted in great part. To a certain degree the inconsistencies in how the philosophers of his age understood such questions as the nature of consciousness, the rationality of thought, and the relationship between idea and act, corresponded with the *lagunae* in his own thought. In his discourse Sarmiento compensated, at least in part, for these inconsistencies or displacements in logic through the creation of a mythological protagonist: writing. In his texts, the written word assumed the role of an omnipotent force which acted upon the institutions of society and the motivations of man.

Undoubtedly a source of intellectual discomfort for Sarmiento and other thinkers was the shallow explanation which the philosophers of the period provided for the relationship between man's subjective and objective experiences. At the outset it is necessary to emphasize the importance of this question, since the whole body of his social thought had the premise that progress would result from the transformations made to the physical environment and the social institutions in accordance with *socialista*, or pre-positivistic, principles. A first problem involves the criteria according to which these principles were derived. How does one know if an idea is logical, reasonable or true? A second problem is the relationship of those ideas to empirical reality. How does one assess their relevancy to concrete situations?

Sarmiento, as is known, was not a rigorous theorist and wrote relatively little on philosophy in general, and almost nothing on the subject of the intellectual faculty of man.[38] In several passages of his many works he treats these issues, but his considerations are almost always brief and fragmentary. In general, his opinions differed little from those of the other thinkers of his epoch. Descartes, who two centuries before had established the philosophical foundations for liberalism, postulated a divine origin for his *cogito*, an idea which Sarmiento seemed to embrace in his conception of history guided by providence. Consistency, however, is not one of the foremost characteristics of Sarmiento's discourse: in other passages he accounts for the origins of man's intelligence in terms of biological inheritance (III, 128; V, xxiii), and in still others he refers to a type of collective conscience (XXXIX, 72).

Andrés Bello, perhaps the most profound and systematic Latin American thinker of Sarmiento's day, and one whose writings Sarmiento was in all probability familiar with,[39] treats the philosophical relationship between thought and reality in rather ambiguous terms. Says Menéndez y Pelayo:

> La idea de substancia queda también vacilante en el sistema de Bello, quien propriamente no reconoce más percepción substancial que la del propio yo, duda mucho de la existencia de la materia . . .; y llega, aunque sea por transitorio ejercicio o gimnasia de la mente, a conclusiones resueltamente acosmistas, que, negando la substancialidad de la materia, convierten el universo físico en un gran vacío poblado de apariencias vanas, en nada diferente de un sueño.[40]

Sarmiento's written opinions regarding this issue differ little from those of Bello. He also was conscious of the abyss that separated the worlds of mental experience and physical material. His doubts regarding ontological questions undoubtedly are related to his tolerance for ambiguity in his views regarding other matters. This, in any case, is a possible interpretation of his words of 1849 concerning moral judgments:

> Y como en las cosas morales la idea de la verdad viene menos de su propia esencia, que de la predisposición de ánimo, y de la aptitud del que aprecia los hechos, que es el individuo, no es extraño que a la descripción de las escenas de que fuí testigo se mezclase con harta

frecuencia lo que no vi, porque existía en mí mismo, por la manera de percibir, trasluciéndose más bien las propias que las ajenas
preocupaciones (V, xii).

Sarmiento admits here the possibility of different points of view existing
in regard to moral questions, but, in continuation, he hesitates in applying
this same idea to the perception of the physical reality:

¿[No es] el mérito y el objeto de un viaje, en que el viajero es for-
zosamente el protagonista, por aquella solidaridad del narrador y
la narración, de la visión y los objetos, de la materia de examen y
la percepción, vínculos estrechos que ligan el alma a las cosas vi-
sibles, y hacen que vengan estas a espiritualizarse, cambiándose en
imágenes, y modificándose y adaptándose el tamaño y alcance del
instrumento óptico que las refleja? (V, xii-xiii)

Some years later he apparently accepted as a fact that people varied in
their modes of perceiving and reasoning:

Triste descubrimiento, por cierto, que nos haría dudar de la solidez
de nuestras propias convicciones y razonamientos, visto que más
tarde la sociedad se reirá acaso de nuestra seguridad y confianza,
pues que el asentimiento que las ideas obtienen del público, deriva
sólo su fuerza y eficacia de su conformidad con los hábitos mentales
de aquellos que las reciben.[41]

This latter quotation suggests that each person perceived the exterior
world in a unique manner which conformed to the nature of his own
"optic instrument." As a result, one's reasoning process was necessarily
related to the idiosyncratic perception of external causes; man's rational
thought was none other than a projector of ideology. Reminiscent is the
thought of Karl Marx, who, in the same period, theorized about the close
relationship between ideology and perception.

But differing from Marx, Sarmiento could not believe—or perhaps this
is a case of *mauvaise foi* in that he could not let himself believe—in the
absence of a fixed reference for men's perceptions. He refused to follow any further the logic of his own intuitions and interrogate his own
somewhat ambiguous ideas concerning what precisely was meant by the
"predisposition" of one's spirit or those "mental habits" which, in the end,
would establish the frontiers for conscious experience. Sarmiento's penetration into the essence of human thought aborts without conclusion. In
this, he contrasts with Nietzsche who, a generation hence, would describe
the dionysiac flood of perceptions and intuitions which constituted the
normal psyche. But Sarmiento, like his romantic and pre-positivistic contemporaries, was not yet ready for that reckoning with subjective chaos
because his thought process was limited, but at the same time protected,
by his belief in providence. Compared to that pantheistic power which
determined the destiny of mankind and the universe, reason was indeed
insignificant. But, at the same time reason was precisely that intellectual
faculty which, according to the social and scientific thought of the period,

would guide man's transformation of nature and society. It was that human faculty which Sarmiento's discourse, like the bourgeois discourse of his epoch, mystified in order to hide its own doubtful legitimacy and in order to justify its pursuit of power in society.

Sarmiento's nebulous ideas concerning the nature of reason formed a mental curtain which spacially limited the play of conscious thought. He probably intuited the fragility of those ideological structures which offered to his consciousness a unified image of the universe. He feared anarchy in the social order as much as the chaos of his own subjective world. Possibly resulting from the first fear were his distrust of the masses, his intolerance for ethnic differences, and his authoritarian practices in government. The possible consequences of that second and more subjective fear were his accentuated egocentrism and impetuous defense of the rectitude of his own ideas.

Sarmiento's discourse, having as its premises these ideas and values, can be compared to a building constructed over an unstable foundation. One receives the impression that writing was for him a protection against the emptiness that he intuited as existing within. An incomparable energy in the construction of civilization occupied his hours of the day. While the gears of the body and the mind are in movement, one seldom has the time or need for self-interrogation about premises. Many individuals compensate for this lack during society's restful hours, when in their solitude they have the opportunity to analyze and contemplate. Similarly, the process of writing for many thinkers accompanies a mental productivity in regard to philosophical issues. One wonders whether this was, in fact, the case with Sarmiento. Several of his biographers–Groussac, Lugones, and others–suggest that philosophical questions and ethical deliberations took a distant second place to Sarmiento's political and journalistic activities.[42]

Sarmiento's writing production–and this is probably true for all impassioned writers–had an obvious subjective function. He was undoubtedly the first person afffected by his writings. The process of writing and the physical presence of his written words served in the function of pacifying the contradictions in his own values and ideas. Perhaps this need for a protection against his own doubts and ambiguities accounts for why the man conferred upon writing what he could not claim for himself: writing, and not he, could demand the unconditional respect of society on account of its disinterested neutrality and circular authority. It was the Chilean press and not he who wrote, Sarmiento ingenuously argued at one point in time:

> Atribuíaseme a envidia, a celos, a deseo de abajar el país la crítica de las cosas que son del dominio de la prensa, y el público se obstinaba en no querer leer *Mercurio* donde decía *Mercurio,* y si, Sarmiento, extranjero, argentino, cuyano, y demás; y yo me exaltaba contra esta injusticia pública, y seguía cada día con más amargura. Era un diario chileno quien hablaba, y yo creí siempre y creo que no debe el

público traslucir a través de las páginas los encogimientos que una situación particular impone al redactor (III, 205).

Sarmiento communicates his irritation with those Chileans who refused to read *El Mercurio* due to the fact that he, being a foreigner, was the principal writer. He answers that the words in print which are subjected to public scrutiny leave behind all traces of their human origin. He wanted to believe that the press transformed the subjective opinions of society's "chosen" leaders into social truths.

Discourse Production and Authority

The etymology of the word "author," which Vico provides us, is helpful for understanding another aspect of *bricoleur* ideation: one's desire to "possess" the world. The Italian historian traced it thus: *auctor: suis ipsius: propsius:* property.[43] Authoring a text is akin to property ownership: the producer of discourse does more than arrange words in a desired sequence, he also limits the space of language. An immediate consequence of discourse production therefore occurs on the psychological level: the author imposes upon his thoughts the illusion of psychic unity upon organizing them sequentially with a beginning and a projected goal. Or, in other words, this illusory temporality groups memories and perceptions and, in doing so, bestows significance upon both those ideas and the author's historical presence.

A second aspect of textual authorization has to do with the idea of social property. The author gives birth to a text, but the text bestows authority upon its author. That is to say, the author is rescued from oblivion only when the reading public grants significance to the text he has produced. Authority, therefore, is the result of the dialectical relationship existing between author and reading public, which has the text as its vehicle of communication and mediation: the author pays homage to the values of the public, and the public reciprocates by granting him recognition. We are inevitably led, then, to consider the relationship existing between Sarmiento and his readers, who in their majority belonged–like Sarmiento himself–to the region's propertied or cultural elite. It was in the intellectual environment sustained by this group that he first formed his ideas and later produced his writing. His values, ideas, and opinions largely coincided with theirs. Similarly, his textual affirmations and suppressions can be said to correlate in large measure to the actions of his group, which was Argentina's dependent bourgeoisie, in its own pursuit of authority.

The illusion of psychic unity which Sarmiento gained through the construction of discourse is evidenced by the recurring theme of beginnings in his writings. In retrospect, what strikes the reader as uncanny in the early writings of the man is this clear statement of intentionality to which in subsequent years he would remain remarkably constant. Anderson Imbert has called this an early "intuición de la propia vida como vida histórica . . . ."[44] Sarmiento often compared his own beginnings to the incipient years of the Argentine nation, and he believed that his own life reproduced on a small scale many of the struggles which characterized Argentina at that period in history. Obviously, a beginning presupposes a context, since it speaks from and to the context. (Sartre says in *La Nausée,* that the beginning presupposes the end.)[45] Writing at an early age, Sarmiento could only project what awaited both himself and Argentina in subsequent years. Promises and ambitions are all that one would normally expect from a young man casting his imagination toward the future. Normally, the historian years hence would grant little importance to these declarations of youthful intention, and instead would study the impact of actual events or final results; indeed, intentions are only meaningful in the light of the resulting action. In this light, Sarmiento's early texts are remarkable: many early predictions for his and his nation's future were eventually born out. One is justified in using the word remarkable, for as Edward Said has succinctly stated, "Beginning is not really a beginner's game."[46] There are few instances in literary and political history where the protagonist of an epoch has written his autobiography near the beginning of his public career and significantly *before* those events which would establish his lasting fame. In Sarmiento's case, autobiography foretold the future as much as it interpreted the past. Was this coincidence of beginnings and ends more an instance of uncanny prophesy or the *bricoleur's* dogmatic enactment of inflexible rules? What is beyond dispute is that Sarmiento, when considered as a producer of discourse, perceived his existence in terms of beginnings and ends. He was one individual who chose to write his prefaces when he was just embarking upon a long and fertile career.

Throughout his early writings he repeated in several forms this idea of a precise and determined beginning to his own existence. He continually applied to his own life the dual myths of self-made man and historical precursor. Both myths involve the historical ascension of the self and a will to discredit the influence of one's tradition or teachers. However, such claims to originality constitute at best a polemical assertion and at worst a subjective fantasy, since all men develop their ideas in interaction with their historical and intellectual environments.

As early as 1843 in *Mi defensa* Sarmiento presented himself as beginning at degree zero in his intellectual formation: "He nacido en una provincia ignorante y atrasada . . . . He nacido en una familia que ha vivido largos años en una mediocridad muy vecina de la indigencia, y hasta hoy es pobre en toda la extensión de la palabra" (III, 6). Then he continues this Adamic theme with an explanation of his intellectual growth: "logré perfeccionarme yo solo, sin modelos y sin maestros" (III, 7). His earlier misfortune at not having obtained a coveted governmental scholarship, and therefore having lost the opportunity to pursue formal instruction beyond the few years of childhood schooling in San Juan, now acquires an accent of pride: "no teniendo maestros ni más guía que mi propio juicio, yo he sido siempre el juez más bien que el admirador de la importancia de un libro, sus ideas, sus principios. De esta falsa posición ha nacido la independencia de mi pensamiento, y cierta propensión de crearme ideas propias sin respetar la autoridad de los otros" (III, 11). Sarmiento's own authority: this idea, reelaborated in various forms, emerges as the principal theme of *Mi defensa*. In this short work it is utilized for explaining different aspects of his character, including his monastic personal habits, his intense concentration, and his perseverance in fulfilling the responsibilities of public writer. He obviously believed that the image of disinterested public servant, which this theme suggests, would promote a favorable disposition on the part of his reading public in a moment of slander and name-calling.

The myth of intellectual founder received a new, albeit less obvious, elaboration in *Facundo*. The explicit axis of the work is the civilization-barbarism opposition, and the implicit one is the personification of those very concepts in the figures of Sarmiento versus Rosas and Facundo. Like all creators of discourse, Sarmiento selected his data and formulated his own interpretations on the basis of the materials and information available to him. What were the factors which influenced him in the construction of this work? There are many possible answers, but one cannot overlook Sarmiento's subjective desire to present himself as founder of movements. In this light we can explain his attention given to *el rastreador* and *el gaucho malo*, for he believed that the passages dealing with such character types and rural scenes would become models for a national literature of the future. That same semi-articulated desire helps to explain the pride of *ecce homo*, the possible Tocqueville of his continent (as he states in the introduction to *Facundo*), who, in rudimentary fashion, presents to his public the first pages of a Latin American sociology. We can account for certain units of content as resulting from the same desire for fame as an initiator, for example the novelistic origin of the protagonist Facundo, a rebellious son who broke ties with family and society in his quest for power (the parallels with how Sarmiento, in other texts, depicted his own origins are all too obvious). Sarmiento's quest for renown as *prócer* –he who comes before–is also seen in his denigration of the *viejos unitarios* and in his near silence concerning the insurrectional activities of the Montevideo-based exiles. After all, what pretender to originality gives testimony as to the value of his precursors? Out of this same pursuit of leadership came the pages devoted to explaining and defending his generation's program for national reconstruction. In other works as well, he promoted unpopular or novel ideas, and thus anticipated the new directions of social dialogue. With *De la educación popular* he advocated for the first time on the South American continent the universal and mandatory education for all citizens, including females and children of workers. *Argirópolis* argued the novel and somewhat fanciful idea of establishing the nation's capital on the island of Martín García, and presented the first written defense of free navigation along the country's internal waterways. *Campaña en el Ejército Grande* marked him as the first figure of national stature to publicly break with Urquiza; in that work he correctly predicted that the new confederation would never succeed in uniting under its banner the internal provinces with the port city. His imagination always gravitated toward the issues of greatest urgency and concern for his countrymen. With untiring energy and Renaissance-like breadth of intelligence, his need to propose and initiate reforms found felicitous realization in an inchoate and unorganized society.

In *Recuerdos de provincia* Sarmiento rectified somewhat his earlier and quite romanticized portrait of himself as the solitary initiator of a new Latin American intellectual tradition. The overriding tone of this work is calculated composure, which contrasts sharply with the fervor, headstrong rebelliousness, and perhaps defensive pride of *Mi defensa*. A principal theme of the work is continuation. The writer situated his own life and beliefs within a long-standing family and regional tradition, and generously recognized his many debts to friends and relatives alike. But this is not at the expense of his ostentatious pride as founder of movements. A good example of this combination of the humble and the haughty is found in the passage reproducing part of the article written by Quiroga Rosas a decade earlier, in which the latter quoted Sarmiento's speech eulogizing the Bishop Oro on the occasion of founding a school for young women in San Juan. Author Sarmiento quotes himself:

> En el discurso de apertura del colegio, que se registra en el núm. 1 del *Zonda,* dando cuenta de la escena el malogrado joven Quiroga Rosas, decía: "La primera voz que sonó, fue la del joven director, don Domingo Faustino Sarmiento, que leía el acta de la independencia . . .: 'Señores, . . . En su ardiente amor por su país, [el obispo Oro] concibió este pensamiento, grande como los que ha realizado, y los que una muerte intempestiva ha dejado sólo en bosquejo. Por otra parte, yo he sido el intérprete de los deseos de la parte pensadora de mi país. Una casa de educación era una necesidad que urgía satisfacer, y yo indiqué los medios; juzgué era llegado el momento y me ofrecí a realizarla. En fin, señores, el pensamiento y el interés general lo convertí en un pensamiento y en un interés mío, y esta es la única honra que me cabe' " (III, 74-75).

In this self-conceived gloss on himself, Sarmiento-author granted Sarmiento-protagonist textuality and therefore authority. This older text, inserted into the pages of *Recuerdos de provincia,* conferred on the newer context a fine tonal balance of pride and humility, origin and continuation. In this, Sarmiento found a convenient substitution for the fragile illusion of intellectual beginnings. In its place, he spun the myth of fidelity to tradition which, in addition to its political convenience, offered a more resistant foundation for his pursuit of psychic harmony.

Sarmiento sensed the ephemeral quality of his illusion of psychic wholeness on account of its dependence upon the reading public's continued interest in his writings. He thrived on controversy precisely because he had an inner need to be continually in the public eye. His fortune was that he was particularly adept in the ways of ideological combat, and his victories in polemic during his Chilean exile far outnumbered his failures. As a consequence, his egomania grew, but at the price of his continued and ever increasing need for public applause. He sensed the precariousness of his position: he, like other producers in the modern world, was subject to the hard laws of competition, which meant that he had to struggle continually against others not only for material gains and social ascendancy, but also for public distinction.[47] He seemed to have believed in society's "Law of Limited Fame," whereby the rise in one person's social stature would be perceived as occuring at the expense of his neighbor's.[48] This suggests the further practice by which Sarmiento's discourse sought its fulfilment as social and psychological property: the campaign of literary fratricide which can be observed throughout his career as a writer. Especially evident were his attempts to prune the fame of both Echeverría and Alberdi (and then later, Urquiza, Mitre, Rawson, etc.), individuals who, along with himself, had a claim for generational leadership in the post-Rosas period.[49]

Sarmiento's attempt to limit the fame of Echeverría was especially dramatic. Echeverría, in addition to his accomplishments as poet, had performed an indispensable role in the philosophical orientation of the young Buenos Aires intelligentsia in the last decade and a half of the Rosas rule. He had to his credit a leadership role in the Salón Literario of 1837, his early attempts at organizing the Buenos Aires youth against the Rosas tyranny, and the principal authorship of *Dogma socialista,* which was the 1837 Generation's philosophical justification and ideological guide for the renovation of their country. Striking on account of its absence in Sarmiento's writing is any mention of these contributions by Echeverría.[50]

Sarmiento did provide, however, a guarded praise for Echeverría's verses, but it must be pointed out that his lauditory comments were sometimes accompanied by ambiguous words masking a potentially hostile criticism.[51] In *Facundo* Echeverría was the *cajetilla* –or haughty *porteño* –whose principal occupation was exciting uncivilized gauchos with his verses set to the music of the guitar (VII, 39). In *Viajes* he was "pobre Echeverría, enfermo de espíritu y cuerpo" (V, 54), implying that Echeverría, with a corroded spirit due to his residence in the interior, had been distracted from more important social and political tasks and now preferred to pass his time contemplating the fine refractions of an abstract and sterile beauty. Echeverría, Sarmiento implied, could contribute little or nothing on the two principal battlefronts against the Rosas regime: journalism and the military campaign.

With Alberdi we see a similar attempt at literary fratricide. Sarmiento's relationship with Alberdi, who is recognized today as the most rigorous social and political theorist of the 1837 Generation, passed from distant admirer to fellow conspirator, then, beginning in 1852, to embittered slanderer. Before 1852, the two had collaborated as leaders for the Argentine exiles' struggle against Rosas. The two were their generation's most authoritative and respected advocates of a liberal program for Argentina's future reconstruction. With the fall of the dictator, however, their friendly ties disintegrated when they chose differing political options: Alberdi aligned himself with Urquiza and the Confederation, while Sarmiento's immediate choice was neutrality, but he eventually embraced the cause of Buenos Aires against the internal provinces. The difference in political positions accounts in great part for the heated polemic which exploded between the two. Alberdi, in *Cartas quillotanas,* attacked Sarmiento's ideas and actions. True to form, Sarmiento responded in writing. The letters constituting *Las ciento y una* criticized in full force Alberdi's politics and the government of Urquiza. More important here was the fact that Sarmiento spared no possible argument or insult in his attempt to discredit Alberdi on both professional and personal levels. In the next several years this vendetta against Alberdi would negatively affect his own ability to judge with impartiality the causes and issues of Argentina's regional rivalry.

Alberdi's appraisal was entirely correct: Sarmiento thrived on polemic.[52] In the long years of his Chilean exile, the charged political environment led Sarmiento, with romantic sensitivity, to view the world in terms of dramatic conflicts between opposing forces. This tendency accounts in part for the success of *Facundo,* with its powerful account of *caudillo* barbarism's onslaught against the forces of progress. But the same sensitivity also came to be directed against liberal compatriots and former allies. His unjust treatment of Echeverría and his verbal assaults on Alberdi exceeded the limits of a disinterested pursuit of truth. Instead, Sarmiento was engaged in an ideological campaign to purge the world and his own discourse of Alberdian and Echeverrían traces. One of many hypotheses for this refusal to grant due recognition to his ideological and generational brethren was his defensive pursuit of fame: his campaign to establish himself as his country's patriarch in the period following the days of the tyrants.

Sarmiento's quest for personal authority inevitably influenced his perception of the desirable role which his writing would perform in the larger society. When he argued that it was the Chilean press, and not the writer, who spoke through the newspaper's printed page, he promoted a myth of an omnipotent writing which could penetrate exterior reality and alter the contours of society. To be more precise, this formidable worldly power of writing belonged only to journalism, and not to any type of writing. We remember that he suggests this distinction in *Viajes* upon explaining that Echeverría's poetry served well for the relatively esoteric project of "la contemplación de la belleza," but was next to useless in the vital struggle against Rosas or in the enterprise of reconstructing national institutions. "Pobre Echeverría"–this passage concludes–"no es ni soldado ni periodista" (V, 54). The journalistic press, Sarmiento continually communicated, constituted one of modern man's most effective instruments in the service of progress. A most glorious event must have been the victory march into Buenos Aires on an afternoon in 1852, following the rout of Rosas' armies at Monte Caseros. Sarmiento, the *boletinero* –or battlefield newspaper writer-editor-printer–received even greater applause from the population than did Urquiza, the victorious general. He believed, and perhaps with good reason, that the pen had finally sallied forth and achieved an equal status with arms in society's ongoing struggle for progress.

The comparison between journalism and weaponry is revealing since, in the opinion of Sarmiento, the social project of writing involved as much violence as did a military battle. There was his hope that ideas in printed form, now objectively valid, would participate as autonomous agents in imposing rational structures upon empirical reality. His written ideas did not constitute an epistemological language; on the contrary, Sarmiento had for them the goal of social transformation and not philosophical precision. Lugones, one of Sarmiento's most perceptive biographers, saw clearly that "Ideas y aún ideales no son para el nada más que un medio: armas o instrumentos de acción."[53] His writing could define no pre-existing truth because for him no truth existed outside of language itself. An idea proved its utility through social performance and not through mere articulation. It originated largely as the product of an individual's deliberations. But that subjective truth could also become, through persuasion or forceful imposition, the truth for society.

Sarmiento was conscious of the fact that one's continually flowing discourse had an essential role in transforming subjective truths into social goals. As ideological *bricoleur,* he began with an intuition and a desire. Then, his writing production channeled all possible means in order to achieve the predetermined objective. Any rhetorical device could prove its usefulness in the writing enterprise. One's calculating reason organized discourse toward the chosen goal, but the struggle did not consist in an appeal to reason. On the contrary, it was the writer's determination and force of persuasion which dictated the terms of battle. Victory would belong to he whose desire prevailed. "¿Concediose jamás el triunfo a quien no sabe perseverar? . . . ¡No! no se renuncia a un porvenir tan inmenso, a una misión tan elevada, por ese cúmulo de contradicciones y dificultades; ¡las dificultades se vencen, y las contradicciones se acaban a fuerza de contradecirlas!" (VII, 10-11)

This passage suggests one of the sources of Sarmiento's incredible energy and will to act: he intuited that the contradictions of the world had no final resolution, but that if the superior individual possessed sufficient resolve and energy, then those contradictions could be neutralized. Subsequently, one could construct upon that foundation of frozen contradictions his own non-dialectical edifice. His writing had a primary role in this operation: while it was powerless to synthesize the disharmonies of the world, it could at least provide a myth of harmony. Journalistic writing, on account of its role of supplanting presence, was Sarmiento's arm in his struggle for social ascendancy.

Notes for Chapter 3

1. Leopoldo Lugones, *Historia de Sarmiento* (Buenos Aires: Otero & Co., 1911), p. 197.

2. Ricardo Rojas, "Prólogo," *Bibliografía de Sarmiento* (Buenos Aires: Coni Hermanos, 1911), p. xv.

3. Lugones, *Historia de Sarmiento*, pp. 131-34.

4. Manuel Gálvez, *Vida de Sarmiento: el hombre de autoridad* (Buenos Aires: Emecé, 1945), pp. 349-50.

5. Claude Lévi-Strauss, *The Savage Mind* (Chicago: University of Chicago Press, 1970), pp. 17-18.

6. C. R. James, *Notes on Dialectics, Hegel and Marxism*, 2nd ed. (New York: Friends of Facing Reality Publications, 1971), p. 5.

7. Louis Althusser, *Lenin and Philosophy and Other Essays*, trans., Ben Brewster (New York and London: Monthly Review Press, 1971), p. 160.

8. Eric Hoffer, *The True Believer: Thoughts on the Nature of Mass Movements* (New York: Harper and Row, 1966), pp. 134-37.

9. Georg Lukàcs, *History and Class Consciousness: Studies in Marxist Dialectics*, trans. Rodney Livingstone, (Cambridge: M.I.T. Press, 1971), p. 154, describes the proletarian mode of perception in a stage prior to attaining class consciousness in terms similar to those of Lévi-Strauss: the "habits of thought and feeling of mere immediacy where the immediately given form of the objects, the fact of their existing here and now and in this particular way appears to be primary, real and objective, whereas their 'realtions' seem to be secondary and subjective."

10. Lévi-Strauss, *The Savage Mind*, p. 20.

11. *Ibid.*, p. 19.

12. *Ibid.*, p. 21.

13. Américo Castro, "En torno al *Facundo* de Sarmiento," *Sur*, 7, No. 47 (1938), 26-34.

14. Ezequiel Martínez Estrada, *Sarmiento* (Buenos Aires: Argos, 1956), p. 202: "Si la actitud de lucha puede adquirirse como un doblez desde las primeras decisiones, las primeras decisiones responden a una predeterminada tesitura ética, a un destino, a una irremediable gracia, para usar el lenguaje de las esencias. Esta actitud ética nativa de Sarmiento era flexible, no obstante. Dentro de límites amplios, su necesidad de acción adecuaba la rigidez de sus principios con las sinuosidades del terreno, del status. Esto es lo que no podemos perdonarle; ante todo porque ahí está su debilidad, las quiebras por donde se lo vulnera."

15. Augusto Belín Sarmiento, *Sarmiento anecdótico: ensayo biográfico* (Buenos Aires: Imprenta Belín, 1929), p. 324.

16. Noé Jitrik, *Muerte y resurrección de 'Facundo'* (Buenos Aires: Centro Editor de América Latina, 1968), p. 11.

17. Ramón Doll and Guillermo Cano, hijo, *Las mentiras de Sarmiento: por qué fue unitario* (Buenos Aires: Ediciones del Renacimiento, 1939), p. 6, who quote Ricardo Rojas.

18. Enrique Anderson Imbert, *Genio y figura de Sarmiento* (Buenos Aires: Editorial Universitaria de Buenos Aires, 1967), p. 22.

19. *Ibid.*, p. 26.

20. *Ibid.*, p. 42.

21. Howard J. Wiarda, "Law and Political Development in Latin America: Toward a Framework for Analysis," in *Politics and Social Change in Latin America: The Distinct Tradition*, ed. Wiarda (Amherst: University of Massachusetts Press, 1974), pp. 199-229, describes the corporate political system which has profound historical roots in most Ibero-Latin countries, as a "series layers, 'stages', each superimposed upon the other, with new elements continually being appended on and adapted to an older tradition, but without that older tradition being slugged off or eliminated or even undergoing very many fundamental transformations" (p. 215).

22. A most interesting reading of Sarmiento's thought and acts–indeed, of Latin American liberal thought and governmental action in general–would be according to the ideas proposed by Richard M. Morse, "The Heritage of Latin America," in *Politics and Social Change in Latin America*, ed. Howard J. Wiarda (Amherst: University of Massachusetts Press, 1974), pp. 25-69, who argues that more or less constant factors in Latin American political life are the principles defined by Thomist sociopolitical thought, for example "organicism" and "patriarchialism." According to these two principles, social unity is perceived as being architectonic, and not derived from rationalistic definitions of purpose or strategy; casuistry is more important than human law. The supposition here is that principles of utopian liberalism, which contradicted the philosophical foundations of the traditional Hispanic American order, would have little chance of substantially altering the basic structures of that society.

23. Ezequiel Martínez Estrada, *Meditaciones sarmientinas* (Buenos Aires: Editorial Universitaria, 1968), pp. 75-6.

24. Sarmiento repeats and counters Alberdi's charge in XV, 134-35.

25. Valentín Alsina was the first to observe, and at the same time criticize, Sarmiento's practice of "systematizing" his observations according to *a priori* categories:

> Estas [exageraciones en *Facundo*] tienen que ser en Vd. una necesidad: ¿sabe por qué? porque creo –aunque puedo estar muy engañado–que es Vd. propenso a los *sistemas* y estos, en las ciencias sociales como en las naturales, no son el mejor medio de arribar al descubrimiento de la verdad, ni al recto examen, ni a la veraz exposición de ella.

The quote is taken from "Notas de Valentín Alsina al libro 'Civilización y Barbarie,"' *Facundo,* by Domingo Faustino Sarmiento, ed. Alberto Palcos (Buenos Aires: Ediciones Culturales Argentinas, Ministerio de Educación y Justicia, 1962), p. 350.

26. Murray Krieger, *The Tragic Vision: The Confrontation of Extremity,* (Baltimore and London: Johns Hopkins Unaversity Press, 1973), I, p. 254.

27. In the introduction to *Facundo's* 1881 translation into Italian, Sarmiento writes that the original version was inspired in a "rapto de lirismo" and "exaltación mental", that it was similar to the "especie de sonambulismo que ha producido a los Moisés, los Garibaldi . . ." In spite of its many errors and distortions, he exhorts, "No vaya el escálpelo del historiador que busca la verdad gráfica a herir en las carnes del *Facundo,* que está vivo: ¡no lo toquéis! así como así, con todos sus defectos, con todas sus imperfecciones, lo amaron sus contemporáneos, lo agasajaron todas las literaturas extranjeras, desveló a todos los que lo leían por la primera vez, y la Pampa Arjentina es tan poética hoy en la tierra, como las montañas de la Escocia diseñadas por Walter Scott, para solaz de las inteligencias." Quoted from *Facundo,* ed. Alberto Palcos, pp. 452-55.

28. Gálvez, *Vida de Sarmiento,* p. 95, explains that in spite of the near universal admiration enjoyed by Sarmiento in Chile on account of his energy and talent, he still had enormous problems in making friends: "En poco más de tres años, Sarmiento ha reñido con sus tres mejores amigos chilenos: Núñez, Minvielle y Lastarria. Esta facilidad para pelearse con todos, hace creer que la culpa no está en ellos sino en la naturaleza volcánica del otro."

29. One of the first of Sarmiento's hagiolaters was his sister, Bienvenida Sarmiento, *Rasgos de la vida de Domingo Faustino Sarmiento,* introd. Antonio P. Castro (Buenos Aires, 1946), p. 34: "Jamás tuvo rencores por política, sus enemigos políticos eran sus amigos." This view is contradicted by Sarmiento himself, who quotes Alberdi's accusation in *Cartas quillotanas* (1852) that "El *mal éxito* que usted ha experimentado entre sus antiguos correligionarios le hace ver que su pluma, tan bien templada en los últimos an nos, no sirve hoy a los intereses nuevos . . . ." Sarmiento responds that this accusation is, in part, "superchería" –or false– in that the Argentine exiles in Chile who before were united in the struggle against Rosas, still supported him in his criticisms of Urquiza. It was, however, "verdad parcial que no está en nuestras manos remediar," says Sarmiento, who also quotes Alberdi: "Me es indiferente que tomen este o aquel partido en cuanto de mí, yo no desmayaré por los desdenes *(desprecios)"* [sic]. He realized that the public figures who stood firmly on principle would always be the brunt of other's attacks.

30. Krieger, *The Tragic Vision,* p. 20.

31. *Le Rire: Essai Sur la Signification du Comique* (Paris: 1969).

32. Critics of the liberal school have tended to emphasize the innocent side of Sarmiento's humor. Belín Sarmiento, *Sarmiento anecdótico,* compiles anecdotes of his grandfather's humorous interaction with his contemporaries. Mauricio Rosenthal, *Sarmiento y el teatro: la musa recóndita de un titán* (Buenos Aires: Kraft, 1967), is unconvincing in his chapter entitled "Loco me fecit," in which he projects Sarmiento's "parentesco con Erasmo" on account of, among other qualities, the latter's "apitud histriónica," "homéricas carcajadas," "desaprensión

y picardía" in language, and a general "incitación al humor." Martín García Merou, *Sarmiento*, pref. Rodolfo Trostine (Buenos Aires: Ayacucho, 1944), more realistically sees "las crudezas rabelesianas" (p. 38) as the foremost characteristic of Sarmiento's humor. It is probable that Sarmiento inspired more seriousness and distanced respect in his contemporaries than light humor. Lastarria's retrospective portrait of Sarmiento (written in the experimental orthography of the period), who had recently arrived in Chile, was hardly one of mirth: "El hombre realmente era raro; sus treinta i dos años de edad parecían sesenta, por su calva frente, sus mejillas carnosas, sueltas i afeitadas, su mirada fija pero osada, a pesar del apagado brillo de sus ojos, i por todo el conjunto de su cabeza, que reposaba en un tronco obeso i casi encorbado. Pero eran tales la viveza i la franqueza de la palabra de aquel joven viejo, que su fisonomía se animaba con los destellos de un gran espíritu, i se hacía simpática e interesante." J. V. Lastarria, *Recuerdos literarios: datos para la historia literaria de la América española i del progreso intelectual en Chile*, 2nd ed. (Santiago: Librería de M. Servat, 1885), pp. 81-82.

33. Lévi-Strauss, *The Savage Mind*, p. 22.

34. Hoffer, *The True Believer*, p. 137.

35. Krieger, *The Tragic Vision*, pp. 261-62.

36. Jacques Derrida, *Of Grammatology*, trans. Gayatri Chakravorty Spivak (Baltimore and London: Johns Hopkins University Press, 1976), p. xxxii.

37. Tulio Halperín Donghi, "Una nación para el desierto argentino," in *Proyecto y construcción de una nación (Argentina 1846-1880)*, ed. Halperín Donghi (Caracas: Biblioteca Ayacucho, 1980), p. xiv, states that the "Nueva Generación" of 1837, to which Sarmiento belonged, "en esta primera etapa de actuación política, parece considerar la hegemonía de la clase letrada como el elemento básico del orden político al que aspira . . . . La hegemonía de los letrados se justifica por su posesión de un acervo de ideas y soluciones que debiera permitirles dar orientación eficaz a una sociedad que la Nueva Generación ve como esencialmente pasiva, como la materia en la cual es de responsabilidad de los letrados encarnar las ideas cuya posesión les da por sobre todo el derecho a gobernarla."

38. Concerning Sarmiento's ideas on the intellectual faculty of mankind, see XXXVII, 125; and XXXIX, 72; in addition to the other passages which are quoted here.

39. According to Juan David García Bacca, "Prólogo," in Andrés Bello, *Obras Completas*, (Caracas: Ministerio de Educacion, 1951), Vol. III, p. xxviii, Bello published ten essays between June 1, 1843 and February 1844 in Santiago's *El Crepúsculo* on different aspects of what he called the "Teoría del entendimiento." It was only in 1872, four years after Bello's death, that these essays and other previously unpublished materials were assembled under the title of *Filosofía del entendimiento*.

40. Marcelino Menéndez y Pelayo, *Antología de poetas hispano-americanos: Cuba, Santo Domingo, Puerto Rico, Venezuela*, (Madrid: Impresores de la Casa Real, 1893), II, p. cxxiv.

41. Domingo F. Sarmiento, *Obras Completas* (Paris: Belín Hermanos, 1895-1909), XXX, 117. This article, entitled "Universidades," is not included in Volume XXX of the 1948-1956 edition of Editorial Luz del Día.

42. The lack of philosophical penetration is undoubtedly one of the reasons why so many critics have emphasized the *journalistic* nature of Sarmiento's writing. Paul Groussac: "Baste decir que su campo primero y último ha sido el periodismo. Sarmiento, pues, ha sido periodista, y casi podría afirmarse que no ha sido otra cosa." (quoted by César H. Guerrero, *Sarmiento: el pensador* [Buenos Aires: Depalma, 1979], p. 189). Leopoldo Lugones expresses a similar point of view: "Porque en Sarmiento, las letras fueron un medio, no un fin. Si tomó el procedimiento más natural y eficaz de expresar las ideas, es porque éstas constituyen la civilización, o, por mejor decir, la libertad sinónima . . . . Sarmiento subordinó sus dotes de escritor a estos rasgos de periodista." *(Historia de Sarmiento, p. 132).* There are others, however, who argue that Sarmiento's ideas were profound, in spite of his journalistic means. See César H. Guerrero, *Sarmiento: el pensador,* and Luis Franco, *Sarmiento entre dos fuegos* (Buenos Aires: Paidos, 1968).

43. Edward W. Said, *Beginnings: Intention and Method* (Baltimore and London: Johns Hopkins University Press, 1975), p. 49.

44. Anderson Imbert, *Genio y figura*, p. 26.

45. Jean-Paul Sartre, *La Nausée* (Paris: Libre de Poche, 1957), pp. 62-63.

46. Said, *Beginnings*, p. 30.

47. This is the argument of Adolfo Prieto, *La literatura autobiográfica argentina* (Rosario: Editorial Biblioteca, 1968), p. 40.

48. George W. Foster, *Tzintzuntzán: Mexican Peasants in a Changing World* (Boston: Little, Brown Co., 1967), speaks of the "law of limited good" in relation to the ideology of certain peasant communities, according to which an individual's increase in wealth and fame is believed to result from a corresponding loss on the part of his neighbor.

49. Roberto Tamagno, *Sarmiento, los liberales y el imperialismo inglés* (Buenos Aires: A. Peña Lillo, 1963), pp. 168-77, documents how Sarmiento also attempted to discredit the accomplishments of Belgrano and San Martín.

50. According to Paul Verdevoye, *Domingo Faustino Sarmiento: éducateur et publiciste (entre 1839 et 1852)* (Paris: Institut des Hautes Etudes de L'Amérique Latine, 1963), p. 60, Sarmiento mentions Echeverría's *Dogma* only two times in his volumnous writings: in the pages of *Viajes* treating his visit with the poet in Montevideo (V, 51-56), and a very short necrology upon the latter's death in 1851 (III, 339-40).

51. Some critics, among which is Alberto Palcos, *Sarmiento: la vida, la obra, las ideas, el genio* (Buenos Aires: Emecé, 1962), pp. 83-84, interpret Sarmiento's comments about Echeverría in *Viajes* (V, 35-56) as a strongly favorable judgement. My own reading of Sarmiento's words, quite distinct, is characterized by the title of my article, "Echeverría según Sarmiento: la personificación de una nación ultrajada por la barbarie," *Cuadernos Americanos,* 255 (1984), 165-85.

52. Halperín Donghi, "Una nación para el desierto argentino," p. xliii, states: " . . . Sarmiento guarda una inconfesada nostalgia de la guerra civil, y es de temer que esa inclinación secreta sea demasiado compartida en un país largamente acostumbrado a ella."

53. Lugones, *Historia de Sarmiento*, p. 28.

CHAPTER 4

'Facundo': Historical Context and Derivative Aesthetics

With good reason Anderson Imbert warns us about the difficulties of classifying Sarmiento according to the study of his written work: "Cada vez que queramos meterlo en las hormas ya consagradas de las escuelas filosficas, Sarmiento se nos escapará por los costados."[1] This is precisely the problem one confronts in analyzing the aesthetic ideas that seem to be operative in *Facundo*. The work, originally a libel and written under the pressure of meeting weekly installment deadlines, is characterized by contradictions and a fluctuating ideology. It could very well be true that Sarmiento, as he said, sacrificed "toda pretensión literaria" (VI, 160) in its composition. But this does not minimize the fact that generations of readers have accepted this work as one of the monuments of Latin American literature.

Accepted, yes, but not studied in all its magnitude. It is a paradox, as Noé Jitrik explains, that the greater part of the existing criticism has ignored the literary aspects of this work and has focused instead on its sociological or historical content.[2] Some recent studies, however, tend to emphasize those aspects of what could be called the unconscious aesthetics of the writer.[3] Sarmiento himself, months after writing *Facundo*, refused to correct the errors and distortions of his original composition, because he was aware that his impetuous manner of writing harmonized with an impassioned style of confronting problems and interacting with others. He wrote to his friend Valentín Alsina that *Facundo's* achievement was far more than he had originally intended: it was "ensayo y revelación para mí mismo de mis ideas . . ." (VII, 15). There was a certain magic about that work which elevated it above the human realm and bestowed upon it an autonomy of its own. He wrote in the introduction to the 1881 Italian translation that the work, conceived in an "especie de sonambulismo" (XLVI, 301), had already served as a prophesy of Argentina's future for two generations. In those few weeks while he was writing the original version of *Facundo,* an intellectual fervor and not an elaborated artistic theory best accounts for his powerful language and evocative images. The idea of an unconscious verve in the writer resolves for the critic certain problems of textual or archetypal interpretation, but creates others for understanding Sarmiento's rationalist pedagogy.[4]

After giving due consideration to what could be called an unconscious aesthetic criterion in Sarmiento's creative production, there remains the question of his conscious artistic intentions. Here we arrive at the heart of the matter, but also a number of problems. Well known is his sociopolitical program: the transformation of the "deserts" to cities and cultivated fields and the "improvement" of the race, that is to say, the substitution of the Indian and the gaucho with a new population of European immigrants. But these objectives contradicted in large part the goals of his romantic aesthetics. Ana María Barrenechea documents this contradiction in *Facundo*, which she calls Sarmiento's "double intention."[5] On the political side, the author wanted to attack the centers of barbarism that he believed existed in the vast plains of the interior and in the institutions and customs of rural society. But on the aesthetic side, Sarmiento wanted to pay homage, through his writing, to the singular natural environment and the picturesque way of life of his native country. Many passages from the text convince us of the truth of this double intention, but still there is no adequate explanation for the psychology of the author who tolerated so many contradictions in his ideas. This question has already been addressed, albeit in an indirect way, in the first three chapters.

It is understandable that the young Sarmiento, totally committed to the struggle against Rosas, had little regard for a literature, and in general a cultural activity, which did not address itself to the crying needs of a country only recently weaned from a feudal past. His adult thought was fairly consistent regarding this pragmatic view of writing. In *Viajes*, he displayed his disdain for the exiled Argentinian poets in Montevideo, who although personally suffering the abuses of Rosas' tyranny, nevertheless expended much of their creative energy in the writing of verses. Similarly, one biographer tells of how Sarmiento, at a later moment when he was national director of public instruction, allowed only a few works of fiction to be present in the newly established public libraries–the *Aeneid*, the *Quijote*, the *Iliad*, *Gil Blas*, and others–and only these because of the supposed exercise of skills that they provided to the reader. He refused to admit that fiction had any other value or that it played a role in moral education.[6] Similarly, a few years before his death in 1888, he is said to have written with pride, "Yo no he probado a escribir una novela en mi vida," as if he had never given in to that particular weakness.[7] Nevertheless, these reactions do not mean that he disdained literary accomplishments, per se. On the contrary, he firmly believed that a measure of a society's advancement was the time and energy which its people devoted to literary pursuits. He wrote in 1856: "Caramelos y novelas andan juntos en el mundo, y la civilización de los pueblos se mide por el azúcar que consume y las novelas que leen" (XLVI, 150). What do these views of the mature thinker suggest concerning the ideas held by him in an earlier period, and specifically, when he was in the process of writing *Facundo?*

One must consider the possibility that aesthetic ideas different from those considered by Professor Barrenechea influenced the composition of *Facundo,* aesthetic ideas that the author believed would also serve in the sociopolitical enterprise. Sarmiento possessed an activist temperament and dedicated himself completely to the political struggle. He was totally involved in his mission of promoting his idea of the desirable form of civilization for the countries of South America. Consequently, it does not surprise us that he would integrate certain artistic ideas of the period into his ideological campaign. It would be an error to say that these new aesthetic ideas were nothing more than a mask for his political interests, just as much as it would be a distortion to think that the political ideas of the writer were subordinated in *Facundo* to an aesthetic practice. Both suppositions are simplifications. Here, political creed and aesthetic practice mutually influenced each other. This is seen in almost all of his early writings, especially in those articles which he had published in Chilean journals in the months preceding the publication of *Facundo.*

The Definition of a Militant Aesthetics

The utilitarian social role that Sarmiento assigned to creative literature in the Chilean polemics of 1841 and 1842 has not been emphasized enough by the critics.[8] He was in strong agreement with the idea of Victor Hugo, which Echeverría and other Argentine writers echoed in their own writings,[9] that romanticism was nothing more than political liberalism in literary form. Accordingly, we can understand the relationship which Sarmiento established between romanticism and the struggles for independence which the Spanish colonies had waged a generation before: "El romanticismo era, pues, una verdadera insurrección literaria como las políticas que le han precedido. Ha destruído todas las antiguas barreras que se creían inmóviles, lo ha revuelto y destruído todo" (I, 310). Although Sarmiento believed that romanticism already belonged to the past (I, 293), he defended many of the ideas associated with that movement because they still carried a symbol of progress. It was typical of Sarmiento that he accepted, but never substantiated in any rigorous analysis, a strict relationship between social tendencies and aesthetic ideas. While he attacked romanticism because it belonged to an age that was already past, he found in the works of Larra, Dumas, and Hugo worthy examples for a national literature that could shake the South American societies from their inertia and provoke positive change.

Given that Sarmiento directed his own literary praxis toward the transformation of society, it is understandable that he had a low regard for those works which merely treated abstract or fictional themes. He tried to convince his reading public of the merits of a literature that portrayed the characters, customs, and events of the region, and analyzed social problems with the hope of arriving at possible solutions. He exhorts the student of literature:

> pero cambiad de estudios, y en lugar de ocuparos de las formas, de la pureza de las palabras, de lo redondeado de las frases, de lo que dijo Cervantes o Fray Luis de León, adquirid ideas de donde quiera que vengan, nutrid vuestro espíritu con las manifestaciones de los grandes luminares de la época; y cuando sintáis que vuestro pensamiento a su vez se despierta, echad miradas observadoras sobre vuestra patria, sobre el pueblo, las costumbres, las instituciones, las necesidades actuales, y en seguida escribid con amor, con corazón, lo que se os alcance, lo que se os antoje. Que eso será bueno en el fondo, aunque la forma sea incorrecta; será apasionado, aunque a veces sea inexacto; agradara al lector, aunque rabie Garcilaso; no se parecerá a lo de nadie; pero, bueno o malo, será vuestro, nadie os lo disputara; entonces habrá prosa, habrá poesía, habrá defectos, habrá bellezas (I, 230).

In his *Facundo,* published a few years later, Sarmiento realized in practice many of the ideals which are outlined here.

This ethical and only minimally aesthetic interest indicates a significant change in his beliefs regarding expressive literature. In his young adult years he strove to be up-to-date with the European thought of his time, and to that end he read every work of literature and history that fell into his hands. Little trace remains of his first attempts at writing according to the criteria assimilated through these readings, but we do know that in 1838 the young writer sent a poem, "Canto a Zonda," to Juan Bautista Alberdi, signing it with a pseudonym and requesting a critical evaluation. Alberdi, only a year older than Sarmiento, already enjoyed a reputation among the youth of the country due to his progressive views on literature and society. No copy exists of Alberdi's answer to this request, but we do know from a subsequent letter of Sarmiento that Alberdi praised the would-be poet's attempt at creating a "particular" and "nacional" expression.[10] It is probable that Alberdi also criticized those efforts at versification because Sarmiento, shortly afterward, abandoned the genre and dedicated himself to the task of organizing the youth of the country around the need for cultural activities and institutions in general. Indeed, there were other projects of far greater urgency that should occupy the talents of an ambitious youth while the country was still in a formative stage; it was necessary to promote progressive and liberal institutions in all spheres of social life. He probably realized poetry's limited role in the advancement of an unschooled population; it was an exquisite fruit that could only grow from a mature and well-groomed tree.

Sarmiento's ideas regarding the need for a national expression must be interpreted in the light of his preference for a literature treating useful ideas. In one essay he used the ideas of Larra in order to fortify his own thesis: "No queremos esa literatura reducida a las galas del decir, que concede todo a la 'expresión' y nada a la 'idea,' sino una literatura hija de la experiencia y de la historia pensándolo todo, diciéndolo todo en prosa, en verso al alcance de la multitud ignorante aún . . ." (I, 249).

He was convinced that romantic expression had a certain utility for the South American societies of his time, but he nevertheless believed that a newer type of literature would promote even better those desired changes. This new expression would retain certain ideas of past literary practices, redirecting them toward the new object of social progress. As a consequence, he embraced a literary aesthetics which included many romantic ideas. The definition he gave to *socialista* literature (I, 310) reveals an important aspect of Sarmiento's literary thought: the precedence he gave to social and political goals. The ultimate purpose of his writing was the transformation of society, and he summoned all textual means in order to achieve that objective. He firmly believed that his writing production should be directed toward the most crying needs of his country: the battle against gaucho barbarism, and the struggle for political reconstruction and social and economic modernization.

Sarmiento, among the other writers of his generation, defended a literary production with a pronounced ethical focus. Emilio Carilla, in his excellent study on romanticism in Latin America,[11] documents the general agreement of Domingo Sarmiento, Esteban Echeverría, Juan María Gutiérrez, Juan B. Alberdi, and Vicente Fidel López regarding how the aesthetic experience of the individual worked toward his own moral elevation and, also perhaps indirectly, toward social progress. Art, they believed, developed certain intellectual faculties which were indispensable for the ruling class of any society. An integral aspect of the program for social action embraced by these thinkers was the necessity of producing a literature which would promote their underdeveloped society's transformation according to liberal criteria.

There were, however, notable differences separating the ideas of Sarmiento from those of other writers. The following statement by Juan María Gutiérrez provides an initial basis for comparison and contrast, and consequently helps us appreciate the particularity of Sarmiento's aesthetic thought. Gutiérrez' text, which treated the social function of poetry, was known to Sarmiento.[12] After attacking the Spanish artists of recent years for their limited talent and lack of imagination, Gutiérrez called attention to the need for Argentinians to cultivate, among other things, an aesthetic sensitivity. This, he believed, played an important role in the total cultural experience of the individual:

> Sobre la realidad de las cosas, en la atmósfera más pura de la región social, mueve sus alas un genio que nunca desampara a los pueblos; que mostrando al hombre la nada de sus obras, le impele siempre hacia adelante, y senalándole a lo lejos bellas utopías, repúblicas imaginarias, dichas y felicidades venideras, infúndele en el pecho el valor necesario para encaminarse a ellas, y la esperanza de alcanzarlas. Este genio es la poesía.[13]

Gutiérrez, in contrast to Sarmiento, manifested an idealist conception of art in the general formation of the individual. Art, through its stimulation of the imagination, offered to the subject an alternative which was more profound than lived experience; the subject could modify his situation when he tried to incarnate that poetic ideal into practice. Sarmiento, however, did not have a high regard for the function of the imagination—as will be demonstrated below—and conceived the function of art almost exclusively in its pragmatic, i.e., "materialist," dimension. Gutiérrez supposed that the individual would become spiritually transformed upon experiencing art; but he did not assume the existence of any direct relation between this and the improvement of society. Sarmiento, in contrast, appreciated art for the social transformations which it might bring about; its value was relative to its effectiveness for promoting progress.

There are other characteristics of Sarmiento's aesthetic ideas which can be noted upon examining his principal sources. In his autobiographical writings he listed the names of the many philosophers and thinkers whose works had influenced his own ideas. As a young man he demonstrated a defensive attitude with regard to his irregular self-education in the provinces, which accounted for, at least in part, the lack of structure or method in his intellectual formation. A consequence was his need to exhibit evidence in front of his reading public attesting to his erudition and the prestige which his ideas enjoyed in renown North American or European texts. One must not devalue Sarmiento's ideas on this account; on the contrary, his genius manifested itself in the original manner in which those derived ideas became transformed and redirected toward his own objectives.

Two writers seem to have had a preponderant influence in the formation of Sarmiento's pragmatic aesthetics: Alexis de Tocqueville and A. W. Schlegel. Mitre justifyably accredited Tocqueville's *Democracy in America* as the "libro de cabecera" among the intellectual influences of his and Sarmiento's generation.[14] The importance of this work upon Sarmiento has yet to be investigated in detail.[15] He quoted Tocqueville frequently during his early years as a writer, and there is little doubt that he had carefully read the entire work of the French writer. It is evident that certain aesthetic ideas of Sarmiento were formulated under the influence of Tocqueville, for instance his materialist conception of the artistic function and the slight appreciation—in comparison with Gutiérrez and others—for the human imagination.

Tocqueville, in the chapter entitled "Of Some Sources of Poetry Among Democratic Nations," describes in glowing terms the poetic practice which he believed was characteristic of democratic nations. He concludes: "I have shown how the ideas of progress and of the indefinite perfectibility of the human race belong to democratic ages,"[16] leaving little doubt as to his favorable evaluation of those countries' culture in which the liberal social and political ideas of his age were already a reality. He explains in detail what for him were the diverse functions of the imagination in different types of society. Referring to those nations with "aristocratic" institutions, he writes:

it sometimes happens that the body acts as it were spontaneously, while the higher faculties are bound and burdened by repose. Among these nations the people will often display poetic tastes, and their fancy sometimes ranges beyond and above what surrounds them. . . . An aristocratic people will always be prone to place intermediate powers between God and man. In this respect it may be said that the aristocratic element is favorable to poetry (pp. 75-76).

Tocqueville disdained the role of the imagination in the aristocratic tradition because it encouraged repose, rather than activity, of man's "higher" intellectual faculties. Similarly, he held a low opinion of poetry because it distracted the attention of the subject away from the lived situation of mankind and encouraged instead the relatively useless contemplation of ideal or remotely possible realities. The opinion of the French writer concerning the literary practice of men living in democracy, however, had a special thrust:

But in democracies the love of physical gratification, the notion of bettering one's condition, the excitement of competition, the charm of anticipated success, are so many spurs to urge men onward in the active professions they have embraced, without allowing them to deviate for an instant from the track. The main stress of the faculties is to this point. The imagination is not extinct, but its chief function is to devise what may be useful and to represent what is real. The principle of equality not only diverts men from the description of ideal beauty; it also diminishes the number of objects to be described (pp. 75-76).

The imagination had a utilitarian function in democratic societies; one could say that its role was the promotion of equality. According to Tocqueville, the work of art fulfilled its aesthetic mission in this type of society when it treated the daily preoccupations and concrete necessities of the population. In essence, Tocqueville criticized formalist poetry's objective of searching for or describing ideal beauty on account of its narrow elitist appeal.

With respect to A. W. Schlegel, Sarmiento mentions in *Recuerdos de provincia* that he had read one of his works in the months just before departing for Chile on route to his second exile (III, 172). It is even more probable, however, that he had learned of the ideas of the German critic through the writings of Echeverría. We remember that in *Facundo* he praises the poetry of the latter, especially *La cautiva*. We can only imagine Sarmiento's reaction to Echeverría's explanations in the critical introduction which accompanied the poem's first edition. Echeverría, frequently quoting Schlegel, states that the lyrical treatment of the deserts is not only "riqueza para nuestro engrandecimiento y bienestar, sino también poesía para nuestro deleite moral y fomento de nuestra literatura nacional."[17] He goes on to explain that other parts of the poem

present "la pasión manifestándose por actos . . . ." But those passions of
the written page, which Echeverría apparently compared with the reader's
literary reaction, ought to be experienced in moderation, "porque el estado verdaderamente apasionado es estado febril y anormal, en el cual
no puede nuestra frágil naturaleza permanecer mucho tiempo, y que debe
necesariamente hacer crisis . . . ." Art, writes Echeverría in another of
his essays, highlights the conflict between man's spiritual and material
aspects, and accordingly dramatizes his moral dignity.[18]

It is highly probable that Echeverría was referring to the well-known
essay by Schlegel entitled "Sources of Pleasure Derived from Tragedy," in
which is stated:

> The moral freedom of man . . . only manifests itself when in conflict
> with his sensuous impulses: so long as no higher call summons it
> to action, it is either actually dormant within him, or appears to
> slumber, since otherwise it does but mechanically fulfill its part as
> a mere power of nature. It is only amidst difficulties and struggles
> that the moral part of man's nature avouches itself. If, therefore,
> we must explain the distinctive aim of tragedy by way of theory,
> we would give it thus: to establish the claims of the mind to a
> divine origin, its earthly existence must be disregarded as vain and
> insignificant . . . .[19]

The German writer proposed that romantic art, through its representation of the irregularities of nature or the mysteriousness of human events,
stimulated the emotions up to the point where the individual's reason,
until then semi-dormant, would rise up and impose itself over the inferior faculties of the intelligence. The particular function of tragedy, says
Schlegel, is to exercise man's "moral liberty" and confirm the spirituality
of reason.

Many passages in the first part of *Facundo* suggest a close association
between the aesthetic ideas of Sarmiento and those of these two European writers. For example, one finds this statement about the possible
sources of a romantic literature in Argentina: "Si un destello de literatura nacional puede brillar momentáneamente en las nuevas sociedades
americanas, es el que resultará de la descripción de las grandiosas escenas naturales, y sobre todo de la lucha entre la civilización europea y la
barbarie indígena, entre la inteligencia y la materia . . ." (VII, 34). He
defines two themes for a national literature in the newly organized American states: the descriptions of the majestic natural scenes and the social
conflict resulting from the continent's particular history. Sarmiento states
a few lines further that the particular value of Echeverría's poetry is due
to the fact the poet "volvió sus miradas al desierto, y allá en la inmensi-
dad sin limites, en las soledades en que vaga el salvaje, en la lejana zona
de fuego que el viajero ve acercarse cuando los campos se incendian, halló
las inspiraciones que proporcioná a la imaginación el espectáculo de una
naturaleza solemne, grandiosa, inconmensurable, callada . . ." (VII, 35).
This passage seems to affirm the Schlegelian idea that romantic poetry
incites the emotions and at times the imagination. But what happens

to the reason? Up until here Sarmiento provides no explanation. Upon continuing, he emphasizes the reactions to romantic literature of man's inferior intellectual faculties:

> La poesía, para despertarse, porque la poesía es como el sentimiento religioso, una facultad del espíritu humano, necesita el espectáculo de lo bello, del poder terrible, de la inmensidad de la extensión, de lo vago, de lo incomprensible; porque sólo donde acaba lo palpable y vulgar empiezan las mentiras de la imaginación, el mundo ideal. . . . ¿Dónde termina aquel mundo que quiere [el habitante] en vano penetrar? ¡No lo sabe! ¿Qué hay más allá de lo que ve? La soledad, el peligro, el salvaje, la muerte. He aquí ya la poesía. El hombre que se mueve en estas escenas, se siente asaltado de temores e incertidumbres fantásticas, de sueños que le preocupan despierto (VII, 36).

It is necessary to reconstruct somewhat this disorganized flow of ideas and complete Sarmiento's implicit scheme of reader reactions to romantic literature. In general, he believed that poetry originated in man's dionysiac encounter with primitive nature, and that the nature of this experience marked the stage in which the individual had advanced toward civilization. Here it is convenient to consider separately the different groups of persons and their respective reactions to the romantic stimulus.

With those individuals of fairly primitive intellectual faculties, poetry realizes itself exclusively on the sub-rational level, and is a "palpable and common" sensation which ignites sentiments such as fear and incertitude. The savage force of nature stimulates in this category of men a degrading psychological reaction since they are completely dominated by their most rudimentary emotions and impulses. In this light we can interpret his treatment in *Facundo* of the *montonera,* which is summarized by his description of their "carácter de ferocidad brutal, y ese espíritu terrorista" (VII, 58). In a similar manner he describes the stare of Facundo, "el *tigre de los Llanos*": "Sus ojos negros, llenos de fuego, y sombreados por pobladas cejas, causaban una sensación involuntaria de terror en aquellos en quienes alguna vez llegaban a fijarse . . ." (VII, 69). Sarmiento is fairly consistent in his treatment of the gaucho as a being who was psychologically dominated by the romantic environment of the wild interior. Except for the *gaucho cantor* and perhaps *el rastreador,* he offers no examples of how the aesthetic experience of this first class of people could have a more edifying effect.

Sarmiento continues onto a different level of poetic reactions when he discusses those individuals with an emphasized imaginative faculty. In many of his descriptions of the man of the pampa, one can observe an explicit relation between a hyperactive imagination and a propensity for violent action. He explains in detail how the pristine desert develops the imaginative faculty at the cost of one's reason. The common gaucho, the *montoneros,* and Facundo Quiroga are similar in that even the smallest provocation could cause in them a violent reaction. "En esta vida tan sin emociones, el juego sacude los espíritus enervados, el licor enciende

las imaginaciones adormecidas" (VII, 50)—and as a result the most innocent of encounters could develop toward a tragic end. Even worse in
Sarmiento's eyes was the meager effort made by rural inhabitants to go
beyond that life governed by the imagination; and it even happened that
they defended it as a merit. He writes about Quiroga's exaggeration concerning the fourteen deaths attributed to his alterego, the *macho de los*
grillos: "Acaso es ésta una de esas idealizaciones con que la imaginación
poética del pueblo embellece los tipos de la fuerza brutal que tanto ad-
mira . . ." (VII, 75). Here, Sarmiento shows his disdain not only for
the narrow pride of the gaucho, but also for the manner in which the
semi-barbarous life of the rural interior came to be idealized in popular
poetry.

In other passsages Sarmiento carries his criticism of the imaginative
world of the gaucho into the area of social customs. The rural inhabitant,
he says, has descended to the cultural level of vulgar superstitions on account of an imaginative faculty hyper-stimulated by an extended contact
with the telluric force of the countryside (VII, 37). What results from the
active imaginative faculty is not necessarily and always violence, but at
times antiquated customs or distorted cultural expression. An example
would be the poetic expression of the gaucho singer which is "pesada,
monótona, irregular . . ., metafórica y pomposa" (VII, 47).

Sarmiento presents us with another division of mankind in relation to
the imaginative faculty, a classification which he makes no attempt to sustain with sociological criteria. This new class of persons, more developed
than semi-barbarous individuals, but still inferior to the public formed
in a rational tradition, are susceptible to fantasy and have a propensity
to dream impossible projects. Their contact with the savage countryside
stimulates the imagination, creating in their thought something similar to
"un sentimiento religioso." Sarmiento had little regard for those individuals who, because of a dominant imagination, were unable to distinguish
between an impossible dream and a realizable goal. This is the reason for
his criticism of poets in general, whose priorities were out of touch with
the social needs of the country:

> ¡Yo os disculpo, poetas argentinos! Vuestras endechas protestarán
> por mucho tiempo contra la suerte de vuestra patria. . . .
> ¡Qué de riqueza de inteligencia i cuánta fecundidad de imagi-
> nación perdidas! ¡Cuántos procesos para la industria i qué saltos
> daría la ciencia si esta fuerza de voluntad, si aquel trabajo de ho-
> ras de contracción intensa en que el espíritu del poeta está exaltado
> hasta hacerle chispear los ojos, clavado en su asiento, encendido su
> cerebro i, agitándose todas sus fibras, se empleara en encontrar una
> aplicación útil de las fuerzas físicas para producir un resultado útil![20]

Two other examples of Sarmiento's contempt for the imaginative temperament are seen in his criticism of the old Unitarians, with their "desacier-
tos y sus ilusiones fantásticas" (VII, 103) or of his own father, who failed

repeatedly in his services to the country on account of his "imaginación, fácil de ceder a la excitación del entusiasmo . . ." (III, 135).

In order to present as complete a picture as possible of Sarmiento's aesthetic ideas, reference must be made to his writings on painting and theater art, in which the ideas he expressed concerning the imagination's function correlated with the critical mainstream of his time, and consequently stand in contradiction to the discussion above. Similar to Coleridge, he postulated that the imagination in certain instances performed a strictly positive role of orienting the individual toward an achievable ideal.[21] In these instances, he depicted the imagination as performing the function of organizing the individual's diverse sensations and impressions, and therefore assisting the reason in its function of discovering the truth inherent in visual or dramatic expression.

Sarmiento was hardly consistent in his aesthetic opinions, as is evident in *Facundo*. In this work he put aside any notion of the imagination's ennobling function, and instead emphasized its negative role in human behavior. One explanation for this was his original intention that the work would belong more to the discourse of politics than to the province of art.

How did Sarmiento perceive the reaction of the educated and civilized reader to the romantic stimulus? It must be admitted that in the passages from *Facundo* quoted above, Sarmiento left incomplete his scheme of the different types of aesthetic reactions. He briefly considered the aesthetic response of the least advanced classes of mankind, but in that work he did not go on to describe the mental experience of the group which—we can assume—constituted his ideal reading public, i.e., the cultured reader.[22] The ideas of Schlegel and Tocqueville once again prove their relevance in filling this lacuna. It is well known that Sarmiento believed that the individuals who constituted the superior order of humanity structured their lives according to reason. Only they were able to control their sub-rational inclinations on the psychological level and guide their imagination in the task of understanding individual and social realities according to concrete categories. Only they were able to comprehend the necessity of taming nature and modernizing society. Consequently, it can be argued that Sarmiento, like these two European mentors, believed that the poetic experience of educated men involved the exercise of passions and imagination with the objective of channeling them toward a useful result.[23] This is the aesthetic principle that seems to predominate not only in *Facundo*, but also in many of the early works of Sarmiento.

An Aesthetics in Practice

It is convenient to remember that this aesthetic principle plays a more important role in some sections of *Facundo* than it does in others. As it

has already been mentioned, the passages of the work with perhaps greatest artistic value were composed without undue calculation regarding the
eventual consequences of his words or ideas. But in other passages, for
which social or political objectives guided their composition, the literary
result was generally less remarkable. At times, however, the irrepress-
ible spirit of the writer manifested itself in his expression in spite of the
conscious intention of the imposed thesis.

Already quoted is a passage from *Facundo* in which Sarmiento defined
the two most probable themes for a romantic national literature: the
descriptions of untamed nature and the struggle between the forces of
civilization and barbarism. Concerning the first of these themes, critics
are substantially in agreement that the work contains some of the finest
landscape descriptions in Hispanic American literature. Leopoldo Lugones, for example, states about Sarmiento, that "Su memoria fidelísima
del colorido y de los detalles, su imaginación constructora, su nativo arte
de contar, formaban el don característico de reproducir el paisaje y el
hombre."[24] José León Pagano, who has focused on the aesthetic aspects
of Sarmiento's psychology, concurs with Lugones in his observation that
"En el *Facundo,* Sarmiento mueve masas de luz y sombras como si estu-
viese mezclando colores en la paleta. Determina el tono según la gradación
de los planos."[25]

As accurate as these artistic assessments might be, one is left with
the question of what were the intentions of the writer in that precise
moment of penning words to the page, and particularly in the light of
the intense political passions that possessed him both then and always.
Might we discover evidence of his *bricolage* psychology upon examining
the construction of those passages treating the landscape and customs of
his country's rural areas?

As an entrance into this matter, I profess my agreement—at least in
part—with Paul Groussac, that Sarmiento's reputation as *paisajista* (during the period under study) is not entirely justified. Groussac writes:

> Y si se me preguntara qué dotes literarias fueron—entre algunas otras,
> como la delicadeza y el gusto—negadas en absoluto a Sarmiento, de-
> signaría precisamente la visión luminosa y el sentimiento apasionado
> de la naturaleza, que hacen a los grandes paisistas [sic] y descrip-
> tivos. Esto no importa comprobar una inferioridad absoluta del es-
> critor, sino señalar una faz característica del talento literario, cuya
> deficiencia le excluye de cierto grupo—acaso no el más grande.[26]

Indeed, Sarmiento wrote few passages in which we can detect an intention
of capturing, by means of its literary recreation, the pure essence of the
natural landscape. Stated in another way, Sarmiento only rarely was
interested in scenes of nature or the countryside because of an immanent
value; instead, natural descriptions had importance for him primarily as
a pretext for discussing his ethical objectives.

In the following landscape description from *Facundo* it can be observed that the narrative voice never lets itself be carried away by the emotions it supposedly gives rise to; instead, it maintains a firm control over its subject matter:

> Esta extensión de las llanuras imprime . . . a la vida del interior cierta tintura asiática que no deja de ser bien pronunciada. Muchas veces al ver salir la luna tranquila y resplandeciente por entre las yerbas de la tierra, la he saludado maquinalmente con estas palabras de Volney en su descripción de las Ruinas: *La pleine lune a l'Orient s'elevait sur un fond bleuâtre aux plaines rives de l'Eufrates.* Y en efecto, hay algo en las soledades argentinas que trae a la memoria las soledades asiáticas; alguna analogía encuentra el espíritu entre la pampa y las llanuras que median entre el Tigris y el Eufrates; algún parentesco en la tropa de carretas solitaria que cruza nuestras soledades para llegar, al fin de una marcha de meses, a Buenos Aires, y la caravana de camellos que se dirige hacia Bagdad o Esmirna. Nuestras carretas viajeras son una especie de escuadra de pequeños bajeles, cuya gente tiene costumbres, idioma y vestido peculiares que la distinguen de los otros habitantes, como el marino se distingue de los hombres de tierra (VII, 24).

In this description, the countryside in itself is of secondary interest to Sarmiento. Beginning the paragraph, it would seem that the narrator attempts to communicate the powerful reactions which a scene of the pampas incites in the spectator, the same effects–it is assumed–that one would experience upon viewing the "tint" of an exotic Asiatic land. He makes an allusion to the words of Volney, which come to mind "maquinalmente." In the next sentence the narrator, now transformed into social scientist, abuses the previously established romantic tone with the excessive repetition–four words in one sentence–of the association between the sensation of solitude and one's residence in the pampas: "hay algo en las soledades argentinas que trae a la memoria las soledades asiáticas; . . . algún parentesco en la tropa de carretas solitaria que cruza nuestras soledades . . . ." Does this repetition mean that the narrator does not trust sufficiently the effects of his own expression? The paragraph, in its totality, has an obvious development: the emotive voice cedes to the scientific voice, and those elements most appropriately called romantic now assume the function of a type of *pharmakos* which is absorbed by the socio-historical thesis.[27]

In another passage, Sarmiento repeats this exemplification of how the Argentine countryside stimulates the development of only the most rudimentary intellectual capacities of mankind:

> De aquí resulta que el pueblo argentino es poeta por carácter, por naturaleza. ¿Ni cómo ha de dejar de serlo, cuando en medio de una tarde serena y apacible, una nube torva y negra se levanta sin saber de dónde, se extiende sobre el cielo mientras se cruzan dos palabras, y de repente el estampido del trueno anuncia la tormenta que deja frío al viajero, y reteniendo el aliento por temor de atraerse un rayo

de los mil que caen en torno suyo? La oscuridad se sucede despues
a la luz; la muerte está por todas partes; un poder terrible, incon-
trastable, le ha hecho en un momento reconcentrarse en sí mismo,
y sentir su nada en medio de aquella naturaleza irritada; sentir a
Dios, por decirlo de una vez, en la aterrante magnificencia de sus
obras. ¿Qué más colores para la paleta de la fantasía? Masas de
tinieblas que anublan el día, masas de luz lívida, temblorosa, que
ilumina un instante las tinieblas y muestra la pampa a distancias
infinitas, cruzándola vivamente el rayo, en fin, símbolo del poder
(VII, 36-37).

Few have described as well as Sarmiento (and one of those few is undoubtedly Güiraldes in *Don Segundo Sombra*) the terrible power of a
pampa storm; few have captured with such expressive prose the effect
which primitive nature has over man. But in the sentences that immediately follow, this eulogy turns to attack, and the euphoric style dissolves
before the social scientific thesis:

Estas imágenes han sido hechas para quedarse hondamente graba-
das. Así, cuando la tormenta pasa, el gaucho se queda triste, pen-
sativo, serio, y la sucesión de luz y tinieblas se continua en su imaginación, del mismo modo que cuando miramos fijamente el sol nos
queda largo tiempo su disco en la retina.

Preguntadle al gaucho, a quien matan con preferencia los rayos, y
os introducirá un mundo de idealizaciones morales y religiosas, mezcladas de hechos naturales pero mal comprendidos, de tradiciones
supersticiosas y groseras. Añádase que si es cierto que el fluido
eléctrico entra en la economía de la vida humana, y es el mismo
que llaman fluido nervioso, el cual excitado subleva las pasiones y
enciende el entusiasmo, muchas disposiciones debe tener para los
trabajos de la imaginación el pueblo que habita bajo una atmósfera
recargada de electricidad hasta el punto que la ropa frotada chis-
porrotea como el pelo contrariado del gato (VII, 37).

In this passage, there is a physiological explanation, perhaps inspired by
the theories of Galvanism, according to which an electric or nervous fluid
"subleva las pasiones y enciende el entusiasmo" of the rural inhabitant.
This man of the pampa does not perceive the forces of nature with scientific categories, but rather with badly comprehended idealizations that
are "mezcladas . . . de tradiciones supersticiosas y groseras." In this
passage, then, the expressive prose serves principally as an entrance into
a pseudo-medical justification for the stunted intellectual powers of the
inhabitant of the countryside.

These examples demonstrate that in Sarmiento's pragmatic aesthetics
the countryside is indeed the object of poetic evocation, but not because
of any intrinsic value it might possess. Sarmiento, we can assume, had in
mind an aesthetic reaction that was even more refined than the emotion
produced by romantic poetry. For him, this new sensation would occur

when the bourgeois reader, inspired by the ideal of material progress, contemplated the transformation of deserts into farms, factories, and cities. And continuing one step further with the same logic, nature's magnificence would be in porportion to its degree of primitivism–that is to say, in proportion to the amount of energy which civilized man, armed with the most advanced technology of his age, would have to expend in order to impose his order over savage nature.

The Romantic Struggle Between Civilization and Barbarism

After having considered the descriptions of the "grandes escenas naturales"–which Sarmiento considered to be the first subject appropriate for a romantic literature in the new American nations–it is now our task to explore the second subject, which is the social dimension of the struggle between "la inteligencia y la materia" (VII, 34). In *Facundo* we read that this imposing conflict offers "escenas tan peculiares, tan características, y tan fuera del círculo de ideas en que se ha educado el espíritu europeo, porque los resortes dramáticos se vuelven desconocidos fuera del país donde se toman, los usos sorprendentes, y originales los caracteres" (VII, 34-35). Then, in the following paragraph, Sarmiento continues with the explanation of how the romantic writer can reveal new aspects of the social struggle in his literature. He praises James Fenimore Cooper, whose writings draw the reader's attention to the scenes occurring "al límite entre la vida bárbara y la civilizada, al teatro de la guerra en que las razas indígenas y la raza sajona están combatiendo por la posesión del terreno" (VII, 35).

Raúl Orgaz has called attention to the influence which Cooper's descriptions of the struggle between the white and indigenous races in North America must have had in the formulation of Sarmiento's historical ideas.[28] One could go a step further and project that Sarmiento, with *bricolage* imagination, probably perceived in Cooper a literary praxis that well suited his own sociopolitical objectives. That is to say, he understood that the reader of literary descriptions such as those offered by Cooper would experience aesthetic pleasure upon contemplating the social struggle taking place "at the limit between barbarian and civilized cultures," because it was there that the European tradition manifested most dramatically its superiority over the American reality. Reconstructing this logic, one could say that, in the first moment, the reader would relive this struggle as a psychological conflict between class values. The reader, educated in accordance with the "espíritu europeo," would experience aesthetic delight upon contemplating how his bourgeois values would inevitably come to predominate in the institutions and beliefs of the rural inhabitants. Then there would be a second moment of aesthetic pleasure when the reader would comprehend how the literary passage had aroused within him certain affective and imaginative reactions, that is to say how his rational facilites became fortified against the backdrop of romantic emotion. These two types of psychological satisfaction are similar to Schlegel's idea of "moral liberty": poetry, in both cases, occurs when the white bourgeois reader contemplates the military victory and the social domination of his race and class over rural barbarism.

It seems that Sarmiento was aware of a certain paradox in his aesthetic ideas, that when the reader took into consideration what was strange or unknown, there began an intellectual process which ended in an act of self-knowledge and a sensation of self-satisfaction. The reader, one could say, arrived at a higher level of identification with the ideology of his class and encountered a complacent image of self in the mirror of discourse.

Doctrines proclaiming an opposition between reason and the sentiments, science and literature, prose and poetry, were widely disseminated throughout the Occidental world in the second half of the nineteenth century.[29] Sarmiento had probably assimilated these ideas through his readings of not only Schlegel, but also Vico, Herder, Condillac, and Rousseau, writers whom he mentioned with frequency.[30] Consequently, it comes as no surprise to learn that he, with social scientific inclination, embraced many arguments proposed by these writers, especially ones treating the imaginative and instinctual orientation of primitive cultures, the prevalence of poetry among the American Indians, and the emotional origin for poetry.

For one who believed in the superiority of modern society and scientific understanding, it was understandable that he also applied these ideas in artistic considerations. This is one explanation for Sarmiento's deploring—surely an unjust position—of Echeverría's useless rebellion; Echeverría was, according to Sarmiento, "el poeta de la desesperación, del grito de la inteligencia pisoteada por los caballos de la pampa . . ." (V, 54). Evidently, Sarmiento granted little importance to the prose works of Echeverría which he had read, such as *El dogma socialista* and *El matadero,* and chose to consider only the poetic side of Echeverría's career and writings. Sarmiento would probably have been in agreement with the words of Thomas Macaulay, who also possessed positivistic inclinations, that no person of his enlightened period could write or enjoy poetry "without a certain mental unbalance."[31] Consequently, what was original in Sarmiento was not the formulation of these aesthetic ideas concerning a primitive expression, but rather their insistent application to all aspects of South American life.

In spite of Sarmiento's suggestion that the romantic poetry of his land ought to address itself particularly to the struggle between the forces of progress and indigenous barbarism, one has to admit that he hardly mentions the Indian in the pages of *Facundo.* A consideration of the Indian simply had little to do with his central topic, which was the life and death of Juan Facundo Quiroga, and the geographic, historical, and social factors which accounted for the *caudillo's* predominance. However, well known was his conviction that there was no place for the indigenous race in Argentina's future; he believed that any nation possessing a significant number of Indians was burdened with an inferior genetic pool, and consequently could never aspire to equal status among the powerful nations of the world.

In contrast, the gaucho and the gaucho society of the interior are the principal focuses of *Facundo*. Passing from the Indian to the gaucho, Sarmiento's attitude became more complex, since the gaucho–either biologically stained by his mixture of European and indigenous bloods, or child of morally fallen Europeans due to his excessive contact with the savage pampas[32] –lay midway on the path of development. Following his French enlightenment mentors, Sarmiento divided history into two categories: moral and physical. The gaucho had only developed physically owing to his constant involvement in "esta lucha del hombre aislado con la naturaleza salvaje, del racional con el bruto . . ." (VII, 32); he had triumphed over all natural resistence and consequently was "fuerte, altivo, y enérgico" (VII, 33). But in spite of that development, the gaucho's intelligence remained stunted: "La vida del campo, pues, ha desenvuelto en el gaucho las facultades físicas, sin ninguna de las de la inteligencia" (VII, 33). The gaucho, considered superior to the Indian, was still inferior to the white European; he was neither entirely barbarian nor civilized, but shared characteristics of both.

In spite of its predominantly historical focus, the first part of *Facundo* offers two clear examples of Sarmiento's anti-gaucho aesthetics. The first corresponds to the magnificent literary portraits of the four well-known gaucho types. The expressive force of the writer exalts these figures, but only after an introductory sentence of social-scientific intent "Yo quiero sólo notar aquí algunos [tipos generales] que servirán a completar la idea de las costumbres, para trazar en seguida el carácter, causas y efectos de la guerra civil" (VII, 39-40). It would seem that Sarmiento had the original intention of providing through his character sketches some concrete examples for his sociopolitical discussion. Again, it is paradoxical that the literary effect of his prose–as judged by a century and a half of criticism–celebrates those character types which his social and political ideology led him to disdain.

The second example is the well-known episode treating Sarmiento's visit to the home of the *estanciero,* whose two occupations were "rezar y jugar" (VII, 31). In the whole work, perhaps this passage achieves best what we call a romantic tone. The narrator compares the rural setting to "los tiempos primitivos del mundo anteriores a la institución del sacerdocio" and proceeds to draw an "escena homérica": the patriarch, of "fisionomía noble," lived among "una docena de mujeres y algunos mocetones" in the domestic environment, while outside there roamed "las majadas . . . con sus confusos balidos," and "caballos, no bien domados aún. . . ." The narrator adds that the *estanciero,* similar to a medieval feudal lord, "Había edificado una capilla en la que los domingos por la tarde rezaba él mismo el rosario, para suplir al sacerdote y el oficio divino de que por años habían carecido" (VII, 31). The admirers of creole culture could find in this episode an evidence of the rural inhabitant's adaptable intelligence and free spirit which qualified him as the worthy prototype of a national race.

The evocative tone still predominates when we continue on to the description of the *estanciero* in his act of devotion: "Concluído el rosario, hizo un fervoroso ofrecimiento." And what follows demonstrates the spiritual pact between narrator subject and described object:

> Jamás he oído voz más llena de unción, fervor más puro, fe más firme, ni oración más bella, más adecuada a las circunstancias, que la que recitó. Pedía en ella a Dios lluvias para los campos, fecundidad para los ganados, paz para la República, seguridad para los caminantes... Yo soy muy propenso a llorar, y aquella vez lloré hasta sollozar, porque el sentimiento religioso se habia despertado en mi alma con exaltación y como una sensación desconocida, porque nunca he visto escena más religiosa; creía estar en los tiempos de Abraham, en su presencia, en la de Dios y de la naturaleza que lo revela; la voz de aquel hombre candoroso e inocente me hacía vibrar todas las fibras, y me penetraba hasta la médula de los huesos (VII, 31).

In this account, which undoubtedly bears the influence of Rousseau's ideas on natural religion, one can detect many elements of a romantic expression: there is the "primitive" scene, the "Homeric" protagonist, an environment responsive to the described personages, and the fervor and emotion that overcome not only the protagonist, but also the narrator-observer.

That is one reading; but the narrator suggests an entirely different interpretation. In the paragraphs immediately following the section quoted above, the narrator turns upon himself and denounces that which he has previously described with such feeling. The religious practice of the *estanciero,* he now states, is an example of how the infested environment of the rural areas has corrupted social relationships and cultural practices:

> He aquí a lo que está reducida la religión en las campañas pastoras, a la religión natural; el cristianismo existe, como el idioma español, en clase de tradición que se perpetua, pero corrompido, encarnado en supersticiones groseras, sin instrucción, sin culto y sin convicciones. . . .

> A falta de todos los medios de civilización y de progreso, que no pueden desenvolverse sino a condición de que los hombres estén reunídos en sociedades numerosas, ved la educación del hombre del campo (VII, 31-32).

Is there some way of reconciling these two contradictory focuses that inspire in the reader totally distinct reactions? What appears at the beginning to be the narrator's romantic embellishment of the customs of the rural interior, in the end is revealed as a rhetorical posture for the sociopolitical thesis. Sarmiento, a naturally gifted writer, intuited–if he did not realize consciously–that a self-description as emotional Everyman convinced better than abstract arguments. In this passage the rational narrator gradually overshadows the romantic persona. This rhetorical procedure in literature prefigured for the writer a similar domination of European institutions over the gaucho in Argentine society.

The realist narrative voice predominates in the first part of *Facundo,* but in the second part, which treats the life and death of Juan Facundo Quiroga, the romantic imagination upstages the judgment of the sociologist. Without doubt the second part is more literary and novelistic: there is a protagonist inserted within a suspense-filled plot, and there unfolds a conflict with a tragic end which seems fitting for the personage who attempted to transgress the very laws of barbarism. Also, there is an attempt–whether conscious or unconscious–to look beyond the historical anecdote for the profound truth of human acts. Sarmiento, states Armando Zárate, "Busca, como un supersticioso, en los hechos humanos, valores imaginarios que una escritura de combate exalta y define. Pero en el fondo, Facundo es un símbolo espectral y como tal, un mito cuyo gesto sólo puede definirse según la energía de la ficción, en su realidad entera, en su *folktale.* He aquí el movimiento primitivo de una densidad constitutiva, congruentemente literaria."[33]

As correct as Zárate's views are regarding Sarmiento's attempt to express the mythical underpinnings of the events surrounding the life and death of the protagonist, one must not underestimate the sociopolitical orientation of his aesthetics. The paragraphs on the battle of Tablada, certainly some of the most accomplished portions of the work in regard to literary criteria, serve well for demonstrating the *socialista* ideas that guided the author's composition. The narrator clearly explains that the objective data, in this instance, are not of primary importance: "La batalla de Tablada es tan conocida, que sus pormenores no interesan ya. En la *Revue des Deux Mondes* se encuentra brillantemente descrita; pero hay algo que debe notarse" (VII, 127). Sarmiento does not tell us what that "algo" consists of, but a reading of the passages following this statement suggests that it is nothing other than the providential force guiding civilization in its struggle against barbarism.

Before and after the paragraphs in question the narrator makes explicit the relationships between the protagonists and their respective social forces. We read about Quiroga and the barbarous character of his followers when they are preparing to enter into an open-field battle: "Facundo estaba en su elemento . . . . [I]gnorante, bárbaro . . . no conoce más poder que el de la fuerza brutal, no tiene fe sino en el caballo; todo lo espera del valor, de la lanza, del empuje terrible de sus cargas de caballería. ¿Donde encontraréis en la República Argentina un tipo mas acabado del ideal del gaucho malo?" (VII, 127-29) He was the sworn enemy of the city and his goal was its total destruction. His antagonist is General Paz, "el hijo legítimo de la ciudad, el representante más cumplido del poder de los pueblos civilizados. . . . Algo debe haber de predestinado en este hombre" (VII, 129). The narrator elaborates about this clash of epic forces: "En la Tablada de Córdoba se midieron las fuerzas de la campaña y de la ciudad bajo sus más altas inspiraciones, Facundo y Paz, dignas personificaciones de las dos tendencias que van a disputarse el dominio de la República" (VII, 128). What happens on the level of discourse is the transformation of the historical anecdote into a romantic narration with tinges of the epic.

Sarmiento has framed his painting and has established the ideological limits of his narration; the only thing left to do is describe the passion of the battle, but not without emphasizing that the eventual result is the victory of the forces representing progress over those of barbarism. Facundo, impatient to begin the battle with his *montonera* horsemen, had ignored almost completely his own infantry and artillery–those military components which Sarmiento generally associated with progress. Facundo considered them "inútiles," and marched to battle with only his cavalry, which had "sin embargo de triple número que el ejército enemigo. Allí fue el duro batallar, allí las repetidas cargas de caballería, ¡pero todo inútil!" (VII, 128). Then Sarmiento describes how Facundo's army, although far outnumbering the the forces of Paz, continues on the path of inevitable destruction.

What follows is one of the most evocative descriptions of the entire work. Sarmiento, faithful to the aesthetic theory elaborated on in the first part of his work, describes the violent clash between the country's two conflictive societies, the *ciudad* and the *campaña* (throughout the chapter these two words are consistently italicized). He emphasizes the terrible energy of those "inmensas masas de jinetes" who are repulsed by the superior military technology and precise strategy of General Paz. This battle, on a small scale, represented for Sarmiento the logical result of a much larger struggle. In the narration he employs such literary techniques as anticipation and antithesis in order to highlight the "firmeza de los vencedores" and the failure of barbarism, and also to drive home his sociopolitical thesis of an invincible civilization which he extolled and exalted.

The Prose of Progress

There remains one final aspect of Sarmiento's militant aesthetics which is appropriate for the discussion here, and that is the supposed superiority of prose in comparison to other forms of literary expression. Universally accepted are the affirmations of Juan Alfonso Carrizo–rigorously subjected to "la duda eterna"–that Sarmiento transcribed almost word for word the "El cantar tradicional a la muerte del General Juan Facundo Quiroga" in the last chapter of *Facundo's* second section.[34] Above we have already considered some of the ideas of the period which perhaps influenced Sarmiento in the composition of these chapters, one being the idea that poetry was the vehicle of expression for the emotions and instincts of primitive societies. It is true that the majority of European theorists did not believe in an inevitable conflict between scientific perception and poetry, but it was widely felt that the development of the former had far outstripped that of the latter in recent decades.[35] Sarmiento, however, did not see the matter in this light. He had little regard for popular poetry. His belief in the necessity of going beyond this mode of social communication is clearly expressed in the first part of *Facundo:*

> El Cantor está haciendo candorosamente el mismo trabajo de cróni-ca, costumbres, historia, biografía, que el bardo de la edad media; y sus versos serían recogidos más tarde como los documentos y datos en que habría de apoyarse el historiador futuro, si a su lado no estuviese otra sociedad culta con superior inteligencia de los acon-tecimientos, que la que el infeliz despliega en sus rapsodias ingenuas (VII, 46).

Sarmiento, like other intellectuals who defended the liberal ideals of his time, returned to the tradition of Aristotle in the belief that history was the antithesis of poetry; he defended the necessity of replacing an emotive expression with the language of science.[36]

Theory, however, is at times an unfaithful guide for praxis, and this seems to be the case in Sarmiento's writing. He didn't call for a total substitution of prosaic in the place of poetic language—not yet anyway—because his aesthetics called for the evocative presentation of the social struggle, in addition to the depiction of barbarism as an evil that must be overcome. In this light, his writing had to satisfy simultaneously the literary demand of evoking a romantic or emotive reaction, and the social-scientific demand of transcending poetry in the affirmation of a prosaic discourse. Sarmiento's solution was to convert the popular poem into combative prose, and in doing so, prune the former of a part of its evoca-tive force and tint it with ideological possibilities.

These two operations become quite visible upon comparing the popu-lar poem and Sarmiento's transcription. First, with respect to the sup-pressions, it is undoubtedly true that he made certain changes simply to facilitate its rendering into prose. But there also exists the possibility that the production of his discourse followed the determined plan of reducing the evocative nature of the poem to a more measured and controlled ex-pression. Two examples will suffice. We read from the traditional ballad:

> En cada posta que llega
> pregunta muy afligido
> la hora que ha pasado un chasqui
> de Buenos Aires venido.[37]

Sarmiento transformed this into: "En cada posta a que llega, hace preguntar inmediatamente: '¿A qué hora ha pasado un chasque de Buenos Aires?'" (VII, 184) The transcription replaces the popular spelling of "chasqui"–which reflects the word's origin in the Quechua language–with its more Europeanized form "chasque" when referring to the stagecoach; in addition, it leaves aside the suggestion of Facundo's great affliction. In another strophe the ballad reads:

> Al entrar en Santa Fe
>   se le aumenta su inquietud,
> y en desesperada angustia
>   se pone con prontitud.

And in *Facundo* we read: "Al entrar en la jurisdicción de Santa Fe la inquietud de Quiroga se aumenta, y se torna en visible angustia . . ." (VII, 184). Again, one can note the small modification in emphasis, which is caused by the deletion of those words referring to the hurried transition in Quiroga's psychological mood and the change of "desesperada angustia" to "visible angustia." These two examples reveal, it would seem, the writer's effort at neutralizing somewhat the ballad's effects of foreboding and anticipation.

Even stronger evidence of the political thesis which motivated Sarmiento's transcription are the phrases in his account which have no correlation whatever to the traditional poem. We read in *Facundo:* "Quiroga se enfurece . . . . La brutalidad y el terror vuelven a aparecer desde que se halla en el campo, en medio de aquella naturaleza y de aquella sociedad semi-bárbara . . ." (VII, 184). Obviously, the presence of this phrase is accounted for by the thesis of telluric barbarism in the interior. Further on Sarmiento–as Carrizo explains–"agrega un largo párrafo para pintar el ambiente caldeado por las pasiones que había en esos días en la ciudad de Córdoba . . . ."[38] It is evident that Sarmiento included this historical information in order that the reader not lose sight of the more important sociopolitical issues that were at hand. And in this ingenious manner, his prose once again demonstrates the superior presence of civilization.

Romantic Poetry

As we have seen, Sarmiento, in accordance with his pragmatic aesthetics, believed that romantic poetry inspired in the reader a sub-rational enthusiasm which was similar to what one experienced upon contemplating the sublime aspects of nature or the epic conflict between different societies. But instead of esteeming that sub-rational enthusiasm as an end in itself, he preferred the man who dominated his instincts and imagination with reason. He especially admired that poetic expression which excited the emotions as a means of demonstrating reason's final ascendancy in the heirarchy of human responses. His socio-historical context was especially appropriate as the subject for a literature which produced this type of aesthetic play: In Argentina, civilized society's two overriding concerns were its confrontation with the savage nature of the pampas, and its brutal conflict with barbaric Indians and primitive gauchos. Sarmiento believed that both of these experiences were historical manifestations of a more basic clash pitting man's reason or intelligence against the emotions, instincts, and even the imagination. He believed that the *romancista* literature produced by such writers as Echeverría and Cooper coincided wth society's modernization project in its exaltation of civilization over barbarism.

Romancista literature was the appropriate expression for his time and age. But Sarmiento, in several of his writings on social, political, and historical topics, already projected the future resolution of those two epic conflicts (civilization's conquest of barbarian social groups and savage nature) which were the essence of his romantic age and its *romancista* literature. What would be the status, then, of poetry in the civilized society of the future, when the problems associated with the pampa's underpopulation and the gaucho or Indian menace would no longer exist? Would poetry cease to exist also? Perhaps even more important, what would be the function of the emotions and the imagination within the hierarchy of intellectual faculties for the supposedly civilized man of the future?

He suggests in various passages that romantic poetry, because it arose primarily in a transitory setting, was a cultural phenomenon of little permanence. He talks of "las condiciones de la vida pastoril tal como la ha constituído la colonización y la incuria," which gave rise to "un destello de literatura nacional [que] puede brillar momentáneamente en las nuevas sociedades americanas . . ." (VII, 34). Romantic expression arose from temporary "conditions" which "momentarily" predominated; it, like the conditions engendering it, was a passing phenomenon. Could one assume then, that in the future romantic poetry would be of interest to only those historians studying the cultural relics of a period which modernity would just as soon leave in the shadow of oblivion?

Because of the strict relationship between the primitive "conditions" of the country in its formative stage and the "momentary" existence of romantic poetry, it is logical that Sarmiento did not appreciate completely those individuals who were characterized by a singularly "poetic" disposition. We remember that he disdained the poetically inclined gaucho because of his "mundo de idealizaciones" (VII, 37) and his "temores e incertidumbres fantásticas" (VII, 36) which arose from his intimate contact with untamed nature. Consequently, there is a note of reproach and perhaps resignation in the frequently quoted words that "el pueblo argentino es poeta por carácter, por naturaleza" (VII, 36). And for this very same reason one can understand better Sarmiento's negative and ambiguous attitude toward Echeverría: although a leader in the ideological and political struggle against Rosism, he was above all a poet, that is to say, an individual misdirected in regard to his objectives due to an excessive contact with the barbarism of the countryside.

In other passages, however, Sarmiento–always contradictory–seems to accredit romantic poetry with a positive and enduring value. For example, he states in *Facundo:* "no puede . . . negarse que esta situación [de la lucha con la barbarie] tiene su costado poético, fases dignas de la pluma del romancista" (VII, 34). And a few paragraphs further: "Del centro de estas costumbres y gustos generales se levantan especialidades notables, que un día embellecerán y darán un tinte original al drama y al romance nacional" (VII, 39). Sarmiento was convinced that the romantic expression of his own day would constitute the foundation of a lasting national literature. In effect, he was absolutely correct; the entire cycle of expression treating the Argentine pampa–from Bartolomé Hidalgo to Güiraldes–is testimony to that vision.

According to Sarmiento, romantic poetry–whether contagious or constructive for modern society–was destined to disappear. In this belief he was joined by many utilitarian thinkers of the period. Macaulay had written in 1825: "We think that, as civilization advances, poetry almost necessarily declines."[39] It would be impossible to identify all of the influences which inspired Sarmiento concerning this belief, but surely one of them was Tocqueville's *Democracy in America*. In one of his more polemical passages, the famous French traveler wrote that life in democratic ages would be markedly "anti-poetic" due to the people's preoccupation with constructing a new nation and their little need for exercising the imagination in creating a fantastic or dream-like art.[40]

It was Sarmiento's belief that a new type of poetry would bloom in the soil of modernity, when primitive society and the romantic expression which it engendered would have passed into history. In the pages of *Facundo* he is silent concerning this possibility, but he wrote a few years later, in a letter to Valentín Alsina which now forms part of *Viajes*, these words about Echeverría:

> He aquí al verdadero poeta, traduciendo sílaba por sílaba su país, su época, sus ideas. El Hudson o el Támesis no pueden ser cantados así; los vapores que hienden sus aguas, las barcas cargadas de mercaderías, aquel hormiguear del hombre . . ., no deja ver esta soledad del Río de la Plata, reflejo de la soledad de la pampa que no alegran alquerías, ni matizan villas blanquecinas que ligan al cielo las agujas del lejano campanario (V, 56).

The Hudson or the Thames river valleys, with nature harnassed for agriculture and society engaged in commerce and industry, could not possibly engender the same type of literature as that of Argentina's *romancista* poets who wrote in the midst of barbarism.

He believed that in the future Argentine writers would develop their own representative forms of expressive literature in accordance with the particular social needs and patterns of development experienced by the region. While undergoing the painful eradication of barbarism and the slow cultivation of progress, the nation would need a pragmatic and militant literature, one not unlike the *socialista* writing which he advocated. Then, once barbarism were largely superceded, the nation would need an expression that would serve as an ideological force for resolving problems and proposing creative possibilities for the future. Like the art and the architecture which he observed in his travels to North America between 1847 and 1848, that literature would be elegant in its extreme simplicity; modest in expressing the high aspirations of a people in pursuit of a noble national ideal; and accessible in its form for a people united by common interests and not by human suffering.[41]

This optimistic vision for Argentina's future literature and society corresponds largely to the utopian liberal values that largely characterized Sarmiento's thought in the period prior to the fall of Rosas in 1852. But there was also that other voice which expressed the dramatically contrasting values of intolerance for social and ethnic differences and the need for the forceful imposition of order. This second voice advocated a literature of the future characterized by ideological and combative furor.

Related to Sarmiento's conviction of the social benefits that would accrue from an anti-poetic literature was his preference for essayistic prose over other forms of expression. With his ambiguous, but essentially negative, opinion of poetry and fictional writing in general, he would have been in agreement with the words of Octavio Paz: "El poeta pone en libertad su materia. El prosista la aprisiona."[42] Paz would probably consider fictional prose as sharing characteristics of both poetry and essayistic prose, and consequently as occupying a middle position between the two. Fictional prose approaches essayistic expression in the use of a language with limited significations and an institutionalized syntactic structure, but it also resembles poetry on account of its relative invention of scene and personages. Consequently, one can understand that when Sarmiento spoke as a social scientist and as a precursor of positivism, he demonstrated comtempt for the language of poets and *romancistas* because it harkened back to the primitive origins of human experience on account of its lack of concreteness and the way it opened itself to varied and ambiguous meanings. Far preferable, according to this frame of thought, was the analytical language of science that could "shrink the province of poetry" and promote the civilizing project of modernity.[43] Consequently, Sarmiento often sought in his writing a language that could substitute multidimensional signs for a meaning that was literal and one-dimensional. Paradoxically, his goals for renovating society were promoted through a writing practice which many times interpreted complex individual and social realities with simplistic categories.

Sarmiento's desire to limit language's signifying power seemingly contradicts what is universally considered to be the unsurpassed literary quality of his prose. It is evident, however, that the two opposing properties coexist in his writing. One can observe evidence of both the author's rational or conscious designs, and his spontaneous writing energy. The tension between these two, if it be characteristic of all discourse in the form of the dialectic between social and personal languages, is particularly evident in the case of Sarmiento, as many of his critics have observed. Allison Williams Bunkley identifies an emotional or irrational "intent" subsuming a conscious "intention."[44] Ana María Barrenechea observes the "incorporación dinámica de su persona a la aventura."[45] Noël Salomon, in reference to the costumbrista sketches in Facundo's first part, sees "l'identification d'une conscience au sujet traité."[46] Noé Jitrik suggests that Sarmiento, in his discourse, persuades through affective rather than logical conduits.[47] These critics seem unanimous in their affirmation of a romantic quality to Sarmiento's discourse, in which expressive impact overshadows a rationally prescribed thesis. This movement from objective to subjective, from "scientific" to "romantic" languages, has usually been interpreted as evidence of his ideological openness to new ideas both in the social and literary realms. Indeed, it correlates well with the widely disseminated image of Sarmiento as stalwart promoter of freedom and democracy for Argentina's liberal future.

However, we have seen in this chapter a second type of stylistic movement in his discourse: the manner by which the writer assumes a romantic or literary pose, and then proceeds to destroy it with social-scientific arguments. This stylistic phenomenon suggests a conservative side to Sarmiento's personality and thought: his desire to cut off discussion and limit social options; his attempt to impose his own personality and his own organizing principles upon reality. Sarmiento's tranformation of the popular poem dealing with the death of his protagonist, his rationalist conclusions about the religious estanciero, and the physiological description of the individual's reaction to a pampa storm, all demonstrate the narrative closure of an essentially expressive or emotive experience. In contrast to the prevailing view of the literary critics mentioned above, this type of inner movement is not an emotive voice infringing upon or even absorbing what is prosaic; instead, the narrator's social values supplant a previously established stylistic appreciation. Rationality predominates over emotion, and science over romanticism. This procedure, which acts to limit signification, occurs as frequently in Facundo as the "literary" stylistic movement which serves to open interpretation.

However, rather than emphasize the differences between types of stylistic movement, perhaps it is more important to call attention to what they have in common: frequently, the favored value or mode of expression, introduced late, comes to predominate over what has been previously presented. After a rhetorical display of tolerance, the "I" of the narrator firmly asserts itself over the narrative material. Both stylistic movements (the outbreak of emotive prose and the rationalist containment of emotive prose) are indicative of the writer's indomitable inner vision that sought to exclude other possibilities. Reminiscent is "la volonté de vérité," as described by Michel Foucault,[48] which is "comme prodigieuse machinerie destinée a exclure."

This new reading suggests that Sarmiento perceived the literary text as a metaphor for society: the oppositions and ambiguities in discourse corresponded in his mind to the struggles between groups and interests in the social sphere. In the process of writing, the narrative voice imposes itself over the narrative material, and discourse attempts to possess language. It is evident that aesthetic theory and practice were merely components of Sarmiento's larger rhetorical strategy which had as its objective the replacement of the existing signifiers with those of his own choosing, and therefore the creation of authority for himself and the group of liberal thinkers whose principles he defended.[49] Paradoxically, his abstract ideals of utopian liberalism–liberty, democracy, constitutionalism– would require forceful means for their implementation. The literary journalist and the military man together would serve as midwives for the emergence of the new social order. interior.[6]

Notes for Chapter 4

1. Enrique Anderson Imbert, *Genio y figura de Sarmiento* (Buenos Aires: Editorial Universitaria de Buenos Aires, 1967), p. 26, observes about Sarmiento's historical thought–but the idea is equally applicable to his aesthetic ideas: Era un sentidor, no un teórico; y como leía y oía mientras peleaba a grandes saltos de un sitio a otro, su 'filosofía de la historia' no tenía coherencia sistemática. Cada vez que queramos meterlo en las hormas ya consagradas de las escuelas filosfícas, Sarmiento se nos escapará por los costados. A veces opina como iluminista, a veces como romántico, a veces como 'socialista' o 'positivista,' sin que sus opiniones sean lo bastante originales para fundar una posición nueva.

Specifically concerning *Facundo*, Sarmiento himself made a similar observation in a letter to his grandson, Augusto Belín Sarmiento, calling the work "una especie de poema, panfleto, historia . . ."–Domingo Faustino Sarmiento, *Facundo*, introd. Alberto Palcos (Buenos Aires: Ediciones Culturales Argentinas, 1961), p. 447.

2. Noé Jitrik, *Muerte y resurrección de 'Facundo'* (Buenos Aires: Centro Editor de América Latina, 1968).

3. Jitrik, *Muerte y resurrección,* and Armando Zárate, "El *Facundo:* un héroe como su mito," *Revista Iberoamericana,* 44, Nos. 104-105 (1978), 471-48.

4. Jitrik, *Muerte y resurrección,* suggests a conflict between the conscious thesis (that of tracing the lines of national conflict in terms of a romantic opposition between civilization and barbarism) and quite distinct values that were revealed only on the expressive level. In a similar fashion, Adolfo Prieto, *La literatura autobiográfica argentina* (Rosario: Universidad Nacional del Litoral, Facultad de Filosofía y Letras, Instituto de Letras, 1962), sees a contradiction between Sarmiento's political ideas and those class values which he had formed in childhood years. Sarmiento lived that conflict, according to Prieto, "con terrible dramatismo, desgarrado interiormente, puesta la cabeza en el nuevo orden, atrapado el corazón en el antiguo . . ." (p. 48). A similar hypothesis, which also has interesting implications, is that of Hernán Vidal, *Literatura hispanoamericana e ideología liberal: surgimiento y crisis (una problemática sobre la dependencia en torno a la narrativa del boom)* (Buenos Aires: Hispamérica, 1976), about the relationship between the socio-economic dependency of the Hispanic American countries and the different discourses which ideologically governed the production of literary fictions–and, one must add–the historical and philosophical thought of Sarmiento and his generation.

5. Ana María Barrenechea, "Función estética y significación histórica de las campañas pastoras en el *Facundo,*" in *Sarmiento: educador, sociólogo, escritor, político,* Juan Mantovani, et al. (Buenos Aires: Universidad de Buenos Aires, Facultad de Filosofía y Letras, 1963), p. 43, recognizes the coexistence of aesthetic and historical objectives, but does not explain the relationship between the two: "la pampa, el gaucho y ciertos rasgos de su vida primitiva figuran en el *Facundo* con una doble función. Por una parte entran en la explicación racional

de un hecho histórico-cultural, y por otra tienen una justificación estética dentro de la obra."

6. These anecdotes are told by C. O. Bunge, *Sarmiento: estudio biográfico y crítico* (Madrid: Espasa Calpe, 1920), p. 172. See Sarmiento's own opinions in XXVII, 310, where he presents a quite favorable opinion concerning the value of fictional prose.

7. *Ibid.*

8. An exception is Raul H. Castagnino, "Estética de la energía en Sarmiento," in *Historias menores del pasado literario argentino (siglo XIX)* (Buenos Aires: Huemul, 1976), pp. 23-38, who utilizes the phrase of Leopoldo Lugones *(Historia de Sarmiento)* as the title of his short study and also for this conclusion about Sarmiento: "Su temperamento no admitió la gratitud del arte en general, del teatro en particular, y reclamó sus servicios para la conducción social, para la educación popular por el medio directo de los principios puestos en acción, visualizados" (p. 38).

9. Esteban Echeverría, "Clasicismo y romanticismo," in *Obras Completas*, Vol. V: *Escritos en prosa*, ed. Juan María Gutiérrez (Buenos Aires: Imprenta y Librerías de Mayo, 1874), p. 100.

10. Domingo Faustino Sarmiento, "Carta a Alberdi" (San Juan, July 6, 1838), in *Sarmiento: cartas y discursos políticos*, (Buenos Aires: Ediciones Culturales Argentinas, 1965), Vol. III, p. 4. Over the years, critics have granted near-unanimous acceptance to the claim by Alberdi that it was indeed Sarmiento who submitted to him this early poem, and to whom Alberdi answered with the letter quoted in the text here. However, there is no evidence of this exchange of letters among Sarmiento's papers. Agusto Belín Sarmiento, grandson and intimate companion of Sarmiento in his later years, died with the conviction that the poem was not of his grandfather: "en toda su vida no hizo un verso, malgrado haber pretendido Alberdi que era de Sarmiento una poesía que fuese sometida a su crítica. . . . Tenemos de Sarmiento la afirmación de no haber escrito un verso; pero es lícito afirmar que era poeta. Su prosa está impregnada de sentimiento poético . . . ." From "Prólogo," in *El joven Sarmiento: escenario en 5 actos* (Saint Cloud: Imprenta Pablo Belín, 1929). p. 15.

11. *El romanticismo en la America hispánica* (Madrid: Gredos, 1958), p. 145.

12. According to Paul Verdevoye, *Domingo Faustino Sarmiento: éducateur et publiciste (entre 1839 et 1852)* (Paris: Institut des Hautes Etudes de l'Amérique Latine, 1963), p. 17, Sarmiento declared in July of 1838 that he had read the speeches commemorating the inauguration of the Literary Salon, among which was that of Gutiérrez. In *Facundo* Sarmiento states: "Tengo, por fortuna, el acta original del Salón a la vista . . ." (VII, 219), possibly referring to the texts of those speeches and the "Palabras Simbólicas" written by Echeverría with a few passages by Alberdi.

13. Juan María Gutiérrez, "Fisonomía del saber español: cual deba ser entre nosotros," in *Antecedentes de la Asociación de Mayo: 1837-1937*, ed. Consejo Deliberante de la ciudad de Buenos Aires en el centenario de su fundación

(Buenos Aires: Canteillo y Co., 1939), p. 58. Two studies treating the relationship between Sarmiento and Gutiérrez are Alberto Palco's prologue to *Facundo*, by Domingo F. Sarmiento (Buenos Aires: Ediciones Culturales Argentinas, 1961); and Roberto Tamagno, *Sarmiento y el imperialismo inglés* (Buenos Aires: A. Peña Lillo, 1963), pp. 245-49. At the end of the first work there are reproduced several letters from the correspondence between the two men.

14. Alejandro Korn, *Influencias filosficas en la evolución nacional*, in *Obras* (La Plata: Universidad Nacional de La Plata, 1940), Vol. III, p. 208.

15. Raúl A. Orgaz, *Sarmiento y el naturalismo histórico*, in Vol. III of *Obras Completas*, introd. Arturo Capdevila (Córdoba: Assandri, 1950), pp. 279-88, dedicates a chapter to the influence of Tocqueville over the social and political thought of Sarmiento, but does not mention the possible influence on the latter's ideas with regard to literature and culture.

16. Alexi de Tocqueville, *Democracy in America*, ed. P. S. Bradley (New York: Random House, Vintage, 1945), Vol. II, p. 78.

17. Esteban Echeverría, *Páginas literarias seguidas de los fundamentos de una estética romántica* (Buenos Aires: El Ateneo, 1928), pp. 208-13. Echeverría names A. W. Schlegel many times in these essays; see, for example, pp. 141, 165, and 175. Emilio Carilla, "Ideas estéticas de Echeverría," in *Estudios de literatura argentina (siglo XIX)* (Tucumán: Universidad Nacional de Tucumán, Facultad de Filosofía y Letras, 1965), p. 159, argues that much of what has been considered original until now in the thought of Echeverría is little more than "la transcripción o el aprovechamiento absorbente" of the writings of A. W. Schlegel, Madame de Staël and Victor Hugo.

18. Echeverría, *Páginas literarias*, p. 169, in the essay "Reflexiones sobre el arte."

19. A. W. Schlegel, "Sources of Pleasure Derived From Tragedy," Lecture V, *Lectures on Dramatic Art and Literature, Ancient and Modern* (1808). My edition is from *Literary Criticism: Pope to Croce*, ed. Gay Wilson Allen and Harry Hanyden Clard (Detroit: Wayne State University Press, 1962), p. 179. It is also possible that Echeverría was familiar with the critical writings of Friedrich von Schiller (certainly Schlegel was), who, in such essays as "On the Pathetic" (1793), expressed similar ideas as Schlegel concerning the final exaltation of man's reason which results from a confrontation with the instincts, the emotions, and the senses. See *Literary Criticism*, pp. 147-59.

20. Castagnino, "Estética de la energía," p. 31, who provides no information regarding the text or date of these words.

21. In an 1843 essay on painting he states:

Un cuadro, lo mismo que un poema, se compone necesariamente de dos partes: de la realidad concebida por la inteligencia, recogida por la memoria, y de la metamórfosis impuesta a esa realidad por la imaginación. Ver o saber, acordarse, comparar, agrandar, transformar, es decir, imaginar, tal es la ley de la pintura también. Negarlo sería negar el estrecho parentesco que tienen entre sí el pincel y la pluma. La imaginación es la misma bajo cualquier aspecto que se mire, y cualquiera que sea la variedad de formas que ella dé a sus creaciones.

Quoted by J. A. García Martínez, *Sarmiento y el arte de su tiempo* (Buenos Aires: Emecé, 1979), p. 154. In the same period he wrote about theatre art (using the new Spanish orthography which he promoted):

Después que la representación pasa, en el fondo del alma del espectador queda depositado un sentimiento de contento interior, una sensación de lo que ha visto y oído, y la fisonomía del señor Casacuberta, sus actitudes heroicas, sus movimientos convulsivos y sus menores gestos, pasan y repasan por la imaginación, se agrupan, se borran unos a otros, y se reproducen sin cesar.

Nace esto de que hay un fondo de verdad en la representación del actor, que se sobrepone a todos los incidentes de la figura, las palabras o las actitudes; nace de que no sólo cuida el actor de reproducir la naturaleza en la representación de la tragedia heroica, sino que la embellece, tomando todas las actitudes que el consentimiento universal atribuye a la perfección humana, i la escultura griega i romana han consagrado a las estatuas . . . .

This quote is taken from Castagnino, "Estética de la energía," p. 36.

22. A topic deserving of separate study is the public to which Sarmiento initially directed his *Facundo*. Well known is the wide diffusion of the work from its first moment, a fact that—it must be supposed—surprised Sarmiento himself. He writes in the "Carta-Prólogo" that accompanied the second edition of *Facundo* in 1851:

Tal como él era, mi pobre librejo ha tenido la fortuna de en aquella tierra cerrada a la verdad y a la discusión, lectores apasionados, y de mano en mano deslizándose furtivamente, guardado en algún secreto escondite, para hacer alto en sus peregrinaciones, emprender largos viajes, y ejemplares por centenas llegar, ajados y despachurrados de puro leídos, a las oficinas del pobre tirano, a los campamentos del soldado, y a la cabaña del gaucho, hasta hacerse el mismo, en las hablillas populares, un mito como su héroe (VII, 16).

Sarmiento, however, probably had not expected such a passionate reception for his work in the few months of its hurried composition. In the original introduction to the work, in addition to several passages in the text, he reveals that one of his intended publics is none other than the "partido europeo" of South America (VII, 8), that group of citizens who would respond to his ideological appeals and enter into the struggle against Rosas. Sarmiento would be "ecce homo" who would reveal through the impartiality of his historical and sociological methodologies the infrastructure of barbarism in his native land (VII, 22). In addition, *Facundo* would be his attempt to teach to those "hábiles políticos" of France and England about what type of government in Argentina was in their true interest (VII, 224-25). He had the remote hope of influencing the regional politics of those European nations. This work would be his contribution to "la prensa libre" (VII, 11), with the objectives of unifying the Argentinian exiles in the struggle against tyranny, and offering them "un tesoro inmenso de conocimientos prácticos, de experiencia y datos preciosos que pondrán un día al servicio de la patria . . ." (VII, 232). What's more, the arguments on the "aesthetic" level that this chapter continues to develop also reinforce the thesis that it is the cultured public which Sarmiento originally intended as the principal recipient of his work.

23. Especially dramatic readings—and ones which reveal how Sarmiento perceived this dionysiac core of impulses and emotions in his own character—treat

his visit to the volcano Vesuvius (V, 277-83), and his testimony about Spanish bullfights (V, 154-65).

24. Quoted by J. A. García Martínez, *Sarmiento y el arte de su tiempo*, p. 41.

25. *Ibid.*, p. 46, from the Pagano study entitled "El problema estético en la psicología de Sarmiento," dissertation in the Academia Providencial de Bellas Artes, Mendoza, 1938, and published in the following year by the same institution.

26. Paul Groussac, *El viaje intelectual: impresiones de naturaleza y arte* (Buenos Aires: Jesús Menéndez, 1920), pp. 26-28, tells of some personal experiences with Sarmiento near Montevideo in 1883 that further reveal the latter's apparent lack of an appreciation for natural beauty. José Bianco, "Así es Sarmiento," *Vuelta*, No. 26 (1979), pp. 5-14, believes that many of Groussac's opinions concerning Sarmiento's literary talents were unfounded.

27. Armando Zárate, who carefully read a draft of this chapter and whose valuable recommendations I have incorporated into many of its paragraphs, comments about the tendency of Sarmiento to channel different rhetorical procedures toward his determined objective. "A este efecto Sarmiento le escribía a su amigo Anselmo Rojo: 'La circulación de ese librejo vale para mí tanto como un escuadrón de coraceros mandado por un jefe arrojado.' (See Manuel Gálvez, *Vida de Sarmiento: el hombre de autoridad* [Buenos Aires: Emecé, 1945], p. 159)." Rodolfo Borello, *"Facundo:* heterogeneidad y persuasión," *Cuadernos Hispanoamericanos*, Nos. 263-64 (1972), 283-302, observes a similar rhetorical practice in Sarmiento: an "actualidad narrativa" is added to the geographical or sociological observation i.e., a human factor or a concrete detail is added in order to lend drama to an apparently neutral description.

28. See Orgaz' chapter "Un ensueño literario: 'el Cooper de la pampa,'" in *Sarmiento y el naturalismo histórico*, pp. 297-303.

29. M. H. Abrams, *The Mirror and the Lamp: Romantic Theory and the Critical Tradition* (London y New York: Oxford University Press, 1977), pp. 79-94, 299, etc.

30. *Ibid.*, pp. 79-82, where Abrams discusses these ideas in the works of Herder, Vico, Condillac, Rousseau and others.

31. *Ibid.*, p. 306.

32. It is a polemical issue today whether there existed a significant population of mixed-race gauchos in the Plata region before the early decades of the nineteenth century. Carlos Alberto Leumann, *La literatura gauchesca y la poesía gaucha* (Buenos Aires: Raigal, 1953), defends the position that the early gauchos were in the majority European descendants who had adapted themeselves to rural life and who did not differ in racial composition from other European groups residing in the country. Sarmiento, however, states that the descendants of interracial unions (he includes Africans in this) had become "un todo homogeneo que se distingue por su amor a la ociosidad e incapacidad industrial" (VII, 25). He suggests, furthermore, that the Spaniards residing in the American countryside shared the same moral characteristics as the Indian: "no se ha mostrado mejor dotada de acción la raza española cuando se ha visto en

los desiertos americanos abandonada a sus propios instintos" (VII, 25). John
Lynch, *Argentine Dictator: Juan Manuel de Rosas (1829-1852)* (Oxford: Claren-
den Press, 1981), pp. 54-124, offers an intelligent study of the gaucho in the
early nineteenth century, and particularly in relation to the social and economic
conditions of the time.

33. Zárate, "El *Facundo*," p. 475.

34. Juan Alfonso Carrizo, "Sarmiento y 'El cantar tradicional del General
Juan Facundo Quiroga,"' *Sustancia*, 1 (1930), 9-18.

35. Abrams, *Mirror and the Lamp*, pp. 79-94.

36. Sarmiento, at another moment, took the opposite point of view, arguing
that poetry, by nature, is thought limiting:

La poesía rimada nos ha parecido siempre una perfectación(?) [sic] de la
época actual, pues la belleza ideal se resiste a entrar en aquellos moldes
y cajoncitos que se llaman versos, sin tener que encogerse y perder sus
formas para no sobresalir, o bien llenar el espacio con algodoncitos a fin de
que la idea no quede como diente flojo bailando en un alvéolo demasiado
grande. Es un hecho notable que grandes poetas modernos, Lamartine,
Victor Hugo, dejaron de ser versadores cuando descendieron a la gran liza
de la vida pública, lo que prueba que aquellas formas vienen estrechas al
pensamiento moderno práctico, expansivo, popular, en la forma y en el
objeto.

These words were written in response to Bartolomé Mitre's jesting prologue to
Rimas: "Esta colección de versos, viene dedicada al general Sarmiento, quien,
como se sabe, es poco dedicado a la poesía." Quoted from Ricardo Rojas,
*Historia de la literatura argentina: ensayo filosfico sobre la evolución de la cultura
en el Plata*. Vol. II: *Los proscriptos* (Buenos Aires: Guillermo Kraft, 1957), p.
606.

37. Carrizo, "Sarmiento y 'El cantar tradicional,"' p. 13.

38. *Ibid.*, p. 15.

39. Abrams, *Mirror and the Lamp*, p. 306, quotes Macaulay.

40. Tocqueville, *Democracy*, pp. 78-81, after describing the "anti-poetic"
environment of the United States, projects what might be the themes of a
literature of the future: "Looking at the human race as one great whole, they
[the men in democratic ages] easily conceive that its destinies are regulated
by the same design; and in the actions of every individual they are led to
acknowledge a trace of that universal and eternal plan by which God rules our
race. . . . The great events . . . commemorate[d] with the general providential
designs that govern the universe . . . , [The search] below the external surface . . .
in order to reach the inner soul . . . . The destinies of mankind, man himself
taken aloof from his country and his age and standing in the presence of Nature
and of God, with his passions, his doubts, his rare prosperities and inconceivable
wretchedness, will become the chief, if not the sole, theme of poetry among these
nations."

41. In the section of *Viajes* entitled "El arte americano," Sarmiento detailed
his impressions of the monuments commemorating the United States' greatest

leader, George Washington. Washington's tomb, which was located beside his home at Mount Vernon, impressed Sarmiento on account of a "cierta elegancia" and its "extrema simplicidad" in "aquel acompañamiento de bosques primitivos" (V, 470-71). The home and tomb fittingly represented the pragmatic orientation of a people whose civilization was slowly emerging victorious from its struggles with barbarism. He extolled this modest structure by contrasting it to the pompous grandeur of similar monuments honoring other national heroes such as Napoleon, Adrian, and Rafael. The scene in Mount Vernon symbolized the worthy ideals of an optimistic and hardworking people. Sarmiento confirmed the observations of Tocqueville decades before that the people of the United States generally paid little attention to great artistic works, given the disposition of their energies toward achieving material well-being and eradicating social inequities. The Washington Monument in its half-finished state exemplified for Sarmiento a noble art which was lived rather than imagined or collected: its technology suggested the genius of an industrious people; its projected magnitude represented their high aspiration in pursuit of a national ideal; and the plan for its public finance indicated their commitment to mass participation and economy. Sarmiento realized the unique place which that monument when completed would occupy in the history of civilization: its magnificence would commemorate a people united by noble common interests and not by untold human sufferings.

42. Octavio Paz, *El arco y la lira: el poema, la revelación poética, poesía e historia* (México: Fondo de Cultura Económica, 1973), p. 22.

43. Abrams, *Mirror and the Lamp,* p. 312, explains that the theorists of the German idealist tradition (whose thought Sarmiento knew by way of his readings in A.W. Schlegel, Mme. de Staël, and others) believed in the primitive origins of poetry (p. 91). Pre-positivist and positivist thinkers, and among them Sarmiento, had little regard for poetic inspiration, which Keble called that "desire to relieve thoughts that could not be controlled" (p. 146 Abrams, *Mirror and the Lamp),* and put their faith in the supposed analytical language of science. It is to be expected that Sarmiento, in other passages, also takes the opposite point of view. See the quote in Note 36.

44. Allison Williams Bunkley, *The Life of Sarmiento* (New York: Greenwood Press, 1952), pp. 199-200.

45. Ana María Barrenechea, "Notas al estilo de Sarmiento," *Revista Iberoamericana,* Nos. 41-42 (Jan.-Dec. 1956), 275-94.

46. Noël Salomon, "A propos des elements 'costumbristas' dans le *Facundo* de D. F. Sarmiento," *Bulletin Hispanique,* 70 (1968), 400.

47. Jitrik, *Muerte y resurrección,* p. 11.

48. Michel Foucault, *L'ordre du discours: leçon inaugurale du College de France prononcée le 2 décembre 1970* (Paris: Gallimard, 1971), p. 22.

49. I explain this function of Sarmiento's style in "Discourse Production and Sarmiento's Essayistic Style," in *Simposio: El ensayo hispánico. Actas,* eds. Isaac Jack Levy and Juan Loveluck (Columbia: Univ. South Carolina, 1984), pp. 147-56.

CHAPTER 5

'Facundo': An Exercise in Bricoleur Historiography

Sarmiento was a precursor in Latin Amercian historiography. He was the first to take into account factors of climate, geography, and demography in his attempt to present a holistic account of social life. His work *Facundo* was the first attempt at incorporating psychology and biography as an instrument of social history. These crude attempts, however, have largely been superseded. Correct is the appraisal that Sarmiento's historical ideas are as alive today as they were a century and a half ago,[1] but it is misleading in the implication that what presently survives is Sarmiento's attempt to comprehend and describe the concrete reality of Latin American society on the basis of social-scientific theory. On the contrary, his attempts at social science survive today largely in reference to their literary and political qualities. Generations of Latin American school children do not remember Sarmiento so much as a historian or social scientist, but rather as he who popularized the historical antithesis of civilization versus barbarism; it was he who utilized that romantic-political formula as the ideological cornerstone in his supurb literary rendering of *caudillo* life and the early nineteenth-century civil wars in Argentina.

Sarmiento's writing on historical matters offers a number of problems to the contemporary reader. First, he and other writers of the period often combined materials or methodologies of inquiry which the present-day reader would consider as belonging to two separate and distinct disciplines: history and literature. This was due, in part, to the lack of a tradition which would have offered guidance, and perhaps conversely, incumberance, to the writers of Sarmiento's generation who had the ambition of establishing a national literature. Consequently, his practice of enhancing historical writing through the inclusion of expressive passages was an acceptable option according to the prevailing ideas on both historical and literary writing. Indeed, most writers of his time generally coincided in the belief that there existed a common ground where literature and historical writing came together: in their focus on the past and their edifying or didactic function. In these circumstances, it is understandable that much of what was then intended to be historical writing would be considered today as belonging more appropriately to the literary tradition.[2]

In addition to the fusion of literary and historical categories, critics have another principal reason for criticizing Sarmiento's historical writing: his inconsistent application of critical terminology.[3] More than one potential critic has opted for worshiping the formidible edifice rather than risk confronting the contradictions in the conceptual labyrinth. Historical writing, Sarmiento believed, was more akin to an art than a science:

> La *Historia* en general, lo sabéis, tiene su asiento entre las musas. . . . No es pues la historia la sencilla narración de los humanos acontecimientos; es además una de las bellas artes, y como la estatuaria, no sólo copia las producciones de la naturaleza, sino que las idealiza y las agrupa armonicamente. . . . El libro que narra los hechos sociales, es una creación del ingenio que toma por materia la vida de los pueblos, por cincel el lenguaje y las ideas, por tipo, un pensamiento supremo (XXI, 86-87).

This rare passage sounds almost contemporary in how it questions the nature of truth. The historian, he says, idealizes events and harmoniously groups his material according to an idea or goal which has been decided before hand; he does not attempt to merely repeat or reproduce the reality as he has experienced it. Sarmiento's idea of an "artistic" manner of grouping data is suggestive of Nietzsche, who, a generation later, would theorize about the social function of discourse in the absence of an objective knowledge. Nietzsche appropriately stated that "The so-called drive for knowledge can be traced back to a drive to appropriate and conquer."[4] According to this logic, Sarmiento understood historical writing to be similar to almost any other form of discourse: it was a means to an end; historiography was one among many components of an all-encompassing political text.[5]

His political goals in writing are perhaps most clearly expressed in relation to *Facundo:* the work was conceived, then hastily published, with the foremost objective of discrediting the Rosas regime, albeit by any means available. A few months after its writing, Sarmiento admitted how in his analysis he had intentionally distorted certain facts and loaded his arguments in the interest of improving its propagandistic effectiveness.[6]

Political objectives predominated, but he also had other goals. In several passages it is evident that he was sincerely committed to an impartial and scientific focus for his work. He was a man of many passions, and his ambitions as social scientific investigator many times contradicted his goals as social reformer. He states in the letter-prologue to the 1851 edition of *Facundo:*

> Tengo una ambición literaria [. . .]; aquellos políticos de todos los países [europeos], aquellos escritores que se precian de entendidos, si un pobre narrador americano se presentase ante ellos con un libro, para mostrarles [la realidad americana . . .], con unción en las palabras, con intachable imparcialdad en la justipreciación de los

hechos, con exposición lúcida y animada, con elevación de sentimientos, y con conocimiento profundo de los intereses de los pueblos, y
presentimiento, fundado en deducción lógica, de los bienes que so-
focaron con sus errores y de los males que desarrollaron en nuestro
país e hicieron desbordar sobre otros . . . ¿no siente usted que él
que tal hiciera podría presentarse en Europa con su libro en la mano
[. . .]? (VII, 16-17)

Facundo was his attempt, albeit preliminary, of analyzing the South
American reality of his time "con intachable imparcialidad en la justi-
preciación de los hechos." His diction suggests a confusion between science and politics, between describing and judging. As Chapters Six and
Seven demonstrate, his supposed scientific study exists within a predetermined ideological context. One might assume that the haste with which
Sarmiento wrote would discount in his own eyes its historical merits. Indeed, he had labored under the political passions of the moment and the
constraints of editorial deadlines in composing the work's first edition, and
he admitted at the time that each page revealed the haste with which it
had been written (VI, 160). Since his goals in writing were largely political, he did not dispose sufficient time nor did he possess the necessary
scholarly disposition in order to carry out the important task of the historian. He dreamed of one day more rigorously examening the historical
roots of *caudillismo* and the factors which gave rise to the civil wars in
his land. In an article published the day preceding the publication of *Facundo's* first installment, he announced his intention of someday rewriting
the work in a more systematic fashion: "Un interés del momento, premioso
y urgente a mi juicio, me hace trazar rápidamente un cuadro que había
creído poder presentar algún día, tan acabado como me fuese posible. He
creído necesario hacinar sobre el papel mis ideas tales como se me presentan, sacrificando toda pretención literaria a la necesidad de atajar un
mal que puede ser trascendental para nosotros" (VI, 160).

Although Sarmiento was critical from the very beginning of the form
with which he presented his ideas in *Facundo,* one must not mistake this
apparent humility for self-criticism of the ideas themselves. He states in
the 1845 introduction: "Este estudio . . . nosotros no estamos aún en
estado de hacer por nuestra falta de instrucción filosófica e histórica . . ."
(VII, 7). One should not be fooled by his modest pose since it is well
known that a lack of formal preparation never prevented him from pursuing certain answers, and sometimes with brilliant results. He hints at
his ambition of becoming the Tocqueville of South America: "premu-
nido del conocimiento de las teorías sociales, como el viajero científico
de barómetros, octantes i brújulas, [vengo] a penetrar en el interior de
nuestra vida política, como en un campo vastísimo i aún no explorado ni
descrito por la ciencia . . ." (VII, 6). He suggests the social value of such
a study based on the latest theories of social organization and historical
conflict. However, what he intended and what he accomplished are two
different matters, for his resolve to study the recent events of his country

from the perspective of sociological and historical theory was generally overshadowed by the political thesis of his writing.

Facundo, written when Sarmiento was just beginning his long years of public life, contains the essence of his mature political and social thought. In fact, some forty years later he again would treat many of the same ideas in *Conflicto y armonía entre las razas en América* (1883), fulfilling at long last his youthful promise. In the introduction to this latter work, he called attention to the continuity between the ideas of his youth and those of his old age: There were "presunciones vagas" of *Conflicto y armonía* in *Civilización y barbarie* (XXXVIII, 11). Accordingly he called this later work his "*Facundo* llegado a la vejez" (XXXVIII, 19). Martínez Estrada confirms the similar ideas which unite these two works when he observes: "*Conflicto y armonía* es una culminación de pruebas que se puede incorporar en el texto de *Facundo* sin añadirlo nada en sustancia."[7] The important matter here is the continuity in Sarmiento's historical ideas throughout a lifetime of writing and political activism. *Facundo* is the text in which he first elaborated in an organized form his mature historical thought.

Sarmiento was aware that his writing on historical matters combined a number of textual strategies. Indeed, his inconsistent application of methodological categories was criticized harshly by several of his peers. His own lack of formal instruction in philosophy and historiography was a painful cause for Sarmiento's sensed–but highly compensated for–inferiority:[8] Neither Sarmiento nor the young intellectuals of Santiago, however, doubted the breadth and profundity of his comprehension in matters of philosphical and historical interest. That was not the issue. Rather, it was his use of those ideas. His compatriot Valentín Alsina, upon reading the first draft of *Facundo,* succinctly identified the problem: the author, he stated, was very prone to organizing his data according to rigid systems.[9] Indeed, Sarmiento, with his pragmatic orientation toward writing, utilized several different modes of historical inquiry, but in contradictory fashion. Alsina suggested that Sarmiento expressed himself more as a politician than as a historian. His systematization was typical of the political activist who simplified complex problems in order to resolve in his mind the contradictions existing between doctrines and actual possibilities for action.

Sarmiento was aware of many of the difficulties confronting those South American intellectuals who attempted to understand the fluid social realities in which they themselves were immersed. Foremost was the problem that the greater part of the social and historical theory which they utilized had been formulated in relation to the European experience. Several times in his early writing he called attention to the discrepancies existing between an analysis made on the basis of such theories and American social fact. Unfortunately, he observed, Argentina's leaders throughout the early decades of his century had continually relied upon theoretically acceptable, but nevertheless distorted, analyses in the formation of social policy. The consequences were predictable: programs failed and attempts at much needed reforms were discredited. This was precisely the cause for the Rivadavia administration's failure: "¿Qué había de suceder, cuando las teorías de gobierno, la fe política que le había dado la Europa [a Rivadavia], estaba plagada de errores, de teorías absurdas y engañosas, de malos principios . . .?" (VII, 100). Rivadavia's objectives had been admirable, but he had been blind to the problems in adapting them to the local reality for their realization. His failures constituted an important lesson for Sarmiento's generation of intellectuals, because they too sought the transformation of their society according to liberal principles.

A second obstacle confronting South American intellectuals who attempted to understand the social reality of their continent was the rapidly changing theoretical context. Sarmiento writes that after 1830,

las ciencias sociales toman nueva dirección, y se comienzan a desvanecer las ilusiones. Desde entonces empiezan a llegarnos libros europeos que nos demuestran que Voltaire no tenía mucha razón, que Rousseau [sic] era un sofista, que Mably y Raynal unos anárquicos, que no hay tres poderes, ni contrato social, etc., etc. Desde entonces sabemos algo de razas, de tendencias, de hábitos nacionales, de antecedentes históricos (VII, 100-101).

Sarmiento's own generation was heir to a significant development of historiographical theory which demonstrated the irrelevance of many ideas previously articulated. In truth, he was writing in a period of theoretical transition, when the advocates of scientific tendencies heatedly challenged the enlightenment and romantic ideas articulated by previous generations of theorists.

Sarmiento intelligently identified some of the problems confronting the socially concerned intellectuals of his period, but he was less than successful in avoiding them in practice. This and future chapters point out several instances in which his own analysis was flawed on account of an apparent copying or uncritical application of methodologies then in vogue. In addition, his writings do not reveal to the contemporary reader as accentuated a rupture between the historical ideas of the past and the ideas of his own generation, as the quoted passage above might lead one to believe. What impresses the contemporary reader is the diversity of his ideological influences. His particular style of learning accounts for this heterogeneous grouping of historical systems. He read widely, but over time the newer systems of analysis which he learned did not replace older schemes in his analysis, but rather came to coexist in the same textual space. He was an historical *bricoleur* who assimilated new elements by appending them to an older base of thought; rarely did those new elements cause a significant rearrangement of his previously held ideas or values.

Precisely because of their inconsistent and contradictory content, one could argue that *Facundo* and his other early works provide the investigator with an invaluable perspective into Sarmiento's process of ideation. *Facundo's* seemingly unfinished condition is evidence that the writer refused to submit its content to the process of ideological reduction: he was hardly concerned with altering his expression in order to conform to a single philosophical or logical system. As a rule, he did not subject the contradictions and inconsistencies of his thought to rigorous examination; he did not conceal them underneath a facade of harmonious systems and ideological wholes. Consequently, the reader finds that in many passages Sarmiento's tapestry of ideas lies bare and accessible to analysis.

The voluminous criticism identifies traces of at least three ideological systems in Sarmiento's historical writing: the enlightenment, with the rationalist idea of progress; historicism, which in its practice of evaluating reality, progressively prepared the way for a type of action-oriented positivism; and a romanticism which was individualist, spontaneous, imaginative, impassioned, and pathetic.[10] This chapter documents how Sarmiento borrowed from all of these historiographical readings, each of which constitutes in *Facundo* a coherent and global interpretation for the data presented. The following pages also demonstrate his combination of the information gained from written sources to the knowledge learned from personal experience and observation, a practice which often made for inconsistencies in his logic. The first section discusses his historicist reading of the past, which borrowed primarily from the enlightenment historiographical tradition in the postulation of the necessary stages for a society's development. The second section discusses the influence of social romanticism, which drew primarily from the ideas of Saint-Simon in the projection of a social structure that man could act upon, and consequently shape, in its development. The third section discusses the function of two related methodological procedures in his writing, normally associated with the influence of European romantic thought, which project a telluric universe of predetermined social possibilities: antithetical historical categories (specifically, civilization versus barbarism), and the anthropomorphization of social forces. The intent of these pages is not to exhaust the possibilities for a critical treatment of these topics, but rather to demonstrate the *bricolage* construction of an important aspect of Sarmiento's historiographical thought. In accomplishing this, the chapter also demonstrates the diversity of historiographical views which contributed to liberalism's multifaceted and contradictory presence in nineteenth-century Argentina.

Historicism's Enlightenment Roots

Nineteenth-century historicism, one of several aspects of the social romanticism which predominated in the historical thought of the time, was constructed upon the Enlightenment's doctrine of progress. Enlightenment writers such as Voltaire, Turgot, and Condorcet had viewed human history as unfolding in a single process whereby individual societies would pass through necessary organization stages in their development toward an infinite future. Over and above the specific climatic, geographic, or historical factors which would influence but not alter those stages, all cultures obeyed the same "ley del progreso humanitario."[11] In general, enlightenment thinkers had not questioned the efficacy of reason. Being that they believed ignorance was the source of disparity between stages of historical development, they projected the eventual progress of any society to occur through the raising of the cultural level of its population. Human history, then, was seen as the development of the individual organism over time. Accordingly, Condorcet proposed a universal standard of conduct for all of humanity based upon the common possession of reason.[12]

The French historicist school of early and mid-nineteenth century accepted the enlightenment historians' central contribution of the doctrine of progress, but altered significantly the standards against which they assessed the value of a particular society's advancement. Whereas the enlightenment thinkers insisted on an eternal standard of value (i.e., reason) against which specific achievements and errors were to be measured, the historicists assessed man's achievement in terms of the category of development in itself. "Historicism is the belief that an adequate understanding of the nature of any phenomenon and an adequate assessment of its value are to be gained through considering it in terms of the place which it occupied and the role which it played within a process of development."[13] Historicists rejected the enlightenment belief in the individual character of an historical event that could be grasped apart and without seeing it embedded within a pattern of development. For the historicists, progress had a connotation of increase in value. This means that the historian who was familiar with the standards of progress could compare the relative development of one society against that of another. Theorists embracing these general views believed that the societies of Northern Europe offered the standards of progress against which all other societies had to be compared.

At the root of these differences between enlightenment and historicist analyses were contrasting world views. Enlightenment thinkers affirmed the natural goodness of mankind and his inherent capacity for moral improvement; each being, regardless of race or ethnicity, could progress through the exercise of his reasoning capacity. Historicist thinkers, in contrast, affirmed a determinist universe in which certain societies advanced and others did not, in accordance with the natural laws governing the direction of change. Reason, accordingly, was not the universal possession of mankind, but belonged only to those select societies that had already manifested their superiority through social, material, and technological advancement. In contrast to the enlightenment thinkers' projection of man's natural goodness, the historicist thinkers perceived a universe dichotomized between those societies (or individuals) blessed by natural law with the primacy of reason in their development, and those whose reason was lacking or dominated by emotions or instincts.

In *Facundo,* Sarmiento's analysis of the different human societies existing within Argentina reveals his continual passage between enlightenment and historicist focuses. At times he is reminiscent of the enlightenment historians in his portrayal of a given society as an organic expression of climatic, geographic, and sociological factors. Approaching impartiality, he describes and explains the origin of cultural differences and does not judge or condemn. In other passages, however, the historicist voice predominates, when—especially in those treating the gaucho—his judgment of social practices is explicitly negative. In these latter passages he portrays a people who approach the brutality of animals on account of reason's weak or negligible influence, and who are therefore exiled from the domain of progress.

An enlightenment-inspired conception of historical progression and social development predominates in *Facundo's* first part, where Sarmiento traces the relationship between the patterns of land occupation and society's predominant social and cultural institutions. Implicit in his analysis is an abstract scheme of historical stages, beginning with the most rudimentary, and progressing up through the most advanced. He calls attention to the disturbing realization that different social groups living in Argentina represented widely contrasting stages of developement. His message is that the lack of uniformity or homogeneity among the population was one of the foremost causes of the country's present turmoil.

Sarmiento identifies the indigenous people as the least developed social group that was currently occupying national territory. When not skirmishing with the white settler population or winning their livelihood through raids and banditry, these people normally spent their time hunting game and gathering nuts, fruits, and other foodstuffs growing in the wild. The Indian tribes rarely if ever practiced agriculture, and therefore seldom occupied an established territory. A migratory pattern of existence contributed to the relatively small size of their social unit. Consequently, these people needed only a minimal degree of group organization. The simplicity of their needs determined that little if any division in labor or specialization in community function arose. With scarce surplus food production, there could be limited leisure and, consequently, little cultural activity. Few were the industrial skills passed on from one generation to the next. Due to all these factors, Sarmiento implicitly classifies the Indian as the most backward of social groups. The Indian people were least likely of all to assimilate the values and traits of modernity and participate in the predominant social practices of the century.[14]

According to enlightenment historiography, the nomadic tribe occupied a higher position than the Indian in the stages of historical development. In a bold and somewhat forced comparison, he likens the gaucho society of the Argentine plains to that of the Bedouin tribes of Asia: "Ya la vida pastoril nos vuelve impensadamente a traer a la imaginación el recuerdo del Asia . . . . La tribu árabe que vaga por las soledades asiáticas, vive reunida bajo el mando de un anciano de la tribu o un jefe guerrero; la sociedad existe, aunque no esté fija en un punto determinado de la tierra . . ." (VII, 28). In his opinion, the people of Argentina's *hinterland* were situated at an intermediary stage of development since their migratory life and clan-like social unit afforded only a partial development of industry. Because there was no permanent possession of the land, educational institutions were largely non-existent and commercial interchange among the different regions was insignificant. The isolation of these people and their infrequent social contacts made it nearly impossible for the culture as a whole to progress.

Sarmiento adopts the focus of the historicist in his depiction of the gaucho as especially prone to violence. Again forcing an historical analogy, he compares Argentina's rural inhabitants to the nomadic groups of North Africa in their propensity for violence and warlike behavior:

> Las hordas beduínas que hoy importunan con algaras y depredaciones la frontera de la Argelia, dan una idea exacta de la montonera argentina, de que se han servido hombres sagaces o malvados insignes. La misma lucha de civilización y barbarie de la ciudad y el desierto, existe hoy en Africa; los mismos personajes, el mismo espíritu, la misma estrategia indisciplinada, entre la horda y la montonera. Masas inmensas de jinetes vagando por el desierto, ofreciendo el combate a las fuerzas disciplinadas de las ciudades, si se sienten superiores en fuerza . . . (VII, 57).

In this horse and cattle-centered existence, the warrior-chieftain was the only one who, by reason of force and strict authoritarian rule, could control his individualistic followers. The violent character of gaucho society was evident to Sarmiento even in the children's warlike games. His portrait of gaucho society was consistently one-sided because he ignored totally the human dimension of individual experience. For him, Argentina's rural life was typified by "el predominio de la fuerza brutal, la preponderancia del más fuerte, la autoridad sin límites y sin responsabilidad de los que mandan, la justicia administrada sin formas y sin debate" (VII, 24).

Sarmiento argues that in all such societies under the iron grip of a despot, where there reigned terror and crime, the higher pursuits of the spirit were impossible:

> Con esta sociedad, pues, en que la cultura del espíritu es inútil e imposible, donde los negocios municipales no existen, donde el buen público es una palabra sin sentido, porque no hay público, el hombre dotado eminentemente se esfuerza por producirse, y adopta para ello los medios y los caminos que encuentra. El gaucho será un malhechor o un caudillo, según el rumbo que las cosas tomen en el momento en que ha llegado a hacerse notable (VII, 52).

There was only the barest hint of civilized manners in this society since force was the sole bond of attachment between men. Individualism and selfishness predominated without there existing to any large degree the respect for mutual obligations and the sacrifice for a larger good.

All regular and systematic order became impossible in gaucho society, where the individual was free from economic necessity and the need to subject himself to a higher civil authority. The gaucho, who for Sarmiento typified Argentina's nomadic presence, was by nature lazy and indolent and not prone to spend his energies in the creation of private or collective wealth. The gaucho, he says, was incapable, even under compulsion, of dedicating himself to hard and frequent labor (VII, 25). With all the necessities of life already provided by a bountiful nature, the gaucho had a minimum of responsibilities: "Los límites de la propiedad no están marcados; los ganados, cuanto más numerosos son, menos brazos ocupan; la mujer se encarga de todas las faenas domésticas y fabriles; el hombre queda desocupado, sin goces, sin ideas, sin atenciones forzosas; el hogar doméstico le fastidia, lo expele, digámoslo así" (VII, 49). Out of this need for fulfilling his unoccupied leisure time in the pastoral environment, the gaucho had created a "sociedad ficticia," the *pulpería,* where he met with other menfolk to participate in violent activities and corrosive vices. Hard liquor inflamed the imagination. The gaucho often accepted physical challenges that ended in the spilling of blood. The gaucho, as depicted by Sarmiento, had developed physically because of his contact with the rude environment; he was constantly engaging in "esta lucha del hombre aislado con la naturaleza salvaje, del racional con el bruto . . ." (VII, 32). Unfortunately, there were few stimuli for the intelligence; no institution, such as school, municipality, or church, fostered a similar development of the rational faculties: "La vida del campo, pues, ha desenvuelto en el gaucho las facultades físicas, sin ninguna de las de la inteligencia" (VII, 33). Consequently, the gaucho, living in culturally stagnant surroundings, rarely came into contact with new ideas and took pride in his stubborn opposition to change.

Sarmiento forces another comparison, this time between Argentine gaucho society and European feudalism. In the enlightenment tradition, feudal society was believed to be the intermediary stage between nomadism and civilization. When he lables Argentina's Spanish colonial past as "feudal," Sarmiento merely repeats the denunciations of Northern European writers about Spain's backward and decrepit colonial order. Problems arise, however, when he attempts to account for civilization's most recent defeats in the country's civil wars. He argues that the gauchos, who had put asunder the reforms of the May Revolution, were representatives of feudal society. Having argued elsewhere that the gauchos were essentially nomadic in their social organization, he somewhat confuses the distinctions between historical stages. In addition, when out of polemical zeal he labels the gauchos as barbarians, his confusing argument is that the gaucho barbarians wished to reestablish the feudal institutions of the colony.

Sarmiento's treatment of gaucho society exemplifies well how he perceived enlightenment categories through the prism of his romantic consciousness: he attempted to interpret each fact of Argentina's past and present by integrating it into a vast totality of significance. His model for this operation was undoubtedly the French historian, Guizot, whose *History of Civilization in Europe* presented for Sarmiento a prototype scheme for society's advancement through different historical stages. Sarmiento's gaucho society bears a strong resemblance to Guizot's "barbarian" society which preceded the European civilization of the current period.[15] His interpretation of Argentina's current crisis is also remarkably similar to Guizot's explanation of the European feudal society's emergence during the medieval era: it resulted from the landowners of the countryside besieging the cities and pillaging the interior (VII, 29). Sarmiento, convinced that he had assimilated the universal scheme of historical development, had little or no need for studying the historical particular. His critics have consistently pointed out how his treatment grossly distorts one's understanding of the historical circumstances which gave rise to the gaucho class and what others have considered to be the positive role of the *montonera* in the formation of the nation.[16]

His historical judgments based on the romantically-interpreted enlightenment scheme of historical progression upstaged other important aspects of Argentina's rural society. For example, Sarmiento entirely ignored class differences or heterogeneity in gaucho society. His equating of Rosas with the gaucho masses of the country was an act of historical mistification of gigantic proportions. Sarmiento emphasizes that Rosas, one of the largest landowners of the Buenos Aires Province, had excelled as a youth in the skills related to horsemanship. He points out that Rosas' successes as *patrón de estancia* were a result of his intimate knowledge of the gaucho character and jargon and his close association with his workers. But Sarmiento fails to point out that Rosas' interests as landowner, cattle producer, *saladero* manager, and meat and hides exporter, were entirely distinct from those of the rural proletariat whom he either ruthlessly pursued or controlled with an iron hand.[17] Sarmiento, in his generalized treatment of gaucho barbarism, failed to understand the objectives of the landowners in their pursuit of social and political hegemony over the region and the nation. Similarly, his analysis makes clear that he had an utter lack of sympathy for the másses of rural poor whose primary concerns were economic and physical survival.

In his *guerra santa* against any and all forces opposing historical progress, Sarmiento also ignored factors of a moral nature. The life of Facundo Quiroga, for example, was of interest to him only in so far as it revealed the secret temper of Argentine barbarism. As such, in *Facundo* he either skips over or treats in very light fashion the protagonist's positive contributions to provincial society and his drive for national organization under a Federalist constitution, an effort that brought him into direct confrontation with Rosas.

With similar zeal, Sarmiento distorts enormously the historical presence of José Gervasio Artigas, a *caudillo* whose high moral example and humanitarian reforms in the Banda Oriental (now Uruguay) during the period of the war for independence from Spain have won wide recognition elsewhere. In Sarmiento's inflexible scheme, Artigas is reduced to an "instrumento ciego, pero lleno de vida, de instintos hostiles a la civilización europea y a toda organización regular, adverso a la monarquía como a la y la consagración de la autoridad" (VII, 57). Historicism, for Sarmiento, justified his reduction of a multifaceted socio-historical reality into a simplistic script; it was an invitation to opportunistic propagandizing.

It is understandable that Sarmiento wrote little or nothing about Argentina's significant black population in the pages of *Facundo*, given that his primary objective was to trace the origins of *caudillo* despotism, which be believed to be fundamentally a problem associated with the country's mestizo, or Spanish-Indian descendant, population. One must also suppose that he lacked firsthand information about blacks or mulattos, being that they were concentrated in Buenos Aires (where they constituted a quarter of the population) and were hardly represented in the Andean provinces.[18] Sarmiento's other writings of the period indicate that unlike the Indian and the gaucho, he believed them to be prime candidates for civilization. In his biography, *El General Fray Felix Aldao* (1845), he praises El negro Barcala, whom he believed was one of the most distinguished figures of Argentina's independence struggles a generation before (VII, 259-60). In general, he esteemed the moral qualities of blacks and mulattos and lauded their educability (see his favorable comments about the mulatto population in Río de Janeiro, V, 60). Toward the end of his life he would again treat the blacks' contribution to South American civilization in the first chapter of *Conflicto y armonía de las razas en América* (1883–XXXVII, 64-69).

Sarmiento's comparison of gaucho society with "barbarism" and "feudalism" is accomplished largely out of polemical enthusiasm, but his discussion of the feudal tendencies still surviving from Argentina's colonial past merits the attention of the historian. He prefaces the chapter treating the Argentine city of Córdoba in 1825 with a quotation in French from Chateaubriand to the effect that several different forms of both liberty and servitude were equally prevalent in feudal European society. Sarmiento and other thinkers of his day were hardly proponents of unbridled "liberty," as he interpreted the advocation of the ideologues of the French Revolution a half century before. Indeed, liberty was, for Sarmiento, a less than desirable social goal. The Chateaubriand quote at the beginning of the chapter establishes an implicit comparison between the feudal practice of liberty, and the social structure the Argentine pampas in his own day. His message was that liberty led to licentiousness in the behavior of society's leaders who had not yet arrived at the threshold of civilization.

The principal basis for comparison between feudal European society and that of Argentina's rural interior, was the strongman government of the two. In *Facundo*, Sarmiento's utopian liberal voice communicates the belief that when the dictatorship by the few stifled the will of the majority, then poverty and ignorance would result. There was no such thing as "enlightened despotism" since all states under tyrannical rule suffered from an intellectual sclerosis, whether it was observable on the superficial level of events or not. In *Aldao* he states that despotism, even when exercised by good leaders, was for the people like tuberculosis was for the human body: the sick man in both cases hardly felt any pain, and his behavior was quite normal even though every step he took carried him a little nearer to the tomb (VII, 278). Despotism in the organ of the state, then, was to be resisted. His example of Córdoba demonstrated that a lack of intellectual stimulation in society caused inertia, indolence, and complacency in its people who, consequently, would lack the will and intellectual means for breaking out of their condition of servitude.

Religion, as practiced by the Spanish church of the colony, had the same effect. Sarmiento emphasizes the constricted intellectual life of Córdoba in the pre-independence period, which was due to the preponderant influence of the church. He states that on every city block there stood a monastery, a convent, or a house for religious devotion. In addition, each family of any means had its own monk, nun, or singer of religious hymns. Similarly, the poorer families tried to have among their number at least one sacristan or altarboy (VII, 95). Sarmiento lends authority to this description of Córdoba's religious environment with a quote from the respected Dean Funes to the effect that theological studies corrupted philosophical pursuits. The writings of one such as Aristotles were interpreted in theological fashion, and therefore there resulted an absurd mixture of sacred and profane arguments. The cultural dialogue of this feudal intellectual environment was characterized by "sutilezas, sofismas engañosas, cuestiones frívolas e impertinentes" (VII, 95). Sarmiento then hurls additional criticisms upon the Cordoban church. Not only did it censor the media and control the flow of information, but in addition it prohibited the activity of those institutions which in other societies played a prominent role in disseminating the new ideas of the century: the public theater, the opera, newspapers, the printing industry. The total effect was a stagnant cultural life. This web of social and religious institutions perpetuated the death of the intellect:

> La ciudad es un claustro encerrado entre barrancas, el paseo es un claustro con verjas de fierro; cada manzana tiene un claustro de monjas o frailes; la Universidad es un claustro en que todos llevan sotanas, manteo; la legislación que se enseña, la teología, toda la ciencia escolástica de la edad media, es un claustro en que se encierra y parapeta la inteligencia contra todo lo que salga del texto y del comentario (VII, 96).

Córdoba, the cloistered city, was the asylum of the Spanish *intelligentsia,* the city where the progressive ideas of the European Enlightenment never penetrated. Feudalism of the intelligence was evident in the minds disciplined by years spent memorizing and then repeating Scriptural passages, which firmly opposed any new idea. They were minds, like the enclosed cloister, which had an immovable idea in the center and were surrounded by a lake of stagnant water (VII, 97). Sarmiento believed that the entrenchment of religious institutions and beliefs in the interior was a formidable obstacle to progress and that it would still be many years before Argentine society would again undertake a clerical reform of progress, similar to what the Rivadavia administration had promised, but could not deliver, a generation before.

Like his enlightenment mentors, Sarmiento believed that a society's progress culminated in the life of the city guided by liberal principles, where the close association of people would make possible the continual development of industry and culture. He believed, as they did, that the heights of civilization would be attained exclusively by those people who permanently occupied a given territory and developed an agricultural base that guaranteed a surplus production. Agriculture, according to this theory, gave rise to the institution of private property, and as a further consequence, law. Legal needs led to other community concerns and associations. Surpluses in food created the possibility for a diversification in productive functions and an expansion of the social infrastructure. Leisure and work specialization, if realized with the proper guidance of educators and planners, would then make possible literary and artistic pursuits.

He stressed many times in his writings that the rise of this Edenic community life was dependent upon society first achieving a necessary population density. The pastoral society, for example, could not develop beyond a limited cultural environment because of a lack of possibilities for association. Sarmiento states that only in the city or the municipality did the conditions exist for intimate association, which was necessary for a people's social development. The landed class of the interior had few public needs which needed to satisfied through association. In short, there was no *res pública* (VII, 30). Only in the city could progressive institutions flourish. Regardless of the society, the city was the place where one found workshops, stores, schools, and institutions associated with the interpretation and enforcement of the law (VII, 27). Sarmiento hypothesized that the concentration of population was a *sine qua non* of civilization—an idea correlated to the etymology of the word *citizen,* which derives from *civis,* meaning, in Latin, city.

He called attention to the fact, but did not stress it, that in Rome and Sparta an economic surplus, which freed citizens to pursue other concerns, was achieved at the cost of slave labor. Free citizens thus channeled their time and energy into constructive social functions and the promotion of culture. However repugnant the Roman institution of slavery seemed, he did appreciate how that institution made possible the civilization of others. But in his own time the exploitation of man by man was neither desirable nor necessary since bountiful providence had provided a land that could sustain a large and prosperous urban population with a rationally organized agriculture.

The Roman municipality, with its public law, egalitarian economy, and accomplished cultural life, served enlightenment thinkers well for their prototype of the ideal social experience. With Sarmiento, however, there undoubtedly were additional reasons which accounted for his fascination with classical antiquity. In his time, Argentina had a latifundium-based cattle economy with a sizable rural working class. Sarmiento correctly understood that the vanquishing of *caudillo* rule could not be accomplished merely by replacing certain individuals in the country's government. He knew that *caudillo* political power was only the most visible indication of a far more pervasive type of domination: Argentina's endless expanses of unpopulated pampas, its cattle economy, and its majority population of rural gauchos, together constituted a network of impediments to the nation's progress. Sarmiento's plan of civilization therefore entailed the promotion of agriculture, the elimination of large land holdings, and the promotion of settlement programs for European immigrants. These changes, in their turn, would bring about the end of the gaucho as a social group and the rise of an agrarian and even industrial economy, which would replace the cattle economy which then prevailed.

Rome, with its agricultural economy, therefore had a certain status as a model of development for Sarmiento and others of his generation. Prevalent in ancient thought, continuing throughout the Enlightenment, and even present in the writings of Guizot, Niebuhr, and other historians writing contemporary to Sarmiento, was the idea that agriculture constituted the proper business of free men because of the healthy moral and physical life it engendered. According to this belief, the citizen working in the fields and exercising his rights as a small landholder became morally and socially prepared for his participation in the democratic institutions of the municipality. Like his enlightenment mentors, Sarmiento believed that this type of economic system naturally engendered a desirable degree of political and social equality. In *Facundo* he praises the life style of Roman citizens who found the nucleus of their communal life in the municipality (VII, 29). Sarmiento and other avid readers of Tocqueville's *Democracy in America* found a contemporary example for Rome's municipality in the New England township. The French visitor to North America had realized the strength of a constitutional system founded upon civic participation. In the daily exercise of rights and responsibilities of the North American township, Sarmiento envisioned a model for successful democratic experience.

He therefore promoted for Argentina a representative government which granted to citizens the freedoms of discussion and association, both of which would be guaranteed by a written constitution. He defended the ideal of equality in the realm of economics as well as civic affairs, but this was a long-range objective. He believed that the masses had to be firmly guided in their social participation as long as they were uneducated and unpracticed in democracy. Handing over the powers of government to the ignorant and uncultured majority would spell civil disaster, as he believed had happened to a certain degree under Moreno and Rivadavia (IX, 102). After all, Sarmiento and his generation of exiles were aware of the fact, but they rarely cared to emphasize it, that their sworn enemy, Don Juan Manuel de Rosas, was supported by the vast majority of Argentinians during the greater part of his presidency. So instead of a popular democracy, Sarmiento advocated, at least in the first stage of constitutional rule, a representative democracy in which leadership roles would be exercised by an educated and economic elite.[19]

In economics, he admired the private and public promotion of industry, an encouragement of free trade through the lowering of tariff barriers, the stimulation of commerce by opening rivers and constructing canals and railways, and the sponsorship of new settlements for increasing agricultural production and exports. Liberal economics, for Sarmiento, was only one of several facets of a "civilized" society. Only rarely did he seem to accept the Saint-Simonian idea of emphasizing production and commerce above all other social needs (see V, 312 for his criticism of this). Instead, Sarmiento viewed material progress as occurring simultaneously with social and political reform in addition to the general improvement of the cultural level of the people.

Coupled with his defense of a vigorous private sector, Sarmiento also defended a strong central authority, both local and national, which would have as its principal function the promotion of society's productive forces. His support for governmental activism was motivated not so much out of the fear of an unfettered individualism in the society of the future (as articulated by Leroux), but out of the knowledge that the private sector, while following the logic of commercial advantage, would not develop to a desirable level all of the institutions that would be needed to guarantee a high level of culture and development for society as a whole. He defended liberal social and economic principles with the understanding that local and national governments could and should take an active, indeed principal, role in community life. In seeming contradiction to his ideas on individual liberty, and in anticipation of his own hard-handed style of governing after 1862, he believed that a certain amount of social guidance and authoritarianism would be necessary to compensate for public mismanagement in the past and to guarantee the prosperity of the future liberal society.

Following his enlightenment mentors, Sarmiento believed that the economic prosperity and quality of life of a people improved in relation to their levels of culture and morality. He was willing to tolerate social inequalities in the short run (good examples of this are his opportunistic support for Chile's Conservative Party in 1840 and his adherence to the cause of Buenos Aires against the interior beginning in 1855), provided that sound programs in eduation and land distribution slowly worked toward a reduction in that division between the rich governing minority and the poor ignorant majority. A progressive community spirit would foster healthy values and what a legislator of his time called "public reason" (IV, 255). Ideally, all citizens would cultivate a spirit of examination and, through their reading of the press, would remain informed of the issues affecting their lives. They would, in turn, utilize the press for exercising their control over government and other social institutions. Individuals, acting through their collective institutions, would involve themselves in learning new industrial techniques, increasing production, and in general, improving their individual and social situations.

Historicism and the Prescription for Progress

In Sarmiento's early writings, the enlightenment-inspired interpretation of the stages of historical development combined and at times became confused with the historicist, or pre-positivistic reading of events. The enlightenment text projected a rational universal order in which all nations participated in the same process of development, but were situated at different stages according to the nature of their technological, productive, and social relationships. It offered primarily a descriptive scheme relating the cultural and moral attainments of a population to its characteristic patterns of production and land occupation. It held that a society attained its highest level of development when the enlightenment ideals of liberty, participatory democracy, and equality came to be embodied in the everyday experiences of its population. The historicist text was intimately linked, but offered distinct points of contrast. While accepting many of the differences between societies which the enlightenment focus detailed, it evaluated different social practices and at times prescribed a precise plan of action for institutional change based on what was held to be a scientific analysis of a given society's inner dynamics. The highest goal was "positive" transformation, or progress, which would be measured primarily in quantifiable or utilitarian terms.

Historicism anticipated by several decades the rapid acceptance and application of positivistic ideas throughout European and Latin American centers of culture.[20] "Positivism" refers to the late-nineteenth century social and historical thought for which scientific study was perceived to be the key to unlocking the secrets of human development and guiding the transformation of man's institutions toward a more perfect order. The term came from Auguste Comte's *Cours de philosophie positiviste*, which was first published in 1852 (and only much later known to Hispanic American thinkers). For our purposes here, "pre-positivism" refers to the thought of several theorists, foremost among them Saint-Simon, who are considered to be precursors to Compte, the "father of positivism."

It is documented that by 1838 several of the young intellectuals of Sarmiento's generation had assimilated the writings of Saint-Simon and were advocating his brand of "social science" as a means toward achieving the harmonious development of society.[21] The mission of his generation of leaders was to study on the basis of scientific principles the forces which held back the country's development. Then, through deliberate action (military force, educational programs, political indoctrination through the press and the arts), they believed they could right the abuses of tyranny and propel Argentina into the age of progress. Science, in their thought, had a strange and not altogether compatible bedfellow: metaphysics. They believed that providential will, speaking through scientific principles, defined their goals and justified their actions. Providence subsumed science; its unrestrainable march guaranteed that a rational and scientific civilization would eventually prevail. They believed that their role as leaders in that struggle was to anticipate the inevitable and to precipitate the unfolding of social and political events.

The subject of the day was History. Sarmiento and the other progressive intellectuals of the time believed themselves to be standing at the threshold of a new era when society's leaders would possess knowledge about all aspects of man's social and physical needs. This knowledge, in its turn, would become a source of social and political power:

> El estudio de la historia forma, por decirlo así, el fondo de la ciencia europea de nuestra época. Filosofía, religión, política, derecho, todo lo que dice relación con las instituciones, costumbres y creencias sociales, se ha convertido en historia, porque se ha pedido a la historia razón del desenvolvimiento del espíritu humano, de su manera de proceder, de las huellas que ha dejado en los pueblos modernos y de los legados que las pasadas generaciones, la mezcla de las razas, las revoluciones antiguas han ido depositando sucesivamente. Porque la historia, tal como la concibe nuestra época, no es ya la artística relación de los hechos, no es la verificación y confrontación de autores antiguos, como lo que tomaba el nombre de historia hasta el pasado siglo. Es una ciencia que se crea sobre los materiales trasmitidos por las épocas anteriores. El historiador de nuestra época va hasta explicar con el auxilio de una teoría, los hechos que la historia ha trasmitido sin que los mismos que los describían alcanzasen a comprenderlos (II, 202).

Each historical period has its particular type of social hero: the warrior, the writer, the scientist. According to Sarmiento, one such personage for his own day was the historian. This new intellectual actor would not only interpret the past, but would utilize his knowledge in order to guide society's development into the future.

For an activist historian like Sarmiento, the criterion of progress was of utmost importance in the study of social relationships. A society's customs, beliefs, and institutions were to be judged on the basis of their effectiveness in providing the well-being of the public and their promise of continuing to do so in the future. Of special interest were those institutions having to do with the dissemination of information. His ideas on language provide a clear example. He chided those who held up as a model for contemporary expression the language of Calderón and Cervantes, because in his opinion the emulation of past models only served to retard the development not only of language, but also of society in general. It was absurd to seek in a past century the standards for language, as if it were remotely possible that a language could arrive at a stage of perfection in an otherwise backward age. Instead, Sarmiento believed that the development of a society's ideas and language kept pace with the advancement of technology and social institutions (I, 252). Swept up by his theory of progress and perhaps his desire for polemic, Sarmiento argued that changes in language usage paralleled society's historical development: a language contained the ideas of a people, and one would therefore expect that a modernized society would possess a means of communication that was itself experiencing continual renovation. It is evident that Sarmiento's criterion of progress precluded, and in fact, preempted, all other considerations regarding the nature and function of language in human communication.

In their search for the laws of human behavior and social development, the "social scientists" of Sarmiento's period naturally looked to the physical sciences for inspiration. The lexicon of the latter disciplines filtered into the vocabulary of historiography, and the discourse of Sarmiento was no exception. For example, he wrote: "Aseméjase el mundo moral al mundo físico. La historia de la tierra se encuentra en las capas geológicas que revelan el mundo monstruoso que ha precedido al nuestro . . . . La historia es, pues, la geología moral" (V, 467). Sarmiento's comparison of social history to geological history—very much like what Hippolyte Taine was to popularize some decades later[22] —was far more than a descriptive metaphor. The historical past was perceived as having left its indelible stamp upon the present; those who attempted to understand the life surrounding them had to utilize their analytical tools in order to penetrate beyond surface manifestations and study a more timeless infrastructure in which present tendencies and future possibilities were integrally linked to the surviving traces of past realities.

Sarmiento implicitly accepted the idea fashionable in positivistic and pre-positivistic circles that human thought had progressed through its religious and metaphysical stages, and had now arrived at its highest, that is, its scientific period. Empirical and mathematical sciences were seen as having displaced speculative pursuits, and as such, mankind had for the first time laid the foundation for rapid technological advances and more advanced forms of social and economic life. The Italian historian Vico, a century earlier, had stressed that history was made by men and that the investigation of the past brought to one a critical awareness of the present. Following this lead, Herder had emphasized the existence of eternal laws governing man's social development. Turgot and Cordorcet had pointed out the importance of education and government in bringing about political reform and moral improvement. From these ideas, it was a short jump to Saint-Simon's belief that man's productive energies could be fully guided and channeled. War and poverty, which were believed to result from social, political, and economic anarchy, could now be permanently held in check. In general agreement with the ideas of all these thinkers, Sarmiento believed that no limits could be placed on the advancement of man toward his own perfection.

He rejected the idea of circular history, for which adherents offered the convenient example of the rise and fall of Rome and then the rebirth, some eleven centuries later, of civilization in the western European countries (V, 90). In contrast, he believed that humanity's highest manifestation of moral and physical development could only exist in the present, and that all previous moments of imperial grandeur, scientific discovery, or artistic creation, merely anticipated the greater glories of the present. Rome, the jewel of the ancient world for its widespread social and legal institutions, ultimately fell to invading forces. It was Sarmiento's belief that when the barbarians absorbed that city they in fact assimilated themselves into it, and thus became a part of the civilized mass. The Middle Ages, then, were not times of darkness, but rather the period of fusion that necessarily preceded the rebirth of classical culture and empirical science in Renaissance Europe.

Similarly, Sarmiento rejected the fatalistic notion of a cyclical development for Latin America, which for others was evidenced by the regression to a reign of tyrants and the subversion of the reforms which had been accomplished in the two decades after independence. For Sarmiento, the situation in Argentina prior to the defeat of Rosas in 1852 did offer cause for worry, but he remained convinced that his generation was witnessing no more than a temporary setback in the continent's inevitable advancement.

A corollary to his conviction regarding humanity's unfaltering forward development was the belief that no person or institution could retard that movement for any extended period of time. No individual, whether he be Facundo or Rosas, could ever bring society's forward march to a complete halt: "¿Es acaso dado a la mano del hombre paralizar las leyes del mundo y del pensamiento? No lo creemos. Un elemento social cualquiera que sea, necesariamente se desenvuelve; se le paralizará dos o más momentos, pero no siempre" (VI, 13). In spite of society's inevitable advancement, Sarmiento was not content to merely await the unfolding of events, for he was resolved to take appropriate action in order to do away altogether with those social "elements" retarding humanity's progress. In this light one can understand his opposition to such *caudillos* as Rosas, Aldao, and later Peñalosa, and throughout his life the disdain he felt for gauchos and Indians.

Sarmiento's unshakable commitment to society's progress accounts in large part for the extreme actions he sometimes advocated, and then directed, against those individuals or groups whom he believed stood in its way. His vision of future progress required not only political conformity of the masses, but also social homogeneity. As he saw it, the rural culture of the interior gave rise to the gaucho's violent social life and their authoritarian *caudillo* rulers. He therefore argued for the government's stern measures in order to contain such social malignancies: "Costumbres de este género requieren medios vigorosos de represión, y para reprimir desalmados se necesitan jueces más desalmados aún" (VII, 52), he wrote in *Facundo*. The violent treatment he prescribed for society's barbarians contrasts sharply with the generosity implicitly promised by his enlightenment-inspired beliefs. The forceful measures that he called for hardly typified the harmoneous society, founded on liberal principles of mutual respect, mass participation, and democratic rights, which he promoted in other passages of the same work. However, to his way of thinking, there was no contradiction in the simultaneous advocation of these radically differing programs; forceful measures against those social groups unfit for civilization would have to precede the liberal promise social harmony. His rendering of *socialista* principles therefore implied society's ability to take giant steps in its development. He believed that social harmony, as defined by utopian liberal thought, would arise naturally upon the ashes of destruction,[23] and that freedom would emerge out of a previous but necessary intolerance.[24] How these seismic tranformations were to occur he does not explain. He overlooked entirely the rage and thirst for revenge which his policies would inspire among a terrorized population. Macabre is his suggestion that a society or its leaders, who, weaned on holocaust, could aspire the philosopher's highest ideal of sociability.

Although many prestigious thinkers of his age aspired to a similar religion of progress, Sarmiento stood out on account of the inflexible and uncompromising means he proposed for achieving such an otherwise admirable objective. His assuredness of the eventual victory of his struggle is communicated well in the introduction to *Facundo,* where he exhorts others to join in the present ideological and future military struggles against the Rosas tyranny:

> ¿Para qué os obstináis en combatirlo, pues, si es fatal, forzoso, natural y lógico? ¡Dios mío! ¡para qué lo combatís!... ¿Acaso porque la empresa es ardua, es por eso absurda? ¿Acaso porque el mal principio triunfa, se le ha de abandonar resignadamente el terreno? [. . .] ¡Por qué lo combatís!... ¿Acaso no estamos vivos los que después de tantos desastres sobrevivimos aún; o hemos perdido nuestra conciencia de lo justo y del porvenir de la Patria, porque hemos perdido algunas batallas? [. . .] ¿Somos dueños de hacer otra cosa que lo que hacemos, ni más ni menos como Rosas no puede dejar de ser lo que es? ¿No hay nada de providencial en estas luchas de los pueblos? ¿Concedióse jamás el triunfo a quien no sabe perseverar? [. . .] ¡No! no se renuncia a un porvenir tan inmenso, a una misión tan elevada, por ese cúmulo de contradicciones y dificultades . . .(VII, 9-11).

Carried on by the powers of his own rhetoric in writing this passage, he momentarily abandoned the more empirical aspects of his vision and affirmed a metaphysics of history. The laws governing man's development, he suggests, were providential, fatal, natural, and logical. With this belief Sarmiento found a common cause with the revolutionary of any period; so fervorously did he believe in his own truth that the campaign to impose it upon society became in his eyes akin to a religious crusade. Sarmiento, in this, resembles the intellectual philosopher, as defined by Ortega y Gasset, who clings to truth at the cost of abandoning life.[25] Sarmiento exhibited an undiluted faith in the rational mechanisms of the the universal order. His duty, then, was to preach anti-traditional doctrines at the center of the revolutionary stage. This assuredness in his own historical mission was both his strength and his weakness: a strength, because it gave him confidence that in turn nourished an amazing energy for social struggle, an energy that few times in his long career suffered the vicisitudes of doubt or hesitation; a weakness also, for Sarmiento's civilizing plan was nurtured by his intolerance for compromise and an arrogant belief in his own superiority.

Romantic Historicism: Society's Telluric Foundations

In addition to the enlightenment and the historicist or pre-positivistic interpretations of events, there is also perceivable in *Facundo* and other early writings of Sarmiento a romantic historicism which manifests itself in three related forms: his depiction of character and society as manifestations of a telluric *Volksgeist,* his description of social forces in terms of antithetical categories, and his anthropomorphization of historical tendencies. The following chapter discusses in detail how Sarmiento organized *Facundo* according to the general idea of the *Volksgeist.* This section explains how the civilization-barbarism antithesis and the anthropomorphization of historical forces function as organizational principles for his historical thought. Then, Chapter Seven reconsiders many of these same issues, but from the perspective of the socio-economic and cultural links between Europe and South America.

Toward 1845, Sarmiento was becoming more and more convinced that the old political division between Unitarians and Federalists no longer adequately accounted for the conflict of interests which fueled the group and regional rivalries in his troubled land. It had become the object of distortion and lie. It was more fit for the purposes of yellow journalism and propagandistic bombasts than for an intelligent interpretation of his country's present impass. Rosas, for example, was a self-proclaimed Federalist, but it was he who had fulfilled the Unitarian Party's quest of uniting the country under a centralist structure with its nerve center in Buenos Aires. Then there was the case of Sarmiento himself, whose childhood formation and provincial origins linked him with the Federalist tradition, but who, as an adolescent, embraced many of the principles of Unitarianism. Now, at the age of thirty four, he understood many of the shortcomings of that movement and distrusted its leadership. He continued to embrace many of its long-range goals, but was more and more critical of the means proposed to realize those goals. Through his readings about the United States, he was becoming convinced –an intuition which he confirmed during his travels there in 1847–of the advantages of a federalist organization for that country and his own. His was a new type of federalism, not the type defended by Rosas and his allies, but one which had much in common with the progressive ideas of Rivadavia, Paz, Valentín Alsina, Florencio Varela, and other prevalent figures in the Argentine Unitarian tradition.[26] How could he explain this contradiction? Rosas was neither Federalist or Unitarian; nor was Sarmiento himself. It was natural that he seek a wholly new opposition that would better account for the differences between the likes of Rosas and himself. The dictator's acts were those of a barbarian, for he was at war with civilization and civilized men. The opposition of civilization-barbarism took into account Sarmiento's largely *moral* perception of Argentina's civil wars. But was it also useful for evaluating his country's past progress and its possibilities for future development?[27]

Sarmiento's application of the civilization-barbarism opposition as an explanation for Argentina's conflict was not the result of weighted deliberations, but rather precipitated events. In the early months of 1845 a diplomat arrived in Santiago with instructions from Rosas to demand of the Chilean government that it prohibit the publication of journalistic propaganda against the Argentine regime, and very possibly that Sarmiento be either exiled from Chile or turned over to the Argentine government on account of his alleged seditious activities. Sarmiento, true to form, decided to counterattack through the press. Under these circumstances he first wrote, and published *Facundo*, which appeared in successive issues of *El Progreso* from the second of May till the end of June. Although he had considered undertaking a similar type of historical and sociological study for some time, the urgent circumstances of 1845 obligated him to write each page with great precipitation. He wrote the work, then, as he confessed some time later, "sin archivo en país extranjero" (XLVI, 303), "dándose originales a medida que se imprimía, y habiéndose perdido manuscritos que no pude reemplazar" (III, 218).

The title he originally gave to the work was *Civilización y barbarie. Vida de Juan Facundo Quiroga. Aspecto físico, costumbres y hábitos de la República argentina,* which suggests the importance that he held initially for this opposition as the organizing principle for the study. The plan of analyzing Argentine history and society on the basis of this opposition must have intrigued him initially, but he must have realized that it would never serve as a guide for rigorous analysis. That was no great matter, however, in the light of his urgent propagandistic mission. As he progressed in his writing, he realized the need of broadening his focus. As a consequence, the opposition becomes progressively more flexible in its application and in passages it is dispelled with altogether. In the spirited introduction (which was not included in the second and third editions), one reads of barbarism's presence in the countryside and its role in the formation of *caudillos* such as Facundo and Rosas. Civilization receives its first characterization as the populous cities and the European nations, where a democratic public life enjoyed the latest fruits of progress. Progressing through the work, the conflict between civility and backwardness broadens into a multifaceted struggle between commerce and progress versus economic and cultural stagnation, and reason and the intellect versus the passions.

By the work's end, the categories of civilization and barbarism have become even more complex and contradictory. Barbarism, either explicitly or implicitly, is associated with: the practice of economic nationalism, the Spanish feudal institutions of the colony, the Jesuit university education in Cordoba, the nomadic tribes of northern Africa, the great expanses of

Argentine pampas, the *montonera,* or groups of mounted gaucho fighters, the cattle industry, the Indian and gaucho–in all, a chaotic grouping of personalities, institutions, and ideas. The progressively developing conception of civilization is equally diverse: the Revolution of 1810, General Paz, the constitution, and in general the liberal program of economic, political, and social reforms already discussed in a previous section. In short, the original opposition between civilization and barbarism becomes so frayed with contradictions and inconsistencies that it loses a great deal of the value it otherwise might have had as a tool for either historical investigation or propagandistic journalism.

A first example of the contradictory nature of these categories is found in the character sketches of the gaucho singer and the pathfinder, two of the figures presented by Sarmiento as social types representative of the population of the pampas. The writer aludes to their base association with barbarism, but his frank admiration for their highly developed skills is evident nevertheless. Another example of contradictions arising from the writer's aplication of this unwieldy historical opposition is found in the description of the city of Cordoba. That city, it is stated, was a center of feudalism at the time of the May Revolution on account of its stagnant intellectual life and monastic atmosphere. But this analysis contradicts a previous demarcation according to which the cities were the vanguard of progress and the countryside was the bastion of barbarism. In short, the antithesis of civilization and barbarism breaks down within the work. Obviously, contradiction and inconsistent reasoning resulted from his attempt to describe a multifaceted human society with simplistic concepts.

Critics have continually pointed out the errors and contradictions in *Facundo* that result from this dualistic interpretation. The question arises as to why Sarmiento was led to portray the social realities of his country in such a confused fashion. Ricardo Rojas convincingly explains the matter in terms of political expediency: the writer sacrificed consistency and historical accuracy for the sake of a "momentánea eficacia polémica" in order to counter the equally distorting sophism of "Unitarians and Federalists" that Rosas exploited so adroitly.[28] Rojas implies that in a later period, when Sarmiento was no longer engaged in the passionate struggle, he adopted a more realistic criterion for describing Argentine society. However, it is evident in several of his works written subsequent to *Facundo* that Sarmiento did not return the civilization versus barbarism slogan to its rightful place in the mausoleum of propagandistic pamphleteering.

Many of the ambiguities in his later writing are due precisely to the same tendency of portraying social problems in a schematic manner. In *Viajes,* written during his long trip to Europe, North Africa, and the United States between 1845 and 1847, and published finally in 1849, Sarmiento's continued use of a rigid categorization for progressive and retrograde tendencies is evident. Observations made during a rapid visit to Spain merely reaffirmed his previous preconceptions of the country's barbarian public spectacles, its lack of industrial production and commerce, and its people's poverty of inquisitive intellectual spirit. He even expressed contempt for a certain cordiality of the people, perhaps out of the need to explain all social manifestations–including those potentially beneficial–in terms of his already established demarcation which situated Spain among the barbarian nations of the earth. For example, he states: "En los círculos de literatos que he frecuentado, he encontrado el mismo espíritu, la misma llaneza, que haría amar al español por aquellos mismos que, como yo, detestan todos sus antecedentes históricos y simbolizan en la España la tradición del envejecido mal de América" (V, 178).

In *Viajes* one encounters further examples of his application of simplistic and ahistorical dualisms for evaluating human societies. In North Africa he noted an irreconcilable struggle between the barbarian Arabs and the progressive European race. Similarly, in France, his disappointment upon perceiving the social inequality and the technological backwardness of the countryside was more than compensated by his awe upon personally witnessing a session of the national parliament. His category of civilization would not disintegrate in the face of discordant data, but rather would become transferred to the new setting of the North American republic.

Although Sarmiento continued to utilize the distorting opposition in his writings subsequent to *Facundo,* he was not entirely inflexible with regard to which aspects of society pertained to civilization and which to barbarism. A good example is his changing opinion regarding the question of European immigration in Argentina. In the period of his Chilean exile, European immigration to South America was one of his panaceas for development. But beginning with the publication of *Viajes,* one can perceive the doubt in his mind about the relative benefit which the settlement of European peoples had for his homeland. He remarks that immigration in the United States did not always constitute a positive force for change; in fact, it had on occasion impeded progress (V, 397). This reversal began to affect his thought concerning issues relevant to South American society as well. As early as 1850 he observed that the presence of European immigrants had little affected the dismal level of culture and industry of the native people (XIII, 89). Some years later, his opinions regarding the benefit of immigration in Argentina would change dramatically. He would become highly critical of the immigration programs implemented since the fall of Rosas, because the net result was disunion and social problems (XXXVI, 234, 290). Then, when president of Argentina, he wrote in reaction to the change in title which the English version of *Facundo* (1868) had undergone at the suggestion of Mary Mann, wife of the famous Bostonian educator: " ... *Life in the Argentine Republic,* que Mrs. Horace Mann ha puesto al frente del libro en lugar de *Civilización y barbarie* que traía originalmente, acaso porque no siempre se puede por los hechos saber de qué lado está la barbarie cuando se agitan las pasiones políticas en estos pueblos infantiles."[29] These words indicate Sarmiento's realization that he had previously erred in blaming the countryside and rural society for the ills besetting Argentina. But, what is more important, the quote indicates that in his later years he continued to utilize the dogmatic opposition,—only now in revised form—in order to explain the social reality of his land.

The civilization-barbarism equation constituted a cornerstone of Sarmiento's social and historical thought, in spite of the obvious confusions it caused in his empirical historical analysis. His mind, geared toward action, oftentimes sought schematic interpretations, even if they were inexact and imprecise. He was a journalist and a polemicist, and he often sought an expression providing an instantaneous propagandistic effect, even though it be wrought with ambivalence. Ironically, his distorted social and historical analyses based on antithetical categories would eventually serve him in his political mission. That he continued using them in his writings suggests a certain amount of public acceptance, not only by the unlettered public, which would be most susceptible to rhetoric and slogans, but also by informed readers who constituted the principal public for his writings.

The civilization-barbarism historical opposition is joined by a second aspect of romantic historicism in Sarmiento's writing: the practice of anthropomorphizing social forces and events. His tendency to depict historical conflict in terms of representative clashes between individuals and social types was probably influenced by Herder's treatment (and that of such Herder disciples as Cousin and Guizot) of national character,[30] but there is another possible explanation for the presence of this tendency in Sarmiento's historical writing: his belief that history was best understood through biographical writing. He wrote in 1842: "La biografía de un hombre que ha desempeñado un gran papel en una época y país dados, es el resumen de la historia contemporánea, iluminada con los animados colores que reflejan las costumbres y hábitos nacionales, las ideas dominantes, las tendencias de la civilización y la dirección especial que el genio de los grandes hombres puede imprimir a la sociedad."[31] The biographies of figures such as Washington, Franklin, and Napoleon not only provided worthwhile examples for the reader's moral consciousness, but also an indispensable source of information about the societies and events of the respective periods. He was not alone in this opinion, judging from the fact that decades later Bartolome Mitre, Sarmiento's erstwhile intimate friend and one of the foremost historians of the period, chose to relate the events preceding and following national independence through his biographies of San Martín and Belgrano.

Sarmiento's personification of the conflicting parties engaged in Argentina's civil war brings together both his enlightenment and romantic historical influences. The practice relates, first of all, to the enlightenment idea of the successive stages of historical development: "Tal es la época actual que se ocupa de explicar los hechos históricos y de colocarlos, no en el orden cronológico en que se han sucedido, sino en el orden progresivo de los desenvolvimientos de las sociedades. Cada hombre ocupa su lugar en esta serie; y cada uno de los caracteres que parecen echados al acaso en el camino que siguen las naciones, tiene su deducción lógica, su representación determinada" (VI, 9). By focusing on representative lives, the historian not only conceptualizes the order of events which constitute the evolution of a given society, but he also situates each individual life in relation to that development. Sarmiento continues the passage above by integrating into the discussion his general conception of the *Volksgeist:*

> Por numerosas que se consideren las excepciones de esta regla, hay sin embargo, cierto encadenamiento en los hechos históricos, cierta analogía entre las tendencias y necesidades de las sociedades, y el carácter y fisonomía moral de los hombres que sobresalen en ellas, por lo que este hecho ha llamado la atención de los filósofos, que han hallado en el estado de civilización de un pueblo y las diversas ideas que luchan en él, la explicación, y si es posible decirlo, el sentido simbólico que envuelven los nombres históricos (VI, 9-10).

He calls attention to the "tendencias y necesidades" of a given society that give rise to the personality and values of its superior citizens. Consequently, it is a short step to his synthesis, which is stated as a rhetorical question: "¿No llama la atención, en efecto, que Washington sea tan idéntico con la sociedad norteamericana, y Napoleón con la francesa?" (VII, 10) There is logic to the idea that a society's outstanding leaders personify their respective epochs because they advocate the fundamental ideas of the time and struggle to shape the social and economic institutions according to those ideas.

Fundamental to the organization of *Facundo* is the idea that the representative individual's thoughts and actions exemplified the predominant tendencies of an historical period.[32] The work's explicit focus is the life of Facundo Quiroga, but Sarmiento's broader concern was to describe the civil institutions and events in that period of *caudillo* rule. He drew Facundo and then Rosas—whom he portrays as the successor of the former—not only as individuals incarnating the worst aspects of the society against which his civilizing campaign was waged, but also as representative types. His thesis is that both Rosas and Facundo Quiroga were barbarians since their personalities had been formed in the same wilderness environment and had been subjected to similar corrupting influences of an infested society. But he notes a fundamental difference between the two. Rosas, in relation to Facundo, was

> su heredero, su complemento; su alma ha pasado a este otro molde más acabado, más perfecto; y lo que en él era sólo instinto, iniciación, tendencia, convirtióse en Rosas en sistema, efecto y fin. La naturaleza campestre, colonial y bárbara, cambióse en esta metamorfosis en arte, en sistema y en política regular capaz de presentarse a la faz del mundo como el modo de ser de un pueblo encarnado en un hombre que ha aspirado a tomar los aires de un genio que domina los acontecimientos, los hombres y las cosas (VII, 5).

Rosas was many times more dangerous than Facundo because he had learned from the latter's brute force and had transformed it into a systematic web of control. Under the regional tyranny of Quiroga the barbarian elements of the country had simply subjugated the "intelligence" of the country. Rosas, however–according to Sarmiento's perspective–now recruited intellectuals for the defense of his own crimes. He had advanced a giant step in the art of despotism: without doing away entirely with Facundo's heavy-handed tactics of police control and discriminate application of terror, Rosas now rationalized his violence against society through propaganda disseminated through the press. Ironically, he identifies Rosas as "hijo de la culta Buenos Aires, sin serlo él" (VII, 5). He presents the contradiction that Rosas, whose social barbarism was the continuation of Facundo's totalitarianism, was now highly "civilized" on account of an adroit manipulation of language.[33] These hyperboles follow the quoted passage above: "¡Rosas! ¡Rosas! ¡me posterno y humillo ante tu poderosa inteligencia! ¡Sois grande como el Plata; como los Andes!" (VII, 169) Sarmiento sarcastically admits the superior dimension of Rosas, because he wielded writing, that instrument and product of the most advanced societies of the time, against civilization itself.

Whatever the differences between Rosas and Quiroga, Sarmiento's reductionist scheme held both of them to be expressions of the same rural *Volksgeist.* The *caudillo,* whether exemplified by either Quiroga or Rosas, was not "un hecho aislado, una aberración, una monstruosidad. Es, por el contrario, una manifestación social; es una fórmula de una manera de ser de un pueblo" (VII, 9). The *caudillo* was the personification of the *Volksgeist* for the rural countryside; he was the individualized expression of the telluric forces of the pampa.

Sarmiento, who had a natural talent for the dramatic, understood the expressive potential of presenting history in terms of personality. In general, the reader's interest increases when he can focus his attention upon concrete and vitalized figures. The popularity in our own day of sentimental and mystery novels suggests that the reader's emotional participation increases to the degree that he identifies with or projects his own values upon the protagonist. When utilizing biography to explain historical events, Sarmiento simultaneously appealed to the reader's intellectual desire for facts and logical argument, and at the same time addressed the more subliminal dimension of the reader's emotive or fantasized involvement.

Consequently, the personification of social forces in *Facundo* blurs the traditional division between historical and literary writing. The equation of Facundo as the *Volksgeist* of the countryside provided and continues to provide a powerful literary symbol, but it creates problems for the historical reading. Sarmiento's obligation as a historian was to seek consistency in his arguments. Out of the need for presenting the ideas and acts of his protagonist as the surface manifestations of the land's telluric forces, he had to ignore or change much of the available information. Consequently, the resulting narration is a web of weighted arguments and distorted evidence. His application of the civilization and barbarism dualism produced very similar results: he minimized the individuality of the historical actor so that his own account might better conform to pre-existing ideological schemes. His biographies of Facundo, Aldao, and "El Chacho"–this trilogy of barbarians–likewise are characterized by one-sided portrayals.

The personification of barbarism has won for Sarmiento his most devoted and hostile followers, both then and now, but it must be pointed out that the theme to which he devoted perhaps even greater attention was the personification of civilization. In *Facundo* it stands to reason that a figure representing progress would counterbalance Facundo, the representative of barbarism–and thus the work would gain a semblance of aesthetic equilibrium. This is especially so because the work's principal structure is a series of historico-politico-aesthetic oppositions: civilization versus barbarism, Buenos Aires versus the pampas, the proponents of liberalism versus Rosas and Facundo, and Argentina's Europeanized future versus the retrograde *americanismo* of the past and present. From an aesthetic point of view, it therefore comes as no surprise to find midway into the work the presence of a personage representing the cities and civilization: General Paz. Sarmiento depicts him as incarnating better than any other individual the dreams of all the previous defenders of liberal ideals in the Río de la Plata region. Even more than San Martín, Rivadavia, and Lavalle, Paz is portrayed as the worthy counterpart of Facundo: "En la Tablada de Córdoba se midieron las fuerzas de la campaña y de la ciudad bajo sus más altas inspiraciones, Facundo y Paz, dignas personificaciones de las dos tendencias que van a disputarse el dominio de la República" (VII, 128). The battle of Tablada typified the epic struggle occurring throughout the New World, which was the confrontation between civilization and barbarism.

Sarmiento's explanation of why Paz best represented the forces of the city reveals not only some of his values regarding civilization, but also a few of the more idiosyncratic tendencies in his thought. Paz, he states, is

> el hijo legítimo de la ciudad, el representante más cumplido del poder de los pueblos civilizados. . . . Paz es militar a la europea; no cree en el valor solo si no se subordina a la táctica, la estrategia y la disciplina; apenas sabe andar a caballo; es, además, manco y no podría manejar una lanza. La ostentación de fuerzas numerosas le incomoda; pocos soldados, pero bien instruídos. [sic] . . . Es espíritu guerrero de la Europa hasta en el arma en que ha servido; es artillero y por tanto matemático, científico, calculador. Una batalla es un problema que resolverá por ecuaciones, hasta daros la incógnita, que es la victoria. . . . [E]s, en una palabra, el representante legítimo de las *ciudades,* de la civilización europea, que estamos amenazados de ver interrumpida en nuestra patria (VII, 129).

Sarmiento was firmly convinced that a progressive military leadership, and especially one that was European-trained, could play an important role in the civilizing process of Argentina. Consequently, he held in high regard General Paz' efforts to create a disciplined military unit that would rely upon tactics and strategy, and not merely on the physical prowess of its participants. His praise of Paz was based on some more subjective reasons, also. For example: Paz is praised, ironically, for his inexperience with horses and his inability for hand-to-hand combat. Sarmiento therefore proposed a different type of hero than the gaucho chieftain who sought the glamor and glory of personal combat, and whose prowess depended upon the highly coordinated movements of man and beast. His new social hero was the theoretician whose ideas were tested in the heat of battle, the intellectual planner who harnessed the resources at his disposal in order to impose a rational order over the rural society's passion and brute force.

The association of General Paz with the *Volksgeist* of the city was not the first time that Sarmiento personified civilization in his writing. Being above all a political strategist, he wrote *Facundo* with the primary purpose of attacking Rosism, albeit through ideas. Other works written during his Chilean exile also had the objective of defending the person he considered to best incarnate the ideas and values that he envisioned for Argentina's future: himself.

Between 1843 and 1852 Sarmiento's stature as a public figure grew dramatically, and along with it his self-confidence and perhaps a sense of predestination regarding his own important role in Argentina's future. This progressive fortification of his self-image is quite evident to the reader of his successive writings. After the literary success of *Facundo*, and upon returning from his extensive travels to Europe, Africa, and North America, he enjoyed the reputation as one of the leaders of Rosas' exiled political opposition. People already were mentioning him as a possible candidate for the country's presidency once the dictatorship was ended. Sarmiento was quick to internalize this sentiment. In an article of 1849 he presented the program of governmental action which he would implement if he were Argentina's president, and in doing so he criticized point for point what he considered to be the failures of the Rosas regime (VI, 231). The clash between Sarmiento and Rosas, he stated, was "una lucha de titanes" (VI, 227).

By 1850, Sarmiento's incessant writing against the Rosas regime had earned him both the wrath of the tyrant and the admiration of a broad following. Rosas had utilized whatever means available for silencing the indominable writer: petitions for his expedition, government-financed slander campaigns through a rival Chilean press, and possibly even an attempt at assassination. In that year Sarmiento wrote *Recuerdos de provincia,* which can be described as a mixture of autobiography and *costumbrista* sketches of the Province of San Juan. This, like *Facundo,* was a "libro de combate," written in the hope of uniting Chilean opinion against the Rosas government and its slander of him. In the introduction he presents himself as a model citizen and an example for youth on account of his "sentimientos morales, nobles y delicados . . . . Hay una nobleza democrática que a nadie puede hacer sombra, imperecedera, la del patriotismo y el talento" (III, 27).

Modesty did not figure in the catalogue of Sarmiento's moral characteristics. In this work he went on to portray himself as the personification of Argentina's future. His *Facundo* had already drawn the *caudillo* as representing that period in the nation's history when the countryside exercised its hegemony over the nation's cities and urban life. His new representative figure would now possess the qualities needed for bringing together a badly divided country. Sarmiento perceived that his own experience figuratively bridged the abyss between the countryside and the city, the past and the future. In this, he portrayed his own existence as the culmination of a family tradition that chronologically paralleled the recent history of the country:

> Aquí termina la historia colonial, llamaré así, de mi familia. Lo que sigue es la transición lenta y penosa de un modo de ser a otro; la vida de la República naciente, la lucha de los partidos, la guerra civil, la proscripción y el destierro. A la historia de la familia se sucede como teatro de acción y atmósfera, la historia de la patria. A mi progenie, me sucedo yo; y creo que siguiendo mis huellas, como las de cualquier otro en aquel camino, puede el curioso detener su consideración en los acontecimientos que forman el paisaje común, accidentes del terreno que de todos es conocido, objetos de interés general, y para cuyo examen mis apuntes *biográficos,* sin valor por símismos, servirán de pretexto y de vínculo, pues que en mi vida tan destituida, tan contrariada, y sin embargo tan perseverante en la aspiración de un no sé que elevado y noble, me parece ver retratarse esta pobre América del Sud, agitándose en su nada, haciendo esfuerzos supremos por desplegar las alas, y lacerándose a cada tentativa, contra los hierros de la jaula que la retiene encadenada (III, 150-51).

Sarmiento believed that his family line represented Argentina's past and that his own life projected the course for the country's future. Significantly, he portrayed himself as having overcome the barbarism in his own life (that is, his own formation in the provinces) because of a redeeming self-education in the latest European ideas and his incomparable determination and will to act. He considered himself to be an incarnated idea, a principle—which still lacked a definitive definition—in the form of a man. Sarmiento, here, transformed history into a romantic narrative with himself as protagonist.

Ambiguous philosophical orientations, the lack of methodological consistency, and the confusion of literary and social scientific procedures, are characteristic of Sarmiento's historical writing. Above, it has been demonstrated that the information contained in *Facundo* lends itself to at least three coherent and mutually independent historiographical readings. Each reading, with its underlying methodological and ideological assumptions, suggests a somewhat different interpretation for the underlying

causes of Argentina's civil wars and the possible resolutions to those conflicts. The differences which distinguish one reading from another could
not be more dramatic. The normative analysis of Argentine society on
the basis of enlightenment categories contrasts with the judgmental thrust
of historicism and the deterministic interpretation of the romantic reading. The liberal social ideals of freedom, democracy, and social harmony
which are projected by the enlightenment reading stand in stark contrast
to his pre-positivistic call for harsh measures of repression against agents
of political dissent and cultural differences. In his methodology of analysis, respect is afforded to supposedly opposing frames of reference, such
as teleological design and scientific method. Rather than reduce social
and historical reality to a single ideological thread, Sarmiento's writings
instead join several of the prevalent schools of historiographical thought
into one fragmentary text. *Facundo* is a compendium of theoretical possibilities, and for that reason, is a reflection of the multifaceted intellectual
environment of Sarmiento's time. The *bricolage* composition of *Facundo*
forces one to reject an ordinary reading which would reveal philosophical or epistemological truth on the level of surface content. Historical
writing has traditionally been considered as differing qualitatively from
other forms of discourse. However, it is apparent that Sarmiento's historical writing is subject to the same laws of production as any other writing: it does not necessarily "reproduce" or "represent" a socio-historical
lived experience with any greater fidelity than, say, fictional or political writing.[34] An intellectual *bricoleur*, Sarmiento selectively borrowed
his symbols from the totality of society's linguistic and conceptual codes
and constructed out of these his expression. He organized his data in
accordance with complex, and at times conflicting criteria. In the construction of his discourse, he was guided not so much by a fidelity to
philosophical or rationalist systems, but rather by the pragmatic goal of
substantiating–however imperfectly–his extra-textual objectives.

Notes for Chapter 5

1. Rodolfo Borello, "El ensayo argentino: 1959-1976," *Los Ensayistas*, 4, No. 6 & 7 (1979), 19, states: "*Facundo* (1845) es el primer intento realizado en el continente de comprender y describir la realidad concreta de un país hispanoamericano, a partir de su historia, de su realidad social y de sus componentes geográficos. . . . Casi todos los que han repensado o examinado esa realidad [argentina e hispanoamericana] han partido de sus puntos de vista. [Algunos] rechazaron, acataron o ignoraron sus ideas. Pero todos le son deudores, en un sentido o en otro. Sarmiento está allí, acatado, denostado, rechazado o superado. Lo que quiere decir que sigue vivo, como hace un siglo."

2. Bernardo Subercaseaux, *Cultura y sociedad liberal en el siglo XIX. Lastarria: ideología y literatura* (Santiago: Editorial Aconcagua, 1981), pp. 90-100, investigates this cross-fertilization of literary and historical expressive systems in relation to the writing of José Victorino Lastarria and the ideas prevalent in Chile's intellectual environment of the mid-century.

3. See in particular, Alfredo L. Palacios, "Civilización y barbarie: dualismo simplista inaceptable," *Cuadernos Americanos*, 105, No. 4 (1959), 162-202; and Ricardo Rojas, *El profeta de la pampa: vida de Sarmiento* (Buenos Aires: Losada, 1945), pp. 205ff. Both discuss the ambiguities and distortions which the civilization-barbarism formula causes in Sarmiento's writing.

4. Edward W. Said, *Beginnings: Intention and Method* (Baltimore and London: Johns Hopkins University Press, 1975), p. xxii.

5. Noé Jitrik, "El *Facundo*: la gran riqueza de la pobreza," in *Facundo o civilización y barbarie*, by Domingo F. Sarmiento (Caracas: Biblioteca Ayacucho, 1977), pp. xi-lii, discusses the "informidad," or intention of the author which would account for such a mixture of styles and ideas.

6. In a letter of December 22, 1845, he wrote to General Paz: "Remito a S. Ex un ejemplar del Facundo qe e escrito con el objeto de favorecer la revolución i preparar los espíritus. Obra improvisada, llena de necesidad de inexactitudes, a designio a veces, no tiene otra importancia qe la de ser uno de tantos medios tocados para ayudar a destruir un gobierno absurdo, i preparar el camino a otro nuevo." Quoted from Domingo Faustino Sarmiento, *Facundo*, prol. Alberto Palcos (Buenos Aires: Ediciones Culturales Argentinas, 1961), p. 450.

7. Ezequiel Martínez Estrada, *Meditaciones sarmientinas* (Buenos Aires: Ediciones Universitarias, 1968), p. 169.

8. His lack of an ordered educational experience is treated several times in his autobiographical writings. See for example: III, 173, 194.

9. "Notas de Valentín Alsina al libro 'Civilización y barbarie,'" in *Facundo*, prol. Palcos, pp. 349-419. Sarmiento responded to Alsina in what is now known as the "Carta-Prólogo" to the 1851 edition of *Facundo* (VII, 15-18), but made relatively few corrections in the text on the basis of Alsina's notes.

10. Enrique Anderson Imbert, *Genio y figura de Sarmiento* (Buenos Aires: Editorial Universitaria de Buenos Aires, 1967), p. 20, presents these three currents in Sarmiento's historical thought, with one minor change: I have substituted "historicism" for what Anderson calls "romanticismo social." I have also consulted the following sources regarding Sarmiento's historical ideas: Enrique Anderson Imbert, "El historicismo de Sarmiento en el centenario del *Facundo,*" *Cuadernos Americanos,* 22, No. 5 (1945), 158-77; Ana María Barrenechea, "Las ideas de Sarmiento antes de la publicación del *Facundo,*" *Filología,* 5, No. 3 (1963), 193-210; Bernardo Canal Feijóo, *Alberdi y la proyección sistemática del espíritu de Mayo* (Buenos Aires: Losada, 1961); Juan Luis Guerrero, *Tres temas de filosofía en las entrañas del 'Facundo'* (Buenos Aires: 1945); José Ingenieros, *Sociología argentina,* 5th ed. (Buenos Aires: Ediciones L. J. Rosso, 1913); Didier Tisdel Jaén, "Hispanoamérica como problema a través de la generación romántica en Argentina y Chile," Diss. Univ. of Texas 1965; Didier T. Jaén, "La generación romántica argentina y el problema de Hispanoamérica," *Journal of Inter-American Studies,* 8 (October 1966), 565-84; Alejandro Korn, *Influencias filosóficas en la evolución nacional,* Vol. III of *Obras* (La Plata: Universidad Nacional de la Plata, 1940); Ricardo Levene, "Sarmiento, sociología de la realidad americana y argentina," *Humanidades,* 26 (1938), pp. 73-105; Raimundo Lida, "Sarmiento y Herder," in *Memoria del Segundo Congreso Internacional de Catedráticos de Literatura Iberoamericana, Agosto de 1940,* ed. Instituto Internacional de Literatura Iberoamericana (Berkeley and Los Angeles: University of California Press, 1941), pp. 155-71; Raúl A. Orgaz, *Sarmiento y el naturalismo histórico,* Vol. II of *Obras Completas,* introd. Arturo Capdevila (Córdoba: Assandri, 1950); and José Luis Romero, *A History of Argentine Political Thought,* introd. and trans. Thomas F. McGann (Stanford: Stanford University Press, 1963).

11. Esteban Echeverría, *Dogma socialista,* in *Obras Completas* (Buenos Aires: Imprenta y Librería de Mayo, 1873), p. 307.

12. Maurice M. Mandelbaum, *History, Man, and Reason: A Study in Nineteenth Century Thought* (Baltimore and London: Johns Hopkins University Press, 1971), pp. 50-53.

13. *Ibid.,* p. 42.

14. Although Sarmiento's early writings reveal on rare occasion a romantic appreciation of the South American Indian, this perspective is overshadowed by his conviction—which was nourished by his familiarity with the social scientific theories and prestigous historical investigations of the day—that the Indian constituted an impediment to his continent's march toward progress. Daniel E. Zalazar is mistaken in his affirmation that "Sarmiento fue, en realidad, un defensor de los indígenas americanos frente a la dominación y explotación hispánicas." ("Las posiciones de Sarmiento frente al indio," *Revista Iberoamericana,* 50, 127 [1984], p. 426). It is true that Sarmiento dedicated far more energy and words to attacking mestizos than he did to attacking Indians, but that was because the former then constituted the overwhelming majority of the country's population, and the latter were already threatened by the extermination—as Sarmiento saw it—that awaited any inferior "race" or culture in front of the inexorable march of progress. In "Las ideas de D. F. Sarmiento sobre la influencia de la religión en la democracia americana," *Discurso Literario,* 2, No. 2 (1985), p. 546, he corrects this opinion in part by explaining that Sarmiento censured those Americans with indigenous mates, because "al mezclarse con razas en estados inferiores de

evolución, las que, por eso mismo, carecían del bagaje espiritual ya acumulado por la raza europea, produjeron un descenso en el progreso evolutivo en relación con la raza europea a que pertenecían." In this last opinion, he wisely concurs with the most important studies treating Sarmiento's opinions vis-à-vis racial questions: Jaime Alazraki, "El indigenismo de Martí y el anti-indigenismo de Sarmiento," *Cuadernos Americanos*, 140, 3 (1965), 135-57; and Antonio Sacoto, "El indio en la obra literaria de Sarmiento y Martí," *Cuadernos Americanos*, 156, 1 (1968), 137-63; remain the most authoritative ones treating Sarmiento's thought vis-à-vis the Indian.

15. Francoise Pierre Guillaume Guizot, *The History of Civilization in Europe*, trans. William Hazlett (New York: A. L. Burt Publishers, n. d.), portrays Europe's previously existing "barbarian" society as based on "military clientship" where "individuality predominates." "[S]elfishness, in all its brutality, in all its unsociability" (p. 50), caused an "absence of moral conditions" that made culture almost impossible. The French historian describes the "indolent" life of the feudal lord: "the possessor of the castle had nothing to do, no duties, no regular occupation" (p. 65). These moral traits gave rise to the clan's warlike nature, their territorially expansive politics, and their staunch opposition to any social change (p. 372). All these characteristics resemble closely the traits of gaucho society as Sarmiento presents in *Facundo*.

16. Issue could be taken with almost every aspect of this description of gaucho character and society, although it is not my objective to do so here. Palacios, "Civilización y barbarie," points out that Sarmiento, who was no historian and was unworthy of the title of sociologist, misunderstood the causes of the *montonera* and completely misrepresented the nature of rural life. Essential points of contention are the accusations in *Facundo* that gauchos by nature were anti-democratic, and that they had impeded the forces of progress in the country's interior. Palacios counters this idea by quoting Vicente Fidel López, who had voiced the same sentiment as that held by Echeverría and Mitre: the gaucho "Era un europeo que había caído en la vida errante de los desiertos americanos; constituía, ahora, un tipo especial que reunía caracteres americanos. El introdujo—concluye López— una *revolución* social en el seno de la revolución política moviéndola en sentido verdaderamente democrático y en busca de una civilización liberal libre de las trabas del pasado" (p. 188). Two other critics who study Sarmiento's treatment of the *montonera* are: Isaac E. Castro, *Sarmiento ante la montonera* (Corrientes: Imprenta del Estado, 1937); and Alfredo E. Ves Losada, "Facundo ante la montonera," *Cuadernos Americanos*, 81, No. 3 (1955), 169-83.

17. John Lynch, *Argentine Dictator: Juan Manuel de Rosas, 1829-1852* (Oxford: Clarendon Press, 1981), pp. 143-53.

18. George Reid Andrews, *The Afro-Argentines in Buenos Aires, 1800-1900* (Madison: University of Wisconsin Press, 1980), who produces data demonstrating that blacks constituted more than a quarter of Buenos Aires' population in 1836, and had contributed more than half of the enlisted men in the wars for independence a generation before. Buenos Aires' black population would decline precipitiously during the yellow fever epidemics from 1856-1875, until they would constitute only 1.8population by 1887.

19. Studies treating Sarmiento's ideas on equality are: Noël Salomon, "El *Facundo* de Domingo Faustino Sarmiento: manifiesto de la preburguesía argentina de las ciudades del interior," *Cuadernos Americanos*, 39, No. 5 (1980),

154-62; and Tulio Halperín Donghi, "Prólogo," in Domingo F. Sarmiento's *Campaña en el Ejército Grande Aliado de Sud América* (México: Fondo de Cultura Económica, 1958), pp. xx-xxvi.

20. I have consulted the following sources concerning positivism in Latin America: José Ingenieros, *La evolución de las ideas argentinas*, ed. Aníbal Ponce (Buenos Aires: El Ateneo, 1951), Vol. II; Ingenieros, *Sociología argentina*, 5th ed. (Buenos Aires: Ediciones L. J. Rosso, 1913); William Kilgore, "The Development of Positivism in Latin America," *Inter-American Review of Bibliography*, 19 (1966), 23-42; Alejandro Korn, *Influencias filosóficas*, Korn, *El pensamiento argentino*, introd. Gregorio Weinberg (Buenos Aires: Nova, n.d.); Orgaz, *Sarmiento y el naturalismo histórico*, and Romero, *A History of Argentine Political Thought*.

21. Juan B. Alberdi made specific reference to the "social sciences" in 1837 when he wrote: "the Science that seeks a general law for the harmonious development of human beings is *social* science." Germán Arciniegas, *Latin America: A Cultural History*, trans. Joan MacLean (Great Britain: Barrie & Rockliff, Cresset Press, 1969), p. 385.

22. H[ippolyte] A. Taine, in *History of English Literature*, trans. H. Van Laun (New York: T. Y. Crowell, 1873), p. 21: "No matter if the facts be physical or moral, they all have their causes; there is a cause for ambition, for courage, for truth, as there is for digestion, for muscular movement, for animal heat. Vice and virtue are products, like vitriol and sugar; and every complex phenomenon arises from other more simple phenomena on which it hangs. Let us then seek the simple phenomena for moral qualities, as we seek them for physical qualities . . . ."

23. In *Campaña en el Ejército Grande*, p. 12, Sarmiento discusses the fanaticism of the leaders of the French Revolution: "después de la revolución de Thermidor no se necesitó nada para que la sociedad volviese a los hábitos de humanidad que había perdido, que los espíritus se aquietasen y continuasen siendo útiles a su país esos hombres mismos que se habían amancillado con crímenes espantosos. . . " [sic]. In this passage he implicitly justifies his advice, which Urquiza refused to follow, that harsh measures were warranted against surviving Federalist leaders in the interior provinces.

24. Sarmiento's historicist judgment of gaucho inferiority led him to urge harsh social action which went beyond the philosophical argumentation in *Facundo*. In February of 1845, for example, he urged Unitarian military leader Anselmo Rojo to treat Rosas harshly, if and when defeated militarily: "¡Al traidor convicto degollarlo, quemarle la casa, terror por terror!" A similar treatment should await those who disagreed with the new government which would replace Rosism: "si el general Paz fuese encargado de la Presidencia, a los que no lo reconozcan debiera mandarlos ahorcar y no fusilar ni degollar. Esto es el medio de oponer a un sistema de matar otro que lo desacredite y que imponga en los ánimos mayor idea de autoridad." Quoted by Paul Verdevoye, *Domingo Faustino Sarmiento: éducateur et publiciste (entre 1839 et 1852)* (Paris: Institut des Hautes Etudes de l'Amérique Latine, 1963), pp. 358-59.

25. José Ortega y Gasset, "El ocaso de las revoluciones," *Obras Completas*, 2nd ed. (Madrid: Revista de Occidente, 1950), III, p. 219.

26. Campobassi, *Sarmiento y su época*, pp. 219-222.

27. I have consulted the following texts, in addition to those already mentioned, concerning Sarmiento's tendency to describe social forces with antithetical categories: Gaspar P. del Corro, *Facundo y Fierro: la proscripción de los héroes* (Buenos Aires: Castañeda, 1977); Alfredo E. Ves Losada, "Campo y ciudad en *Facundo,*" *Cuadernos Americanos*, 15, No. 6 (1956), 185-200.

28. Rojas, *El profeta de la pampa*, p. 206.

29. *Ibid.,* pp. 209-10.

30. Orgaz, in the chapter entitled "Cousin y la teoría del grande hombre," in *Sarmiento y el naturalismo histórico*, pp. 289-95; and Verdevoye, *Domingo Faustino Sarmiento*, pp. 403ff, offer concise discussions about Sarmiento's tendency to anthropomorphize historical forces.

31. Orgaz, *Sarmiento y el naturalismo histórico*, p. 294, where he quotes from I, 178.

32. D. L. Shaw, "Concerning the Structure of *Facundo,*" *Ibero-Amerikanisches Archiv*, 6, No. 3 (1980), 239-50, provides an overview of the criticism treating this topic.

33. Ernest Renan, *l'Origine du langage*, in *Oeuvres Completes* (Paris: Calmann-Lévy, Ed., 1958), VIII, pp. 90-91, explains that the origin and function of the word "barbarism" have to do with the ideas of muteness and the lack of intelligibility. Rosas, in this regard, was certainly not an appropriate example of primitive "barbarism."

34. Roland Barthes, "Historical Discourse," in *Structuralism: A Reader*, ed. and introd. Michael Lane (London: Jonathan Cape, 1970), pp. 145-55.

CHAPTER 6

Determinism, Idealism
and the Web of History

Sarmiento's treatment of historical issues, as seen in the previous chapter, with contradictions and overlapping philosophical tendencies is the critic's bugaboo. One approach would be to suppose that chaos reigns in his work because of the lack of methodological consistency. However, it is known that this writer was not above feigning madness, if that would bring him one step closer to the realization of his goals.

Sarmiento's verbal play about madness seems, at first glance, to be an insignificant passage in relation to the totality of his writing. However, further inspection reveals its role in relation to his complex psychology which ultimately—and inevitably—will cast its shadow over the productive process of his discourse. The setting was Santiago de Chile, in 1852. Sarmiento had been under constant attack by the Rosas government, and now was threatened with extradition to Argentina's capital in order to stand trial for sedition and conspiracy against the homeland. His Chilean contacts had already perceived in him a special talent, and he was the object of both immense respect and derision. "Loco Sarmiento," as his opponents labeled him, selected a most unusual defense against the attempts to discredit his name: the writing of an autobiography which would convince potential readers of his own moral uprightness and the nobility of his character.

In *Recuerdos de provinicia*, as this long autobiographical and *costumbrista* essay is titled, "Loco Sarmiento" quotes as an epigraph a famous line from *Macbeth*, but he attributes it erroneously to *Hamlet*, as if he wished to substantiate textually the nickname popularly bestowed upon him.[1] Hamlet, for him, was an obsessed personage for whom madness was a means to an end. His quote: "Es este un cuento que con aspavientos y gritos, refiere un loco y que no significa nada" (III, 25). For both Hamlet and Sarmiento, then, madness was a rhetorical stance; it was part of the sound and the fury for getting their own way and making their own obsessions prevail.[2] Can this passage from *Recuerdos de provincia* serve in the task of understanding better some of the unarticulated goals of Sarmiento's historical writing in general? At the very least, it lends legitimacy to the perspective presented here, which sees in his thought the evidence of a *bricolage* knowledge production. It leads the reader to search beyond the contradictory surface content of that writing and seek out a method for that madness.

An appropriate beginning for this enterprise is to briefly consider Sarmiento's understanding of what precisely constituted a methodology for writing history. Historiography, as well as any other area of humanistic investigation, becomes a discipline when its practitioners articulate a methodology and then abide as closely as possible to that methodology in the construction of their discourse. One basis for evaluating a given historical writing practice is to compare the resulting text to its original methodological premises. It is expected that historical writing, more than other types of writing, will be guided by a consistent and coherent methodology. That is to say, the writer will systematically order and select the stuff of his discourse according to what he accepts as rational and coherent criteria.

The philosophical orientation of the writer is one of the fundamental determiners in the selection of a method for historical analysis. Hegel, for example, was an idealist, and nearly the whole tradition of enlightenment historical writing that preceded him was also idealistic, if we understand the word idealism in the very general sense of ascribing a primacy to subjective reality in its role of not only furnishing the impetus for institutional change, but also of providing the measure for being or individual and social achievement. On the other hand, the positivistic tradition was largely materialist in that it's practitioners ascribed primacy to the role of social and productive relations in the formation of the individual's ideas and also in the precipitation of social change. In general, every historical text may be classified in relation to the idealism-materialism continuum. Since this philosophical issue influences the writer in both his selection and arrangement of content units, it is one of the more fundamental constituents of a given historical methodology.

In the previous chapter it was demonstrated how Sarmiento tapped several philosophical systems in order to describe and evaluate the different ideologies, population groups, and social institutions of the time. The many contradictions and inconsistencies in his arguments, and the unwieldy combination of ideas from enlightenment, pre-positivistic, and romantic schools, are indicative of Sarmiento's semi-controlled inventiveness and somewhat creative spontaneity in writing. The task at hand is to hypothesize a "grammar" for his historical writing, that is, to suggest a set of underlying rules which govern the organization of his apparently contradictory ideas.

Such a structural investigation rejects the hypothesis that the totality of Sarmiento's historical ideas merely constitutes an unsystematic *collage*. An initial argument against this *collage* interpretation is based on the idea that the human mind shies from disorder and gravitates unconsciously toward psychic harmony. This is precisely the function of the archetype and the myth, which provide stable categories for man's cognitive and perceptive functions. The idea of the *bricoleur*, as explained in Chapter Three, is relevant here. The *bricoleur*, who differs only in emphasis but not in kind from the "scientific" thinker, presents an apparently disordered array of elements in his discourse. But again, the data constituting his discourse receive their structure from a pre-existing emotion, intuition, or bias. The structural investigation proceeds, then, by seeking an explanation for why the discourse is organized the way it is.

The confusion between philosophical idealism and materialism in Sarmiento's historical writing does indeed have an explanation. The following pages document how the writer, instead of situating himself philosophically in either the idealist or the materialist camp, chose instead, to play both games, but at different times. This results in more than a contradiction in the content of his ideas, for what is at issue is the definition and limitation of the theoretical space that makes historical study possible in the first place. Sarmiento's historical ideas, in short, were philosophically idealist when that stance seemed convenient, and materialist –and even determinist–when the opposite point of view seemed to be tactically relevant. The text is like a rejected child seeking acceptance into one or another of the authoritative historical traditions prevailing even to the present day.[3]

Philosophical Materialism

First of all, Sarmiento was a materialist. This general perspective enters the thought of the time through a distorted reading of the works of Vico and Herder–and then their disciples– who had proposed that the study of geographic, climatic, and historical influences could yield information about the contemporary existence of a people. However, as was frequently the case–and especially in the nineteenth-century intellectual environment of Latin America–, these ideas, by the time Sarmiento came into contact with them, had already developed their own mythology the lengthy process of diffusion, reinterpretation, and intertextual insertions, and did not necessarily retain the spirit of their original formulation.

The methodology of studying the environmental conditions and past history of a people is central to *Facundo*. In this, Sarmiento utilized the general idea of the *Volksgeist*, which proposes that events were largely influenced by the physical environment and that the leaders of social struggles were to a great degree the personifications of the forces of nature.

The *Volksgeist* belongs to a well-defined and prestigious historical tradition. The concept has its roots in the ideas of Vico, whose thought came to Sarmiento via the writings of Herder and the nineteenth- century French historical school, and in particular, through the translations into French by Michelet.[4] Vico was one of the first of the modern European historians to postulate that the study of environment and past history could yield information about man's contemporary existence. Herder, who followed in the tradition of Vico, was in his turn avidly read by the younger generation of European historians. Herder added to these ideas concerning the influence of the environment upon the formation of man. He suggests in a chapter title the power of biology in this regard: "The Genetic Power is the Mother of All Forms upon Earth, Climate Acting Merely as an Auxiliary or Antagonist."[5]

Herder established a methodology of inquiry that Sarmiento would later utilize. Herder states: "We should never overlook the climate from which a people came, the mode of life it brought with it, the country that lay before it, the nations with which it intermingled, and the revolutions it has undergone in its new seat."[6] Herder believed that the historical life of a people could not be understood as existing apart from the environment in which they were formed. Like his mentor Vico, the German historian had perceived the underlying relations between the physical, natural, and human worlds, all of which were governed by God's will, and which the historian could decipher through rational analysis.

Another probable source for Sarmiento's *Volksgeist* orientation was Alexis de Tocqueville, whose *Democracy in America* took into account "the prodigious influence that the social condition appears to exercise upon the laws and the manners of men . . . ."[7] Similar to Vico and Herder, the French aristocrat believed that one must study an individual's racial origins and the past history of his family in order to understand "the prejudices, the habits, and the passions which rule his life" in the present.[8]

The idea of the *Volksgeist* is fundamental for comprehending how Sarmiento sought to analyze the antecedents of *caudillo* rule in Argentina. In the spirit of Herder, he dedicates several pages to such diverse matters as the interior provinces' geography, customs, popular traditions, and character types. The reader not versed in historiographical methodology might mistakenly view these as relatively peripheral concerns, given the writer's primary objective of combating Rosas through his brand of journalistic propaganda. Sarmiento's intentions, however, were more ambitious: he wished to wage a total war against not only the *caudillo* leaders of the country, but also the social and productive systems that made their political ascendancy possible in the first place. He opportunistically seized upon the *Volksgeist* historical orientation as an arm for his own ideological struggle.

The content and focus of *Facundo's* first chapters, in addition to their precise ordering, obey the tight logic of Sarmiento's *Volksgeist* orientation. Chapter one treats the physical aspects of the country, in addition to the derivative "caracteres, hábitos e ideas que [la geografía] engendra," according to its subtitle (VII, 19). Chapter two follows these physical factors to a further point in the line of causal development and focuses more specifically on character types prevalent in this environment. It further develops the thesis that the predominant ideas, values, and dispositions of the inhabitants in Argentina's rural society exist in relation to the peculiar geographical setting. Chapter three then carries the causal chain from psychology to sociology when it considers the group associating institutions which exist of the men living in that environment previously considered. Chapter four completes the scheme by abstracting from the geographic, psychological, and sociological data in order to formulate some hypotheses concerning the past history of the area. Here, Sarmiento specifically deals with the promise, and then the eventual failure, of the post-independence movement to modernize the country as a whole. One reason for the failure in the author's opinion, was the fact that the country's leaders had not taken adequate account of the organic unity existing between the people and the land.

These four chapters establish a thread of causality beginning with the physical environment and ending with social history. Taken together, they comprise the background for what then follows: the presentation of the life of Juan Facundo Quiroga. The work's first and second parts, then, constitute a tight conceptual unity. In the work's second part this *caudillo* is afforded detailed attention, not so much because of his outstanding acts or personality–although it is true that Quiroga in history and legend held an enormous sway over the public consciousness at the time–but because he seemed to be a representative figure for the lawless and violent character of rural life. As such, Facundo's rise to prominence in Argentina's interior prefigured Rosas' ascendancy over the country as a whole:

> en Facundo Quiroga no veo un caudillo simplemente, sino una manifestación de la vida argentina tal como la han hecho la colonización [española] y las peculiaridades del terreno . . . . Pero Facundo en relación con la fisonomía de la naturaleza grandiosamente salvaje que prevalece en la inmensa extensión de la República Argentina; Facundo, expresión fiel de una manera de ser de un pueblo, de sus preocupaciones e instintos; Facundo, en fin, siendo lo que fué, no por un accidente de su carácter, sino por antecedentes inevitables y ajenos de su voluntad, es el personaje histórico más singular, más notable, que puede presentarse a la contemplación de los hombres que comprenden que un caudillo que encabeza un gran movimiento social, no es más que el espejo en que se reflejan en dimensiones colosales, las creencias, las necesidades, preocupaciones, y habitos de una nación en una época dada de su historia (VII, 12-13).

Sarmiento's excursion into philosophical materialism continues in what Anderson Imbert had aptly labeled as his "modo antropomórfico de explicar el mundo."[9] Sarmiento's tendency throughout *Facundo* is to present specific individuals as personifying abstract social forces and ideological principles. Indeed, in several passages he articulates the belief that by analyzing the ideas and acts of individuals, one comes to understand the predominant social conflicts of a period. What results is an especially dramatic presentation of a struggle between those forces which he took to represent his abstract and quasi-metaphysical categories of civilization and barbarism.

Facundo's second part concretely illustrates how Sarmiento's materialist conception of events influenced the construction of discourse. The text's thesis is that barbarism, which is personified by the figures of Facundo and Rosas, threatened the survival of institutions working toward order and progress. As the protagonist, Facundo is portrayed as a child of Argentina's untamed rural interior. An epigraph from Alix's *Histoire de l'Empire Ottoman* heads the chapter treating Quiroga's infancy and youth: "L'homme de la nature et qui n'a pas encore appris a contenir o deguiser ses passions, les montre dans leur energie, et se livre a toute leur impetuosité" (VII, 67). The writer therefore begins with a pre-established conclusion–or call it a methodological bias–which must be substantianted by the available evidence: Facundo, of primitive spirit due to his origins in a savage natural environment, will be largely governed by the emotions and hardly affected by the higher dictates of reason.

Literary critics have little but praise for the artful style in the episode treating the mountain lion which initiates Facundo's biography. From the point of view of historical accuracy, however, that style made for a most biased appraisal. It is obvious that the underlying objective of the writer was the demonstration of how untamed nature had left its indelible imprint on the personality of the protagonist:

> También a él le llamaron *tigre de los Llanos,* y no le sentaba mal esta denominación, a fe. La frenología y la anatomía comparada, han demostrado, en efecto, las relaciones que existen entre las formas exteriores y las disposiciones morales, entre la fisonomía del hombre y de algunos animales a quienes se asemeja en su carácter (VII, 69).

After this beginning, the direction of the narration is obvious. The logic is that Facundo's character developmemt, after having received its initial stamp, followed an unalterable path. Facundo's adolescence is then explained in terms of the *Volksgeist* of the wild pampas which had already possessed that young existence: "Cuando llega a la pubertad, su carácter toma un tinte más pronunciado. Cada vez más sombrío, más imperioso, más selvático, la pasión del juego, la pasión de las almas rudas que necesitan fuertes sacudimientos para salir del sopor que las adormeciera, domínalo irresistiblemente a la edad de quince años" (VII, 71). Even as a child his adult traits were highly visible, according to Sarmiento: "¿No es ya el caudillo que va a desafiar más tarde a la sociedad entera?" (VII, 71). Artistic sensitivity is superimposed over sociopolitical thesis; the writer anticipates the protagonist's entrance into a deterministic web. For the reader, there will be no suprises. Or, better yet, Facundo's childhood is viewed retrospectively: his biography begins *post festum* with already established givens and with the results of his future development already assumed.

To treat in detail how Sarmiento continued in the textual reconstruction of Facundo Quiroga's adult life would only court redundancy. The textual premise is that the protagonist's barbarian character was a direct result of his residence in the primitive countryside. As the narration follows this cardboard cut-out figure, now a mature being, as he erupts onto the national scene, evidence is accumulated of Facundo's undeviating progress toward barbarism. The narrator emphasizes almost exclusively the data which falls within the parameters of philosophical materialism, and progressively tightens the rhetorical noose around the neck of the protagonist in this deterministic textual world. Facundo's assassination at Barranco Yaco is presented as a fitting end for one who in life had so completely internalized the primitive forces of his medium.

Sarmiento was aware of the extremely one-sided nature of his portrait, which he justified out of the objective of presenting a type in the form of an individual:

> Aquí termina la vida privada de Quiroga, de la que he omitido una larga serie de hechos que sólo pintan el mal carácter, la mala educación, y los instintos feroces y sanguinarios de que estaba dotado. Sólo he hecho uso de aquellos que explican el carácter de la lucha, de aquellos que entran en proporciones distintas, pero formados de elementos análogos, en el tipo de los caudillos de las campañas que han logrado al fin sofocar la civilización de las ciudades . . . (VII, 75-76).

He admits to having suppressed certain material that would have contradicted his political thesis and unbalanced the aesthetic harmony of his tautological presentation. He demonstrates in this quote his awareness of the "productive" nature of his writing: he utilized an economy of data in order to engender a particular type of discourse which would achieve a calculated effect upon his idealized public. It is interesting to note the hollow pretense of impartiality: he admits to having left aside certain data, but only that data which would have reinforced the very same conclusions had they been included in the presentation. It is obvious throughout the pages treating Facundo Quiroga that literary and political objectives overshadowed Sarmiento's commitment to historical realism.

Philosophical Idealism and the Future of Society

In the interest of a fidelity to methodological principles—and even out of a desire for artistic balance—it is not surprising that we find in *Facundo* an elaboration of the *Volksgeist* of civilization, and its consequent anthropomorphization, which parallels that which is accomplished in relation to Facundo Quiroga and Sarmiento's conception of barbarism. In fact, this application of civilization's *Volksgeist* is not altogether anathema to the text's political objective of attacking Rosas and promoting the liberal ideas which would guide the country's transformation in the future. Considered from a rhetorical perspective, a *Volksgeist* of the city implies a determinism of final consequences, that is, the inevitable victory of urban and anti-Rosas forces. Whereas the outstanding geographical feature associated with the interior was the endless, nearly unpopulated pampas, that of the coastal areas was the urban settlement, with easy access to European commerce and culture. Buenos Aires, like Montevideo to a lesser degree, enjoyed a highly favorable position: "está en contacto con las naciones europeas; ella sola explota las ventajas del comercio extranjero . . ." (VII, 22). He suggests the causal link between maritime contact and the coastal city's relatively high level of material comforts and progressive social life. However, not only the coastal areas would benefit from the geographical features that make maritime trade possible, since Argentina was also blessed with several rivers which made different interior regions accessible to the sea. Crossing the heart of the interior were several navigable rivers which promised for the surrounding areas a commercial development equal to that enjoyed by the coastal areas. It was Sarmiento's belief that in these areas the commercial way of life was destined to predominate as it already did in the Province of Buenos Aires. He harshly criticized Rosas for keeping the interior rivers of the country closed to international commerce and for opposing liberal institutions in general. According to Sarmiento, Rosas' opposition to the city-*Volksgeist* was tantamount to resisting the inevitable march of History. In Argentina, the city was bound to triumph eventually, since "hay una organización del suelo, tan central y unitaria en aquel país, que aunque Rosas hubiera gritado de buena fe *¡federación o muerte!* habría concluído por el sistema unitario que hoy ha establecido" (VII, 22).

Sarmiento's interest in the historical past was never abstract and impassive: on the contrary, his historical readings and writings always had the object of fortifying or justifying his programs of social and political action. As a result, his politics began where historical theorization ended. He believed that Rosas and what he called the latter's "gaucho government" obstructed the inevitable progress of the city-*Volksgeist*. The *caudillo* dictator, like the Spanish colonial administration generations before, continually failed to realize that it was in the country's long-range interests to open its rivers to international commerce. Historical writing was one means of denouncing the Rosas government, whose program was "absurdo e insostenible" (VII, 232) since it went against what Sarmiento took to be the destiny of the region. He condemned the Rosas government not only for what he believed was it's attempt to resurrect the institutions of the colonial and feudal past, but also for its blind resistance to the providence-mandated development of the region.

Sarmiento's arguments against the Rosas government therefore took two principal directions: first, there was his belief in the necessity for republican government to replace a retrograde feudalism; and second, he advanced the argument that providence ordained the eventual victory of the city-*Volksgeist* over that of the countryside. He envisioned his own generation of political activists to be the midwives of history; it was they who would help to give birth to a new age in which progressive institutions and a commercial orientation would predominate.

According to the *Volksgeist* thesis, an individual could hardly hope to alter substantially the socio-historical reality in the light of the preponderant influence of geographical determinism. The implication is that a powerful man or a determined government would attempt to resist the forces of providence, but that resistance would be brief and it would eventually fail. According to this interpretation, the social revolutionary was not entirely free to choose the direction for society's future development; his ideas, in order to eventually succeed, would have to comform to a predetermined pattern. Sarmiento accordingly stressed that the impetus for successful institutional change must originate in response to the possibilities offered by one's socio-historical and geographical context. This is the intended meaning of his dramatized rhetorical question in *Facundo's* introduction: "¿Somos dueños de hacer otra cosa de lo que hacemos, ni más ni menos como Rosas no puede dejar de ser lo que es? ¿No hay nada providencial en estas luchas de los pueblos?" (VII, 9-10) The voluntaristic and energetic young writer's declaration of a fatal force guiding his actions is decidedly incongruous. More convicing is the explanation that he seized upon the *Volksgeist* thesis as a motor for his discourse out of polemical and artistic passion, and not out of reasoned conviction.

With this idea of a providential design for historical development, Sarmiento's historical ideas enter into contradiction. When he described the mission of his generation as that of reinserting the nation into the providential *Volksgeist* of progress, he depicted their role as the passive actors of history's script, and not as masters of their own destiny.[10] But the liberal program of social transformation which he defended in other pages called for the technological mastery of nature, the construction of cities, the harnessing of rivers, and the formation of governments promoting the free exchange of ideas. In the pages of *Facundo,* the *Volksgeist* actor, guided by providence's fatal laws, coexisted alongside of the voluntaristic liberal. Philosophical determinism shared textual space with philosophical idealism, and why not? Both were rhetorical procedures that served the same god of progress.

Sarmiento's application of the *Volksgeist* therefore reinforced many of the same goals deduced from his enlightenment-oriented analysis of the country's present crisis. From the former he extracted the argument that providence ordained the eventual victory of the city-*Volksgeist* over that of the countryside; associated with the latter was his commitment in theory to republican institutions and his opposition to the establishment of a retrograde feudalism. But his *bricolage* orientation meant that theories took second place to action. It was of little consequence to him whether the justifications provided were of an enlightenment or romantic orientation, or both; but it was convenient that his writing did, in fact, provide some justification (or several justifications) for the actions that he urged upon his cohorts. Sarmiento, however, realized that his long-range goal needed no textual justification whatsoever: he believed that civilization's fatal and eventual victory over barbarism was dictated by providence, not by men.

Liberalism and the Mythical Power of the Idea

In addition to the image of a *Volksgeist* for the water-accessible coasts and inlands, *Facundo* provides a second image of Argentina's urban population of white Europeans and their descendants. This image, harmonizing with the philosophical underpinnings of liberalism, is of an adaptable and progress-oriented elite for whom all change is possible because they possess the idea. If we accept his discussion of the inevitability of the victory over Rosas, as referred to above, Sarmiento is quite consistent in minimizing the relationship between environment and culture when discussing this group. For example, in the introduction to *Viajes en Europa, Africa y Estados Unidos,* written some six years after *Facundo,* Sarmiento articulates how the idea, in certain groups of people–and here he included himself–assumed an active role in elevating human existence above the formative powers of the land:

> la idea de la verdad viene menos de su propia esencia, que de la predisposición de ánimo, y de la aptitud del que aprecia los hechos . . . . El hecho es que bellas artes, instituciones, ideas, acontecimientos, y hasta el aspecto físico de la naturaleza en mi dilatado itinerario, han despertado siempre en mi espíritu el recuerdo de las cosas análogas de América, haciéndome, por decirlo así, el representante de estas tierras lejanas, y dando por medida de su ser, mi ser mismo, mis ideas, hábitos e instintos. Cuánta influencia haya ejercido en mímismo aquel espectáculo, y hasta dónde se haga sentir la inevitable modificación que sobre el espíritu ejercen los viajes, juzgaranlo aquellos que se tomen el trabajo de comparar la tendencia de mis escritos pasados con el giro actual de mis ideas (V, xii-xiii).

In this passage he avoids any reference to a formative *Volksgeist,* but instead talks about a certain predisposition which made a person susceptible to a positive and inevitable modification of the spirit.

These ideas concerning the innate capacity of men for self-improvement situate Sarmiento's thought within the idealist tradition. He, as well as enlightenment thinkers such as Montesquieu, Condorcet, and others, emphasized the ascendancy of man over the organic and animal worlds on account of the transformational power of the idea. But it must be pointed out that he, like his enlightenment mentors, glossed over the difference between one's conceptualization of the idea and one's desire or ability to act according to it in order to transform a concrete situation. In essence, Sarmiento bestowed upon his illusory class of progressive beings a nearly mythical capacity for praxis: "Tenemos una cualidad y hacemos alarde de ella, porque suple a la fortuna y al talento, al saber y a los demás dotes; sabemos querer; y cuando queremos algo, bien y deliberadamente, ponemos los medios de conseguirlo" (XIII, 363).[11]

If his explanation of the individual's passage from ideation to action stretches the reader's credibility, then all the more so will his transition from an individual's moral improvement to a society's historical progress. His belief in the possibility of society's governed development was well within the idealist tradition. For him, human history had succeeded in elevating itself above the natural order as a result of its propensity for change and its impetus for self-improvement. Perhaps it was the gap in his logic, or his abruptness in passing from the individual to society, which caused him to abandon an analytic language in favor of the metaphor. In the longer passage quoted above, Sarmiento's ambiguous use of the word "natural" reveals his contradictory view of humanity. On the one hand, nature—as seen in the previous section—gives rise to barbarism through its telluric force; but on the other hand, nature, as portrayed here, governs the transformational power of the idea:

> Las ideas, ha dicho M. Lamartine, bajan siempre de lo alto. No es el pueblo, sino la nobleza, el clero, y la parte pensadora de la nación, quien ha hecho la revolución. Las preocupaciones tienen a veces su origen en el pueblo; pero las filosofías no brotan sino en la cabeza de las sociedades; y la revolución francesa era una filosofía. Y asísucede siempre, las luchas sociales están de largo tiempo antes escritas en libros, o formuladas en oraciones; y el que quiera estudiar un hecho consumado, ha de ir a buscar sus causas generadoras en los deseos de antemano manifestados, en la conciencia que del bien o del mal tenían formada los hombres que descollaron en un tiempo a la cabeza de las naciones, representándolas por la ciencia, la religión, las preocupaciones y las luces (III, 266-67).

He explains that historical action originates when the intellectual introduces the idea to society, an event which is usually followed by a long period of gestation. The relatively inert physical forces and material interests weigh down even the most pregnant of ideas, but in doing so they necessarily become altered to some degree. Then, when the time is ripe, innovative ideas break to the surface of social discussion and cause violent struggle among the groups vying for social predominance. In another text he continues this mystification of the idea to its logical extreme. Anthropomorphized ideas, upon separating themselves from the human source of articulation, become the protagonists of historical action. If man or hostile governments take action to repress these insurgent ideas, then it will be to no avail:

> Las ideas entonces, lejos de debilitarse por la paralización que intenta obrar en ellas la política, se robustecen por el contrario, se depuran y se presentan cuando llega el caso de manifestarse incorporadas en forma de credo político, con principios fijos, claros y bien precisados (VI, 11).

This metaphorical description of social agitation emphasizes the insurrectional force with which Sarmiento perceived new ideas to act upon society.

This last quote suggests the destiny which he predicted for those ideas whose force was already spent, for example the reforms of the French Revolution or of the May insurrection in Argentina. These progressive movements had held the cards of victory for a few years, but then they lost ground to the ideas of the past which had continued their march "underground," only to surge forth at a later moment (VI, 12). Nonetheless, the laws of providence decreed that the periods of reaction would eventually come to an end, leaving those progressive movements victorious and unchallenged on the fields of battle.

This vision of struggling ideas as the impetus of social change is fundamental for understanding many of Sarmiento's most engaging activities. For example, his devotion to journalism is explained in part by the belief in the revolutionary power of new ideas: in their printed and popularized form, they would sow the social terrain with polemic and thereby cultivate reforms. One reading of the opening lines of *Mi defensa* suggests an impetuous and at times irresponsible frenzy to his early activities in Chile: "he templado las armas con que me he echado de improviso en la prensa, combatiendo con arrojo a dos partidos, defendiendo a otro; sentando principios nuevos para algunos; sublevando antipatías por una parte, atrayéndome por otra afecciones; complaciendo a veces, chocando otras, y no pocas reuniéndolos a todos en un solo coro de aprobación o vituperios . . ." (III, 2). However, another reading suggests that his commitment to foster discussion without undue regard for immediate consequences was guided by this extremely idealistic interpretation for the mechanism of progress. In a similar fashion he frequently expressed the idea that his adamant opposition to tyranny was due in part to the restriction which the tyrants had placed upon the circulation of ideas, that *sine qua non* of civilization.

The emphasis placed on the free exchange of ideas elucidates one aspect of the opposition demonstrated by Sarmiento and others of his generation to the government of Juan Manuel de Rosas. Critics have called attention to the "idealistic" and "dream-like" quality of their projects, and therefore the relative ineffectiveness of their complaints against the dictator.[12] Rosas had already achieved Rivadavia's dream of uniting the country under one political authority (although Rivadavia would have disapproved of Rosas' heavy-handed control for the economic benefit of the cattle oligarchy.) Rosas, in essence, had all but deprived the neo-Unitarian exiles of their political *raison d'être*. Similarly, Rosas, who had developed the *saladero* and had led the cattle industry of the coastal areas into a capital-efficient centralization, was the man of the hour in the economic sphere, though Sarmiento and the other members of his generation of gentile thinkers chose to ignore it. In consequence, the points of contention drawn up by the Asociación de Mayo against Rosas were largely of form, and not of substance. According to Alberto Palcos, when all was over and done, "el único reproche esgrimible contra Rosas sería él de haber apelado a la violencia."[13] Eventually, after the country's torturous journey past Caseros in 1852 and then to Pavón in 1861, the newly ascendant bourgeoisie, and among them Sarmiento, would legitimize many aspects of Rosas' system through the letter of the law.[14] Rosas in great part had provided the political and economic base upon which they would proceed to establish their superstructural reforms. The national unification he had forceably achieved made possible the eventual political ascendancy of Argentina's commercial bourgeoisie with its dependent liberal ideology.

Returning to questions of historiographical methodology, Sarmiento postulated that the ability to learn new concepts and utilize them for creating a new and better pattern of living was precisely what differentiated the primitive tribe from the civilized society. He believed that the education of its children was indispensable for any developed society. He did not hold that man was born good, in the sense of the Rousseauian noble savage, nor that man was born with Locke's *tabula rasa* of innate learning capacity. Man, for Sarmiento, had as many bad instincts as good. He therefore believed that a progressive society would encourage and stimulate the positive qualities of the citizenry through instruction, institutional reform, and political participation, and therefore prepare them for a life governed by reason.

The matter of reason versus the emotions is one of the keys to Sarmiento's thought regarding the class composition of society. His historical doctrine was predicated on the idea that mankind was developing along the path of equality and that a society would eventually emerge in which every able-bodied person would participate in a democratic political process and would enjoy prosperity under a liberal economic system. This classless society was his dream for the future. In the present, however, there was still a need for social difference.

Argentine society, from his perspective, suffered from an enormous cultural gap separating an elite minority from the uncultured masses. The former, who had traveled farther along the civilizing path, were already indoctrinated into the life of reason. The masses, however, whose reasoning faculty still lay largely dormant, were still governed for the most part by the baser faculties of the intelligence. This being so, the wise social planner had the need of providing an acceptable institutional framework in which the masses could exercise their still unseasoned and semi-tamed nature. Even in the most progressive societies of his day he found a justification for such public amusements as bullfights, the romantic theatre, and public festivals:

> Por todas partes se siente la misma falta y la misma necesidad de esas fiestas populares que conmueven profundamente los corazones, que unen los ánimos y representan las creencias, las tradiciones y los votos de la sociedad. Se echan hoy menos aquellos tiempos felices en que el cristianismo era la expresión por sí solo de todas las necesidades de la sociedad . . . . Nuestra época es desgraciadamente una época de lucha, de transición y de escepticismo. Ideas, intereses,

tendencias, todo está en contradicción, y lo que sería bueno para la muchedumbre ignorante, sería ridículo y despreciable para la parte ilustrada: lo que convendría a unos espíritus, sublevaría a los otros. Un día llegará en que las nuevas ideas de que hoy vive la humanidad, tomen sus formas y se ostenten éstas apoyadas en la veneración de las masas y de la sociedad entera (II, 146).

Even popular amusements had their place in his civilizing scheme, at least for a society in transition that still aspired entrance into civilization's fold.[15]

In some passages Sarmiento's enchantment with man's reasoning faculty, and his corresponding disdain for the emotions and the instincts, has an extremist ring to it, and must be accounted for by, among other factors, his pragmatic reading of enlightment texts.[16] Rousseau, the radical educator of the previous generation, had urged man to turn from books and the purely rational considerations of facts in order to find human perfection within his heart or in the "impulse from a vernal wood."[17] Guizot, highly admired by Sarmiento, was of a similar disposition, as evidenced by the very positive function he accredited to the sub-rational faculties of the human intelligence. Guizot wrote about Voltaire, who also had given primacy to the reasoning faculty: Voltaire, famous primarily as a philosopher, nevertheless "was also a poet, and when he gave himself up to his imagination, to his poetic instincts, he found impressions greatly differing from his judgment."[18] For Guizot, poetry was not *erreur,* as Voltaire had called it, but truth, in the sense that it "answered very legitimate needs of human nature."

Sarmiento's insistence on the superiority of reason contrasts with the views of Rousseau and Guizot. He was clearly a precursor of late nineteenth-century positivism, whose advocates sought to utilize scientific analysis for the purpose of transforming man's values and institutions. Linking Sarmiento to them was his highly pragmatic perspective concerning the role of man's rational intelligence. He believed that in the preceding century, civilization's most advanced thinkers had analyzed society and that their criticisms had brought about the destruction of retrograde social forms. Now, the responsibility of his own generation was to examine institutions and values with the objective of creating a new social order (II, 136). Man's most worthy intellectual pursuit, he writes, was the amelioration of all aspects of social life. After his voyage to Western Europe and North America between 1845 and 1847, Sarmiento returned even more convinced that his own continent was progressing in unhealthy directions. The first step in the bitter struggle to right the immense wrongs was to study "las causas profundas y tradicionales" of his continent's turmoil. These he says,

es preciso romper, si no queremos dejarnos arrastrar a la descomposición, a la nada, y me atrevo a decir a la barbarie, fango inevitable en que se sumen los restos de pueblos y de razas que no pueden vivir, como aquellas primitivas cuanto informes creaciones que se han sucedido sobre la tierra, cuando la atmósfera se ha cambiado, y modificádose o alterado los elementos que mantienen la existencia (V, xiii).

His mission, which sometimes reached the level of a cosmic imperative in his eyes, was tantamount to saving South America from a fate comparable to the extinction of inferior animal species because of their failure to adapt to changing natural conditions.

Sarmiento anticipated late nineteenth-century philosophical naturalism in his emphasis upon the ills besetting his continent and the surgical remedies prescribed for their cure. Like that of the literary naturalists, his discourse reveals an artistic sensitivity at play in a social-scientific world. The organic analogy united his view of society to that of the individual. If the principal sickness of Argentina's social organism was "barbarism," then the social planner must perform an operation to remove such a malignant tumor. When the infection was minor, the operation would involve no more than a substitution of defective or sick parts for those which were healthy: "arrancarse una a una las ideas recibidas, y sustituírseles otras que están muy lejos de halagar ninguna de aquellas afecciones del ánimo, instintivas y naturales en el hombre" (V, xiii). If the required surgery on the social organism was more complex, then one could only hope that a knowledge of the causes would assist him in remedying those ills, or at least in blocking their effects (VI, 11). Since the introduction of the desired institution into the social organism was bound to encounter resistance, the social planner could utilize his knowledge in order to determine "su momento oportuno para introducirse" and "encontrarse el medio de regularizar la lucha . . ." (VI, 12,13). But if the evils besetting society went beyond the recently acquired and fairly untested state of the science, then it was advisable to make only an exploratory investigation, "y sus huellas guiarán los pasos de los que quieran en lo sucesivo ilustrar la opinión pública, es decir, formar la razón general haciendo conocer los escollos de que estamos rodeados, para indicar el sendero que nos toca seguir en la azarosa marcha de nuestras repúblicas" (VI, 12-13).

Sarmiento, the literary surgeon, suggests one other possibility for treating the sick social organism: preventive medicine. Upon reaching an agreement with respect to diagnosis and cure, society's elite could coordinate efforts in order to apply the prescribed preventive treatment:

¿Por qué la república, en que los intereses populares tienen tanto predominio, no ha de apetecerse, no ha de solicitarse, aunque no sea más que un paso dado hacia el fin, una preparación del medio ambiente de la sociedad para hacerla pasar del estado de civilización al de *garantismo* y de ahí al de *armonía* perfecta? (V, 91).

In predicting the blissful results which his metaphorical operations would yield for society, his diction leaves the realm of naturalism and enters into that of utopian socialism.

It is evident that his belief in the insurrectional power of the idea and the scientific guidance of society contradicted the determinism which he depicted as characteristic of the "barbaric" sector of Argentina's national population. Idealism, in his view, had to do exclusively with civilized individuals or those whose behavior was governed by reason and who consequently willed for themselves a constant evolution along the path of progress. The people living in intimate contact with nature, however, were not considered capable of self-improvement since they lived both as individuals and as a community under the sign of an unchanging *Volksgeist*. Consequently, Sarmiento's civilization/barbarism dichotomy not only divided the national population into two distinct camps, but also defined two separate methodologies for historical analysis. While discussing those people whom he considered belonging to the civilized sphere, he utilized the philosophical underpinnings of idealism, and while considering those he deemed barbaric, he employed the theories of historical determinism.[19]

Sarmiento, who was an ideologue before he was a scholar, utilized his historical writing to promote partisan politics. He did not hesitate to muster philosophy or historical methodology in the pursuit of power. Seen from this perspective, he differed little from the *científicos* in the Mexico of Porfirio Díaz, those brilliant lawyers and economists who also worshiped at the glittering shrines of Science and Progress. They, like Sarmiento, guided their country to previously unattained heights in the areas of material progress and elitist cultural production. They also made the distinction between civilization for the white, European-stock population of the urban capital, and barbarism for the Indians and people of mixed ancestory who constituted the sub-classes of the city and the countryside. The *científicos*, like Sarmiento, held out to the former group the dream of infinite progress; for the latter group, whom they perceived to be marked with the curse of Cain, they imposed a choice between servitude and annihilation.

Idealism, Materialism and the Education of Man

The preceding section presents examples of how, through the calculated arrangement of ideas, Sarmiento's language constantly projects itself outside of the textual space and obeys the Machiavellian quest for sociopolitical power. The textual shifts from philosophical idealism to materialism—as demonstrated above—also obey the political necessity of promoting Argentina's white bourgeois population and attacking the non-white, non-bourgeois population of the countryside. In his writings this philosophical polarity influences the treatment of ethnic, racial, and social differences. Consequently, one can detect two parallel, but contradictory, views regarding man's potentiality for learning and the role of formal instruction in relation to social progress.

No aspect of Sarmiento's life and thought exemplifies better his ambiguous relationship to the Argentine liberal tradition as his lifelong commitment to public education. His confidence in the moral advancement
of the individual as the motor for social progress reveals his profound
roots in the enlightenment tradition and –as treated in the last chapter–
utopian liberalism. Like Echeverría and the early Alberdi, he believed
in the necessity for slow and not revolutionary change through the educated minority's political conduction and moral instruction of society's
submissive masses. Sarmiento did not question the premises of that educational model nor the basic precepts of the culture upon which that
model was based. His educational theory was aimed primarily at puri-
fying and simplifying that culture of minorities in order that the masses
could absorb it more rapidly. His illuminating visit to the United States
came at about the same time as the frustrated revolutionary outbreaks
across Europe in 1848. Both of these events would crystallize his belief
that public education and a diffusion of wealth (which would be gained
primarily through the state's land distribution policies) were the precon-
ditions for the worthy goals of social equality and broad-based political
participation.[20]

This lifelong utopian focus to his thought and actions acquires its full
meaning in the light of the sociopolitical system that came to predominate in Argentina after 1852. Echeverría already anticipated that new
system in the writings of his later years (he died in 1851) and Alberdi
mapped out its structure in *Bases* (1852): a system characterized by civil
and commercial (not political) liberty which would be guaranteed through
the order imposed upon society by an authoritarian government in which
the cattle-exporting interests, those which had become consolidated during the Rosas period, would predominate. Alberdi quickly conformed
to the theoretical fundamentals of these aspects of the dependent-liberal
system, but Sarmiento judged them to be intolerable. Both advocated
the accelerated introduction of foreign capital and immigration, but with
differing visions of progress. For Alberdi, Argentina's development into a
regime of liberty lay in the remote future; Sarmiento impetuously called
for urgent movement then and there, toward the same goals. The conservative Alberdi advocated a role for public education that did not venture
beyond the instruction of manual or vocational skills; Sarmiento incessantly advocated and practiced a pedagogy aimed at cultivating in the
lower classes a life governed by reason in the exercise of liberty. Given
the new oligarchical dictatorship in which the two men's respective orientations came to be tested, one would have to conclude that Alberdi's was
by far the most realistic. But Sarmiento's post-1852 career was the most
ambiguous: sometimes through accommodation, sometimes through ideological combat, he continually sought the implementation of his liberal
educational and agrarian goals within the limits of what was politically
and socially possible.

In this light I can agree with his liberal hagiographers, that Sarmiento's
was the most progressive voice of his continent in the area of educational

reform and in his lifelong commitment to the dream of social equality through a system of public instruction. His writings on educational issues are unsurpassed for their breadth and profundity, and he correctly perceived them as that part of his total work which would be the most enduring. However, those same pages display a similar philosophical rift as do those treating his ideas on historical change. In educational theory, Sarmiento reveals himself sometimes as a materialist and sometimes as an idealist, depending upon the subject at hand and the convenience for advocating one political philosophy over the other. In the passages treating education within the context of the white bourgeois municipality, his message is one of idealism, optimism, and hope. But in other passages, he discusses the uselessness of education for altering or improving the inferior station of the non-white population inhabiting his continent.

Sarmiento's ideas on education were flavored by the pre-positivistic idea of social amelioration whereby the social planner would transform institutions on the basis of information provided by historicist and empirical analysis. The school teacher, in addition to the military leader and the reform-minded newspaper reporter, was one such individual who could harness knowledge in order to advance society:

> Sólo el maestro de escuela, entre estos funcionarios que obran sobre la sociedad, está puesto en lugar adecuado para curar radicalmente los males sociales. . . . El tiene una sola moral para todos, una sola regla para todos, un solo ejemplo para todos. El los domina, amolda y nivela entre sí, imprimiéndoles el mismo espíritu, las mismas ideas, enseñándoles las mismas cosas, mostrándoles los mismos ejemplos; y el día en que todos los niños de un país pasen por esta preparación para entrar en la vida social, y que todos los maestros llenen con ciencia y con conciencia su destino, ese día venturoso una nación será una familia, con el mismo espíritu, con la misma moralidad, con la misma instrucción, con la misma aptitud para el trabajo un individuo que otro, sin más gradaciones que el genio, el talento, la actividad o la paciencia (IV, 421-22).

It is obvious that when Sarmiento penned the above passage the utopian bent of his consciousness dominated over his sense of realism: one could say that his eyes were so focused upon the final objective of instruction that he lost sight of the student. In this passage, he communicates a Skinnerian pedagogy with the objective of creating a uniform and homogeneous society of individuals possessing the same aptitudes and the same morality as a result of having received similar instruction.

The education of the non-white non-European cultures was not a principal concern for Sarmiento's European mentors, whose works he utilized in the production of his own patchwork discourse. There are exceptions to this however. A brief consideration of the thought of Herder and Tocqueville regarding this subject will help to situate Sarmiento's views within a larger context, since the opinions of these two European writers suggest the breadth of the ideological context out of which Sarmiento's discourse emerged.

Tocqueville's firsthand observations concerning the plight of the indigenous population on the North American continent were recorded in *Democracy in America,* a work which we have already documented as having been closely read and infinitely respected by Sarmiento. Discernible is the French visitor's nominal respect for the enlightenment value of universal equality, but what predominates in his discourse is the diction of class and racial differences. The Indian's inferiority, he states, was not natural but acquired. Having become accustomed to submitting to everything except reason in the course of his life, "he is too unacquainted with her dictates to obey them .... Far from desiring to conform his habits to ours, he loves his savage life as the distinguishing mark of his race and repels every advance to civilization, less, perhaps, from hatred of it than from a dread of resembling the Europeans."[21]

This extremely pessimistic view of the Indian's ability to adapt in the face of changing conditions found its parallel—but in not nearly so damning a form—in the thought of Herder. The German theorist more generously accredited the Indian, and in fact all races, with the power to adapt to new circumstances. But, he cautioned, change would be slow at best, such as that observed in the modifications of customs on account of centuries-long climatic shifts. "The various national forms of people testify that even this, the most difficult change of the human species, is possible."[22] A philosopher might regard these words as a somewhat optimistic view regarding a minority group's assimilation to society's dominant norms. However, a social planner such as Sarmiento, when confronted by the daily challenges of social conflict, might interpret them as a warrant for excluding those groups in order to achieve a projected reform.

As with the topic of social progress, Sarmiento's ideas concerning the education of non-white population groups in his country are almost always expressed in the terms of telluric determinism. He anticipated the "nationalists" of a few decades hence who would consider human behavior for the most part as deriving from biological causes:

> Yo creo firmemente en la trasmisión de la aptitud moral por los órganos, creo en la inyección del espíritu de un hombre en el espíritu de otro por la palabra y el ejemplo. Jóvenes hay que no conocieron a sus padres, y ríen , accionan y gesticulan como ellos; los hombres perversos que dominan a los pueblos, infestan la atmósfera con los hálitos de su alma, sus vicios y sus defectos se reproducen; pueblos hay, que revelan en todos sus actos quienes los gobiernan . . .(III, 128-29).

The contemporary reader would regard Sarmiento's three examples for the transmission of moral aptitudes as exemplifying three entirely different issues. The example comparing young people to their parents suggests the genetic inheritance of not only physical attributes, but also moral traits. In the consideration given to perverse tyrants, there is a suggestion—perhaps intended as a figure of speech—that social practices can be passed from one generation to another, very much like a communicable disease. Lastly, the reference to the relationship between the

rulers and the ruled explicitly defends the transformational power of education, either for better or for worse, in shaping the moral values of a
community. The first two examples suggest the strong causal power of
the material organism over man's moral and social habits, but the third
seems to contradict the original premise about the biological determination of moral aptitudes. The lack of methodological rigor in this passage
suggests Sarmiento's inability and perhaps his discomfort at attempting
to rationalize racial prejudices with a quasi-scientific language.

The above quote is not an isolated occurrence which one could ascribe
to the writer's hasty pen in an unmediated moment of creative exuber-
ance, because the same general idea of a physical or biological determinism
over the behavior of certain groups is repeated throughout his writing. In
the following passage a biological analogy is used to fortify Sarmiento's
discussion on historical change:

> Porque las grandes luchas de las naciones, ni aun las conmociones
> populares, se engendran a sí mismas. La ley inmutable de la natu-
> raleza orgánica es que en la vida la simiente guarde y envuelva el
> germen, y que este germen sometido a cierto grado de temperatura,
> se desenvuelva y produzca el árbol fructífero y saludable, o la planta
> venenosa o erizada de espinas (III, 266).

Here, he suggests that not only social struggles, but also human intelligence and physical growth, are governed according to the immutable
laws of the natural world. The biological metaphor, a commonplace in
nineteenth-century writing, receives at his hands a deterministic thrust.
It is somewhat tautological to argue that whatever ends well originated
in a good seed. But this argument functions on a rhetorical level to draw
attention away from the contradiction of a progressive white bourgeoisie
in a context of telluric determinism. The metaphor also has utility in
substantiating for the social elite a politics of containment, apartheid, or
genocide for an undesirable social group. Within this frame of thought, he
who owns the word also defines the goals and limits of education. He who
speaks or writes assumes the authority for deciding which seed will be allowed to develop into a fructiferous and healthy tree, and which ones will
have to be destroyed before they grow into venomous and spiny plants.

When writing as educator or historian, Sarmiento many times abandoned the quest for impartial truth, and instead strove for rhetorical
efficiency according to the exigencies of his sociopolitical situation. He
portrayed the Indians and gauchos of Argentina as beings whose character and social institutions were overwhelmingly determined by a barbarian
physical environment. Throughout his writing one can encounter many
damning statements regarding racial and ethnic minority groups. Even in
De la educación popular, his most enlightened work for its promise of instruction, and therefore progress, for South America's masses, Sarmiento
excludes the Indian for his "ineducabilidad" (XI, 212) and the people
of mixed race, who were for him "incapaces o inadecuadas para la civilización" (XI, 38).

"Las ideas no tienen patria," Chilean minister Montt had persuaded him (III, 196), and perhaps Sarmiento learned too well the lesson of his lifelong friend and supporter. The original context of the utterance was Montt's assurance to the newly arrived Argentine exile that in Chile he was appreciated by those who mattered, even though others might attempt to defame him with the accusation that he was a foreigner meddling in local affairs. But the words of Montt also have significance within the context of Sarmiento's discourse itself, in the sense that ideas need not be joined through systems, and systems need not be dealt with according to discourse's supposed structure or methodological consistency. Indeed, the epistemological discontinuities and displacements in Sarmiento's discourse are notorious. He was a pragmatic thinker and not a purist. The worthiness of an idea was to be judged not in relation to its ideological "homeland," but rather in relation to the effect which that idea's articulation would have over the body politic.

Perhaps Sarmiento had learned the laws of rhetoric from the old maestros—whose lessons have been incorporated into the deconstructive criticism of the 1980s—that truth is dependent only upon contingent factors which are specific to a particular reading of a text or a given reality. Truth is a function of discourse; it does not exist outside of language itself. A doctrine's pretense to truth illustrates nothing less than its own mystification, its own unwillingness to accept the "ideology of ideology," in the words of Louis Althusser.[23] The truth about truth is that it has no homeland; it can be utilized in the struggle either for or against the ideological masks of oppression.

The official texts of a frozen continent have taught uncritical school children over the last century to esteem the universality of Sarmiento's ideas on education and history and to pay homage to Latin America's first educator-president. But since "ideas have no homeland," they must not be interpreted from an abstract and universal criterion. Ideas, like the tool in the hand, have no worth apart from the objectives which they are used to defend. To Sarmiento's eternal credit, he was his country's and his continent's most constant defender of popular education. When he spoke as an idealist, popular education had the goal of saving the masses of children in the country from a slow economic and social marginalization; it was the indispensable instrument of social articulation in an age of universal progress. But when those ideas are viewed in relation to the social and political context in which they were articulated, one arrives at a somewhat different conclusion. During most of his adulthood he believed that the struggle between civilization and barbarism in his country was more specifically that between the biologically endowed white race and the genetically inferior people of color; between society's urban and educated elite, and the uncultured rural inhabitants. In truth, as Martínez Estrada succinctly states, "Enseñar fue para Sarmiento, siempre, una de las formas de dirigir."[24] For one like Sarmiento, the pursuit of truth was motivated sometimes by a benevolent humanism, and at other moments by the goal of social and racial domination.

Notes for Chapter 6

1. This is not the only misquote by Sarmiento in *Facundo*. Ana María Barrenechea, "Función estética y significación histórica de las campañas pastoras en el *Facundo*," in José Montovani et al., *Sarmiento: educador, sociólogo, escritor, político* (Buenos Aires: Universidad de Buenos Aires, Facultad de Filosofía y Letras, 1963), p. 49, states that the epigraph in French for *Facundo's* first chapter comes not from Francis B. Head, as is indicated, but rather from Alexander Von Humboldt's *Tableau de la Nature* (Paris, 1808). This type of error is never entirely gratuitous; it leads one to hypothesize about the role of mistaken source references in relation to an implicit or explicit function of Sarmiento's discourse production.

2. The editor of Sarmiento's *Obras Completas* provides a brief history of the epithet "loco" as applied to Sarmiento (XIII, 263). Sarmiento himself documents its first use: in an 1848 letter written by José Santos Ramírez, a Federalist military official, who denounces Sarmiento for having urged him to join the opposition. Years later Sarmiento wrote in the margin to his copy of that letter: "Primera aparición en documento oficial del epíteto de loco." The editor continues by stating that Urquiza then adopted the epithet, calling Sarmiento the "loco boletinero." After that, it was only natural that his opponents would refer to Sarmiento in the same manner with the goal of discrediting him and his objectives.

3. A most interesting reading of Sarmiento's works would be this search for universal acceptance, as suggested by Adolfo Prieto, *La literatura autobiográfica argentina* (Rosario: Universidad Nacional del Litoral, Facultad de Filosofía y Letras, Instituto de Letras, 1962), p. 56, who argues that the writer, due to his world of "inseguridad organizada," went to extreme lengths to gain popularity and renown through his writings and acts.

4. Raimundo Lida, "Sarmiento y Herder," *Memoria del Segundo Congreso Internacional de Catedráticos de Literatura Iberoamericana* (Berkeley and Los Angeles: University of California Press, 1941), pp 156-58; and Didier T. Jaén, "Hispanoamerica como problema a través de la generación romántica en Argentina y Chile," Diss. University of Texas, 1965, pp. 41-50.

5. Johann Gottfried Von Herder, *Reflections on the Philosophy of the History of Mankind,* introd. Frank El Manuel (Chicago: University of Chicago Press, 1968), p. 29.

6. Herder, *Reflections,* p. 29.

7. Alexis de Tocqueville, *Democracy in America,* I, Notes by Phillips Bradley (New York: Random House, Vintage, 1945), p. 357. See the chapter, "El modelo lejano: Tocqueville," in Raúl A. Orgaz, *Sarmiento y el naturalismo histórico,* in Vol. III of *Obras Completas,* introd. Arturo Capdevila (Córdoba: Assandri, 1950), pp. 279-88, for a study of Tocqueville's influence on Sarmiento's thought.

8. *Ibid.,* pp. 27-28.

9. Enrique Anderson Imbert, *Genio y figura de Sarmiento*, (Buenos Aires: Editorial Universitaria de Buenos Aires, 1967), pp. 52-53.

10. Juan Domingo Perón's words, as recorded by Eduardo Galeano, "Perón, los gorriones y la Providencia," in *Violencia y enajenación* (Madrid: Nuestro Tiempo, 1971), p. 87, are reminiscent of Sarmiento's conception of providence: "'A los traidores, a los tránsfugas hay que dejarlos volar, pero sin darles nunca descanso. Y esperar a que la Providencia haga su obra. Hay que dejar actuar la Providencia . . .;' y subrayó, guiñándome un ojo: 'Especialmente porque la Providencia muy a menudo la manejo yo.'"

11. "El deseo" constituted a foremost quality of the civilized man, according to Sarmiento. In XV, 222, he argues that "el deseo" is one of the primary qualifications for a successful statesman.

12. Alejandro Korn, *Influencias filosóficas en la evolución nacional*, in Vol. III of *Obras* (La Plata: Universidad Nacional de la Plata, 1940), p. 168, states about the Generation of 1837: "Ninguna época imaginó mayores proyectos y empresas, ninguna realizó menos. Fue necesario que surgiera una generación menos soñadora, que templada en la adversidad, en el ostracismo, en la brega diaria, afrontada con criterio práctico, y sobre todo, con voluntad enérgica la tarea del momento, para llevarla a cabo no en los dominios fantásticos de la imaginación, sino dentro de las realidades y posibilidades precarias y contingentes de la acción viable."

13. Alberto Palcos, *Sarmiento: la vida, la obra, las ideas, el genio* (Buenos Aires: El Ateneo, 1938), p. 91.

14. Tulio Halperín Donghi, "Prólogo," *Campaña en el Ejército Grande Aliado de Sud América* by Domingo F. Sarmiento (México: Fondo de Cultura Económica, 1958), p. xxvii: "El régimen político que bajo máscara republicana organice una dictadura heredera de los instrumentos de compulsión creados por el rosismo, orientados ahora por un plan de progreso económico acelerado, es lo que Alberdi llama la república posible."

15. In some passages Sarmiento is ambiguous about the desirability of such a brave new world, at least for a transitional man such as himself, whose character was tempered as much by the passions as it was by the intellect. In *Viajes*, for instance, he opens himself to introspection upon experiencing the profound emotions stimulated by a visit to the volcano Vesubius: "¡No hay placer como el de tener mucho miedo, cuando esto no degrada, y es solicitado espontáneamente, ni sensaciones que agiten más profundamente el corazón que las del terror! ¡Oh! Yo me he hartado en el Vesubio con estos raros goces . . ." (V, 278). He writes of a similar reaction upon visiting the Spanish bullfight: "He visto los toros, y sentido todo su sublime atractivo. Espectáculo bárbaro, terrible, sanguinario, y sin embargo, lleno de seducción y de estímulo. . . . ¡Oh, las emociones del corazón, la necesidad de emociones que el hombre siente, y que satisfacen los toros, como no satisface el teatro, ni espectáculo alguno civilizado!" (V, 163)

16. Delfina Varela Domínguez de Ghioldi, *Filosofía argentina: los ideólogos* (Buenos Aires: 1938), p. 53, likens Sarmiento to Moreno and Rivadavia in that all studied French scientific theory in its application to educational principles. She is basically correct in the assessment that all rejected the path of the sentiments and the emotions, but she is incorrect in her assertion that this was learned from Rousseau's *Emile*.

17. J. Bronowski and Bruce Mazlish, *The Western Intellectual Tradition: From Leonardo to Hegel* (New York: Harper and Row, 1960), p. 294.

18. Francois Guizot, *The History of France, in Essays and Lectures,* ed. and introd. Stanley Mellon (Chicago: University of Chicago Press, 1972), pp. 357-58.

19. Ezequiel Martínez Estrada, *Sarmiento* (Buenos Aires: Argos, 1956), p. 166, also notes the unresolved contradiction between Sarmiento's optimistic idealism and pessimistic "realism": "El idealismo de Sarmiento se aplicaba a la realidad sin ajustarse a ella, y su realismo era pesimista. Era idealista cuando concebía una legislación y un gobierno democráticos, sanos y decentes, sin profundizar mucho en las posibilidades de que tal utopía se pudiese cumplir; era realista cuando advertía que el móvil de la historia es, con la cruza irracional de razas, la barbarie. Pero ni supo extraer de esa realidad grosera un idealismo realista, ni de aquel idealismo teórico un sistema de aplicaciones prácticas que coincidiera con la realidad."

20. This paragraph is based on the ideas presented by Tulio Halperín Donghi, "Prólogo" to Sarmiento's *Campaña en el Ejército Grande,* pp. xii-xix.

21. Tocqueville, *Democracy in America,* pp. 345-47.

22. Johann Gottfried von Herder, *Reflections on the Philosophy of the History of Mankind,* introd. Frank E. Manuel, abr. ed. (Chicago: University of Chicago Press, 1968), p. 29.

23. Louis Althusser, *Lenin and Philosophy and Other Essays,* trans. Ben Brewster (New York and London: Monthly Review Press, 1971), p. 168, states: "In every case, the ideology of ideology thus recognizes, despite its imaginary distortion, that the 'ideas' of a human subject exist in his actions, or ought to exist in his actions, and if that is not the case, it lends him other ideas corresponding to the actions (however perverse) that he does perform."

24. Martínez Estrada, *Sarmiento,* p. 7.

CHAPTER 7

European Civilization
and American Barbarism:
Historiography on the Periphery

In Sarmiento's lifetime, Argentina evolved from a Spanish colony with a regional subsistence economy, to a constitutional federation participating in a world-wide system of commercial exchange. Within a few decades the predominant economic ideas of its leaders changed from mercantilism to capitalism; from protectionism and regional isolation to laissez faire and internationalism. A related transition occurred in the realm of culture: a hierarchical order based on ecclesiastic dogmas gradually gave way to an intellectual atmosphere characterized by empirical investigation, rational questioning, and the rapid exchange of information. These transitions gave rise to the most pressing and disputed issues in the economic, political, and cultural discourses of the period. Into this framework, one must situate Sarmiento's conception of the ferocious battle between civilization and barbarism, the two forces which were vying to control the destiny of the country.

Indeed, a major tenet of the historical interpretation that Sarmiento gave for the Argentine society of his time was the opposition between Europe and America. On the one hand, he called for the adaptation of social and cultural models originating in Northern Europe (and later in the United States) and the country's insertion into the world economic system in accordance with liberal principles. He understood that Argentina's destiny was intimately tied to those of Europe and North America; the ideas, institutions, manufactured goods, technology, and markets of the latter two regions were the *sine qua non* of Argentina's possible civilization in the future. On the other hand, his conception of barbarism pertained largely to the Hispanic tradition in America: the country's latifundium-structured land tenure system, social institutions associated with feudalism, and culture marked by a heritage of medieval scholasticism. Nevertheless, other aspects of barbarism were predominately American in origin: the uninhabited "deserts" or pampas, the savage wildlife, the Amerindian population, and the primitive culture of the gaucho. His diagnosis of the possibilities and obstacles for the development of his country, according to the multifaceted concepts of civilization and barbarism, largely anticipated the program of liberal reconstruction that was to be implemented in the post-Rosas period. Superseding the short-lived Confederation was the Buenos Aires-centered government which favored the interests of that province; the population there benefited from free trade in the world economic system dominated by England, and aspired to subordinate the other social groups and regions of the country to its own criterion of development.[1]

Sarmiento's admiration for the European and North American cultures is well known. During his Chilean exile (from 1840 to 1852) he wrote many articles defending the British commercial presence in the Río de la Plata region. Of particular note is his passionate praise in *Facundo* for European initiatives, and in particular the French blockade of 1835 to 1838. Also well known is the double focus of his plan for the economic and social development of the Argentine interior: the colonization by European immigrants and the opening of the country's rivers to the European ships that sought to establish direct commercial ties with interior population centers. Another example of his European inclination—more subtle, yet still of unquestionable significance—was the propagation of European and North American values and the promotion of those countries' institutions in his own land. Moreover, he was convinced that the white European race was endowed with a superior biological condition that made it more fit than any other for the society of the future. His respect for the Anglo-European people and institutions accompanied an implicit condemnation of the native cultures that could be found in America. These prejudices are apparent throughout his writings, and even in the works which deal with historical or sociological matters; indeed, his claim to strict honesty and ideological impartiality in the presentation of sociological data must be understood in the context of his ethnic and cultural biases.

Throughout his career he consistently defended the cultural and social institutions of Great Britain. Nevertheless, in the first few years of his Chilean exile his ideas regarding that country's contribution in the Río de la Plata region changed radically. Shortly after initiating his journalistic activities there, he wrote a series of articles in which he criticized the British government's meddling in the official life of his country. Then, a few years later, an opposite perspective began to take precedence, when he defended Europe's modernizing influence in South America. He would advocate this latter perspective up to nearly the end of his long public life. These two perspectives are dealt with in the first two sections of this chapter. Then, the third section explores the affinities between the two oppositions, Europe-South America, and civilization-barbarism, and relates them to Sarmiento's role as an historian for his continent.

Sarmiento: Critic of Neo-colonialism

A recurring topic in Sarmiento's writing is Europe's potential role in the social and economic development of Argentina. Unique among the voluminous writings dedicated to this topic is a series of articles that he published in *El Mercurio* between October of 1841 and August of 1842, that is, at the very beginning of his second Chilean exile.[2] Opposition to Rosas had been particularly fierce in the preceding few years, with France taking an active role in blockading Buenos Aires in 1838 and subsequently providing munitions and supplies to his foes in Montevideo and the interior. Many believed that Lavalle's 1840 military excursion against the dictator would have been successful had the French not abandoned him in their abrupt change of policy, which had the goal of a negotiated peace. Throughout this period, the British government's official neutrality hardly masked its cordial relationship with Rosas and its satisfaction with the regime's relative stability, both of which contributed to a prosperous climate for British commercial interests.[3]

In this series of articles Sarmiento reveals a general desillusionment with the role of the European powers in the Río de la Plata region. Although he was probably resentful of France's fickle opposition to Rosas, he does not single that country's government out for attack, probably out of the hope that it could be persuaded to renew its military opposition to the regime in Buenos Aires. In regard to British policies, however, Sarmiento's disapproval was explicit. He was enraged and perhaps perplexed over Britain's tacit and at times direct support for Rosas' tyrannical regime. The dictator, he noticed, was openly courted by the large British community residing in and around the port city. Sarmiento observes that with regard to diplomatic relations the European governments in general paid more attention to the commercial interests of their own subjects than to the plight of Argentine citizens who were subjected to the harsh measures of a cruel and unjust tyrant. Why, Sarmiento asked, did the British support a leader such as Rosas who in idea and deed opposed the principles of republicanism and freedom of expression, those same ideas which predominated in the governing circles of Great Britain? Sarmiento had difficulty accepting the fact that commercial concerns influenced in the formulation of British foreign policy more than moral or ideological factors. Even less understandable was their continued support for the dictator, in spite of the latter's opposition in opening Argentina's rivers to international, and particularly British, commerce. Meanwhile, Sarmiento and several of the other exiled writers of his generation, in addition to the older leadership of the Unitarian party, received little or no support from the British government, in spite of their continued defense of the liberal policies that the British promoted.[4]

In the most important essay of this series, Sarmiento observes a qualitative difference between the colonial system earlier used by the European powers, and what he calls "colonialismo moderno" (XIII, 310). Under the old style of colonial domination, European nationals had governed the subservient native population and had personally directed the productive and commercial operations of the territory. However, a new brand of colonialism was coming into existence, for which the British empire offered the clearest example of how political and administrative control over the peripheral country was no longer necessary. Local elites now took part in policy making and organized the local production. British nationals now limited their activities to finance and commerce, and the British state provided naval and military protection. Sarmiento notes that this new system, which was as advantageous for the European metropolis as it was for the local elites, had come into being by force of necessity and not by design. In the case of the United States, "Por fortuna suya no encontró [Inglaterra] grandes imperios que destrozar, ni ricos depósitos de plata y oro que purificar con sangre humana" (XIII, 310). In that land, Britain had found neither an easily exploitable mineral wealth nor a docile indigenous population appropriate for forced labor. It had found only uninhabited yet potentially productive lands. Unable to establish there a plantation system that would produce agricultural goods for exportation, as it had done in the islands of the Caribbean, Britain instead promoted industrial production. The original fear of creating a rival supplier of manufactured goods vanished with the realization that commerce between metropolis and colonies continually increased, that the colonial economy admirably complemented its own manufacturing capacities. Britain realized that high profits could be had if it exercised control through indirect commercial means rather than through direct administration. This trade relationship continued, and even prospered, after the independence struggle of the thirteen North American colonies. By the early decades of the nineteenth century, this commercial system, supported by the world's most powerful navy, had extended itself throughout the whole world; in arms and in trade Britain had not one serious rival in the world: "Como un crucero anclado frente a la Europa, las islas británicas sirven en un extremo del océano de punto céntrico que unen los hilos que envuelven ya toda la tierra como una telaraña. Su marina mercante y de guerra cubre todos los mares y su sistema de apostaderos está ya completo" (XIII, 312).

Sarmiento calls attention to Great Britain's especially tenatious campaign to acquire territories with strategic advantages for its naval and commercial objectives. That country had taken control of the former French colonies in India, and had ousted the Dutch from Africa's Cape of Good Hope; it possessed several islands in the Caribbean, in addition to all of Canada. Sarmiento observes that Britain had a predilection for obtaining insular and coastal possessions: Hong Kong, Sierra Leone, and the Guayanas were firmly under its domination. These islands and coastal areas promised an even larger profit: commercial control over the entire continents of Asia, Africa, and South America. Moreover, naval bases in several islands and coastal regions gave that country control over the most frequented passages for maritime traffic: Gibraltar and Malta in the Mediterranean, Santa Elena on the coast of Africa, Asention and Caden in the Red Sea, the Malvinas (Falkland Islands) near Cape Horn, and

Beirut at the mouth of the Suez Canal. Wherever there existed a port that could shelter and supply its fleet, Britain had established its presence, regardless of the question of legitimacy or the right to possession.

The *avant-garde* for British naval and commercial domination had already been established. Its military force influenced the local governments, but did not have the function, as in past colonial experiences, of directly enforcing the local laws. Britain had learned that there was no need to exercise direct authority over the social and political affairs of the peripheral countries. Its ministers and representatives, supported by the overwhelming military and commercial power of their home country, were adept at influencing local laws and governmental programs.

Sarmiento outlines the chain of circumstances that had come to typify public life in many of the poorer nations of the world:[5] The corrupt official, lacking local support and moral force, enters the office of the European consul seeking financial aid and support for his self-serving plans. The price for this assistance is his willingness to enter into a commercial agreement with the companies or individuals from the more powerful country, irrespective of the long-range interests of his own country. Sarmiento writes in his typically dramatic style: "he aquí el pacto que hacen: yo te entregaré, dice el gobierno, el principio económico, y tú ayúdame a sofocar el político. Pactada y firmada esta convención, fácil es decir las consecuencias dañinas que fluyen contra la América y la organización de sus gobiernos" (XIII, 307-8).

Sarmiento claimed that British support for America's worst governments contradicted the former's claim of practicing "universal philanthropy" in its affairs with the peoples of the world. British policy in foreign lands did not follow in practice the "universal values" related to civilization which were so assiduously defended at home, for example the freedom of the press, public education, constitutional government, and *habeas corpus*. On the contrary, British policies pursued what Sarmiento calls an "invasión universal" (XIII, 314). He sarcastically suggests that British "philanthropy," as practiced throughout South America, had the Machiavellian objective of promoting selfish material interests. In some lands, he cynically suggests, it is "El mismo sentimiento de filantropía que hace a la Inglaterra perseguir la esclavatura que produce el azúcar que compite con la de sus colonias" (XIII, 316). British "philanthropy" manifested itself in some lands in the form of a pro-slavery system with an economy based on plantation production. In the case of Argentina, the British contribution was continued support for a despotic *caudillo* who had converted the country into a prison camp.

Up until this point in the essay, Sarmiento has intelligently defended two fundamental issues: first, that the new form of commercial control practiced by Great Britain made unnecessary the military and administrative domination that typified traditional colonialism; and second, that while the agents of that country pursued commercial and political advantages in the peripheral countries, they many times violated several humanitarian and republican principles that were considered almost sacred for their own people.

The section of the essay that follows adds no new ideas to the previous discussion, but is of interest, nevertheless, for what it reveals about how Sarmiento ordered his ideas and constructed his discourse. In what follows, he neither elaborates nor interprets the important themes discussed earlier–indeed the first section of the essay contains one of the first descriptions of the evolving neo-colonial world system, and it therefore anticipates the anti-imperialist thought of the twentieth century. Instead, he proposes a new hypothesis: that the British wished to nationalize Argentina, or a significant portion of it, and convert it into a traditional colony. This argument might have had a certain validity with respect to British policies in the Río de la Plata region some thirty years earlier, but for the 1840s it was hardly convincing. His logic is that British support for Rosas had the goal of undermining the national institutions, and therefore weakening any existing nationalist sentiments. He suggests that the local population and world opinion in such a case would consider necessary and even desirable the territorial usurpation by the British.

This new interpretation of British intentions in the Plata region largely contradicts the arguments presented earlier in the same essay. In addition, one could safely say that few if any of his contemporaries would have been in agreement with any of the implications of the new thesis. His contemporaries had every reason to doubt him when he suggests: Great Britain's intention of seizing Argentine territory; its military potential for doing so; its desire for substituting the new form of commercial and political control for the older form of colonial domination; the sufficiently weakened spirit of national unity among the Argentinians which would have permitted a British invasion; and the possible acceptance by the local population and world opinion for the British usurpation of the national territory.

The question arises as to why Sarmiento would offer such a doubtful and illogical conclusion to an otherwise coherent analysis.[6] One of many hypotheses for such a conclusion is that his predominantly moral interpretation of events (i.e., his emphasis on the need for society's reeducation and his belief in the relatively little importance of economic interests over collective decisions and individual motivation) clashed with what he had personally observed about Britain's preponderantly material interest in the Río de la Plata region. Indeed, the conclusion to the essay converts the discussion of neo-colonial domination (what he had called "el colonialismo moderno") into a moral dilemma: he naively argues that a corrupt British leadership violated that country's longstanding mission by orienting its policies toward the protection of commercial interests rather than the improvement of social institutions on the periphery. He suggests that the short-sighted British leadership favored economic profits in the short run over the promotion of universal civilization in the long run. Hence, the contradiction between the text body and the conclusion of this essay results from a tension in Sarmiento between two different ideological systems: his utopian dreams for Argentina's transformation clashed with a more realistic assessment of the possibilities for such change. Like the volcanic movement along a geological faultline, there occurred a displacement in the logic of his discourse. This tension would be neutralized within a few years, but only after he resigned himself to the subservient role that his country was to play within the world system dominated by Great Britain, and only after he definitively discarded his idea of neocolonial domination in favor of a more optimistic vision for Argentina's future.

The topic of British influence over Argentina's government and commerce, and by extension, the latter country's future socio-economic development, is related to another issue of primary importance: the regional rivalry between the Province of Buenos Aires and the rest of the country. In these same essays of 1841 and 1842, Sarmiento accurately observes that the Buenos Aires oligarchy exploited the interior provinces by reason of its control over the customhouses through which the great majority of the country's exports and imports had to pass on their route to and from the European centers of commerce. Sarmiento argues that this, in addition to Buenos Aires' control over the national customhouses, had the effect of retarding the growth of several interior cities. The excise taxes paid on all goods destined to or proceeding from the provinces significantly reduced commercial opportunities there. The provinces, as a result, could hardly hope to retain their more energetic and enterprising citizens; they could hardly hope to attract an industrious immigrant population. The overall result was economic stagnation. Rosas' greatest crime, in Sarmiento's eyes, was his resistance to the country's eventual and inevitable progress. Rosas obstructed the country's possible emergence from the quagmire of underdevelopment.

Sarmiento's ideas about the necessity for free trade along Argentina's interior rivers as a means of promoting economic prosperity in the provinces remained largely unchanged throughout his long decade of exile in Chile. However, he was to alter significantly his perspective on the role of Buenos Aires in those affairs. In the essays of 1841 and 1842, the geo-political focus predominated: he denounced the selfish and shortsighted interest of the Buenos Aires oligarchy in perpetuating its control over the nation's customhouses and its prohibition of direct commerce along the country's rivers.[7] This analysis, which highlighted the various levels of control and dependence in an international economy, anticipated an important tendency in contemporary thought about developmental economics.[8] In these early essays Sarmiento accurately perceived the intermediary role of the Buenos Aires oligarchy in organizing the country's productive capacity around its own commercial ties to Europe.

The 1841 to 1842 essays reveal a side to Sarmiento's thought which has received little attention to date.[9] They constitute a very brief but lucid chapter which has scant relationship to the rest of his writing production. Open to conjecture is why he soon rejected this interpretation of Argentine geo-political dependence. Previous chapters have dealt indirectly with the importance of European society and ideas in his overall vision of civilization and some of the factors guiding him in writing his sociological and historical analyses subsequent to 1845. The following section considers his employment of the propagandistic opposition between Euorpean or Europeanized civilization and native barbarism in the context of the Europe-South America opposition.

The Europeanization of South America

In the decade after writing these early articles, Sarmiento's ideas changed dramatically with regard to the general impact of the policies and actions of the European imperial powers on the Río de la Plata region. Whereas before he expressed his criticism of England's self-serving military and commercial goals for the region, he later arrived at the position, which would prevail in its general form throughout the rest of his life, that Europe's mission overwhelmingly favored the objectives which he himself held for his country and his region. This change of perspectives in his writing was undoubtedly related to, among other factors, his acquaintance with new and prestigious writings which defended free trade. Also important was the rapidly changing scene of international economic and political tensions in the region.

An avid reader in his youth, Sarmiento had readily absorbed the ideas regarding the benefits of uninhibited commercial exchange which predominated in European intellectual, commercial, and political circles. When he arrived in Chile in late 1840, he was already acquainted with the general enlightenment conception of free enterprise and economic liberty, in addition to Saint-Simon's ideas on economic progress. These influences can be detected in the article of 1842 in which he associates Montevideo's significant progress in recent years with a number of factors, primary among which was the city's free movement of people and commerce. He contrasts Montevideo's relative prosperity and open political environment to the economically deprived and repressive political and cultural environment of Buenos Aires under Rosas (VI, 37-46). Opinions of this nature became further fortified in his mind a few years later while traveling in Europe, when he read of the ideas of Richard Cobden (with whom he later had the occasion to converse extensively) and Robert Peel. Both were renowned British economists and politicians who exercised considerable influence not only in European commercial circles, but also in the government of their country. Sarmiento quickly became a convert to the ideas advocated by these two regarding the overall benefits of absolute free trade and the harm accomplished by protectionism of any kind. In an article of 1851 he quotes with authority an impressive array of economic statistics which demonstrated the undisputed success of the British experience with free trade, an experience which he offers as a worthy precedent for the countries of South America (VI, 383-94).

Beginning around 1845, Sarmiento's theoretical, and later statistical, arguments in favor of British and French assistance for developing the social and economic potentialities of the Plata region were related to those countries' growing opposition to the Rosas government. Their continued demand for the right to free navigation along the country's interior rivers became by late 1845 a major cause for their declaration of war and their joint naval blockade of Buenos Aires shortly thereafter. British opinion in the Plata region, however, was sharply divided on the issue. With few exceptions, the British commercial interests centered in and around Buenos Aires had prospered under the policies of the Rosas government. Furthermore, British citizens residing in Buenos Aires enjoyed a long-standing relationship of "reciprocal predilection" with the local government.[10] But the owners of other British enterprises centered in Montevideo, who enjoyed strong links with Brazilian interests, believed that open access to the internal cities of the region would provide a potentially lucrative trade and would therefore help them to undercut their rivals who already controlled the commercial outlets in and around Buenos Aires. These Montevideo-based interests succeeded in promoting their view upon the British Foreign Ministry, and therefore provoked the intervention of 1846. British historian Ferns points to the fact that the firms whose ships did succeed in reaching some of the interior cities after the pitched battle at the Vuelta del Obligado incurred financial losses. He is probably correct in his assessment that the previous restrictions placed upon such trade had little affected the commercial opportunities of Great Britain and had not seriously benefited or injured any interest in Argentina.[11] However, he is undoubtedly wrong in his implication that future commerce along the internal rivers of the affected regions would not produce significant financial benefits to whatever firms undertaking such ventures.[12]

Sarmiento, living in Chile, was influenced in his interpretation of these events by writings which defended the position of the British faction centered in Montevideo, which reinforced his long-standing respect for the French government's fairly consistent opposition to Rosas. In *Facundo,* he demonstrates his support for the British Foreign Ministry's growing hostility to Rosas, a position which new political forces in London would soon discredit and overturn. He largely ignored the other faction of British interests centered in Buenos Aires which remained faithful to Rosas during the entire conflict and severely criticized their own government's heavy-handed and ill-conceived military actions against the dictator. Similarly, Sarmiento's total opposition to Rosas impeded him from appreciating what other observers admired as the latter's firm resistance to impingements upon national sovereignty. Somewhat dogmatically, Sarmiento and several other young intellectuals (in addition to the exiled leadership of the old Unitarian Party) more and more came to equate progress with free trade and material advancement. England and France, advocating the elimination of tariffs and trade restrictions, became allies for the Argentine exiles in this conflict. Sarmiento's denunciations therefore resembled the complaints of other Argentine exiles and concerned European voices when he interpreted European intervention as civilization's response to Rosas' barbarian menace.[13] In their steady stream of pamphlets and articles they expressed the common protest that the dictator stood in the path of the continent's eventual and, to their way of thinking necessary, transformation according to liberal criteria.

After the fall of Rosas in 1852, Sarmiento's writings in which he contrasted the social and cultural worlds of Europe and South America became more strident for at least two reasons. First was the growing realization that the utopian liberal values he had previously defended would hardly count in Urquiza's plans for reorganizing the country. He realized that Urquiza, with authoritarian leadership style, fidelity to the symbols of Rosism and Federalism, and ties to landed cattle interests, promised a continuation rather than an opposition to many aspects of the recently defeated regime. Second, and perhaps even more important, was the great disappointment Sarmiento experienced upon observing firsthand the type of society flourishing in Entre Ríos which Urquiza apparently offered as a model for Argentina's future civilization. There was a province similar to the other provinces dominated by a *caudillo* government; but instead of being enclosed in an archaic economy, it sought the benefits of world commerce. Barbarism, he observed, survived and prospered under the protection of civilization.[14] Consequently, he came to the realization that Urquiza, the richest landowner and undisputed political boss of Entre Ríos, was the last person who would seek an end to *caudillo* rule in the interior.

His civilization-barbarism scheme in crisis, Sarmiento defended it all the more insistently. Urquiza became his new representative of barbarism, and Sarmiento now equated the cause of civilization with that of the port city.[15] Decades before–according to his interpretation–Buenos Aires had enjoyed a constitutional government and a free press. The rude *estanciero* succeeded in imposing his control over the city and the region and then extended his domination over the provinces. Now, with Rosas defeated and liberty within reach, Sarmiento's admonition was to go "Todo con Buenos Aires, nada con los caudillos provinciales, que no traen sino violencia y ruina, porque son incapaces de comprender la justicia, los intereses económicos y la libertad" (XV, 57). In his passion, he based his arguments almost entirely on issues of political freedom and cultural tradition. He strongly criticized the authoritarian leaders of the provinces, who almost to the man remained in power throughout the transition in national leadership from Rosas to Urquiza. However, the Province of Buenos Aires had returned to its pre-Rosas practice of democratic parliamentary leadership; the cattle oligarchy of that province, now supported by the repatriated liberals, continued to promote economical ties with Europe. Sarmiento now repeated what he had stated in *Facundo,* that Buenos Aires would reassume its leadership role in the modernization of the country. His opinion was that the national leadership which was centered in Buenos Aires must take the necessary measures, including forceful action if warranted, in order to rid the provinces of their *caudillo* legacy.

Sarmiento's attention to the political issues of the post-Rosas period largely outweighed, and perhaps obscured to him, other important factors which were related to the economic reorganization of the country (in spite of his words to the contrary). His support for a centralized national authority under Buenos Aires leadership merely confirmed what Juan Manuel de Rosas, over a period of two decades, had established in fact. In his previous studies of the national reality, which were almost always characterized by a rather light treatment of economic factors, he had largely ignored the close links between the latifundium's economic hegemony and Rosas' political control.[16] Similarly, after writing the series of essays of 1841 to 1842 in which he criticized Britain's intervention in the Río de la Plata, he would scarcely again mention the subject of European political and economic interests and their role in domestic politics. Indeed, Rosas' long tenure in power and his extensive influence throughout the country (to say nothing about his support in European capitals), was undoubtedly due, in large measure, to the fact that his government's program corresponded almost totally to the interests of the estancieros, who, as a social class exercised hegemony over the region.[17] The removal of Rosas from Argentina little altered, if at all, the composition of economic interests of the region and the dominant position of those interests over the rest of the country. Sarmiento surely overestimated the power of the previously exiled intelligentsia to assert its control over the cattle and salted-meat interests of the region. In accordance with his largely moral and idealist theories of development, he believed that the region's commercial bourgeosie would extend its domination over the country and bring an end to Argentina's latifundium order.

During this period he seems to have mistaken the symbols of civilization for real indications of progress. The upper class in San Juan might have seemed to him to have been the proponents of a pre-bourgeois transformation of the region. However, he was mistaken in his association of the Buenos Aires Province's "clase culta" with the "clase propietaria y moral" which wore the "traje del mundo civilizado" (XV, 166). His idea of civilization came to be equated with culturalist values, social order, and civil authority. His contradiction was that he never ceased campaigning for the utopian liberal program for Argentina's transformation which typified his thought in an earlier period (political democracy, education for raising the cultural level of the masses, land distribution in order to promote the growth of a middle class engaged in agriculture). But given the value he placed on social stability, which was tantamount to his support in fact for the Buenos Aires oligarchy's privileged position in the country, and given his silence or ignorance regarding the play of economic interests in the region, that continuing campaign was little more than nominal and symbolic.

What stands out in his writings after 1845 is the growing consciousness of the need for internationalism and of the negative achievements gained through local sentiments or petty nationalism. In *Facundo* Sarmiento consistently denigrates what he calls Rosas' *americanismo,* a word which he frequently italicized on account of its association with the most despicable aspects of rural barbarianism and authoritarian government (VII, 216, 221, 222). He boasts of the support given by himself and other young opponents of the dictator for the French blockade of Buenos Aires in 1838. He admits, but does not explain, that as bellicose as that situation was, the French presence did have positive results for Argentine society (VII, 216). He explains that French support for the exiles' cause had the principle objective of saving "la civilización europea, sus instituciones, hábitos e ideas en las orillas del Plata" (VII, 221). He takes pride in admitting that the "alianza íntima entre los enemigos de Rosas y los poderes civilizados en Europa, nos perteneció toda entera a nosotros" (VII, 221).

In the essays of 1841 and 1842, he vociferously protested British imperial designs on Argentina. In *Facundo* he treats the subject again, but this time without the tone of insult and injury. Representative of his newly evolving perspective is the suggestion that the issue of foreign influence in local government would be of little importance if Great Britain were populating with its sons and daughters the shores of Argentina's mighty rivers as it had done with the Mississippi (VII, 225). If Britain wanted consumers for its own products, then why should a local government stand in its way? Sarmiento set little store by the Hispanic people's potential to develop commercial and industrial enterprises. On this account, he believed that the colonial pattern of trade, that is, the exchange of Europe's manufactured artifacts for America's primary materials, was at that time a most favorable arrangement for his own country. His compatriots would have to tolerate the negative aspects of that servile relationship while they slowly acquired the technological knowledge and commercial skills necessary for development. The major problem in all this, according to Sarmiento, was motivating his countrymen to accept the challenge of self-improvement.[18] In the following years these two themes would become a litany in Sarmiento's writing: the mutual benefits gained by developed and underdeveloped regions alike when they engaged in trade,[19] and Latin America's necessary apprenticeship in the Europe-dominated world capitalist economy as a means of developing its own financial and industrial potential.

In *Viajes,* Sarmiento defends even more strongly Europe's rights when it came to questions of developing the industry and commerce of regions still unaffected by progress. Writing about his visit to North Africa at the end of 1846, he places a greater value on economic exchange than nationalist pride. Perceivable also are his racist and ethnocentric biases:

> ¡Oh, no! Dejemos a un lado todas esas mezquindades de nación a nación, y pidamos a Dios que afiance la dominación europea en esta tierra de bandidos devotos. Que la Francia les aplique a ellos la máxima musulmana. La tierra pertenece al que mejor sabe fecundarla. ¿Por qué ha de haber prescripción en favor de la barbarie, y la civilización o ha de poder en todo tiempo reclamar las hermosas

comarcas segregadas algunos siglos antes, por el derecho del sable, de la escasa porción culta de la tierra? . . . [A]mo demasiado la civilización para no desear desde ahora el triunfo definitivo en Africa de los pueblos civilizados (V, 208-9).

Like his French liberal mentors, he believed that only society's elite–that is, its intellectuals, property owners, and directors of commercial activities–could provide the standard for advancement. Ethnic or racial factors carried relatively little weight when it came to matters related to commerce and social organization. In his eyes the central role of Europeans in North African society justified whatever financial benefit they might derive, for upon their shoulders rested the burden, but also the promise, of civilization.

It comes as no surprise to learn that the same prejudices characterized his understanding of the social and political conflicts of Argentina. In 1852, he and Alberdi entered into their famous polemic. In *Cartas quillotanas* Alberdi minimized the value of Sarmiento's treatment of the struggle between Argentine cities and countryside on account of its highly subjective focus. Sarmiento, counterattacking in *Las ciento y una,* exasperated the passions of the time by declaring that the population of Corrientes and Entre Ríos, on account of their barbarian heritage surviving from the days of Ramírez and Artigas, were the sworn enemies of Buenos Aires (XV, 59). Furthermore, since Urquiza was little more than an unreformable *caudillo* himself, that leader's movement to establish a constitutional government in the country was doomed to fail. "Para [Urquiza] no había pueblos, sino gobernadores de provincia, dueños de ellas como él lo es ahora de Entre Ríos. La Constitución debía, pues, ser un arreglo entre propietarios feudales" (XV, 60). For Sarmiento, the lines of national conflict remained largely the same as they had been during the period of Rosas, but with one major difference. Still, the defenders of an Argentina organized according to liberal principles were pitted against the defenders of local autonomy and cattle latifundia. It was still the civilization of the *frac* against the barbarism of the *chiripá.* Now, however, the defenders of what would come to be known as dependent liberalism, who resided primarily in the Province of Buenos Aires, battled against the *caudillos,* who maintained their economic, social, and political power throughout the interior provinces.

In the eleven years between 1841, when he wrote the essays critical of European influence in Argentina, and 1852, when he authored *Las ciento y una,* his opinions had altered dramatically. The northern European nations in the earlier essays had been depicted in the role of undermining Argentina's civil institutions and supporting its cattle-export economy. In his later essays, however, the northern European countries constituted the principal civilizing influence which combated the backwardness of the region. His opinion on the role of Buenos Aires in the regional political economy also changed. In the essays of 1841 and 1842, he had argued that the power elite of that province ruthlessly imposed its commercial monopoly and political hegemony over the other provinces. Then, in

Facundo, this opposition between port city and the interior was little more than a shadow thesis.[20] And in 1852 Sarmiento angrily labeled as "ridícula patraña" (XV, 349) the idea that Buenos Aires wished to reestablish the trade monopoly which Spain had previously exercised over the Río de la Plata region. In effect, he came to reverse completely his position on this and other issues.

What is even more important for the present investigation, however, is his change in historiographical methodology, which was anticipated by the *non sequitur* conclusion to the 1841 and 1842 essay analyzed above: his early analysis based on the economic and social interests of the different parties to Argentina's conflict became transformed, at least by the writing of *Facundo,* into an eclectic system in which there predominated the Manichaean opposition between the idealist forces of civilization and the deterministic power of American barbarism. In the earlier period, his writing had the goal of freeing the indigenous forces of his country from Europe's constricting bondage in order to continue unobstructed in their struggle to modernize. In the latter period, however, his civilization-barbarism interpretation for Argentina's turmoil would become a justification for Argentina's insertion into the British-dominated world economic system.

In his writings of this latter period one finds the first articulation of several ideas which are considered today to be essential aspects of Sarmiento's mature thought. First, there was his conviction that Argentina's trade alliances with the European powers provided the fastest and perhaps the only possible avenue for his nation's progress. So convinced was he of the relative inferiority of the Spanish-American tradition that he believed his own land could only progress under the guiding wing of Northern Europe. He welcomed his nation's dependency and believed that European intervention in economics, politics, and culture could only benefit Argentina's march toward progress:

> Pertenezco al corto número de habitantes de la América de Sur que no abrigan prevención ninguna contra la influencia europea en esta parte del mundo; como publicista he sostenido de diez años a esta parte que estaba en nuestro interés abrir a la Inglaterra y a todas las naciones europeas la navegación de nuestros ríos para que desenvolviesen el comercio, la riqueza, creasen ciudades, y estimulasen la producción; como escritor, he defendido constantemente los intereses ingleses y europeos en América, fingiendo creer que siempre en las cuestiones que entre Europa y América se suscitan, la razón debe de estar de parte de los europeos (VI, 279).

A corollary to his acceptance of dependency was a disregard for any analysis that took as its point of departure the different social classes and their respective interests in a socio-economic struggle. This was due, in large part, to his confidence in the eventual conciliation of individual, class, and collective interests. This meant that he did not regard as fundamental the clashes between different social, economic, or cultural orientations, such as those represented by gauchos and urbanites, masses and intelligentsia, and the populations of the interior and Buenos Aires. He was convinced that the Europeanized institutions of the urbanites, intellectuals, and the population of Buenos Aires were destined to prevail for all social groups and throughout the entire country. His elitist orientation, in combination with the emphasis he continued to place on the moral reeducation of society, led him to believe in the central role of the country's intellectual leaders for guiding the population as a whole in the creation of a more harmonious social order.

Conversely, Sarmiento explained the apparent exceptions to economic, political, and social harmony largely in moralist terms. For him, England's support for Rosas was due to the greed of a few individuals; France's local failures were on account of Minister Guizot's ignorance about the Río de la Plata region. Similarly, Sarmiento contradicted the Federalist position in his affirmation that Europe's economic gain would benefit America, and that Buenos Aires' regional progress corresponded to the relative advancement of the interior. He gave credibility to the suggestion that the growing prosperity of the agrarian and commercial bourgeoisies in the Buenos Aires region, within decades, would become an impediment to, rather than the vehicle for, the continuing development of the country as a whole. Only toward the end of his life would he come to doubt most of these assumptions which formed the bedrock of his mature social thought, and which he articulated initially in the latter years of the Rosas regime.

One last issue relevant to the relationship between Argentina and Europe was the little importance he granted to economic factors in a group's or a government's formulation of policy, or for that matter in the motivation of individuals. His comments of 1844 with regard to the French government's objectives in the blockade of 1835 to 1838 are revealing. Prime Minister Guizot, he maintains, "ha apurado, hasta en sus últimas consecuencias, un sistema de política que, afectando una desinteresada neutralidad, no ha sido más que nulo, ciego, y contrario a los intereses de la Francia, a su influencia como nación y a sus ventajas comerciales" (VI, 110). These apparently critical words are transformed into praise when he explains what the motivations of Guizot and the French government really were:

> Mr. Guizot, decimos, ha estado contrariando los intereses franceses en el Río de la Plata, malogrando simpatías que habrían sido la base de una influencia francesa superior allí a toda otra, porque se fundaban más en la inteligencia y en los intereses de la civilización, que en los puramente materiales, que no ha sabido consultar siquiera (VI, 110).

In this praise for Guizot's moral –but not pragmatic–government, he reveals the belief that the altruistic motivations of what he calls elsewhere the "grandes potencias del mundo cristiano" (VI, 184) necessarily took precedent over material and commercial interests. According to his world view, moral and economic issues were not in dispute. On the contrary, altruistic aims, rather than clashing with more pragmatic concerns, pointed toward society's long-range benefit. For this reason, actions inspired by good intentions would affect only in a marginal manner the day-to-day transactions of commercial enterprises. For him, the truth of civilization allowed for no possible contradiction. In the utopia that he envisioned, society's distinct interests would inevitably be redirected in a harmonious fashion toward support for collective goals.

The following section builds upon the Europe-South America opposition, as described above, in analyzing some of the theoretical underpinnings for the civilization-barbarism formula in Sarmiento's historical thought, and in situating this latter formula within the context of the European thought of his time.

The Philosophy of History

Sarmiento's belief in the need for his continent to follow the course of development already established by the countries of Western Europe and the United States became transformed into an issue of historiographical study. The historicist school, with roots in the Enlightenment, and now reinforced by the more scientific focus of the "socialist," or pre-positivistic school, provided him with a scheme for understanding the different stages through which his or any society must pass in its development toward civilization. Writing in 1843, he expresses the necessity of studying his own society on the basis of immutable laws as a preparation for undertaking actions on behalf of its transformation (VI, 101). In his writings of that year, one can already detect the methodological bias which would predominate in his later works: the belief in the superiority of Northern European and North American cultures and his own society's relative backwardness. This view would, by 1845, become summarized in the formula of civilization versus barbarism, where the former represented the foreign, principally European, influences which were needed to transform the continent, and the latter represented the legacy of Hispanic influences, combined with America's inferior racial stock and untamed wilderness.

In the early 1840's Sarmiento was a full party to the enthusiastic discussions in Santiago regarding precisely these historiographical issues. The French advocates of a "philosophy of history" turned away from empiricism and the "impartiality" of enlightenment historical writing, and in doing so rejected the idea of Fenelon that "The good historian belongs to no time period and to no history."[21] The new historical tradition, which was in the tradition of metaphysical idealism, attempted to define the "soul" or "spirit of facts" through the analysis of contemporary culture and the events of the past. In France, Chateaubriand's and Cousin's examples of "philosophical history" were highly regarded as offering the standard for this new type of analysis. Guizot, in addition, had his fervent admirers on account of his essentially moralist and ideological notion of the historical fact.[22]

It did not escape the young intellectuals in Santiago that this new current of historiographical thought in France was closely linked with the promotion of liberal ideas, and consequently, with the rise of the bourgeoisie in challenge to the defenders of the *ancien régime*. They embraced the idea of the French theorists that the march toward *liberty* was the basic criterion upon which all the events of the past were to be judged. Integral to the "philosophical" historian's practice of comparing a particular society against the implicit standards offered by liberal Northern Europe, was the pragmatic goal of orienting their society in the future.[23] Sarmiento and others rapidly fell under the spell of this promise. In their own writing, they cast aside whatever pretense to ideological neutrality and transformed their liberal ideas into the criteria for selecting relevant facts and reaching their conclusions. They attempted to imitate the French historicists, whose writings had provided the liberal movement with an effective platform for political action.

The discussions in Santiago over historiography have been well documented, not only by the participants, but also by critics who have correctly viewed them as constituting an important chapter in the intellectual history of a continent. Two of the protagonists of the debate were José Victorino Lastarria, who would become Sarmiento's intimate friend and perhaps the most outstanding literary historian of his generation, and Andrés Bello, the most esteemed intellectual of the continent. In his 1844 response to Lastarria's investigation over the influence of the Spanish colonial system in Chile,[24] Bello argued that the defense of liberty was the basic principle of his intellectual endeavors, but he attacked what was merely "embriaguez licenciosa en las orjías de la imajinación" –as Lastarria quoted him.[25] In regard to historical doctrine, Bello rejected out of hand the currently fashionable idea of a philosophy of history and the practice of writing philosophically the particular history of a period or of a designated people. Lastarria, writing much later in his *Recuerdos literarios,* states:

> El Señor Bello dudaba de esta posibilidad, sosteniéndonos que lo que se podía hacer era filosofar o moralizar sobre los acontecimientos i los hombres, al escribir la historia narrativa de un pueblo; pues, según su juicio, una cosa es la ciencia jeneral de la humanidad, que se llama filosofía de la historia, i otra es la historia de los hechos de una raza, de un pueblo, de una época, sin que aquella pueda conducirnos a la filosofía particular de ésta como nosotros le sosteníamos. El señor Bello establecía una diferencia entre la filosofía de la historia i los hechos, i creía que lo primero era hacer la crónica de los detalles, la narración de los sucesos, para deducir despues el espíritu peculiar de ellos para apreciarlos i juzgarlos, según sus circunstancias, en lo cual, hacía consistir toda filosofía, toda ciencia histórica: de modo que en su concepto había tantas filosofías o ciencias históricas como hai sucesos que se pueden juzgar.[26]

In essence, Bello correctly perceived the ideological bias at the heart of the historicist enterprise and understood how that movement sacrificed the pursuit of truth for objectives related to political expediency.

This exchange of opinions over Lastarria's essay is instructive as an entrance into the underlying premises of the philosophical-historical practice of the young defenders of liberalism, and the weighty criticisms posed by as judicious a thinker as Andrés Bello. Bello criticized Lastarria's analysis for its largely subjective and relative focus and for being "divorciado de los hechos" (in the words of Lastarria). Bello discounted the benefits of such an ideologically oriented writing practice, in spite of Lastarria's claim that it could serve humanity's general advancement according to liberal principles. Bello did not criticize the the aims and objectives of such writing, but rather its methodological assumptions. Whereas he defended the inherent value of a cultural experience in relation to its own circumstances of geography, history, and industry,[27] the young advocates of liberalism such as Lastarria and Sarmiento embraced a more monolithic conception of progress. For them, there was in essence one standard against which all societies were to be evaluated: that offered by England and France. It was in those countries, they argued, that mankind had most developed his capacities in industry, social organization, and culture. Northern Europe provided the example for all other societies in their inevitable and "providential" march toward greater liberty and progress.[28]

Because Lastarria and Sarmiento were insensitive for the most part to the ethno- and geo-centric nature of their ideas on progress, they rejected Bello's observation that they consistently confused assumptions and facts in their studies. It has been pointed out earlier, for example, that Sarmiento modestly perceived his *Facundo* as a hurried, but nevertheless solid, sociological and historical portrait of the Argentine plains; he believed that the work offered in schematic form a portrait of his own continent which was similar to what the French aristocrat Tocqueville had written on North America. Scientific terminology, as applied to historiography, appears quite frequently in this work and in his other writings of this period. He could make mistakes with regard to details, but he considered his methodology of analysis to be above ideological reproach. He rejected criticisms that artistic sensitivity and social or ethnic biases flavored his discourse, and instead reasserted the supposed scientific principles which he followed.[29]

The fervent support of Sarmiento and Lastarria for a largely ethnocentric philosophy of history has two principal explanations.[30] First, there is the "culturalist" perspective predominating in the thought of the two. There is little doubt that Sarmiento's early childhood experiences as part of San Juan's cultured and propertied class came to shape his perceptions on political and social issues. His enlightenment orientation, which was fueled by his adhesion to the principles of the May Revolution and his admiration for the program of Bernardino Rivadavia, came together with the values that predominated in that setting: the premium placed on education and book knowledge, and his belief in the transformational power of the idea in society. The second cause is very much related: the conviction that progress and sociability would be achieved only under the guidance of that social class which most fully embraced the culturalist ideal and most successfully transformed idea into social fact. That class, which we identify with current terminology on the basis of its social function, was the bourgeoisie, although it remained unnamed in his writings. The bourgeoisie, still embrionic and preliminary in form, sought more than its autonomy or self-enrichment; it also strived to absorb all social groups into its fold. In short, the bourgeoisie offered all members of society a share in the benefits of progress. Through the governance of that class, Sarmiento and Lastarria envisioned the universalization of American society, that is, the insertion of their countries into the world community led by White Northern Europe. They embraced the scientific principle as the vehicle through which progress was to be achieved. If applied uniformly, it offered to all an equal participation in the nascent capitalist order. Sarmiento, in this period of his career, perceived the utopian liberal program of social organization not as a means for excluding the majority and favoring the few, but rather as a program for extending society's benefits to everyone. He believed it was the responsibility of the bourgeoisie, that class which largely coincided with the cultured elite and which embraced a similar social doctrine, to guide the whole society into this promised era.

The belief that European (or North American) society and culture had attained a higher degree of civilization than any other in the history of mankind, was to lead Sarmiento and Lastarria into a serious confusion regarding their own mission in South America. In France, ideas related to historicism and philosophical history had become widely accepted after the Revolution of 1789 and were fulfilling, in general, the need of promoting and defending the bourgeoisie as the vanguard of the historical process. It was one thing for the young South American intellectuals to admire the liberal program of reforms that had resulted from that revolution, but they were mistaken to believe that they could situate their own countries within that same conception of history, without there first having occurred a similar unfolding of economic, social, and cultural institutions.[31] Bello clearly perceived the mistaken premises of the young intellectuals in his midst:

> Una máquina—dice—puede trasladarse de Europa a Chile y producir los mismos efectos que en Europa. Pero la filosofía de la historia de Francia, por ejemplo, la explicación de las manifestaciones individuales del pueblo francés en las varias épocas de su historia, carece de sentido aplicada a las individualidades sucesivas de la existencia del pueblo chileno . . . . Abranse las obras célebres dictadas por la filosofía de la historia. ¿Nos dan ella la filosofía de la historia de la humanidad? [sic] La nación Chilena no es la humanidad en abstracto, es la humanidad bajo ciertas formas especiales . . . .[32]

Bello critized the young intellectuals' seduction by European thought. Perhaps he foresaw how this same tendency in subsequent decades would encourage others to defer to the interests of the world-economy's core in the economic, social, and cultural organization of their own societies.

The Genesis of a Mystifying Historical Antithesis

The sad irony of Sarmiento's career is that in spite of his early attempt to erase Argentina's feudal colonial heritage and to modernize the country's institutions according to liberal principles, he became an unwitting accomplice in the consolidation of a neo-colonial class structure and the integration of his country into the commercial empires of Northern Europe. His historical writing provides a glimpse into how he, as an individual, interpreted the transition in the Argentine bourgeoisie's social role, that is, the transition in their advocacy from utopian liberal principles to economic and cultural dependency. In fact, Sarmiento is as responsible as any other writer of his generation for articulating the theoretical path for that transition and for providing a historically based justification for the dependent-liberal order which was emerging.

The civilization versus barbarism opposition, as he came to apply it at will, and more often than not out of reasons of political expediency, provides a link between Sarmiento's discourse and the historical writing which emanated from the capitals of Europe's nineteenth century empires. Many paragraphs have been written about the probable influences on Sarmiento of this civilization-barbarism antithesis, but it is rarely mentioned that the same opposition characterizes the great majority of historical works written by Europeans during the eighteenth and nineteenth centuries. It was, in essence, a widely accepted idea of the period. Fernández Retamar calls attention to the factors accounting for the resurgence and popularization in Sarmiento's time of this time honored formula among the ideologues of the economically prosperous and territorially expansive countries of Western Europe:

> Habiendo llegado a los euroccidentales el turno de considerarse eje de la historia, [se nombraron a sí mismos civilizados], cedieron entonces graciosamente el término 'bárbaros,' como en su momento hicieron los romanos, a otras comunidades humanas: entre ellas, de manera muy destacada, a los habitantes de América con quienes se pondrían en contacto gracias a los paleoccidentales ibéricos. ... No es extraño que el vocablo surja entonces, cuando la burguesía eurooccidental, en pleno auge racionalista, comienza a trazar un balance de su saber, que va de las manos de los enciclopedistas franceses a las de hombres como los Humboldt y Hegel.[33]

Retamar makes explicit the link between Western Europe's newly acquired metropolitan status with regard to its economic and political dominance, and the new appeal of this ideological formula among its population.

Civilization versus barbarism is one of several schemes which, over the last few centuries, has served as an organizing principle in European scientific and social-scientific thought. This scheme, similar to the conception of the "Great Chain of Being" and historicism, is intimately related to the Western European attitude of superiority toward other people and different cultural experiences.[34] These three schemes present a view of the world in which the white European man stands at the top of the hierarchy of beings and at the front of the historical process. Consequently, when Sarmiento studied South America according to the implicit criteria of a "philosophy of history," he viewed his own people disfavorably and ignored the positive aspects of their experience. They could not qualify as civilized, since this term was reserved for the developed capitalist countries of Europe. He even went so far as to accept aspects of the predominant European world view, for instance ethnocentricism and racism, and the derivative contempt for non-Occidental peoples—which in this case were his own. Over the last few centuries, the historians' attempts at justifying European conquests and exploitation are characterized by racist and ethnocentric orientations; this continues to be true even today. However, what is special is the more or less voluntary collaboration of Sarmiento and other thinkers from the periphery who were addicted to such ideas.[35]

Beginning in the late 1830s, Sarmiento had avidly read the texts available to him which treated historiographical issues. What impresses the contemporary critic who surveys his ideological influences is the prevalence in those works of schemes similar to his own civilization versus barbarism formula. This is true even for the writings of those European thinkers who continue to enjoy widespread fame. Hegel and Humboldt are two of the most prestigious writers of their respective centuries who prepared the intellectual terrain for the acceptance of this dichotomy in even the highest circles of Europe's intellectual life. Hegel, for example, posited the existence of a dialectic between spirit and matter which underlay all historical events. His idea of America as a continent dominated by nature which awaited a transformation by the forces of reason, could very well have suggested to more pragmatically oriented readers an historical opposition between a materialistic and barbaric America and the civilized European spirit.[36] Humboldt, in his turn, popularized the image among Europeans of a South American continent burdened by the preponderous force of nature.

Guizot, whom Sarmiento praised as "el historiador de la *Civilización europea*" (VII, 9), followed Hegel in combining an idea of universal historical development to an opposition between "civilized" and "barbaric" cultures. This antithesis, so evident in even his most highly regarded works, could very well have influenced Sarmiento's perspective of South American society.[37] Indeed, the high degree of similarity between the Frenchman's analysis of European history and Sarmiento's treatment of Argentina—as pointed out earlier[38] —suggests a meeting of the minds on this antithetical perspective for analyzing culture and history.

The polarization of historical categories is not limited to the work of philosophers and historians, for it is also evident in the writings of many European writers who had a personal contact with new world society. The travel accounts of Arsenio Isabelle and Francis B. Head are examples of texts, widely read throughout Europe, which treated Southern South America from the same general perspective.[39] Similarly, articles written by other European visitors to the Plata and published in prestigious journals such as the *Revue de Deux Mondes* also emphasized a dichotomy between "the civilized governments" of Europe and the "American" practices of the Rosas government which "seemed to be falling back into barbarism . . . ."[40] Sarmiento was probably familiar with all of these works.

Sarmiento's civilization-barbarism scheme enjoys contextuality with the historical discourse of European writers not only because of a supposed normative basis for describing society, but also on account of the implicit, and sometimes quite explicit, judgment of the relative superiority of the values and institutions of the white European bourgeois tradition. Limiting the discussion to only those historians mentioned by Sarmiento for having influenced his own ideas, a first grouping is constituted by the apostles of historicism: Condorcet, Turgot, Saint-Simon, Fourier, and Guizot. Common to the discourse of all of these is the linear quality according to which they perceived historical development. Progress was seen to have a connotation of increased value. They assumed that the European societies of their day were precisely those which had attained the most advanced stage possible. This Eurocentrism finds perhaps its strongest and narrowest expression in the work of Guizot, who defended France as the most advanced nation on earth because there prevailed in all aspects of individual and social life "the empire of ideas, of reasoning, of general principles, of what is called theory."[41] Sarmiento, in *Facundo,* seems to embrace Guizot's franco-centric conception of civilization, as can be seen in the numerous paragraphs devoted to French politics in the Río de la Plata and the role of the French historian who was, at that time, his nation's prime minister (VII; 9, 221-27).

A second category of neo-colonial historiography is reserved for Tocqueville's *Democracy in America,* a work with unrivaled authority among Sarmiento's generation of writers.[42] Tocqueville's biases regarding the superiority of European society and the derivative Anglo-American culture in the Republican era can be seen in his account of the destruction of the Indians of North America, which occurred "without violation of a single great principle of morality in the eyes of the world. It is impossible to destroy men with more respect for the laws of humanity."[43] In effect, Tocqueville presents this genocide as logically resulting from the Indian's confrontation with the historically superior civilization of white European descendents. This view also finds its echo in the writings of Sarmiento.[44]

Literary and historical critics with the objective of delineating ideological influences have traced the path of knowledge dissemination from liberal European theorists to the work of Sarmiento. Important here are the ideological continuities, or, in other words, the community of values and motives, which unites Sarmiento to the European historians of his time. He shared their ethnocentrism and culturalism, and did his part to mythicize those values under the trappings of scientific study. Sarmiento did create a mimetic discourse, but ironically it is not found in his descriptions of the social and historical conflicts of his time. Instead, it is to be encountered in the act of reading consumption, when the white European reader with liberal philosophical orientation finds in works like *Facundo* a complacent image of himself and his own ethnic and class values. This mimetic factor, perhaps more than any other, accounts for the fame of Sarmiento as a social thinker and the perseverance –even in our own time–of those who have employed similar dichotomous schemes for interpreting South American society.

The relevance or popularity of a given discourse for a specific group of readers depends in large measure upon the degree to which it–whether in semantic content or social function–corresponds to that group's social, political, or economic interests. In effect, Sarmiento's historical dualism must be considered as merely a segment of a centuries-old script which is constituted by many distinct texts, all of which share the same general theme. Within this larger script Sarmiento's rendering of the historical dichotomy enjoys a certain authority, as evidenced by the fact that it has been reinterpreted so many times that its newer versions have all but left behind the original points of reference (i.e., the spoken and lived Latin American reality which those texts pretend to describe). The acid test of *Facundo* as a book of foundation is the continued affirmation granted by its readers of this historical opposition.

The civilization-barbarism opposition has been used time and again to justify the dependent liberal order in Argentina. E. Bradford Burns hypothesizes an "ideology of class" linking the thought of Latin American intellectuals such as Sarmiento to the European historical tradition:

> That ideology rationalized the institutions and the elites who controlled them, a justification which helped legitimize both and contributed to their continuity. The values and goals of that ideology served the elites well as one effective means to coerce larger and larger segments of the population into accepting the institutional structures and social systems of Latin America in the past century, even though those structures and systems were more detrimental than beneficial to an overwhelming majority of the population . . . . Historians successfully shrouded national histories with a sacred mystique which has inhibited broader historical investigations and even ridiculed the posing of some fundamental historical questions which might cast doubt on the efficacy of modernization, progress, development, not to mention the national institutions themselves.[45]

Paradoxically, Sarmiento and other liberal theorists promoted a type of modernization for their continent which implied not merely the subordination of its economy and culture to European interests, but also the annihilation of much of its people. Argentina, as it was known to him, represented a series of anti-values upon whose extinction or disappearance depended his civilizing program.[46] Argentina's intelligentsia, beginning with Sarmiento's generation (with the possible *theoretical* exception of Alberdi and Echeverría) and continuing into the the present century, despised the country, even though a number of them (among which the best example is Sarmiento himself) demonstrated through their writings an uncanny comprehension and admiration for its people and customs.

Notes for Chapter 7

1. Tulio Halperín Donghi, "Una nación para el desierto argentino," in *Proyecto y construcción de una nación (Argentina 1846-1880)*, ed. Halperín Donghi (Caracas: Biblioteca Ayacucho, 1980), p. li.

2. "El aprendizaje de la civilización," *El Mercurio*, 30 Oct. 1841 (XIII, 326-29); "Colonización inglesa en el Río de la Plata," *El Mercurio*, 1 Nov., 1841, 19 23 Aug., 1842 (XIII, 305-20); "Lo que gana el extranjero con nuestra anarquía," *El Mercurio*, 11 Nov., 1841 (XIII, 321-25). The editor states at the end of the second of these essays (p. 320) that "por equivocados que resultasen estos conceptos, revelan una de las preocupaciones que asediaban a los actores en la lucha y no podían omitirse en estas páginas." "No han sido explicados tan satisfactoriamente hasta hoy los *assigments* de la diplomacia inglesa y singulares complacencias con Rosas . . . ." The editor makes another apology in reference to the third essay: "Este escrito dictado por las necesidades de la época, no necesitaría para aplicarse a nuestros inconvenientes del presente, sino sustituir el concepto en que está basado de extranjeros, gobiernos y particulares, fomentando las discordias civiles en Sud América, por este otro que Sarmiento ha desarrollado muchas veces, de la indiferencia y separación del extranjero de nuestra vida civil y política y fomentando así el desorden e inexperiencia del gobierno innatos a nuestra educación y costumbres" (p. 312).

3. John Parish and W. P. Robertson, *Letters on South America comprising Travels on the Banks of the Paraná and Río de la Plata in Three Volumes* (London: John Murray, 1843), p. 277, note the friendship between the British and the Argentinians "as if they belonged to one and the same family."

4. In 1849 Sarmiento would again have occasion to protest British foreign policy in the Río de la Plata region. Mr. Harry Southern, representing the British government, wrote in that year a letter to Rosas, which was co-signed by the agents for eighty of the most important foreign commercial enterprises in Buenos Aires, arguing that the leader's proposed withdrawl from the coming elections would be "a great public calamity" for "the most important interests of the British resident community." Quoted by José Luis Muñoz Azpiri, *Rosas frente al imperio británico: historia íntima de un triunfo argentino*, 2nd ed. expanded. (Buenos Aires: Theoría, 1974), p. 129. In January of the following year Sarmiento published in *La Crónica* a copy of the letter he had sent to Mr. Southern in which he emphasized his support for European, and especially British, presence in the Río de la Plata, and at the same time expressed his preoccupations that the British had violated their own moral and commercial interests in supporting Rosas (see VI, 276-95).

5. Allegations of this nature about British wrongdoing in Argentina are eloquently refuted by H. S. Ferns, *Britain and Argentina in the Nineteenth Century* (Oxford: Clarendon Press, 1960). He states that Argentina clearly was part of Britain's "informal empire," but with regard to exercising control over political power in Argentina, "the verdict for Britain is unquestionably 'Not Guilty'" (p. 487). He explains that British attempts at invading Argentina in 1808, and the

British-French intervention of 1846, were measures which were not only ineffective, but on the whole ill-advised. He argues that the policies leading to those counter-productive ventures violated the normal pattern of British diplomacy in the Río de la Plata region, and were subsequently "corrected" (pp. 275, 487-88).

6. The editors of the *Obras Completas* have taken the liberty of combining articles from 1 November 1841 and 19 & 23 August 1842 into one essay. There is no indication of whether Sarmiento intended the latter article(s ?) to be a continuation of the former. (Julia Ottolenghi, *Vida y obra de Sarmiento en síntesis cronológica* [Buenos Aires: Kepelusz, 1950], does not list an article of 23 August 1842 which would correspond to the information given by the *OC* editors). What is possibly at issue here is the overall logic and consistency of Sarmiento's thought with regard to this one topic within a short period of months, and not merely the internal coherence of what was originally planned and written as a single essay.

7. Sarmiento would treat again the issue of Buenos Aires' desire for economic domination in an essay written in about 1850, "Comercio de Córdoba" (XIII, 292-94). The editor indicates that this essay was first published in volume one of *Sud América*, although no date is given. In this article Sarmiento observes that Córdoba had suffered enormously on account of the restrictions requiring it to buy and sell nearly all its products via Buenos Aires: "Estos hechos mostrarán a los gobernantes de las provincias, que la cuestión que ha agitado a la República es una cuestión simplemente de comercio, de fletes, de caminos, de distancias. Buenos Aires quiere establecer el monopolio del comercio, su gobernador lo sostiene, a fuerza de violencias, atentados y crímenes, para cobrar más derechos en su aduana" (XIII, 294).

8. This three-tiered relationship between metropolis, capital city, and interior is suggestive of the ideas of Immanuel Wallerstein. See for example, "The Rise and Future Demise of the World Capitalist System: Concepts for Comparative Analysis," *Comparative Studies in Society and History*, 16, No. 4 (1974), 387-415.

9. An exception is Ezequiel Martínez Estrada, *Sarmiento* (Buenos Aires: Argos, 1956), pp. 154-58. Roberto Tamagno, *Sarmiento, los liberales y el imperialismo inglés* (Buenos Aires: A. Peña Lillo, 1963), also discusses these essays but fails to recognize their special position within the development of Sarmiento's ideas.

10. Ricardo Rojas, *El profeta de la pampa: vida de Sarmiento* (Buenos Aires: Losada, 1951), pp. 633ff. James R. Scobie, *La lucha por la consolidación de la nacionalidad argentina, 1852-1862*, trans. Gabriela de Civiny (Buenos Aires: Hachette, 1964), p. 19, states that before 1852, 45 percent of those residing in Buenos Aires were citizens of other countries, and even a greater proportion of the commercial establishments and stores were owned and operated by European interests.

11. Ferns, *Britain and Argentina in the Nineteenth Century*, p. 253.

12. As a result of Urquiza's 1852 decree opening the internal rivers to foreign navegation, Thomas Page was commissioned by the United States government between 1853 and 1856 to investigate trade possibilities along the Uruguay and Paraná Rivers. He issued a very positive assessment of such investment and

commercial possibilities in *La Plata, the Argentine Confederation, and Paraguay, Being a Narrative of the Exploration of the Tributaries of the River La Plata and Adjacent Countries During the Years 1853, 54, 55 and 56, Under the Orders of the United States Government* (New York: Harper & Brothers, 1859).

13. How the themes of *Facundo* and other writings interface with the writings of the journalistic campaign against Rosas which was waged mutually by exiled Argentine nationals and interested French and English citizens, has yet to be treated by the criticism. Such a study would have to take into consideration articles such as C. L. B., "Des Rapports de la France et de l'Europe avec l'Amérique du Sud," *Revue des Deux Mondes*, Series 4, 31, No. 15 (1838), 54-69; and Un Voyageur, "Les Deux Rives de la Plata: Montevideo, Buenos-Ayres, Rivera, Rosas," *Revue des Deux Mondes*, 50, Year 13, No. 2 (1843), 5-49. Both articles anticipate Sarmiento's condemnation of the Rosas regime and gaucho society; both utilize a similar civilization-barbarism dichotomy and project a similar Francophile historicist orientation.

14. Halperín Donghi, "Prólogo," *Campaña en el Ejército Grande Aliado de Sud América*, by Domingo F. Sarmiento (México: Fondo de Cultura Económica, 1958), p. 1.

15. Although Sarmiento promoted himself in this period as "provinciano en Buenos Aires," it must be recognized that his prescription for the country's advancement was based on the conviction of Buenos Aires' rightful domination over the internal provinces. "El hecho de que los presidentes que le sucedieron [a Mitre], como Sarmiento, Avellaneda, Roca y Juárez Celman, fueron oriundos de las provincias, no significa en forma alguna que el dominio de Buenos Aires sobre la nación peligrara," says Scobie, *La lucha por la consolidación de la nacionalidad argentina*, p. 9.

16. Juan B. Alberdi was correct in his continual criticism over decades that Sarmiento largely ignored economic factors and excluded from consideration "los intereses" of the different groups or classes. See *Facundo y su biógrafo: notas para servir a un estado con el título que precede* (Tucumán: Signo, 1968), pp. 15-16, 42-63. The entire work is a selection from Alberdi's *Escritos póstumos*, Vol. V. Misleading is Roberto Tamagno's wholesale condemnaton of Sarmiento, in *Sarmiento, los liberales y el imperialismo inglés,* who mistakes this inattention to economics for Sarmiento's support for British commercial interests at the expense of those of his countrymen.

17. John Lynch, *Argentina Dictator: Juan Manual de Rosas 1829-1852* (Oxford: Clarendon Press, 1981), pp. 45-51.

18. He painfully admits in *Facundo* that Hispanic Americans, like the Spanish, "no somos ni navegantes ni industriosos, y la Europa nos proveerá por largos siglos de sus artefactos en cambio de nuestras materias primas, y ella y nosotros ganaremos en el cambio; la Europa nos pondrá el remo en la mano y nos remolcará río arriba hasta que hayamos adquirido el gusto de la navegación" (VII, 226).

19. See also XIII, 60-61, 83-84.

20. Noé Jitrik, *Muerte y resurrección de 'Facundo',* (Buenos Aires: Centro Editor de América Latina, 1968).

21. Philippe Van Tieghem, *Petite histoire des grandes doctrines litteraires en France* (Paris: Presses Universitaires de France, 1950), p. 199.

22. *Ibid.*, pp. 199-201.

23. Bernardo Subercaseaux S., *Cultura y sociedad liberal en el siglo XIX: Lastarria: ideología y literatura* (Santiago: Editorial Aconcagua, 1981), p. 75.

24. "Investigación sobre la influencia de la conquista i del sistema colonial de los españoles en Chile: memoria presentada a la universidad en la sesión solemne de 22 de setiembre de 1844, por don José Victorino Lastarria," *Obras Completas*, Vol. III: *Opúsculos literarios i críticos* (Santiago: Imprenta Pedro G. Ramírez, 1885), pp. 71-88. Paul Verdevoye, "Don Andrés Bello y Domingo Faustino Sarmiento: una polémica y una colaboración," in *Bello y Chile: Tercer Congreso del Bicentenario*, Tomo I (Caracas: Fundación La Casa de Bello, 1981), pp. 103-24, investigates the relationship between Bello and Sarmiento. He concludes that the two, with very similar ideas, mutually respected and admired each other.

25. J[osé] V[ictorino] Lastarria, *Recuerdos literarios: datos para la historia literaria de la América española, del progreso intelectual en Chile* (Santiago: Librería de M. Servat, 1885), p. 232. Lastarria wrote this work in the 1870s, some 30 years after the events had occurred.

26. *Ibid.*, pp. 237-38.

27. Fernando Campo Harriet, "Andrés Bello y la enseñanza de la historia," *Atenea: Revista de Ciencia, Arte y Literatura*, Nos. 443-444 (1981), pp. 309-16.

28. Lastarria, *Recuerdos literarios*, pp. 240-43.

29. Inherent in this "philosophical" approach to historical research was a confusion between artistic writing and historical investigation. See Bernardo Subercaseaux S., "Filosofía de la historia, novela y sistema expresivo en Chile (1840-1850)," *Cuadernos Americanos*, 38, No. 4 (1979), 99-122. Even though Lastarria, Sarmiento, and others of the period brought their "artistic sensitivity" to the task of historical investigation, they were convinced of the objectivity of their enterprise. Thus, the result is a prose which seduces the reader (as Jitrik states in *Muerte y resurrección de 'Facundo'*, p. 11), and convinces with "elocuencia y verbosidad" (as Subercaseaux states concerning Lastarria in "Filosofía de la historia," p. 79).

30. Noé Jitrik, "Para una lectura de *Facundo*, de Domingo F. Sarmiento," in *Ensayos y estudios de literatura argentina* (Buenos Aires: Galerna, 1970), pp. 12-34.

31. Subercaseaux, *Cultura y sociedad liberal*, p. 68.

32. *Ibid.*, p. 86.

33. Fernández Retamar, "Algunos usos de civilización y barbarie," *Casa de las Américas*, 7, No. 102 (1977), 33. In another essay, "Nuestra América y Occidente," *Casa de las Américas*, 6, No. 98 (1976), he quotes Sarmiento to demonstrate that the latter was, at least in part, conscious of the dire consequences of his thought and acts: "Seamos francos: aunque esta invasión universal de Europa sobre nosotros es dañina y arruinosa para el país, todavía es

útil para la civilización y el comerico" (p. 45). Other critics have defended Sarmiento's ethnocentric and racist ideas. See, for example, Carlos Alberto Erro, "La aportación sociológica de Sarmiento," in Juan Mantovani, et al., *Sarmiento: educador, sociólogo, escritor, político* (Buenos Aires: Facultad de Filosofía y Letras, 1963), p. 25-39.

34. Dona Richards, "The Ideology of European Dominance," *The Western Journal of Black Studies*, 3, No. 4 (1979), 244-50.

35. Fernández Retamar, "Civilización y barbarie," p. 33.

36. Georg Wilhelm Friedrich Hegel, *The Philosophy of History*, trans. J. Sibree, rev. ed. (New York: Colonial Press, 1899), pp. 81-99.

37. François Pierre Guillaume Guizot, *The History of Civilization in Europe*, trans. William Hazlitt (New York: A. L. Burt, n. d.), pp. 372 ff.

38. See Note 15 of Chapter Five.

39. Ana María Barrenechea, "Las ideas de Sarmiento antes de la publicación del *Facundo*," *Filología*, 5, No. 3 (1968), 193-210, mentions the possible influence of Isabelle on Sarmiento, although Paul Verdevoye, *Domingo Faustino Sarmiento: éducateur et publiciste (entre 1839 et 1852)* (Paris: Institut des Hautes Etudes de l'Amérique Latine, 1963), p. 383, doubts Sarmiento's familiarity with Isabelle's writings. In *Facundo*, Sarmiento mistakenly ascribes one of his epigraphs to Francis B. Head's *Rough Notes Taken During Some Rapid Journeys Across the Pampas and Among the Andes* (Boston: Wells and Lilly, 1827), which suggests nevertheless that he was at least aware of Head's European fame, and perhaps that he had even read the work at an earlier date.

40. C. L. B., "Des Rapports de la France," pp. 65-66. See also Un officer de la flotte [Captaine Page ?], "Affairs de Buenos Ayres: Expéditions de la France contre la République Argentine," *Revue des Deux Mondes*, 25 (1841), 301-70, who refers to "cette horde sauvage" following the dictator Rosas (p. 351), who was "cet homme extraordinaire," nevertheless "n'était qu' un barbare . . ." (p. 361). Sarmiento often referred to the *Revue* in his writings, which in all respects was a very fine journal. Its 24 issues a year, each a thick volume of writings on history, literature, politics, and philosophy, had a wide diffusion throughout the capital cities of South America.

41. Guizot, *The History of Civilization*, p. 281.

42. Raúl A. Orgaz, *Sarmiento y el naturalismo histórico*, in Vol. III of *Obras Completas*, introd. Arturo Capdevila (Córdoba: Assandri, 1950), pp. 267-332, offers one of the most thorough accounts of the influence upon Sarmiento of Tocqueville's ideas. Unobserved, however, is the very strong resemblance between the methodology of inquiry utilized by the two writers. For example, Tocqueville, like Sarmiento eclectically united a number of methodological presuppositions: First, there is the belief that the "gradual development of the principle of equality is . . . a providential fact . . . . [I]t is universal, it is lasting, it constantly eludes all human interferences, and all events as well as all men contribute to its purposes." *Democracy in America*, (New York: Random House, 1963), I, p. 5. Second, there is the Vico-inspired methodology of studying the geographic, historical, and social conditions, all of which were thought to influence the intelligence of the individual and the institutions of society. And third, there is an a priori schematization of values and systems into the

two categories of "civilization" and "savagery." For example, the Indian, "Far from desiring to conform his habits to ours, . . . loves his savage life as the distinguishing mark of his race and repels every advance to civilization, less, perhaps, from hatred of it than from a dread of resembling the Europeans" (pp. 346-47). The entire Tocqueville work can be read as a criss-crossing of these three methodologies in a similar manner as occurs in the historical discourse of Sarmiento.

43. Tocqueville, *Democracy in America*, p. 369.

44. Tocqueville's influence is likely in this passage written by Sarmiento at the beginning of his second Chilean exile: "Porque es preciso que seamos justos con los españoles; al exterminar a un pueblo salvaje cuyo territorio iban a ocupar, hacían simplemente lo que todos los pueblos civilizados hacen con los salvajes, lo que la colonia efectúa deliberada o indeliberadamente con los indígenas: absorbe, destruye, extermina. Si este procedimiento terrible de la civilización es bárbaro y cruel a los ojos de la justicia y de la razón, es, como la guerra misma, como la conquista, uno de los medios de que la providencia ha armado a las diversas razas humanas, y entre éstas a las más poderosas y adelantadas, para sustituirse en lugar de aquellas que por su debilidad orgánica o su atraso en la carrera de la civilización, no pueden alcanzar los grandes destinos del hombre en la tierra" (II, 217-18). Other writers who expounded a more "relativist" interpretation of culture had little influence over Sarmiento. E. Lerminier, who regarded Vico as his principal influence, believed that progress occurred universally, and did not destroy the originality of each country and people. *(De l'influence de la philosophie du XVIIIè siècle sur la législation et la sociabilité du XIXè* [Paris: Didier, Libraire-Commissionnaire, 1833], p. xvi). Johann Gottfried von Herder, with similar premises, carried this view one step further in the criticism of Eurocentrism *(Reflections on the Philosophy of the History of Mankind,* abr. ed. [Chicago: University of Chicago Press, 1968], p. 7). In one work he sarcastically questioned the Europeans' professed desire to disseminate the Christian gospel and to spread the ideas of Western civilization among the lesser-developed world. A narrative character of Asian ancestry–democratically granted the power of textuality–speaks from these pages: "But do not forget (to mention) that this high mission has nothing whatsoever to do with the East-Indian Company or the propaganda from London," implying that the desire for profits and not altruism was the principal motivation for the enterprises of self-righteous Europeans among the natives of the periphery (quoted by F. M. Barnard, *Herder's Social and Political Thought: From Enlightenment to Naturalism* [Oxford: Clarendon, 1965], p. 102).

45. Bradford Burns, "Ideology in Nineteenth-Century Latin American Historiography," *Hispanic American Historical Review,* 58, No. 3 (1978), 429.

46. Marcelo Sánchez Sorondo, "Sarmiento: hombre de acción," *Sur,* No. 341 (1977), 136-55.

CHAPTER 8

Epilogue:
Sarmiento's Contradictory Voice
in the Argentine Liberal Tradition

    Liberalism in nineteenth-century Argentina is far from being a coherent and unified movement, and in this respect it is comparable to the European movements which preceded it. Argentine thinkers became remarkably adept at applying ideas from the Spanish, English, French, and North American liberal philosophical traditions to their own regional concerns.[1] Spanish liberals taught their American brethren of the benefits to be gained from political diversity, the economic principles of free trade, and the restriction of Church authority. The principal lessons learned from the English were the emphasis on individual rights (as opposed to the power of the state), the encouragement of a small land-holding agricultural sector, and the promotion of industry and trade. The French Enlightenment's principal contributions were the opposition to despotism, the criticism of Spanish feudalism, and the confidence in society's new bourgeois class for providing leadership in the age of progress. And lastly, Argentine intellectuals learned from North American liberals the advantages of constitutional government, protection for individual rights and free enterprise. In Argentina intellectuals and societal leaders chose selectively from these multiple and at times contradictory influences in order to attack Spanish institutions, the Church, the large landowners, and, in general, what they believed to be their country's colonial legacy. Like liberals everywhere, they believed necessary the liberation of physical and human resources under the dual banners of laissez-faire economics and republican government. They founded educational institutions; promoted industry, agriculture, and trade; and sought democratization in the political process and in the ownership of productive resources.

    Although these ideas constituted the general program for liberalism in nineteenth-century Argentina, it is to be expected that the successive generations of thinkers emphasized different aspects of that program according to the specific circumstances and needs they confronted. José Luis Romero, in his celebrated book on the history of Argentine political thought, traces the influence of liberalism in the country prior to the time of Sarmiento and the Generation of 1837.[2] First, there were the liberal reforms initiated in the Plata region by the Spanish Bourbon regime in the latter decades of the eighteenth century which received their inspiration from enlightenment thought. While the Bourbon leaders desired economic liberalism without political reform, the demand of the Argentine creoles for a greater role in local government provided an impetus for the emancipation movement which followed.

A second moment of liberal influence in Argentina united the inspirations of leaders like Rivadavia, Alvear, and Belgrano, who sought to organize the newly independent country according to the doctrines of free trade, as were put forth by the British. Liberalism in politics, however, remained inhibited. But these leaders' fears of an unchecked advance of the masses, as the French Revolution seemed to demonstrate, fueled their desire for a constitution which would insure the social and political stability necessary for development.[3]

Liberal ideas would again constitute the preponderant intellectual influence in Argentina with the thought and writings of the Generation of 1837, whose principal spokesmen were Esteban Echeverría, Juan Bautista Alberdi, and Domingo Faustino Sarmiento. What later came to be known as the *Dogma socialista,* a brief text written in 1838 by Echeverría with the collaboration of a few passages by Alberdi, was intended to provide the country's cultural elite with a new doctrine. This doctrine, it was hoped, would be capable of returning to the country's cultured minority an ideological unity. At the same time it would inspire action aimed at reconquering the political hegemony of the country that had been lost in recent years to the opulent but sometimes rudely mannered rural landowners.[4]

One of the clearest aspects of the *Dogma* was its social theory, which combined aspects of the thought of Saint-Simon, Fourier, Leroux, Lamennais, and others, under the common banner of *socialismo.* This body of ideas, which on the philosophical plane could be designated as belonging to the "Eclectic" school, was associated in a political dimension to the "Restoration." It reflected the lessons learned from the turbulent aftermath of the French Revolution regarding the necessity for society to be governed by a social and intellectual elite in order to assure civil order and protection to property during the period of their society's modernization. Eclecticism was a type of ideological backwater: romanticism had passed and had left its mark, but the enlightenment thought from before reasserted itself and sought an accommodation with the newer ideas. *Socialismo* spoke to the necessity of intensively analyzing the social reality in order to guarantee success for political programs. In a certain sense this philosophy was an opportunistic justification for opposing the spread of the French Revolution's excessively "popular" orientation.[5] Echeverría translated these ideas into the expressed need for Argentina's educated elite to reestablish its influence in society and government. He offered a new image of the revolutionary Commune, which would no longer be the center of creative activity for society's masses, but rather the passive receptical for the teachings of the country's educated patriots.[6]

Other aspects of the *Dogma,* and therefore of the ideas disseminated by Echeverría to an ambitious, but philosophically inexperienced, Buenos Aires youth, escape easy classification. An attraction to many traditional values and older forms of life came to be combined with the romantic advocation of municipal life and organic democracy. Many of its ideas, on account of their diversity and their idealistic and sometimes mystical focus, could only with difficulty be applied to the social and political reality for which they were originally intended.

Critics have called these ideas "utopian," not only on account of the abstract relationship they held to the Argentine circumstances for which they were originally deduced, but also because of the combative environment in which they were advocated.[7] Shortly following the *Dogma's* initial dissemination, its young intellectual adherents found themselves in political exile. Their mixed bags of liberal ideas now served as battle cries in their attacks against the tyrannical Rosas regime. The voices raised against Rosas tended to appeal to idealistic projections rather than concrete and applicable programs in the ideological struggle to win adherents to their cause. They looked to the past in defending largely the same principles (liberty, free trade, republicanism) which had dominated liberal politics a half century before in the revolutionary struggle against the decrepit colonial order. They also held a nostalgic admiration for the old Unitarian administrations' programs for national transformation, although they criticized the inflexibility of Rivadavia and others in the application of those programs.[8]

As months in exile turned into years, their attitude of pure negativity in front of a social reality that was destined to be subdued by a utopian revolutionary project slowly gave way to a more conciliatory attitude in front of the existing social and economic forces of the country and a growing disconfidence in the possibilities for radical change. The liberal intellectuals, from their vantage points in exile, sullenly came to realize that Lavalle's failure in 1842 signaled the underlying strength of the Rosas regime. Later, the European struggles of 1848 taught them that a revolutionary movement surging from the spontaneity of certain forces oppressed by the regime in power, although not altogether impossible, was entirely undesirable.[9] Alberdi's radical pessimism about their previous revolutionary project would receive its clearest expression in *Bases* (1852), a work which advanced authoritarianism at the service of progress. The other liberal intellectuals, while not following Alberdi in his support for the landed oligarchy of the interior, nevertheless followed his lead in putting themselves at the service of the country's existing socio-economic structure, and abandoned their previous project of overthrowing it. In their majority, they would work in conjunction with the social and political hierarchies in the Province of Buenos Aires that had become consolidated during the Rosas era.

In their writings prior to 1852, the young exiled intellectuals anticipated this new period of *dependent* liberalism in Argentine sociopolitical
and economic thought which would accompany the regime replacing Rosism after 1852.[10] Sarmiento's generation began to realize that an adapted
form of their old liberal ideals could simultaneously serve the interests of
the cattle-raising and exporting bourgeoisie, just as it could their own ambitions for directing the nation's progress. The abolition of tariff barriers
and the promotion of free trade along the country's internal rivers were
two such programs which assured the country's integration into the world
economy. On the one hand, the cattle oligarchy would gain the guarantee
of a market for its exports to principally English buyers, in addition to
its right to unrestricted luxury imports. On the other hand, the liberal
intelligentsia would continue to enjoy close social and cultural ties with
the more developed nations of Northern Europe; they would direct local
industrial and agricultural development through European investment,
and would oversee the modeling of the nation's social, educational, and
cultural practices upon reputable European standards.

In their domestic programs, the newly ascendant liberals in the post-
Rosas period slowly put aside their previous ideas of utopian reform and
advocated more pragmatic actions to deal with the immense tasks related
to the modernization of the nation. More and more they favored the
doctrines associated with positivism, which meant the abandonment of
their previous emphasis on freedom in political and intellectual spheres.
In acts and writings, they now supported and justified an hierarchical
social order and the political domination of society by privileged groups.[11]
John Dewey's description of late nineteenth-century liberalism in North
America and Europe applies also to Argentina: the absolutist ideals of the
country's dependent liberals led them "not to prevent change, but . . .
to limit its course to a single channel and to immobilize the channel."
They suffered the contradiction that the reforms achieved by the liberals
of an earlier epoch had given rise to an "era of power" in which the newly
ascendant interests sought to limit and control the advancement of the
masses. The liberals of this second period, then, provided a rationalization
for inequality and privilege.[12]

Given the rivalry that erupted after 1852 between the Province of
Buenos Aires and Urquiza's Confederation, it was natural that the great
majority of the liberal intelligentsia, upon returning from exile, should
align themselves with the former. The most important exception was
Alberdi, originally from Tucumán, who became a leader in the interior
provinces' campaign against Buenos Aires hegemony. Most of the others,
however, had been born and raised in Buenos Aires, were accustomed
to the material comforts which the city offered, and identified with its
relatively advanced cultural setting. Their refined culturalist orientation
contributed to their belief in the port-city's mission of inseminating the
more backward provinces of the interior with their own ideas of progress
and modernity. They were readily received by the upper sectors of the

region, whose families were also of urban origins (family histories demonstrate the predominance of commercial or bureaucratic livehihoods), but who in recent decades had found in cattle production not only economic opportunity but also refuge in an economy dislocated by the effects of the introduction of free trade, in addition to the ruinous wars.[13] The returned intellectuals therefore found a common cause with the cattle oligarchy and other leading interests in Buenos Aires: while the province's economic interests struggled to maintain their commercial monopoly over the rest of the country, the liberal intellectuals would advocate forceful measures in order that the interior provinces' recalcitrant barbarism conform to their new ideas on trade, government, and association.

After a decade of intermittent economic and political struggle, the loose confederation of thirteen provinces finally gave in to the economically dominant and militarily superior Buenos Aires. Beginning with the presidency of Bartolomé Mitre in 1862, that powerful province headed a central government that sometimes brutally imposed its will over the other provinces. That the presidents succeeding Mitre, like Sarmiento and Avellaneda, were originally from the provinces, does not dispute the association of dependent liberal ideology with porteño domination. It would be more correct to say that those presidents were conquered by Buenos Aires, and consecrated their governments, through their liberal creed, to fortifying the domination and prosperity of that city.[14] .sk

While others of his generation would make a more or less clean break with the past in this transition from a utopian to a dependent focus in their ideas, Sarmiento would live in permanent confusion between authoritarianism and freedom, between democratic faith and oligarchical solidarity. The renunciation of a program for the country's revolutionary transformation also meant for Alberdi the renunciation of his and his elitist cultural group's previously held mission of imposing an ideal force over a rebellious reality. For Sarmiento, however, culture never left off being an instrument for liberation. He continued faithful, throughout his long and fertile career, to the creed of 1837 in his belief that the enlightened class, which was constituted by those who possessed an objective and universally valid truth, were obliged to struggle constantly for the incarnation of that truth in society's institutions. This he believed possible in spite of the progressive consolidation of his country's existing socio-economic structures, to whose defense he would dedicate long and loyal service.[15]

That "service" to the Buenos Aires oligarchy had its omnious beginnings immediatelly after the battle of Caseros. Not content with Urquiza's "terrible vengeance" and "controlled terror" against the followers of Rosas in and around the Province of Buenos Aires,[16] he urged to no avail a continuation of such violent measures with the objective of eradicating the vestiges of Rosas' *caudillo* system throughout the interior. His inability to steer Urquiza into more forceful action was merely one of several factors that convinced him of the latter's unwillingness to combat the sociopolitical system that continued to exist almost unmodified throughout the interior even after the overthrow of the dictator. More and more he became convinced that the triumph of civilization throughout the land could only be accomplished by Buenos Aires, where the cultured elite had been restored to political leadership. His definitive break with Urquiza signaled the new lines of national struggle which would shortly erupt between Buenos Aires and the Urquiza-led confederation of interior provinces.

The following decade was perhaps the most anguished in Sarmiento's stormy career. Critics treating the period have taken diametrically opposed positions. Apologists such as Alberto Palcos depict Sarmiento as perhaps the most respected and conciliatory voice in very difficult times.[17] Milcíades Peña, representing the other extreme, calls this period the most shameful in an otherwise brilliant career.[18] Of continuing need is a scholarly treatment of this period of Sarmiento's life that would avoid the pitfalls of political or ideological partisanship.[19]

Between 1852 and 1863, the contradiction between Sarmiento's advocation of a society in which there would predominate liberty and freedom, and the forceful means deemed necessary for that society to emerge, came to be a cause of anguish. Before 1852, the problem had not been so acute: his energies had been entirely absorbed in the propagandistic, and then military, struggle against Rosas, a struggle for which force hardly needed justification. He and his generation of young exiled intellectuals had used their arsenal of liberal ideas primarily for *attacking* a decrepit regime. They had the luxury of defending a sociopolitical program for national reconstruction that was "idealistic and sentimental like the poetry of the time." At the time they had no need to concretize and actualize their "mystical virtuoso ideas."[20]

All this would change, however. In 1852, with Rosas defeated, several members of this group assumed positions of public responsibility in the Province of Buenos Aires. Then, after the battle of Pavón in 1861, this group would extend its influence over the rest of the country. They accepted the task of national unification which necessitated, in the first moment, the reconciliation of idealistic revolutionary principles and oftentimes clashing social and economic forces. Sarmiento, to all appearances, suffered terribly on account of this. In 1852, shortly after Rosas' defeat, he returned to Chile, ostensibly on account of his opposition to both Urquiza's Confederation and the Buenos Aires drive toward autonomy. His writings from that year on can be read in the light of his difficulty, and at times inability, in reconciling old doctrines to the new realities of his personal situation and that of his nation. Not only was he the "porteño en las provincias y el provinciano en Buenos Aires"—which was the slogan he adopted that year for promoting his own political future—he was also the educator among military bosses and the advocate of gaucho pacification among constitutionalists.

A decade later, following the definitive victory of Buenos Aires over the Confederation in the battle of Pavón, Sarmiento had occasion to demonstrate his most violent and authoritarian tendencies. Similar to what he had urged Urquiza following the victory over Rosas at Caseros, he advocated in front of Mitre a military campaign that would have as its goal the total defeat of Federalism's surviving forces. "Southhampton o la horca," he recommended for Urquiza (in reference to the site of Rosas' exile).[21] "Echele 24 batallones de infantería y sublévele a Corrientes." About Santa Fe, he talked about having it disappear as a province.

Two years later, when encharged with the responsibility of putting down the revolt of "El Chacho" and restoring civil order to the northern provinces, he again urged Mitre: "No trate de economizar sangre de gauchos."[22] According to Ricardo Rojas, he conceived the struggle as an episode of civilization pitted against barbarism, and as he depicted it, civilization acquired dimensions of a fantasy bordering on delirium.[23] Mitre, as president, had cautioned him to limit his actions to what would be viewed as a "guerra de policía," not wishing the struggle to be perceived as a civil war or an overt case of urban society imposing its will over an unwilling rural province. Throughout the campaign Mitre urged relatively conciliatory measures and attempted to moderate Sarmiento's more extreme actions and impulses. Although Sarmiento was not directly responsible for the death of Peñalosa, he approved wholeheartedly of the extralegal circumstances of that death and the very brutal manner in which it was accomplished.[24] For Rojas, the entire episode demonstrated the "disconcertante psicología" of one who carried out a "primitive" vengeance against the foes of the new social order while simultaneously defending the abstract ideals which characterized his earlier writings.[25]

His detractors have drawn Sarmiento's presidency from 1868 to 1874 as the continuation of the former period when the man was an ideological and military leader in Buenos Aires' violent political imposition over the interior and its efforts to exterminate the Indian and convert the gaucho into a docile rural proletariat. They have called attention to his forceful supression of the López Jordán uprising in Entre Ríos and the pacification campaigns in Corrientes and Mendoza. The first part of José Hernández' memorable poem, *El Gaucho Martín Fierro,* captures well the widespread hostility throughout the interior to the Buenos Aires-centered regime and its ruthless campaign for national renovation.

Advocates of this negative perspective ironically compare the new liberal regime under such leaders as Mitre and Sarmiento to the Argentina of Rosas, in spite of the mortal battle waged between these two forces only decades earlier. In truth, there were several important similarities: common to both regimes were a cattle-oriented economy with hegemony exercised by Buenos Aires, close ties with British imperialism, a war-ready condition, imperial designs over Paraguay and Uruguay,[26] and possibly the sheer number of enemies and victims from among the country's population.[27] In fact, British historian H. S. Ferns argues that the regimes of Mitre and Sarmiento did not differ substantially from that of Rosas (or those of Moreno, Rivadavia, etc.) in that all directed an internally oriented capitalist order dominated by the economic interests of the *estancieros* and meat processors. He argues that there were no essential political or procedural differences, except that Rosas' "closed" policies to the country's potential social development vis-à-vis an internationally oriented laissez faire economy contrasted with the "openness" of the succeeding liberal regimes.[28]

Again, it is Tulio Halperín Donghi who offers perhaps the most authoritative perspective of Argentine society in the post-Rosas period, and one that largely avoids the rhetoric of political factionism.[29] He argues that the liberalism that was emerging advocated profound modifications in collective life. Its leaders were aware that they represented the interests of a small minority of the nation's population, but made little attempt to broaden their representation. It was a very special situation: the party of Mitre defined as its goal the renovation of society, but acted in the interests of a province that was anxious to preserve its hegemony and its own political traditions. This contradiction bred hypocrisy and a profound immorality in the liberal leaders. Their "Partido de la Libertad" waged relentless campaigns to "pacify" the interior and forcibly implant their own political beliefs upon a largely unwilling population. An inevitable result of their lack of any goal or aspiration that went beyond the sensual exercise of power, their intellectual contribution to national culture rarely rose above crass frivolity.

Halperín Donghi presents convincing evidence that Sarmiento, upon assuming the presidency in 1868, attempted to distance himself from the past trajectory of Mitre's Liberal Party and to seek dialogue with Federalist leaders in the interior.[30] As president, he slowly came to realize some of the mistaken premises which had led him in previous years to condemn the existing social and political order in the interior provinces and to uncritically support Buenos Aires' commercial and financial control over the rest of Argentina. He came to the realization that the preponderant influence of Buenos Aires had impeded the country's development instead of helping it. His writings reveal that his old dreams of an independent, prosperous, and democratic Argentina became rekindled, although he lacked the means for transforming those dreams into social action. His new foe was Mitre, who continued to defend the narrow regional interests of Buenos Aires and its cattle-exporting oligarchy. Alberdi, Sarmiento's most stalwart opponent since 1852, and the country's clearest and most persistent critic of Buenos Aires hegemony and that province's deepening dependence in the economic system governed by Great Britain, had good but begrudging words to say about Sarmiento's administration. In his promotion of national interests, Sarmiento received support from a surprising direction: his old enemy Urquiza. In a letter to the former president of the country, Sarmiento admitted that back in 1852 Urquiza's vision of the realities of the country had been clearer than his own (L, 218). He confessed that his own actions at that time, if not theoretically in error, had been counterproductive in practice. Now he was aware of the problems involved in governing an unruly and politically divided people. Only now could he respect the authoritarian brand of progress which Urquiza had practiced a decade earlier. There reappeared in his thought the exasperating contradiction that had also plagued Urquiza to some degree before: his sincere desire for democratically oriented reform clashed with the recognition that the context which he pretended to influence was destined to conserve for still a long while its oligarchical structure.[31]

During his presidency, these changes in his thought regarding the nature and constitution of "barbarism" were not accompanied by a reevaluation in his ideas with regard to the civilizing influence of European immigration and investment in Argentina. Neither of these two issues was the topic of serious controversy (Sarmiento's disillusionment with the effects of immigration began to be articulated only in 1882). Opponents occasionally criticized the actual results of the country's immigration policies, but they rarely criticized the intentions of those policies. Similarly, Sarmiento's presidency enjoyed a solid consensus in its support of foreign capital as the impetus for the country's economic renovation.[32]

In the latter years of his life, from approximately 1880 to 1888, Sarmiento had further occasion for reflecting back on the circumstances surrounding the fall of Rosism and the rise of the new national order, those two events which summarize best the struggles of his long public career. Up to the last months of his life he was embroiled in the controversies of government and involved in labors of the press. Historians studying this period remember *Conflicto y armonía de las razas en América* (1883) as his unfortunate attempt at documenting through questionable social-scientific practices the inferior racial heritage of his continent. Largely ignored by partisan researchers, however, is the testimony of his deep depression in those final years upon realizing that the programs of immigration and foreign investment, which he had supported throughout his adulthood, many times had produced results contrary to what he had intended. In 1887, he acknowledged his agreement with the words of ex-president Roca that "En Buenos Aires no está la Nación, porque es una provincia de extranjeros."[33] In conversations and writings he repeatedly alluded to his growing disillusionment, although these ideas never received clear articulation. He believed that the survivors of the old provincial aristocracy of Buenos Aires in alliance with foreign commercial interests, and not a new capitalist class of small agricultural producers and industrialists, were the avid beneficiaries of the new society which had emerged largely as a result of his generation's dedication and energy.[34] Largely gone was his faith in those illustrated classes that had guided colonial society, and who he had believed would provide the guiding force for the construction of a republican Argentina.

His pessimism was in response to the society of economic privilege and social stratification that had arisen in large measure as a result of the liberal reforms for which he and his generation had been early advocates and then protagonists. The liberal principles most emphasized in his youth spoke to the utopian dream of society's universal advancement and its people's increased participation in national life. However, three decades of post-Rosas liberal rule had largely betrayed the spirit of those early ideals. In the 1880's, Argentina's ruling elite continued to manifest its support for foreign ideas, commerce, and economic initiative. The coastal oligarchy still maintained its iron grip over the nation's cattle-export economy and its culture continued to justify that predominance. The slogan "civilization versus barbarism" had been conceived initially as a bombast against tyranny and the moral abuses of power. In this subsequent period, however, the slogan came to be used as a justification for the country's dependent order. It was Sarmiento's fate to have been a protagonist in that transition. It was his tragedy to preserve and revive in his old age many of the same ideals that had fueled his struggles as a youth.

Contributing to Sarmiento's tragedy was his failure to embody the preocupations of his latter years in a prose with an expressive power rivaling that of his earlier writings. Neither his new opposition to the Buenos Aires oligarchy, nor the wrath of God (as Borges reminds us) could undo the past. But one would at least expect that his change in ideas and perhaps political orientation be faithfully recorded in the nation's cultural production. That was not the case, however, since his image, for his contemporaries and for posterity alike, no longer responded to his own initiatives, but rather to the political opportunism of others. He no longer possessed the energy or verve of before in order to produce a writing whose critical force could unfreeze his coagulated country. The aged man, confronting the moral wasteland before him, could only tremble before the shadow of his former self.

As a young man he had succeeded remarkably well in the enterprise of writing in order to liberate his society from the tyranny of gaucho *caudillos*. He had appealed to both the power of arms and the press in order to defend his worthy goals: "Nuestra causa es tan respetable que es preciso para hacerla triunfar, tener al compás la pluma y la espada al mismo tiempo," he had written to Anselmo Rojo in the heat of the battle against Rosas.[35] For the young Sarmiento, writing nobly served society's—and even humanity's—highest calling. As public writer his responsibility was to guide society's elite toward the optimum avenues for achieving progress. His writing would also educate the masses as a preparation for entering into society's modern age. At times his pedagogy had as its objective the justification of stern measures taken by society's enlightened leaders. To all indications, the young Sarmiento achieved notable success in this public writing mission, as he defined it. Rosas fell in 1852, not because he was conquered militarily, but because of internal dissent. His supporters of years standing deserted him and then handed over the government of the province and the nation to a new set of leaders. Sarmiento's generation of exiled publicists had done their part in corroding the dictator's popular support and in educating the public about alternatives to his power.

In the decades subsequent to the fall of Rosas, Sarmiento's early writings continued to enjoy considerable esteem, but now as the literary and ideological support for the newly ascendant dependent-liberal regime centered in Buenos Aires. What survived into this subsequent period was the young Sarmiento's commitment to social and material progress and his appeal for a national leadership entrusted to an elite group of cultural priests. The results for Argentina were spectacular: the country's economic development outstripped by far any possible rival on the South American continent. Up through the first few decades of the twentieth century, Argentina's shining example of modernization was universally recognized. The vast majority of conservative, liberal, and even Marxist, writers considered Sarmiento as precursor, and even "hero," of this success story in development.[36]

In recent decades, however, critics have demonstrated greater skepticism toward the idea of Argentina's exemplary status vis-à-vis Latin America. Historians resurrecting the largely forgotten struggles over the last century and a half have called attention to the enormous human costs, in addition to the much praised benefits, of Argentina's modernization. Political economists have documented how national leaders during Sarmiento's lifetime guided the country on a path of development that has resulted in accentuated social inequality and structural economic dependency.[37] The title of Bradford Burns' recent book treating Latin America in the nineteenth century summarizes well these critical views of Argentina's experience during that century: Sarmiento's legacy to his country has been *The Poverty of Progress*.[38]

Ezequiel Martínez Estrada's *Radiografía de la pampa* (1933) anticipated much of the recent criticism treating Sarmiento's role in Argentina's ill-fated development. His profound realization was that Sarmiento's soul coincided with his country and his land: Argentina's areas of greatness derive from the most constructive aspects of Sarmiento's work and thought; but its most ignominious chapters also had his prejudices and acts as a precedent. Few would disagree that Sarmiento's early writing set the tenor and the pattern for Argentina's emergence into the modern world. But his dream for Argentina's future, as Martínez Estrada points out, rested on at least two tragic misconceptions. First, his hatred of Spain's feudal legacy in America became converted into a hatred of anything naturally American. Second, in violently desiring for Argentina a progress similar to what existed in other lands, he failed to understand that people and nations cannot model themselves after utopias. It is unfortunate that his largely mistaken ideas about civilization became the basis for dependent liberalism's program of national transformation. Similarly, it is unfortunate that his mistaken conception of barbarism became transformed into taboos which had to be eliminated, repressed, or supressed.[39] The "humanist" face to his anti-americanist policies in the earlier period became transformed into state policy when the nation's enlightened leaders would direct the liquidation of Argentina's "natural" population in order to make way for the railroad.[40]

Another result, and one which directly pertains to his mission as a public writer, is that a long tradition of writers and opinion formers in Argentina have copied his example of manipulating ideas and values according to each's preferred interpretation of the civilization-barbarism scheme. Unfortunately, perhaps the most enduring effect of Sarmiento's journalistic writing was the denial of social truths in favor of one's own. According to Martínez Estrada, Sarmiento's legacy in the dependent-liberal order has been the practice of relegating significant fragments of the nation's social reality to the subconscious, along with the words which describe them. As a result of Sarmiento's predication, "Los fantasmas desalojaron a los hombres y la utopía devoró a la realidad."[41]

And yet, since each age (and author) determines its own precursors, it is not impossible that a different image of Domingo Faustino Sarmiento becomes popularized midway through the decade of the 1980's, one responding to the new birth of freedom for the country's population and the revival of dignity and goodwill as hallmarks for its leaders. Indeed, among the varied advocacies of Sarmiento during his long public career, one could easily find inspiration for this benevolent image which would take its place alongside of that highlighting his intolerance for racial and ethnic differences, in addition to his authoritarian and even violent militaristic tendencies. The focus undertaken in this work upon his early career as public writer has provided many such examples: his commitment to the "utopian" liberal ideals of liberty and freedom, and his uncompromising "conspiracy" against tyranny. Add to that the man's integrity, honesty, and spirit of service and sacrifice, which characterized his entire career. In the final decades of the present century, Martínez Estrada's earlier judgment still seems exact: Sarmiento's soul continues as a faithful expression of the vital passions of his country. Before, his advocacies promoted and prefigured the liberal state's periods of greatness as well as crisis. Now, his Janus-like image fittingly represents not only the horrors of the "dirty war" in the 1970s, but also the country's heartening attempts to emerge from the depths of despair and inhumanity.

Notes for Chapter 8

1. Iván Jaksić, *The Meaning of Liberalism in Latin America: The Cases of Chile, Argentina, and Mexico in the 19th Century.* (Buffalo: SUNY, Council on International Studies, 1981).

2. José Luis Romero, *A History of Argentine Political Thought*, trans. Thomas F. McGann (Stanford: Stanford University Press, 1963), pp. 8, 53.

3. Jaksić, *The Meaning of Liberalism.*

4. Tulio Halperín Donghi, "Prólogo" to Domingo F. Sarmiento; *Campaña en el Ejército Grande Aliado de Sud América* (México: Fondo de Cultura Económica, 1958), p. xi.

5. Noé Jitrik, "El *Facundo:* la gran riqueza de la pobreza," in Domingo F. Sarmiento, *Facundo, o civilización y barbarie* (Caracas: Ayacucho, 1977), p. xl.

6. Tulio Halperín Donghi, *El pensamiento de Echeverría* (Buenos Aires: Sudamericana, 1951), p. 132.

7. Harry K. Girvetz, *The Evolution of Liberalism*, introd. Arthur Schlesinger Jr. (New York: Collier Books, 1963); and John Dewey, *Liberalism and Social Action* (New York: G. P. Putnam's Sons, 1935). Both recognize two distinct stages of liberalism (classical and contemporary; early and late). My terminology reflects the distinct flavor and structure of Latin America's development which affect the role of culture, and make Latin American ideological movements differ from their sister movements in Europe and North America. The period of "utopian" liberalism receives its best description in Karl Mannheim, *Ideology and Utopia: An Introduction to the Sociology of Knowledge*, trans. Louis Wirth and Edward Shils, (New York: Harcourt, Brace & World, 1936), pp. 219-229, who discusses the "liberal-humanitarian ideal" in relation to enlightenment thought. The period of utopian liberalism in Argentina can be said to extend from the first administration of Rivadavia to the fall of Rosas; during this period there predominated in liberal discourse the utopian social goals of altering the cause of historical and political events, according to Domingo Millani, "Utopian Socialism: Transitional Thread from Romanticism to Positivism in Latin America," *Journal of the History of Ideas*, No. 24 (1963), pp. 515-522. José Ingenieros, *Las direcciones filosóficas de la cultura argentina* (Buenos Aires: Universitaria de Buenos Aires, 1963), pp. 71-72, labels Echeverría's ideas–which nourished the social thought of his generation–as "el socialismo utópico," because of their similarity to the ideas prevalent in France at the time. I have chosen not to follow the definitions of the term "utopia" as offered by Carlos M. Rama, ed., *Utopismo socialista (1830-1893)* (Caracas: Ayacucho, 1977), p. 132, who explains that Sarmiento's own application of the term "utopian" was in criticism of Fourier's utopian ideas for being opposed to science, commerce, social advancement, and the state-guided construction of "civilization;" and that of Juan Guillermo Durán, "Literatura y utopía en Hispanoamérica," Diss. Cornell, 1972, which is in reference to Sarmiento's racist ideas in *Conflicto y armonía*.

8. Sarmiento writes in *Aldao:* "después de tanta gloria, Rivadavia . . . no tuvo más defecto que haberse anticipado dos siglos a su época, asustando a sus contemporáneos cual visión sobrenatural, ridícula y fascinadora a la vez . . ." (VII, 256).

9. Tulio Halperín Donghi, "El espejo de la historia," *Contorno,* No. 9/10 (1959), p 79.

10. The dependent stage of liberalism, which was anticipated by such works as Alberdi's *Bases,* became institutionalized in the decade of the 1860's with the victory of Buenos Aires over the provinces and ascension of liberal intellectuals such as Sarmiento and Mitre to political power. See Tulio Halperín Donghi, ed., *Proyecto y construcción de una nación (Argentina 1846-1880)* (Caracas: Biblioteca Ayacucho, 1980), for a interesting interpretative essay by the editor and a collection of the relevant documents of the period; and James R. Scobie, *La lucha por la consolidación de la nacionalidad argentina, 1852-1862,* trans. Gabriela de Civiny (Buenos Aires: Hatchette, 1964) for a detailed political history. In this dependent period, the country's liberal leaders advocated an acceptance of the cattle-exporting bourgeoisie as the mainstay of the socio-economic order. Later, they would find in the theories of positivism a rationalization for the new emphasis on order and authority; they justified their country's apprenticeship to Europe as the most feasible avenue for developing their own society in all its facets.

11. W. J. Kilgore, "The Development of Positivism in Latin America," *Inter-American Review of Bibliography,* 19 (1969), 23-42.

12. John Dewey, *Liberalism and Social Action* (New York: G. P. Putnam's Sons, 1935), p. 34.

13. Tulio Halperín Donghi, "La expansión ganadera en la campaña de Buenos Aires (18180-1852)," in *Los fragmentos del poder: de la oligarquía a la poliarquía argentina,* by Ezequiel Gallo (h), et al, eds. T. S. di Tella and T. Halperín Donghi (Buenos Aires: Jorge Alvarez, 1969), pp. 21-74.

14. Jame R. Scobie, *La lucha por la consolidación,* p. 9.

15. This paragraph is based on the ideas from Halperín Donghi, "El espejo de la historia," who treats in admirable fashion the contradictory ideology of Sarmiento with regard to social revolution.

16. John Lynch, *Argentine Dictator: Juan Manuel de Rosas, 1829-1852* (Oxford: Clarendon Press, 1981), p. 332.

17. Alberto Palcos, *Sarmiento: la vida, la obra, las ideas, el genio* (Buenos Aires: El Ateneo, 1938), pp. 123-39.

18. Milcíades Peña, *Alberdi, Sarmiento, el 90: límites del nacionalismo argentino en el siglo XIX* (Buenos Aires: Fichas, 1970).

19. Brief but fairly balanced treatments of Sarmiento's career between 1852 and 1862 are: José S. Campobassi, *Sarmiento y su época, I (1811/1863)* (Buenos Aires: Losada, 1975); and Ricardo Rojas, *El profeta de la pampa: vida de Sarmiento* (Buenos Aires: Losada, 1945).

20. R. Picard, *El romanticismo social,* as quoted by Domingo Milliani, "Utopian Socialism: Transitional Thread From Romanticism to Positivism in Latin America," *Journal of the History of Ideas,* 24 (1963), p. 328 fn.

21. Rojas, *El profeta de la pampa,* p. 642.

22. All the quotes from this paragraph are taken from Rojas, *El profeta de la pampa,* p. 442.

23. *Ibid.,* where Rojas states that Sarmiento interpreted the struggle "como un episodio de 'Civilización y barbarie', y representada por él, la civilización, su fantasía exaltóse hasta el delirio, como si fuese el numen de una tragedia."

24. Campobassi, *Sarmiento y su época,* pp. 547-48.

25. *Ibid.*

26. Lynch, *Argentine Dictator,* pp. 307-9, discusses Rosas' war machine and his desire to control Paraguay and Uruguay.

27. It would be difficult to compare the number of internal enemies and Argentine victims of the respective regimes. Lynch, *Argentine Dictator,* attempts to compile such figures for Rosas in the superb chapter treating the dictator's system of terror (pp. 201-46). For the Mitre-Sarmiento presidencies, few studies have come to my attention which treat similar issues with impartiality and an attention to detail. Some texts accuse the forces of Buenos Aires of a veritable slaughter of local militia and *montonera* forces after the battle of Pavón. For example, Fermín Chávez, *Civilización y barbarie en la cultura argentina,* 2nd ed. expanded (Buenos Aires: Theoría, 1965), p. 88, copies an editorial printed in *La Capital* (with no city given, but obviously the capital city of one of the interior provinces—most probably in the Litoral, or the country's eastern border), 9 December 1867, which lists the number of deaths which occurred during the liberal period (that is, up to the last year of Mitre's presidency): Deaths in combat: 24,482; Soldiers and civilians executed: 4,395; Deaths due to injuries in combat: 9,625; Emigrants to foreign countries: 10,000. Accusations of similar atrosities have been made with regard to Sarmiento's battle against "El Chacho" and the pacification campaigns he directed while president in Entre Ríos, Corrientes, and Mendoza.

28. H. S. Ferns, *Argentina* (New York and Washington: Frederick A. Praeger, 1969), pp. 88, 96-97.

29. Tulio Halperín Donghi, "Una nación para el desierto argentino," in *Proyecto y construcción,* pp. xi-ci. The following paragraph draws heavily on the ideas presented on pages xi and lxii.

30. *Ibid.,* p. lxv.

31. *Ibid.,* p. lxxii.

32. *Ibid.,* pp. lxxvi-lxxix.

33. Quoted by Rojas, *Profeta de la pampa,* p. 642.

34. Tulio Halperín Donghi, "Sarmiento: su lugar en la sociedad argentina post-revolucionaria," *Sur,* No. 341 (1977), 121-135. See also Milcíades Peña, *Alberdi, Sarmiento, el 90,* pp. 80-83; and Enrique Anderson Imbert, *Genio y*

figura de Sarmiento (Buenos Aires: Editorial Universitaria de Buenos Aires, 1967), pp. 142-49.

35. Juan Rómulo Fernández, *Sarmiento (semblanza e iconografía)* (Buenos Aires: Librería del Colegio, 1938), p. 29, records the quote from Sarmiento's 1845 letter to Rojo which accompanied a few copies of *Apuntes biográficos: vida de Aldao.* This book contains the best collection of Sarmiento fotos which I have encountered.

36. Elizabeth Garrels, *Mariátegui y la Argentina: un caso de 'lentes ajenos'* (Gaithersburg, MD: Hispamérica, 1982), p. 119, makes these affirmations amidst several serious distortions. She documents how José Carlos Mariátegui admired the legacy of Sarmiento in Argentina's material development, but she is less clear about Mariátegui's ignorance concerning Sarmiento's appeal to largely racist policies for achieving that modernization.

37. Amidst the vast bibliography of works treating this highly ideological, and therefore polemical, topic, the most authoritative are the writings of Tulio Halperín Donghi, as listed in the bibliography, and Aldo Ferrer, *The Argentine Economy,* trans. Marjory M. Urquidi (Berkeley and Los Angeles: University of California Press, 1967).

38. E. Bradford Burns, *The Poverty of Progress: Latin America in the Nineteenth Century* (Berkeley and Los Angeles: University of California Press, 1980). Although Burns is to be praised for his general description of the mixed results for Latin America's modernization in the last century, his treatment of Argentina has several serious distortions, which I hope to address in a future essay.

39. Ezequiel Martínez Estrada, *Radiografía de la pampa,* 6th ed. (Buenos Aires: Losada, 1968), p. 341. See also Chávez, *Civilización y barbarie,* pp. 26-30.

40. David Viñas, *Literatura argentina y realidad política.* Vol. I: *De Sarmiento a Cortázar* (Buenos Aires: Siglo Veinte, 1971), pp. 20-21, 146-47, 166-74.

41. Martínez Estrada, *Radiografía de la pampa,* p. 341.

SELECT BIBLIOGRAPHY

Abrams, M. H. *The Mirror and the Lamp: Romantic Theory and the Critical Tradition.* New York: Oxford University Press, 1977.

Alazraki, Jaime. "El indigenismo de Martí y el anti-indigenismo de Sarmiento." *Cuadernos Americanos,* 140, No. 3 (1965), 135-57.

Alberdi, Juan Bautista. *Cartas quillotanas (polémica con Domingo F. Sarmiento).* Buenos Aires: Talleres Gráficos Argentinos, 1932.

—————— . *Facundo y su biógrafo: notas para servir a un estado con el título que precede.* Tucumán: Signo, 1968.

Althusser, Louis. *For Marx.* Trans. Ben Brewster. New York: Pantheon Books, 1969.

—————— . *Lenin and Philosophy and Other it Essays.* Trans. Ben Brewster. New York and London: Monthly Review Press, 1971.

Anderson Imbert, Enrique. "El historicismo de Sarmiento en el centenario del *Facundo,*" *Cuadernos Americanos,* 22, No. 5 (1945), 158-72.

—————— . *Genio y figura de Sarmiento.* Buenos Aires: Editorial Universitaria de Buenos Aires, 1967.

Andrews, George Reid. *The Afro-Argentines in Buenos Aires, 1800-1900.* Madison: University of Wisconsin Press, 1980.

Arciniegas, Germán. *Latin America: A Cultural History.* Trans. Joan MacLean. Great Britain: Barrie & Rockliff, Cresset Press, 1969.

Austin, J. L. *How to Do Things with Words.* Ed. J.O. Urmson. Cambridge, Mass., 1962.

Barnard, F. M. *Herder's Social and Political Thought: From Enlightenment to Naturalism.* Oxford: Clarendon, 1965.

Barrenechea, Ana María. "Función estética y significación histórica de las campañas pastoras en el *Facundo.*" In *Sarmiento: educador, sociólogo, escritor, político.* Juan Mantovani, et al. Buenos Aires: Universidad de Buenos Aires, Facultad de Filosofía y Letras, 1963, pp. 43-60.

—————— . "Las ideas de Sarmiento antes de la publicación del *Facundo.*" *Filología,* 5, No. 3 (1968), 193-210.

——————— . "Notas al estilo de Sarmiento." *Revista Iberoamericana,* No. 41-42 (1956), pp. 275-94.

Barrenechea, Ana María and Beatriz R. Lavandera. *Domingo Faustino Sarmiento.* Buenos Aires: Centro Editor de América Latina, 1967.

Barthes, Roland. "Historical Discourse." In *Structuralism: A Reader.* Ed. and introd. Michael Lane. London: Jonathan Cape, 1970, pp. 145-155.

Bataillon, Marcel. "Introduction." In *Souvenirs de Province,* by Domingo F. Sarmiento. Trans. Gabrielle Cabrini. Paris: Les Editions Nagal, 1955, pp. 7-21.

Belín Sarmiento, A. "Prólogo." In *El jóven Sarmiento: escenario en 5 actos.* Saint Cloud: Imprenta Pablo Belín, 1929.

——————— . *Sarmiento anecdótico (ensayo biográfico).* Saint Cloud: Imprenta Belín, 1929.

Bello, Andrés. *Filosofía del entendimiento y otros escritos.* In Vol. III of *Obras Completas.* Caracas: Ministerio de Educación. 1951.

Bergson, Henri. *Le Rire: Essai Sur la Signification du Comique.* Paris: 1969.

Bianco, José. "Así es Sarmiento." *Vuelta,* No. 26 (1979), 5-14.

Bóo, Alicia R. "La realidad argentina a través de Varela y Sarmiento." In *Florencio Varela y el 'Comercio del Plata,'* by Félix Weinberg and collaboraters. Bahía Blanca: Instituto de Humanidades, Universidad Nacional del Sur, 1970, pp. 83-110.

Borello, Rodolfo. "El ensayo argentino: 1959-1976." *Los ensayistas,* 4, No. 6 & 7 (1979), 19-30.

——————— . "*Facundo:* heterogeneidad y persuasión." *Cuadernos Hispanoamericanos,* No. 263-64 (1977), pp. 283-302.

——————— . *Habla y literatura en la Argentina (Sarmiento, Hernández, Mansilla, Cambaceres, Fray Mocho, Borges, Marechal, Cortázar).* Tucumán: Universidad Nacional de Tucumán, Facultad de Filosofía y Letras, 1974.

Borges, Jorge Luis. *El aleph.* Madrid: Alianza, 1975. In English: *The Aleph and Other Stories, 1933-1969.* Ed. and trans. Norman Thomas de Giovanni. New York: E. P. Dutton, 1970.

Bouilly, Victor. "L'option romantique au Río de la Plata." *Revue de Littérature Comparée,* 52, No. 1 (1978), 5-22.

Bravo, Héctor Félix. *Sarmiento, pedagogo social: las concepciones sociales en la pedagogía de Sarmiento.* Buenos Aires: Editorial Universitaria de Buenos Aires, 1965.

Bronowski, J. and Bruce Mazlish. *The Western Intellectual Tradition: From Leonardo to Hegel.* New York: Harper and Row, Harper Torchbooks, 1960.

Bunge, C. O. *Sarmiento: estudio biográfico y crítico.* Madrid: Espasa-Calpe, 1926.

Bunkley, Allison Williams. *The Life of Sarmiento.* Princeton: Princeton University Press, 1952.

Burgin, Miron. *The Economic Aspects of Argentine Federalism, 1820-1852.* Cambridge: Harvard University Press, 1946.

Burns, E. Bradford. "Cultures in Conflict: The Implication of Modernization in Nineteenth-Century Latin America." In *Elites, Masses and Modernization in Latin America, 1850-1930,* by E. Bradford Burns and Thomas E. Skidmore. Austin: University of Texas Press, 1979, pp. 11-78.

——————. "Ideology in Nineteenth-Century Latin American Historiography." *Hispanic American Historical Review,* 58, No. 3 (1978), 409-31.

——————. *The Poverty of Progress: Latin America in the Nineteenth Century.* Los Angeles and Berkeley: University of California Press, 1980.

C. L. B. "Des Rapports de la France et de l'Europe avec l'Amérique du Sud." *Revue des Deux Mondes,* Series 4, 31, No. 15 (1838), 54-69.

Campobassi, José S. *Sarmiento y su época: 1811-1863.* Buenos Aires: Losada, 1967. Vol. I.

Canal Feijóo, Bernardo. *Alberdi y la proyección sistemática del espíritu de Mayo.* Buenos Aires: Losada, 1961.

Carilla, Emilio. "Ideas estéticas de Echeverría." In *Estudios de literatura argentina (siglo XIX).* Tucumán: Universidad Nacional de Tucumán, Facultad de Filosofía y Letras, 1965, pp. 147-162.

——————. *El romanticismo en la América hispánica.* Madrid: Gredos, 1958.

——————. *Lengua y estilo de Sarmiento.* La Plata: Universidad Nacional de la Plata, Facultad de Humanidades y Ciencias de la Educación. 1964.

Carrizo, Juan Alfonso, ed. *Cancionero popular de Salta.* Buenos Aires: A. Barocco, 1933.

──────────── . "Sarmiento y 'El cantar tradicional del General Juan Facundo Quiroga.'" *Sustancia,* 1 (1930), pp. 9-18.

Castagnino, Raúl H. "Estética de la energía en Sarmiento." In *Historias menores del pasado literario argentino (siglo XIX).* Buenos Aires: Huemul, 1976, pp. 23-38.

Castro, Américo. "En torno al *Facundo* de Sarmiento." *Sur,* 8, No. 47 (1938), 26-34.

Castro, Isaac E. *Sarmiento ante la montonera.* Corrientes: Imprenta del Estado, 1937.

Chávez, Fermín. *Civilización y barbarie en la cultura argentina.* 2nd ed. exp. Buenos Aires: Theoría, 1965.

Corro, Gaspar P. del. *Facundo y Fierro: la proscripción de los héroes.* Buenos Aires: Casteneda, 1977.

Derrida, Jacques. *Of Grammatology.* Trans. Gayatri Chakravorty Spivak. Baltimore and London: Johns Hopkins University Press, 1976.

Dewey, John. *Liberalism and Social Action.* New York: G. P. Putnam's Sons, 1935.

Doll, Ramón and Guillermo Cano, Jr. *Las mentiras de Sarmiento: por qué fue unitario.* Buenos Aires: Ediciones del Renacimiento, 1939.

Draghi Lucero, Juan. *Cancionero popular cuyano.* Mendoza: Best Hermanos, 1938.

Durán, Juan Guillermo. "Literatura y utopía en Hispanoamérica." Diss. Cornell, 1972.

Echeverría, Esteban. *Dogma socialista.* Buenos Aires: Imprenta y Librerías de Mayo, 1873.

──────────── . *Obras Completas.* Ed. Juan María Gutiérrez. Buenos Aires: Imprenta y Librerías de Mayo, 1874.

──────────── . *Páginas literarias seguidas de los fundamentos de una estética romántica.* Buenos Aires: El Ateneo, 1928.

Erro, Carlos Alberto. "La aportación sociológica de Sarmiento." In *Sarmiento: educador, sociólogo, escritor, político,* by Juan Mantovi, et al. Buenos Aires: Universidad de Buenos Aires, Facultad de Filosofía y Letras, 1963, pp. 25-39.

Fernández, Juan Rómulo. *Sarmiento (semblanza e iconografía).* Buenos Aires: Librería del Colegio, 1938.

Fernández Retamar, Roberto. "Algunos usos de civilización y barbarie." *Casa de las Américas,* 7, No. 102 (1977), 29-52.

—————. "Nuestra América y Occidente." *Casa de las Américas,* 16, No. 98 (1976), 36-57.

Ferns, H. S. *Argentina,* New York: Frederick A. Praeger, 1969.

—————. *Britain and Argentina in the Nineteenth Century.* Oxford: Clarendon Press, 1960.

Ferrer, Aldo. *The Argentine Economy.* Trans. Marjory M. Urquidi. Berkeley and Los Angeles: University of California Press, 1967.

Foucault, Michel. *The Order of Things: An Archaeology of the Human Sciences.* New York: Random House, Vintage, 1970.

—————. *L'ordre du discours: leçon inaugurale du College de France prononcée le 2 décembre 1970.* Paris: Gallimard, 1971.

Foster, George W. *Tzintzuntzán: Mexican Peasants in a Changing World.* Boston: Little, Brown Co., 1967.

Franco, Jean. "Trends and Priorities for Research on Latin American Literature." *Ideologies & Literature,* 2nd cycle, 4 (May-June 1983), 107-20; reprint from The Wilson Center, Working Papers for the Latin American Program, 1981.

Franco, Luis. *Sarmiento entre dos fuegos.* Buenos Aires: Paídos, 1968.

Galeano, Eduardo. "Perón, los gorriones y la Providencia." In *Violencia y enajenación.* Madrid: Nuestro Tiempo, 1971.

Gálvez, Manuel. *Vida de Sarmiento: el hombre de autoridad.* Buenos Aires: Emecé, 1945.

García Bacca, Juan David. "Prólogo." In Andrés Bello, *Obras Completas.* Caracas: Ministerio de Educación. 1951, Vol. III.

García Costa, Víctor. *El periódico político.* Buenos Aires: Centro Editor de América Latina, 1971.

García Martínez, J. A. *Sarmiento y el arte de su tiempo.* Buenos Aires: Emecé, 1979.

García Mellid, Atilio. *Proceso al liberalismo argentino.* Buenos Aires: A. Peña Lillo, 1957.

García Merou, Martín. *Sarmiento.* Introd. Rodolfo Trostine. Buenos Aires: Ayacucho, 1944.

Garrels, Elizabeth. *Mariátegui y la Argentina: un caso de 'lentes ajenos.'* Gaithersburg, MD: Hispamérica, 1982.

Girvetz, Harry K. *The Evolution of Liberalism.* New York: Collier Books, 1963.

Groussac, Paul. *El viaje intelectual: impresiones de naturaleza y arte,* 2nd ed. Buenos Aires: Jesús Menéndez, 1920.

Guerrero, César H. *Sarmiento: historiador y biógrafo.* Buenos Aires: El Ateneo, 1950.

——————. *Sarmiento: el pensador.* Buenos Aires: Depalma, 1979.

Guerrero, Juan Luis. *Tres temas de filosofía en las entrañas del 'Facundo'.* Buenos Aires, 1945.

Guizot, François Pierre Guillaume. *The History of Civilization in Europe.* Trans. William Hazlitt. New York: Al Burt, n.d.

——————. *The History of France.* In *Essays and Lectures.* Ed. and introd. Stanley Mellon. Chicago: University of Chicago Press, 1972.

Gutiérrez, Eduardo. *El Chacho.* Buenos Aires: H. Tommasi, n.d.

Gutiérrez, Juan María. "Fisonomía del saber español: cual deba ser entre nosotros." In *Antecedentes de la Asociación de Mayo: 1837-1937.* Homenaje del H. Consejo Deliberante de la ciudad de Buenos Aires en el centenario de su fundación. Buenos Aires: Canteillo y Co., 1939, pp. 49-60.

Halperín Donghi, Tulio. *The Aftermath of Revolution in Latin America.* Trans. Josephine de Bunsen. New York: Harper and Row, 1973.

——————. "El espejo de la historia." *Contorno,* No. 9/10 (1959), pp. 76-81.

——————. "La expansión ganadera en la campaña de Buenos Aires (1818-1852)." In *Los fragmentos del poder: de la oligarquía a la poliarquía argentina,* by Ezequiel Gallo (h), et al. Ed. T. S. di Tella and T. Halperín Donghi. Buenos Aires: Jorge Alvarez, 1969, pp. 21-74.

——————. "Una nación para el desierto argentino." In *Proyecto y construcción de una nación (Argentina 1846-1880).* Ed. Halperín Donghi. Caracas: Biblioteca Ayacucho, 1980, pp. xi-cii.

——————. *El pensamiento de Echeverría.* Buenos Aires: Sudamericana, 1951.

——————. "Prólogo." In *Campaña en el Ejército Grande Aliado de Sud América,* by Domingo F. Sarmiento. México: Fondo de Cultura Económica, 1958, pp. vii-lvi.

—————————— . *Revolución y guerra: formación de una élite dirigente en la Argentina criolla.* Buenos Aires: Siglo Veintiuno, 1972.

—————————— . "Sarmiento: su lugar en la sociedad argentina post-revolucionaria." *Sur,* No. 341 (1977), 121-135.

Harriet, Fernando Campo. "Andrés Bello y la enseñanza de la historia." *Atenea: Revista de Ciencia, Arte y Literatura.* No. 443-444 (1981), pp. 309-16.

Hauser, Arnold. *The Social History of Art:* Volume III: *Rococo, Classicism, Romanticism.* New York: Random House, Vintage, n. d.

Head, Francis B. *Rough Notes Taken During Some Rapid Journies Across the Pampas and Among the Andes.* Boston: Wells and Lilly, 1827.

Hegel, Georg Wilhelm Friedrich. *The Philosophy of History.* Trans. J. Sibree. Pref. Charles Hegel. Rev. ed. New York: Colonial Press, 1899.

Herder, Johann Gottfried von. *Reflections on the Philosophy of the History of Mankind.* Introd. Frank E. Manuel. Chicago: University of Chicago Press, 1968.

Hernández, José. *Vida del Chacho: rasgos biográficos del General Angel Vicente Peñalosa.* Buenos Aires: A. dos Santos, 1947.

Hoffer, Eric. *The True Believer: Thoughts on the Nature of Mass Movements.* New York: Harper and Row, 1966.

Hudson, Damián. *Recuerdos históricos sobre la Provincia de Cuyo.* Buenos Aires: Juan A. Alsina, 1898. Vol. II.

Ingenieros, José. *Las direcciones filosóficas de la cultura argentina.* Buenos Aires: Universitaria de Buenos Aires, 1963.

—————————— . *La evolución de las ideas argentinas.* Ed. Anibal Ponce. Buenos Aires: El Ateneo, 1951, Vol. II.

—————————— . "Exposición de ideas sociológicas." In *Conflicto y armonía de las razas en América,* by Domingo F. Sarmiento. Buenos Aires: La Cultura Argentina, 1915, pp. 7-40.

—————————— . "La filosofía social de Echeverría y la leyenda de la 'Asociación de Mayo,'" *Revista de Filosofía, Cultura, Ciencias . . . ,* 4 (1914), 225-97.

—————————— . *Sociología argentina.* 5th ed. (Buenos Aires: Ediciones L. J. Rosso, 1913).

Jaén, Didier Tisdel. "La generación romántica argentina y el problema de Hispanoamérica." *Journal of Inter-American Studies,* 8 (1966), 565-84.

──────────. "Hispanoamérica como problema a través de la generación romántica en Argentina y Chile." Diss. University of Texas 1965.

Jaksić, Iván. *The Meaning of Liberalism in Latin America: The Cases of Chile, Argentina, and Mexico in the 19th Century.* Buffalo: SUNY, Council on International Studies, 1981.

James, C. R. *Notes on Dialectics, Hegel and Marxism.* 2nd ed. New York: Friends of Facing Reality Publications, 1971.

Jameson, Fredric, *Marxism and Form: Twentieth-Century Dialectical Theories of Literature.* Princeton: Princeton University Press, 1974.

──────────. *The Political Unconscious: Narrative as a Socially Symbolic Act.* Ithica: Cornell University Press, 1982.

Jitrik, Noé. "El *Facundo:* la gran riqueza de la pobreza." In *Facundo o civilización y barbarie,* by Domingo F. Sarmiento. Caracas: Biblioteca Ayacucho, 1977, pp. ix-lii.

──────────. *Muerte y resurrección de 'Facundo'.* Buenos Aires: Centro Editor de América Latina, 1968.

──────────. "Para una lectura de *Facundo,* de Domingo F. Sarmiento." *Ensayos y estudios de literatura argentina.* Buenos Aires: Galerna, 1970, pp. 12-34.

Katra, William H. "Discourse Production and Sarmiento's Essayistic Style." In *Simposio: el ensayo hispánico. Actas.* Eds. Isaac Jack Levy and Juan Loveluck. Columbia, S.C.: University of South Carolina, 1984. Pp. 147-56.

──────────. "Echeverría según Sarmiento: la personificación de una nación ultrajada por la barbarie." *Cuadernos Americanos,* 255 (1984), 165-85.

──────────. "El *Facundo:* contexto histórico y estética derivada." *Cuadernos Americanos,* 236 (1981), 151-76.

Kilgore, William. "The Development of Positivism in Latin America." *Inter-American Review of Bibliography,* 19 (1966), 23-42.

Korn, Alejandro. *Influencias filosóficas en la evolución nacional.* In Vol. III of *Obras.* La Plata: Universidad Nacional de la Plata, 1940.

──────────. *El pensamiento argentino.* Introd. Gregorio Weinberg. Buenos Aires: Nova, n.d.

Krieger, Murray. *The Tragic Vision: The Confrontation of Extremity.* Vol. I. Baltimore and London: Johns Hopkins Press, 1973.

Lastarria, [José] V[ictorino]. "Investigación sobre la influencia de la conquista i del sistema colonial de los españoles en Chile: memoria presentada a la universidad en la sesión solemne de 22 de setiembre de 1844, por don José Victorino Lastarria." In *Obras Completas,* Vol. III: *Opúsculos literarios i críticos.* Santiago: Imprenta Pedro G. Ramírez, 1885, pp. 71-88.

——————. *Recuerdos literarios: datos para la historia literaria de la América española, del progreso intelectual en Chile.* Santiago: Librería de M. Servat, 1885.

Lerminier, E. *De l'influence de la philosophie du XVIIIè siècle sur la legislatión et la sociabilité du XIXè.* Paris: Didier, Libraire-Commissionnaire, 1833.

Leumann, Carlos Alberto. *La literatura gauchesca y la poesía gaucha.* Buenos Aires: Raigal, 1953.

Levene, Ricardo. "Sarmiento, sociólogo de la realidad americana y argentina," *Humanidades,* 26 (1938), pp. 73-105. Reprinted in *Sarmiento: homenaje de la Facultad de Humanidades y Ciencias de la Educación.* La Plata: Universidad Nacional de La Plata, 1939, pp. 83-116.

Lévi-Strauss, Claude. *The Savage Mind.* Chicago: University of Chicago Press, 1970.

Lida, Raimundo. "Sarmiento y Herder." *Memoria del Segundo Congreso Internacional de Catedráticos de Literatura Iberoamericana, Agosto de 1940.* Ed. Instituto Internacional de Literatura Iberoamericana. Berkeley and Los Angeles: University of California Press, 1941, pp. 155-71.

Lizondo Borda, Manuel. "Sarmiento, Posse y Tucumán." *Humanidades,* 37, No. 3 (1961).

Lugones, Leopoldo. *Historia de Sarmiento.* Buenos Aires: Otero & Co., 1911.

Lukács, Georg. *History and Class Consciousness: Studies in Marxist Dialectics.* Trans. Rodney Livingstone. Cambridge: M.I.T. Press, 1971.

Lynch, John. *Argentine Dictator: Juan Manuel de Rosas, 1929-1852.* Oxford: Clarendon Press, 1981.

Mackenna, Benjamín Viñuna. *La Argentina en el año 1855.* Introd. V. Lillo Catalán. Buenos Aires: Edición de la Revista Americana de Buenos Aires, 1936.

Mandelbaum, Maurice M. *History, Man, and Reason: A Study in Nineteenth Century Thought.* Baltimore and London: Johns Hopkins University Press, 1971.

Mannheim, Karl. *Ideology and Utopia: An Introduction to the Sociology of Knowledge.* Trans. Louis Wirth and Edward Shils. New York: Harcourt, Brace and World, 1936.

Martínez Estrada, Ezequiel. *Los invariantes históricos en el 'Facundo'.* Buenos Aires: Casa Pardo, 1974.

———————. *Meditaciones sarmientinas.* Buenos Aires: Ediciones Universitarias, 1968.

———————. *Radiografía de la pampa.* 6th ed. Buenos Aires: Losada, 1968.

———————. *Sarmiento.* Buenos Aires: Argos, 1956.

Menéndez y Pelayo, Marcelino. *Antología de poetas hispano-americanos,* Vol. II: *Cuba, Santo Domingo, Puerto Rico, Venezuela.* Madrid: Impresores de la Casa Real, 1893.

Millani, Domingo. "Utopian Socialism: Transitional Thread from Romanticism to Positivism in Latin America." *Journal of the History of Ideas,* No. 24 (1963), pp. 515-522.

Mitre, Bartolomé. *Obras Completas.* Buenos Aires: Congreso de la Nación Argentina, 1938.

Morán, Fernando. *Novela y semidesarrollo: una interpretación de la novela hispanoamericana y española.* Madrid: Taurus, 1971.

Morse, Richard M. "The Heritage of Latin America." In *Politics and Social Change in Latin America: The Distinct Tradition,* Ed. Howard J. Wiarda. Amherst: University of Massachusetts Press, 1974, pp. 25-69.

Muñoz Azpiri, José Luis. *Rosas frente al imperio británico: historia íntima de un triunfo argentino.* 2nd ed. Buenos Aires: Theoría, 1974.

Orgaz, Raúl A. *Sarmiento y el naturalismo histórico.* Vol. III of *Obras Completas.* Introd. Arturo Capdevila. Córdoba: Assandri, 1950.

Ortega y Gasset, José. *Obras Completas.* Madrid: Revista de Occidente, 1950-1962.

Ottolenghi, Julia. *Vida y obra de Sarmiento en síntesis cronológica.* Buenos Aires: Kapelusz, 1950.

Page, Thomas. *La Plata, the Argentine Confederation, and Paraguay, Being a Narrative of the Exploration of the Tributaries of the River*

La Plata and Adjacent Countries During the Years 1853, 54, 55 and 56, Under the Orders of the United States Government. New York: Harper & Brothers, 1859.

Palacios, Alfredo L. "Civilización y barbarie: dualismo simplista inaceptable." *Cuadernos Americanos*, 105, No. 4 (1959), 162-202.

Palcos, Alberto. *Echeverría y la democracia argentina.* Buenos Aires: El Ateneo, 1941.

——————. *El 'Facundo.' Rasgos de Sarmiento. Génesis y peripecias del 'Facundo.' Sarmiento y Rosas. Sarmiento íntimo. Sarmiento y el voto secreto.* Buenos Aires: El Ateneo, 1934.

——————. "Prólogo." In *Facundo: civilización y barbarie*, by Domingo F. Sarmiento. Buenos Aires: Editorial Cultura Argentina, 1961.

——————. *Sarmiento: la vida, la obra, las ideas, el genio.* Buenos Aires: Emecé, 1962.

Parish, John and W. P. Robertson. *Letters on South America comprising Travels on the Banks of the Paraná and Río de la Plata in Three Volumes.* London: John Murray, 1843.

Paso, Leonardo. *Los caudillos y la organización nacional.* Buenos Aires: Sílaba, 1970.

Paz, Octavio. *El arco y la lira: el poema, la revelación poética, poesía e historia.* México: Fondo de Cultura Económica, 1973.

Peña, Milcíades. *Alberdi, Sarmiento, El 90: límites del nacionalismo argentino en el siglo XIX.* Buenos Aires: Ediciones Fichas, 1970.

——————. *La clase dirigente argentina frente al imperialismo (seguido de Orígenes y resultados de la nacionalización de los ferrocarriles).* Buenos Aires: Fichas, 1973.

Ponce, Aníbal. *Sarmiento: constructor de la nueva Argentina. La vejez de Sarmiento.* Buenos Aires: Héctor Matera, 1958.

Prieto, Adolfo. *La literatura autobiográfica argentina.* Rosario: Universidad Nacional del Litoral, Facultad de Filosofía y Letras, 1965.

——————. *Literatura y subdesarrollo: notas para un análisis de la literatura argentina.* Buenos Aires: Biblioteca 1968.

Rama, Carlos M., ed. *Utopismo socialista (1830-1893).* Caracas: Ayacucho, 1977.

Renan, Ernest. *Oeuvres completes.* Vol VIII: *l'Origine du langage.* Paris: Calmann-Lévy, 1958.

Ribeiro, Darcy. *Las Américas y la civilización: proceso de formación y causas del desarrollo desigual de los pueblos americanos.* Trad. R. Pi. Rev. ed. Buenos Aires: 1972.

Richards, Dona. "The Ideology of European Dominance." *The Western Journal of Black Studies.* 3, No. 4 (1979), 244-50.

Rodríguez, Augusto. *Sarmiento militar.* Buenos Aires: Edición G. Kraft, 1950.

Rojas, Nerio. *Psicología de Sarmiento.* Buenos Aires: Kraft, 1961.

Rojas, Ricardo. *Historia de la literatura argentina: ensayo filosófico sobre la evolución de la cultura en el Plata.* Vol. I: *Los proscriptos.* 2nd ed. Buenos Aires: Guillermo Kraft, 1957.

——————. *El pensamiento vivo de Sarmiento.* Buenos Aires: Losada, 1941.

——————. *El profeta de la pampa: vida de Sarmiento.* Buenos Aires: Losada, 1945.

Romero, José Luis. *A History of Argentine Political Thought.* Introd. and trans. Thomas F. McGann. Stanford: Stanford University Press, 1963.

Rosenthal, Mauricio. *Sarmiento y el teatro: musa recóndita de un titán.* Buenos Aires: Kraft, 1967.

Sacoto, Antonio. "El indio en la obra literaria de Sarmiento y Marti." *Cuadernos Americanos,* 156, No. 1 (1968), 137-63.

Said, Edward W. *Beginnings: Intention and Method.* Baltimore and London: Johns Hopkins University Press, 1975.

Salomon, Noël. "A propos des elements 'costumbristas' dans le *Facundo* de D. F. Sarmiento." *Bulletin Hispanique,* 52 (1968), 342-412.

——————. "El *Facundo* de Domingo Faustino Sarmiento: manifiesto de la preburguesía argentina de las ciudades del interior." *Cuadernos Americanos,* 39, No. 5 (1980), 121-76.

Sánchez Sorondo, Marcelo. "Sarmiento: hombre de acción." *Sur,* No. 341 (1977), pp. 136-55.

Sarmiento, Bienvenida. *Rasgos de la vida de Domingo Faustino Sarmiento.* Introd. Antonio P. Castro. Buenos Aires: 1946.

Sarmiento, Domingo Faustino. *Campaña en el Ejército Grande Aliado de Sud América.* Prol. Tulio Halperín Donghi. México: Fondo de Cultura Económica, 1958.

——————— . *Facundo.* Ed. and prol. Alberto Palcos. Buenos Aires: Ediciones Culturales Argentinas, 1961.

——————— . *Obras Completas.* 52 vols. Buenos Aires: Editorial Luz del Día, 1948-1956.

——————— . *Obras Completas.* Paris: Belín Hermanos, 1895-1909, Vol. XXX.

——————— . *Sarmiento: cartas y discursos políticos.* Buenos Aires: Ediciones Culturales Argentinas, 1965. Vol. III.

Sartre, Jean-Paul. *La Nausée.* Paris: Livre de Poche, 1957.

Schlegel, A. W. *Lectures on Dramatic Art and Literature, Ancient and Modern.* In *Literary Criticism: Pope to Croce,* eds. Gay Wilson Allen and Harry Hanyden Clark. Detroit: Wayne State University Press, 1962, pp. 172-84.

Scobie, James R. *Argentina: a City and a Nation.* 2nd ed. New York: Oxford University Press, 1971.

——————— . *La lucha por la consolidación de la nacionalidad argentina, 1852-1862.* Trans. Gabriela de Civiny. Buenos Aires: Hachette, 1964.

Shaw, D. L. "Concerning the Structure of *Facundo.*" *Ibero-Amerikanisches Archiv,* 6, No. 3 (1980), 239-50.

Suárez, Matías E. *Sarmiento: ese desconocido.* Buenos Aires: Theoría, 1964.

Subercaseaux, Bernardo. *Cultura y sociedad liberal en el siglo XIX. Lastarria: ideología y literatura.* Santiago: Editorial Aconcagua, 1981.

——————— . "Filosofía de la historia, novela y sistema expresivo en Chile (1840-1850)." *Cuadernos Americanos,* 38, No. 4 (1979), 99-122.

——————— . "Filosofía de la historia, novela y sistema expresivo en la obra de J.V. Lastarria, 1840-1848." *Ideologies & Literature,* 3, No. 11 (1975), 56-84.

van Tieghem, Philippe. *Petite histoire des grandes doctrines litteraires en France.* Paris: Presses Universitaires de France, 1950.

de Tocqueville, Alexis. *Democracy in America.* New York: Random House, 1963. Vol. I.

Taine, H[ippolyte] A. *History of English Literature.* Trans. H. Van Laun. New York: T. Y. Crowell, 1873.

Tamagno, Roberto. *Sarmiento, los liberales y el imperialismo inglés.* Buenos Aires: A. Peña Lillo, 1963.

Varela Domínguez de Ghioldi, Delfina. *Filosofía argentina: los ideólogos.* Buenos Aires: 1938.

Verdevoye, Paul. *Domingo Faustino Sarmiento: éducateur et publiciste (entre 1839 et 1852).* Paris: Institut des Hautes Etudes de l'Amérique Latine, 1963.

——————. "Don Andrés Bello y Domingo Faustino Sarmiento: una polémica y una colaboración." In *Bello y Chile: Tercer Congreso del Bicentenario,* Vol. 1. Caracas: Fundación La Casa de Bello, 1981, pp. 103-24.

Ves Losada, Alfredo E. "Campo y ciudad en *Facundo.*" *Cuadernos Americanos,* 15, No. 6 (1956), 185-200.

——————. "Facundo y la montonera." *Cuadernos Americanos,* 81, No. 3 (1955), 169-83.

Vidal, Hernán. "*Amalia:* melodrama y dependencia." *Ideologies & Literature,* 1, No. 2 (1977), 41-70.

——————. *Literatura hispanoamericana e ideología liberal: surgimiento y crisis (una problemática sobre la dependencia en torno a la narrativa del boom).* Buenos Aires: Hispamérica, 1976.

Viñas, David. *Literatura argentina y realidad política.* Vol. I: *De Sarmiento a Cortázar.* Buenos Aires: Siglo Veinte, 1971.

——————. *Rebeliones populares argentinas.* Vol. I: *De los montoneros a los anarquistas.* Buenos Aires: Carlos Pérez, 1971.

Un Voyager [pseud.]. "Les Deux Rives de la Plata: Montevideo, Buenos-Ayres, Rivera, Rosas." *Revue des Deux Mondes,* 50, Year 13, No. 2 (1843), 5-49.

Wallerstein, Immanuel. "The Rise and Future Demise of the World Capitalist-System: Concepts for Comparative Analysis." *Comparative Studies in Society and History,* 16, No. 4 (1974), 387-415.

Weinberg, Félix. "El periodismo en la época de Rosas." *Revista de Historia,* No. 2 (1957), 81-100.

Wiarda, Howard J. "Law and Political Development in Latin America: Toward a Framework for Analysis." In *Politics and Social Change in Latin America: The Distinct Tradition.* Amherst: University of Massachusetts Press, 1974, pp. 199-229.

Zalazar, Daniel E. "Las ideas de D. F. Sarmiento sobre la influencia de la religión en la democracia americana." *Discurso Literario,* 2, No. 2 (1985), 541-48.

——————— . "Las posiciones de Sarmiento frente al indio." *Revista Iberoamericana,* 50, No. 127 (1984), 411-27.

Zárate, Armando. "El *Facundo:* un héroe como su mito." *Revista Iberoamericana,* 44, No. 104-105 (1978), 471-48.

INDEX

Aberastain, Antonio: 28

Alberdi, Juan Bautista: aesthetic ideas, 75; against Buenos Aires, 200-01, 204; commitment to social change, 159; contrasted to Sarmiento, 159; liberal ideas, 198; member of Gen. of 1837, xv, 12, 190; directs *La Moda*, 27; views after 1852, 199, 202; rivalry with Sarmiento, 21, 61-62, 179; Sarmiento sends poem, 74, 99n.10; on Sarmiento's presidency, 204; on Sarmiento's intelligence, 49

Aldao, El fraile: 9-10; Sarmiento denounces, 19

Alsina, Valentín: 65n.25, 71, 94; critizes *Facundo*, 108

Althusser, Louis: xiii, 163; concept of *bricoleur*, 43

Alvear, Carlos María de: 198

Andean regions (Bolivia & Peru): 1; economic decline of Argentina's Andean provinces, 2

Anderson Imbert, Enrique: xiii; on Sarmiento's ideas, 48; on Sarmiento's anthropomorphizations, 71

Aquinas, St. Thomas: 65n.22

Argentina
—bourgeoisie: xv; European models, 188; growth in 1900s, 36; and liberal intellectuals, 200; progressive, 158, 185; post-1852 economic role, 201; Sarmiento's critique after 1880, 205; transition in mid-1900s, 186. *See also* liberalism; Sarmiento: liberalism
—Buenos Aires vs. interior: 5, 10, 16, 118-19, 173-74; "natural" population, 207
—economy: British imperialism, 169-70; pre-independence, 1; tariff policy of Rosas, 22n.8
—history: Spanish colonialism, 1, 114; colonial Córdoba, 117; colonial culture, 16, 24n.28; May Revolution, 114, 154, 184; British role in development, 168-75; *terratenientes*, 5; civil wars, 4, 127, 155; transition in 1900s, 167; liberalism, 197-

98; liberal reconstruction post-1852, 168, 200-08, 211n.27; presidencies of Mitre & Sarmiento, 203-04, 211n.27; railroads, xi, 207; "dirty war" of 1970s, xv, 208. *See also* Buenos Aires
—immigration: proposed by Rivadavia, 5; results of, 129; Sarmiento's support for, 205. *See also* Sarmiento: "civilization"
—interior provinces: economic decline, 1-2, 4; rivalry with Buenos Aires, 173; source of barbarism, 176; after 1852, 203
—liberalism: in post-1852 period, 168; in national history, 197-208
—oligarchy: x
—Rosas. *See* Rosas; Sarmiento: Rosas

Aristotle: 91, 117

Artigas, José Gervasio: 115, 179

Avellaneda, Nicolás: 201

Balcarce, Marco González: 27

Asociación de Mayo: 154. *See also* Generation of 1837

Banda Oriental. *See* Montevideo, Uruguay

Barcala, "El negro": 116

Barranco Yaco: 149

Barrenechea, Ana María: 72, 73, 96

Barthes, Roland: xiv

Bases (Alberdi): 159, 199

Belgrano, Manuel: 198

Bello, Andrés: 17; neoclassical ideas, 29; ontological ideas, 54; historiographical debates in Santiago, 183-86

Benavides (Colonel, then Governor of San Juan): 9, 10; Federalist military leader, 19; confronts Sarmiento over *El Zonda*, 28

Bergson, Henri: 51

Bible readings by Sarmiento, 11

Bravo, Héctor Félix: xiii

Borges, Jorge Luis: xi, xii, xiv, 206

Brazil: 175

bricoleur: 41-63; Lévi-Strauss' definition, 42; Althusser's definition, 43; to possess, 57; begins with a desire, 63. *See also*: Sarmiento: *bricoleur*

Buenos Aires (city and province): center of civilization, 150; clash with interior provinces, 173; desire for economic domination, 192n.7; post-1852 period, 176, 199-208; produces Rosas, 1, 132; Sarmiento's changing ideas vis-à-vis, 179, 204-05; Sarmiento defends, 193n.15, 201-04. *See also* Argentina: history

Bunge, Carlos Octavio: xiii

Bunkley, Allison Williams: xiii, 96

Burns, E. Bradford: 189, 207

Campobassi, José S.: xiii; on Sarmiento's conversion to unitarianism, 23n.13

"Cantar . . . a la muerte del General Facundo": 90-92

Carilla, Emilio: 75

Carrizo, Juan Alfonso: 90-92

Cartas quillotanas (Alberdi): 62, 66n.29, 179

Caseros, battle of (1852):63, 155, 201, 203

caudillos: British support for, 171; rise of, 1, 4-5; and Rosas, 10; struggle against, 118-19. *See also* Sarmiento: *caudillos*

Cautiva, La (Echeverría): 77

Chile: politics of 1841, 29; Sarmiento's participation in, 120

Castro, Américo: 46

Chateaubriand, François René de: 116, 182

científicos. See Positivism

Cobden, Robert: 174

Coleridge, Samuel P.: 81

Comte, Auguste: 121

Condillac, Etienne de: 86

Condorcet, Antoine-Nicolas de: 110-11, 152; historicist views of, 188

Confederation: 202-03; Alberdi's support for, 62; Sarmiento's opposition to, xi. *See also*: Argentina: history

Cooper, James Fenimore: 85, 93

Córdoba (city): 116-17, 127-28. *See also*: Argentina: history

"corporate" Latin American culture: 49

Corrientes (province): 179, 203

costumbrismo: 59, 96, 134

Cours de philosophie positiviste (Comte): 121

Cousin, Victor: 12, 130, 182

Cuyo. *See* San Juan

Democracy in America (Tocqueville): 146; historicist views, 188; Indians, 161, 188, 195n.42

dependency: xv; Alberdi's view of, 159; definition, xvi; dependent liberalism, 179, 200-08; material successes of in post-1852 period, 207; Sarmiento anticipates, 186; Sarmiento welcomes, 180

Derrida, Jacques: xiii-xiv, 53

Descartes, René: 54

Dewey, John: 200

Díaz, Porfirio: 158

discourse production: xiii; and authority, 57-63; definition, 57

Dogma socialista (Echeverría): xv, 68n.50, 86; and liberalism, 198

Don Segundo Sombra (Güiraldes): 84

Duhalde, Eduardo Luis: xii

Echague, Juan Pablo: xiii

Echeverría, Esteban: xv; commitment to social change, 159; exception to Generation of 1837, 190; and Joven Argentina, 12; and liberalism, 198; and romanticism, 73, 93; and Salón Literario, 27; and Sarmiento, 39n.14; Sarmiento's negative views of, 61-62, 94; Sarmiento's views on literature of, 77-78; "useless rebellion," 86. *See also*: Generation of 1837

"Eclectic" School: 198

England. *See* Great Britain

Entre Ríos (province): xi, 176, 179

Enlightenment: and historicism, 111, 182; and liberalism, xv, 1; overview, 197; power of ideas, 152; Sarmiento's familiarity with, 11; in Sarmiento's historicist thought, 110-21. *See also* liberalism

Europe: imperialism and culture, 186-92; Europeanization of South America, 174-82; Europeans and progress, 152; as symbol for civilization, 150, 186-92; provides standard for historicism, 183, 185

Facundo Quiroga, Juan: 8; before Rosas, 131; and decline of interior, 10; described in *Facundo*, 50, 89-90, 148-49; Sarmiento confronts, 19; Sarmiento denounces, 14; *tigre de los Llanos*, 79-80. See also Sarmiento: *Facundo*

Ficciones (Borges): xii

Federalist Party: xii; dispute with Unitarians, 1, 10;and Mitre, 204; Sarmiento against after 1852, 203; Sarmiento's federalist ideas, 126-28. *See* Unitarian Party

Fénelon, François de Salignac: 182

Fernández de Lizardi, José Joaquín: 36

Fernández Retamar, Roberto: 186

Ferns, H. S.: 175, 191n.5, 203-04

feudalism: 114; and liberal thought, 197; Sarmiento's opposition to, 151, 167, 207; and Rosas, 150. *See* Argentina: history

"Figarillo" (pseudonym for Alberdi): 27

Fourier, Charles: 188, 198

France: blockade of 1835-1838, 2, 168; Commune, 198; intervention in Río de la Plata, 178, 181; and liberalism, 185,

198; Revolution, 154; Sarmiento's support for, 169; standard for progress, 184

Franco, Jean: xiii

Foucault, Michel: xiv, 97

Freud, Sigmund: 52-53; in Althusser's thought, 43

Funes, Gregorio (Dean): 11, 16, 117

Galvanism: 84

Gálvez, Manuel: xii, xiii; on Sarmiento's writing, 42; on Sarmiento's interpersonal relationships, 66n.28

García Mellid, Atilio: xiii

García Merou, Martín: xiii, 35

gaucho: 102n.32; 139n.16. *See also* Sarmiento: gauchos

El gaucho Martín Fierro (Hernández): 203

Generation of 1837: xv; aesthetic ideas, 75; change from utopian to dependent liberalism, 200-01; despised Argentina, 190; dreamlike plans, 165n.12; and education, 159; idealistic, 154; according to Halperín Donghi, 67n.37; and Joven Argentina, 12; and liberalism, 198-107; opposition to Rosas, 199, 206; in post-1852 period, 199, 200-03; and Salón Literario, 27, 99n.12

Great Britain: imperial manoeuvres (middle 1900s), 168-70; intervention in Río de la Plata in 1846, 2, 175; Sarmiento criticizes role, 168-74, 178; Sarmiento's support for 174-82, 191n.4; as standard for progress, 184; trade system (early 1900s) 2. *See also* Argentina: history

"Great Chain of Being": 187

Groussac, Paul: 68n.42; on Sarmiento as *paisajista*, 82

Guerrero, César H.: 66n42

Guerrero, José H.: xiii

Güiraldes, Ricardo: 84

Guizot, François: 12, 114-15, 119, 130; civilization/barbarism in, 139n.15, 187; moral interpretation of French intervention, 181; on philosophy of history, 182; sub-rational faculties of man, 156

Gutiérrez, Juan María: 12, 75. *See also* Generation of 1837

Halperín Donghi, Tulio: xiii; on Sarmiento's presidency, 204

Head, Francis B.: 188

Hegel, Georg Wilhelm Friedrich: 43, 144, 186-87

Hemingway, Ernst: 20

Herder, Johann Gottfried von: 86, 130, 145-46; criticizes ethnocentrism, 196-n.44; on non-white populations, 160-61

Hernández, José: 203

Hernández Arregui, Juan José: xii

Histoire de l'Empire Ottoman (Alix): 148

historicism: 182, 187-88. *See also* Sarmiento: historicism

History of Civilization in Europe (Guizot): 114-15

"history of consciousness": xiii

Hoffer, Eric: 51

Hugo, Victor: 73

Humboldt, Alexander von: 186-87

immigration. *See* Argentina: immigration; Sarmiento: civilized institutions

Indians: in Herder, 161; in Tocqueville, 161, 188, 195n.42. *See also* Sarmiento: Indians

Ingenieros, José: xiii

Isabelle, Arsenio: 188

Jameson, Frederic: xiii

Jitrik, Noé: 47, 71, 96, 98n.4

journalism in Argentina: 13, 27. *See also* Sarmiento: journalism

Joven Argentina. *See* Generation of 1837

Korn, Alejandro: xiii, 16, 165n.12

Krieger, Murray: 51-52

Lamartine, Alphonse Marie Louis de Prat de: 153

Lamennais, Félicité Robert de: 198

Larra, José María de: 27, 34; romantic ideas, 73; Sarmiento uses ideas of, 74; timely writing, 32

Lastarria, José Victorino: 29; describes Sarmiento, 67n.32; in historicism discussions, 183-85

Latin America: independence movement, xv, 1, 27; Hegel's continent of nature, 187

Lavalle, Juan: 169, 199

"Law of limited fame": 61

Lerminier, E.: 196n.44

Leroux, Pierre: 12, 120 198

Lévi-Strauss, Claude: 42, 51; on *bricoleur*, 42-43; engineer vs. *bricoleur*, 45; imprisoned *bricoleur*, 47; on mythical thought, 46

Liberal Party (of Mitre): 204

liberalism: xii, xiii; in Argentina, 197-208; dependent, xv, 199-203, 205-06, 210-n.10; in post-1852 period, 168; orthodox, xiii; utopian, xv, 65n.22, 97, 116, 209n.7; *See also* Sarmiento: liberalism; Argentina: history

Life in the Argentine Republic (Eng. trans. of *Facundo*: 129. *See* Sarmiento: *Facundo*

Life of Franklin (Benjamin Franklin): 11-12

Literatura autobiográfica argentina (Prieto): 6

literature polemics of 1841-1842 in Santiago: 34, 73

Locke, John: 155

López, Vicente F.: 75. *See also*: Generation of 1837

López Jordán, Ricardo: 21, 203

Lugones, Leopoldo: xii, xiii; on Sarmiento's ideas, 63; on Sarmiento's journalism, 33, 39n.7, 41, 68n.42; on Sarmiento as *paisajista*, 82

Macaulay, Thomas: 86

Machiavelli, Niccolò: 158

Mann, Mary (Mrs. Horace): 129

Martí, José: 36

Martínez Estrada, Ezequiel: xiii; compares *Facundo* and *Conflicto*, 108; on Sarmiento's ahistorical ideas, 47; on Sarmiento's book knowledge, 49; on Sarmiento and education, 163; on Sarmiento's inner conflicts, 165n.19; on Sarmiento and liberal order, 208; on Sarmiento as soul of Argentina, 207-08

Marx: Marxists on Sarmiento, xii, xiii; in thought of Althusser, 43; and ideology and perception, 43, 55

Matadero, El (Echeverría): 86

materialism, philosophical: 145-49; and education, 160-62; and telluric determinism, 161-62. *See also* Sarmiento: historiography; Sarmiento: *Volksgeist*

mauvaise foi (term of Jean-Paul Sartre): xiii; in *Facundo*, 55

Menéndez y Pelayo, Marcelino: 54

Mercurio, El (newspaper): 29, 30, 56, 169

Mexico: 158

Michelet, Jules: 145

Middle Ages: Sarmiento compares Argentine colony with, 113-15, 124; Sarmiento's comparison with Córdoba, 128; Guizot's description of, 139n.15

Mitre, Bartolomé: xi; and "El Chacho" campaign, 203; as historian, 130; his Liberal Party, 203-04; as military leader against Rosas, 203; poetic ideas, 103n.36, as president, 201-203; Sarmiento opposes, 204

Montalvo, Juan: 36

Monte Caseros. *See* Caseros

Montesquieu, Comte Robert de: 152

Montevideo (city): 150, 169, 174-75

montonera: 8-9, 79, 90. *See also* gauchos; Sarmiento: gauchos

Moreno, Mario: 119, 204

nationalism, aristocratic: xii; and racism, 161

naturalism: 157. *See also* materialism; Sarmiento: *Volksgeist*

Niebuhr, Barthold Georg: 119

Nietzsche, Friedrich Wilhelm: 47, 55, 106

Montt, Manuel: 29, 30, 163

oratory: 13

Orgaz, Raúl: xiii

Oro, Domingo de: 11; oratory of 12-13

Ortega y Gasset, José: xiv, 125

Pagano, José León: 82

Palcos, Alberto: xiii; on Sarmiento from 1852-1865, 202; on Asociación de Mayo, 154-55

Paoli, Pedro: xii

Paraguay (country): 203; Triple Alliance War, xi

Paso, Leonardo: xiii

Pavón, battle of: 155, 202, 203

Paz, General José María de: 50, 89; Sarmiento's letter to, 137n.6; Sarmiento's personification of "civilization," 133-34

Paz, Octavio: 95

Peña, Milcíades: xiii, 202

Peña, Rodolfo Ortega: xii

Peñalosa, Angel "El Chacho": Sarmiento's book on, 35; Sarmiento's complicity in killing, xi; Sarmiento's opposition to, 21, 203. *See also* Sarmiento: *"El Chacho"*

Peel, Robert: 174

pharmakos: 83

phenomenology: and *bricoleur* ideation, 46

"philosophy of history": 90, 182-86, 194-n.29. *See also:* Sarmiento: historiography

Ponce, Aníbal: xiii

positivism: 121, 144; and *científicos* of Mexico, 158; and historicism, 182; and historiography, 121-26; in post-1852 Argentina, 200-08; pre-positivist age, 53; pre-positivism and art 104n.43; Sarmiento's ideas, 151, 156, 180-81. *See also* Sarmiento: positivism

Poverty of Progress, The (Burns): 207

Prieto, Adolfo: 6; Sarmiento's ambiguous ideas, 7, 15, 98n.4

Quiroga Rosas, Manuel: 12, 28; founds school with Sarmiento, 60

Radiografía de la pampa (Martínez Estrada): 207

raideur (concept of Bergson): 51

Recuerdos literarios (Lastarria): 183

Ramírez, Francisco: 179

"Restaurador, El." *See* Juan Manuel de Rosas

revisionism, populist and nationalist: xii, xiii

Revue des Deux Mondes (journal): 89, 188

Río de la Plata: 169; British role in, 170-72, 174-82; French role, 178

Rivadavia, Bernardo: 1; on value of education, 184-85; economic policies, 4; reasons for failure, 109, 119; liberal thought, 198; political goal of unity, 154; similar to Rosas, Mitre, Sarmiento, 204; Sarmiento admires, 5

Roca, Julio: 205

Rojas, Ricardo: xii, xiii; on Sarmiento's action orientation, 42; on Sarmiento's civilization vs. barbarism scheme 128; on Sarmiento as *genio pragmático*, 47; on Sarmiento's hatred for "El Chacho," 203; on the political goals of *Facundo*, 35; on Sarmiento and underdevelopment, 36-37

Rojo, Anselmo: 206

Romanticism: in *Dogma socialista*, 199; historicism, 126; and public amusements, 155; social, 138n.10; 1841-1842 polemics in Santiago, 34, 73. *See also romancista* literature

romancista literature: 92-97; social function, 155-56

Rome: fall of, 123; municipality, 118-19

Romero, José Luis: 197

Rosa, J. M.: xii

Rosas, Juan Manuel: authoritarianism, xv; censorship, 27; fall from power, xv, 206; and Federalism, 2, 10; French view of, 188; his government compared to that of Mitre, 203-04; vis-à-vis Grea Britain, 169; opposed by liberals, 198; popularity, 119, 177; resistance to imperialism, 175-76; rise to power, 1; Sar miento combats in press, 30-31; Sarmiento's opposition to, 202, 154-55. *See also* Sarmiento: Rosas; Argentina: history

Rousseau, Jean-Jacques: 86, 156; natural religion, 88; noble savage, 155

Said, Edward: 58

Saint-Simon, Claude-Henri de Rouvroy, Comte de: 121, 174; and historicism, 188; and *socialismo*, 198

saladero: rise of, 2; and Rosas, 154; Sarmiento doesn't consider, 4

Salomon, Noël: xiii; on Sarmiento and free trade, 22n.9; on *costumbrismo* and Sarmiento, 96; on Sarmiento and liberty, 7

Salón Literario: 27, 99n.12. *See* Generation of 1837

San Juan (province): 1; and *caudillos*, 10; culture after independence, 14, 18; society after independence,3, 177, 184

San Luis (province): 4; decline of, 10; Sarmiento founds school in, 15

San Martín, José de: 29

Santa Fe (province): 4, 203

Santiago, Chile (city): 28; discussions on historiography, 182-86; opposition to Sarmiento, 143; young intellectuals of, 108

Santiago de Estero (province): 4

Sarmiento, Bienvenida: 66n.29

Sarmiento, Domingo Faustino: biography
—youth: 3, 13; intellectual formation, 41, 58; parents, 6; political views, 5-7
—exile period: 28; with Chilean politics, 29; as journalist, 27-37, 208; opposition to Rosas, 38n.4. *See also* Santiago; Sarmiento: journalist; Sarmiento: Rosas
—educator: youthful activities, 11-14; views about 158-63
—military experience: youthful, 18-21; against "El Chacho," 203; "pacification" campaigns as president, 202-03; educator among military bosses, 202
—post-1852 period: 159, 197-208
—presidency: 203-05
—1880-1885: 205-08

Sarmiento: character (judgements about)
—*bricoleur*: 41-63, 82, 144; conflict between idealism and realism, 165n.19; in views on education, 163; in views on historiography, 105-36, 151
—intelligence: ambiguous, 15; confident, 125-26, 135; demonaic aspects, 16; egocentric, 56, 61; his emotional core, 165n.15; humorous, 66n.32; impetuous, 44; "loco," 51, 143, 164n.1, 164n.2; romantic, 101n.23
—values: aristocratic, 7-9; culturalist, 11-18, 200; elitist, 120; moralist and idealist, 177; racist, 160-63, 168, 194n.33; utopian, 17, 157, 173, 176-77; violent: 69n.52, 124, 176-77, 140n.23, 140n.24, 201-02

Sarmiento's opinions on:
—aesthetics: 71-97; art in U.S., 103n.41; history versus poetry, 91; novels, 72; poetry, 74-75, 80, 94, 103n.36; *romancista* literature, 92-97, Schlegel's influence, 76-78; Tocqueville's influence, 76-77
—Africa: 9, 102n.32, 127; civilization versus barbarism, 129; in *Viajes*, 178-79; violence of, 113
—barbarism: *americanismo*, 178; against European presence, 175-76; against progress, 167; and naturalism, 157; personification of Facundo, 115, 148-49; post-1880 reappraisal, 204-05; and Urquiza, 176
—biography as history, 130-35
—Blacks: 116, 139n.18
—*caudillos*: *Facundo's* focus, 131; Facundo Quiroga typifies, 147; hatred of, 19, 118-19, 124; urges violence against, 140n.23, 140n.24, 201-02; such as Urquiza, 176; as *Volksgeist*, 146. *See also caudillos*; Sarmiento: gauchos

—"civilization": 205; and circulation of ideas, 154; and coastal areas, cities, 149-52; and commerce, 150; and Europe, 178-79; and imperialism, xv; and social institutions, xii; liberal program for, 167; *Volksgeist* of, 149-52

—civilization/barbarism opposition: in aesthetic theory, 82; anthropomorphization of, 147-52; explained in *Facundo*, 45, 182; in historiography, 167-90; determines methodology of inquiry, 158; origin and development of, 127-30, 206; and political expediency, 186-90; as romantic struggle, 85-90

—economics: of "civilization," 120-21; free trade, 22n.9, 173-74, 180; material advancement, 175; silences about 4, 177, 193n.16

—education: 11-18, 158-63

—equality: 139n.19, 205-06

—gauchos: 7-11, 87-90; condemns, 162; historically viewed, 113-17; hyper-active imagination, 93-94; during presidency, 203

—historiography: 105-36; developmentalism, 155; enlightenment influence, 110-11; historicism defined, 110-11; historicist views, 186-92; historicism vs. enlightenment, 110-21; lack of attention to sociopolitical data, 180-81; moralist, 181; philosophical idealism, 144, 149-52; "philosophy of history," 182-86; philosophical materialism, 145-49; power of the idea, 152-58; pretense of impartiality, 149; role of agriculture, 119-20; role of city, 118-19

—ideas: power of, 14, 152-58; in May Revolution, 184-85

—imagination: 75-81

—imperialism: xvi; 1841-1842 critique of, 168-74; subsequent support for, 175-82, 194n.33, 205; treated in *Facundo*, 178; post-1880 views, 206

—Indians: 7, 138n.14, 162, 167; in *Facundo*, 86-87; historical development, 112-13; in Tocqueville and Herder, 161, 188, 195n.42; justifies annihilation, 196-n.44; views during presidency, 203

—journalism: newspaper definition, 28; and progress, 13; superiority over oratory, 23n.13; as weapon, 62-63; and writing, 33, 68n.42, 130

—language: organizes experience, 52-57; parallels history, 122-23

—liberalism: xii-xiv, 6-7; and aesthetics, 91; dependent, xv, 200-08; and education, 7; and historiography, 184; and power of ideas, 152-58; promoted through the press, 31; Rosas' opposi-

tion to, 2; and social harmony, 125; and social transformation, 151; utopian, xv, 65n.22, 97, 116

—nature: and barbarism, 167; and Facundo Quiroga, 148; "natural" man, 153

—*paisajista* (literary rendering of landscape): 82

—positivism: 80-81; progress sought, 151; as precursor, 156; pre-positivism, 121-26. *See also* positivism

—Providence: 121; and march of history, 151-52, 154; and voluntarism, 165n.10

—race: 9, 160-63, 168, 178, 194n.33, 208. *See also* Sarmiento: Indians; Sarmiento: gauchos

—reason: 156

—revolutionary ideas: 18, 154; contradictory, 201; youthful goals, 206

—Rosas: against commerce, 150; aginst progress, 173; and barbarism, 115; compared to self, 134; failure of government, 174; post-1880 view, 205; successor of Facundo Quiroga, 131-32; *Volksgeist* of barbarism, 147, 151. *See also* Rosas; Sarmiento: barbarism; Sarmiento: *Volksgeist*

—slavery: 7

—society: economic privilege, 205-06; lower classes, 8-9, 56; post-1852 period, 176; social goals in writing, 33ff, 206; upper classes 5, 6-8

—utopian thought: clash with realism, 173; definition, 199; and education, 160; goals of harmony and prosperity, 185; and liberalism, 65n.22, 209n.7; in post-1852 period, 176-77, 200; in post-1880 period, 205-06; and progress, 17, 24-n.26, 157; as tragic error, 207. *See also* liberalism; dependency

—voluntarism: 151-53

—*Volksgeist*: 126-32; anthropomorphization, 130; of barbarism, 145-49; of civilization, 149-52

—writing: public writer, xiv, 27-37; "performative" goals, 32, 63; power of, 12, 30, 63, 158-62; "productive" activity, 149; for social ascendancy, 63. *See also* Sarmiento: journalism

Sarmiento: works

—*Aldao (El General Fray Félix Aldao,)* (1845): 50, 116

—*Argirópolis* (1850): xi, 35

—*Campaña en el Ejército Grande* (1852): 35, 59

—*"Chacho, El"* (1863): 50

—*Las ciento y una* (1852): 35, 62, 179

—*Conflicto y armonía de las razas en América* (1883): 180, 205; racism, 116

—*Educación popular, De la* (1849): xi, 59;

views of Indian and gaucho, 162
—*Facundo (Civilización y barbarie: vida de Juan Facundo Quiroga, y aspecto físico, costumbres, y hábitos de la República Argentina)* (1845): xi; *americanismo*, 178; Alsina's criticisms, 65n.25; book of foundation, 189; born of free press, 33; *bricoleur* style, xiv, 44-45, 48; Buenos Aires vs. interior, 180; colonial mentality, 16; civilization vs. barbarism, 45; Cuyan focus, 4; Echeverría, 61-62; Facundo Quiroga, 50; fatalism and idealism, 151; first part, 146-47; Guizot's francocentrism, 188; historiography, *(bricoleur)* 105-36, (enlightenment) 112-20, 137-n.1, 180; imperialism, 178; as motivations in writing, 50, 66n. 27; 71; myth of founder, 59; public, 101n.21, 189; publication of, 127; social science, 184; San Juan, 8; support for British, 175
—*Mi defensa* (1843): 9; early successes in journalism, 13; intellectual formation, 58-59; style, 43, 154
—*Recuerdos de provincia* (1852): xi; activities in Chile, 30; article on San Martín, 29; on education, 14; epigraph from *Hamlet*, 143; ideology, 7, 11; intellectual formation, 12, 77; "libro de combate," 35; military leader, 20; objectives in writing, 134; old families of San Juan, 3; style, 60
—*Viajes por Europa, Africa y América* (1849-1851): xi; disdain for poets of Montevideo, 72; Echeverría, 61, 68n.51, 94; Europe's rights in the Plata, 178; power of ideas, 152; rigid categories, 128-29
Sartre, Jean-Paul: xii, 58
Schlegel, A. W.: 76-78, 81, 86
Scobie, James R.: xiii
Skinner, B. F.: 160
social science: 121-23; 140n.21; Sarmiento's pretense to, 184
socialista ideas: 11-12, 95; and development, 75, 125; and historicism, 182; intellectual sources, 198; as pre-positivist ideas, 54; Sarmiento's support for, 32, 34. *See also* positivism
Spain: colonial system, 183; legacy to New World, 16

Taine, Hippolyte: 123
Tamagno, Roberto: xiii, 23n.9
telluric determinism: *See* materialism
Tocqueville, Alexis de: 12; 81; aesthetic ideas, 76-77, 103n.40, 94; and historicism, 188; influence in Sarmiento, 100-n.15; on non-white populations, 160-61; Sarmiento as the T of America, 59, 107, 184; similarities with Sarmiento, 195n.42; and *Volksgeist* of civilization, 146
Triple Alliance, War of: xi
Tucumán (province): 200
Turgot, Anne Robert Jacques: 110, 188
Unamuno, Miguel de: 52
Unitarian Party: xii; and British, 169; and Federalists, 1, 10, 126-28; in power, 9; and progress, 175; and Rosas, 154; and Sarmiento, 5-6, 18-19, 23n.13; Sarmiento on "viejos unitarios," 59
United States: 126, 170; model for progress, 185; seen by Tocqueville, 188; and Washington, 131
Urquiza, José de: and Confederation, 200-03; "controlled terror" by, 201; governmental program, 176; jealousy for Sarmiento, 63; Sarmiento's opposition, xi, 21, 60, 202-03; Sarmiento praises, 204-05
Uruguay (country): 115, 203. *See* Montevideo
Verdevoye, Paul: xiii
Varela, Florencio: 38n.5
Vicuña Mackenna, Benjamín: 17
Vico, Giambattista: 57, 86, 123, 145-46
Vidal, Hernán: 98n.4
Viñas, David: xii, xiii, 17
Voltaire, François Marie Arouet: 110, 156
Vuelta de Obligado, Battle of: 175
Weinberg, Féliz: xiii
Wiarda, Howard: 49
world economy: 1; and Argentina post-1852, 206; and culture, 185-86; Sarmiento ignores, 5
Zonda, El (newspaper): 28, 60
Zárate, Armando: 89
Zuviría, José María: xiii